Politics
in Transitional Societies

The Challenge of Change
in Asia, Africa, and Latin America

Politics
in Transitional Societies

The Challenge of Change
in Asia, Africa, and Latin America

edited by

harvey g. kebschull
North Carolina State University at Raleigh

APPLETON-CENTURY-CROFTS
EDUCATIONAL DIVISION
MEREDITH CORPORATION

New York

To
SUSAN KIM

Preface

No student of politics can today afford to ignore the vast regions of Asia, Africa, and Latin America. Whether interested primarily in contemporary events and the difficult problems confronting policy-makers as they seek to direct the destinies of their nations, or in the comparative analysis of political institutions and processes, the student must take into account the political kaleidoscope presented by the nations in these areas. Never before in history have so many societies—with over two billion persons—been involved in such basic and complex social, economic, and political changes. Since the end of World War II, over seventy new states have been carved out of former colonial territories and, together with the older states in Latin America, their problems and aspirations have injected a new dimension into world politics. Their institutions, processes, and policies compel the attention of scholars and policy-makers alike. Social scientists have, at the moment, a unique opportunity to observe the processes of nation-building and development in fascinatingly diverse settings. While our knowledge of these states and societies is still fragmentary and incomplete, a rapidly expanding body of literature is available to students who seek to understand the characteristics and problems of these varied nations.

The inclusion in one study of nations as disparate as those in Latin America, Asia, and Africa is, of course, fraught with difficulties and dangers. Every generalization about them as a group is subject to many exceptions and qualifications. Each state has its distinctive pattern of resources, institutions, and processes, and each confronts a particular array of problems. Even within a single region, as in Latin America, wide variations exist among the nations in their social structures, political institutions, levels of economic development—indeed, along any dimension that might be suggested. Yet, if the dangers of overgeneralization are obvious, the dangers of regarding each nation as totally unique—with little or nothing in common with others—must also be avoided. To identify both similarities and differences and to account for their importance is the task of the social scientist, a task greatly complicated by the varying types and rates of change occurring in these societies. Careful analysis of these complex changes is required if well-founded conclusions concerning the nature of these societies are to emerge.

The study of transitional societies and their search for social, economic, and political development has had a profound impact on the discipline of political science. New concepts and approaches to the study of politics have been stimulated by the need to adequately account for the broad range of factors that are relevant for a systematic analysis of political systems and political change. Today, the scope of political studies requires an essentially interdisciplinary approach. The relationship of economic development to political stability in the new states, for example, demands an understanding of many economic and political factors. Even more broadly, the attempt to conceptualize "nation-building" and "modernization" imposes upon the political scientist a need to account for a variety of economic, cultural, and political factors, among others, many of which have not been, traditionally, of more than very marginal interest to political scientists.

Central to the study of transitional societies is the search for an acceptable definition of political development. Many of the present definitions may readily be faulted as being based on Western social, economic, and political values and institutions, which may be rejected by non-Western societies as meaningless or undesirable. Some authorities, indeed, deny the possibility of any universal definition of political development, in the belief that each society must determine for itself on the basis of its values and goals what constitutes development. Thus, at present, social scientists are grappling with the enormously complicated problem of conceptualizing the process of political development, and students of the transitional nations confront the exciting challenge of identifying and relating the complex and dynamic variables that promote development. Simultaneously there must be concern for the development of theory and the collection of data, and in each area difficulties exist. For reasons that are discussed in more detail in Chapter II, much of the data on transitional societies required by social scientists is unavailable or difficult to accumulate. Since accurate information is required for the construction and testing of theories, this problem imposes a major barrier to our understanding of political change and development. In addition to this problem, the familiar and difficult hurdle to theory-building in any discipline remains: the difficulty of stating propositions that accurately relate individual elements of phenomena to each other. Thus, much work remains before an under-

standing of the fundamental nature and problems of transitional societies is achieved. At the same time, however, great opportunities for
intellectual creativity and original research exist to challenge the student interested in these nations.

The purpose of this collection of materials is twofold: to supply
some useful information on the nature of transitional societies and their
problems as a foundation for more advanced study, and to sharpen the
analytical skills of students of politics, whatever their foremost interests
may be. To undertake this dual purpose, both primarily descriptive and
primarily analytical works are included in the reading selections. Since
only a small sampling of the extensive literature is possible in a collection of this type, students are urged to explore at greater length the
periodical literature and the books available on the many aspects of
politics in developing nations.

The principal debts of any editor are immediately apparent, and I
should like to express my appreciation to the authors and publishers
whose works are included in this book for permission to reproduce
their materials. Less apparent is my debt to those scholars whose works
are not included in this compilation, but whose writings have contributed to my understanding of the developing areas. In addition, I
have profited from my many discussions with students and scholars, and
I am particularly indebted to C. Barclay Kuhn and Richard Chapman
for their stimulating critical comments on my manuscript. I am also
grateful to Mrs. Annette Gottfried for compiling the statistics found in
the Appendix, and especially to my wife, Georgia, for her extensive help
in preparing this work. Errors of fact and judgment must, of course,
remain mine alone, despite the generous aid of all these persons.

H. G. K.

CONTENTS

CONTENTS

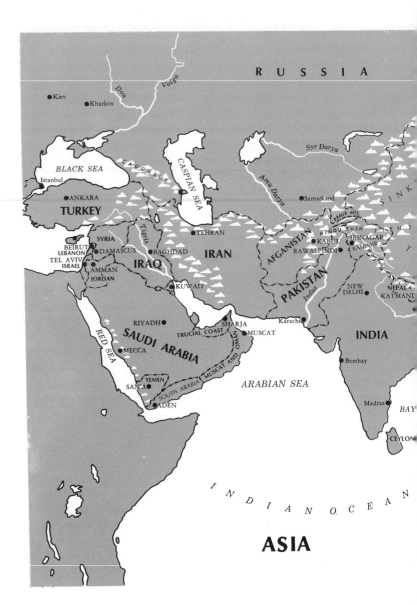

AFRICA

LATIN AMERICA

introduction

During the past two decades, one of the great revolutions of modern history has been drastically altering the structure and the dynamics of many societies, and as well, the whole arena of world politics. One phase of this revolution—that of securing political independence—is now virtually completed. The once great colonial empires of European powers have almost disappeared, and few colonies remain that, likely, are soon to experience the exhilaration accompanying the achievement of independence. The attention of leaders and scholars is currently concentrated on the other dramatic changes that collectively constitute the "revolution of modernization." Confronting the societies in Latin America, Asia, and Africa are the challenging goals of social, economic, and political development. Widely varying in their specific dimensions within these societies, difficult, complex problems must be solved in order to attain these goals. Many hopes and expectations have disintegrated already under the impact of hard, unyielding barriers to progress. Nevertheless, few societies in these areas have remained immune from ideas postulating goals whose achievement does not involve profound changes in traditional values, structures, and processes. The search for stable, effective political institutions and processes, for economic growth, the development of a sense of national unity and purpose, and the establishment of useful relationships with other states encompasses almost all societies in these vast areas.

Until the outbreak of World War II, the dominant position of the European colonial powers in Asia and Africa seemed secure. Even then, however, the long-term effects of colonial policy were creating aspirations for independence, self-determination, and economic development. The education of a small number of natives, the injection of Western values and beliefs, the construction of transportation and communication

1

systems, and the development of bureaucracies and armed forces all helped to fuel the demands within the colonies for fundamental political and economic changes. After the war, when their power was shattered and they were under intense pressure from the new world powers—the Soviet Union and the United States—to grant independence to their colonies, the colonial powers began to yield to the demands of leaders of the independence movements. The United States itself set the example when, in 1946, it granted full independence to the Philippines in fulfillment of its promise made before the war. The following year, India and Pakistan achieved their independence from the British, establishing a precedent that seemingly could not be reversed. At an unprecedented rate in world history, colonies attained their political independence, only to confront the diverse problems of survival and growth largely through their own initiatives and resources. Many Latin Americans, as well, have been seeking the means to modernize their societies; and while the particular obstacles to development that they confront are often quite different from those in Asia or Africa, a core of similar problems is widely shared throughout these areas.

Since attaining independence and undertaking to modernize their social, economic, and political systems, the transitional societies in Asia and Africa have attracted considerable scholarly interest from political scientists, economists, sociologists, and others. Similar interest in Latin American societies—long in the hinterland of social science studies—has been stimulated by the concern to understand development on a universal basis. Attention has been focused on the process of social change, the development of the nation–state, and the stages of economic growth, among other topics, in an effort to identify and describe the patterns of change now occurring in these societies and to compare them with those that have taken place in "modern" Western societies. Are the processes of development similar among the presently developing states? Must they pursue the same course as in Western states? What, indeed, constitutes development and modernization? What are the relationships between different types of development? Few definitive answers are as yet available to these and to similar complicated questions. The search for answers requires careful analysis of the momentous changes now occurring in transitional societies.[1]

[1] Neither of the terms "transitional" or "developing" which are commonly used, as in this text, to describe most of the states in Asia, Africa, and Latin America is fully satisfactory. As with other frequently used terms such as "underdeveloped," "backward," "emerging," or "The Third World," they fail to establish a clearly defined category into which certain states may be placed to the exclusion of all others. The problem lies in the multiplicity of factors that must be accounted for—along with the changes occurring in these factors—which together constitute an adequate description of a state or society. The term "transitional" can, of course, be applied to virtually all societies, the "modern" as well as the "underdeveloped." Again, the term "developing" may be inaccurate for some societies included in our coverage since, with

The scope of our study encompasses a large number of states that differ in many important respects. Yet they also share some fundamental characteristics and problems that set them apart, as a group, from the "modern" states of the mid-twentieth century.

First we may note some of the striking differences among these states. These variations partially account for the different specific problems confronting the individual developing states, the range of alternative courses of action that can be pursued in attempting to resolve them, and the political institutions and processes that have been established. Some of the developing states are, of course, very large; indeed, several of them are among the largest in the world.[2] Others, however, are among the smallest. In contrast to such giants as mainland China and Brazil—both of which are larger than continental United States—are such diminutive states as Malta and Singapore, each of which is less than 250 square miles. In between these extremes, sizes range widely. Several states—India, Argentina, Saudi Arabia, the Congo (Leopoldville), and the Sudan—are approximately one third the size of the United States. Many others are considerably smaller: Laos, Ghana, and Ecuador, for example, are about the size of Arizona or Western Germany, while Guatemala, Honduras, Jordan, and Mali are approximately the size of Ohio or New York.

Similar variations are found in the size of the populations of these states. China's estimated 750 million or India's 470 million contrast sharply with the 95,000 in the Maldive Islands. A few states, such as Brazil, Nigeria, Pakistan, and Indonesia, have populations in the 50 to 100 million range, but most states have considerably smaller populations, a number of which are under 5 million, e.g., Burundi, Tunisia, Costa Rica, and Paraguay.

Although a few states—Bolivia and Laos, for example—are land-locked, and a few others such as Cuba and the Philippines are composed wholly of islands, most states have both land and sea boundaries. Many of them are reasonably compact, but others are confronted with the many social, economic, and political problems that arise from their peculiar shapes. Pakistan, for example, is divided by a hostile India into two areas almost 1,000 miles apart; it lacks direct land communication and transportation within its sole control. Indonesia is also faced with difficult problems of communication and transportation, since its 3,000 islands extend over 3,000 miles. In Latin America, Chile stretches like a

respect to some of their characteristics, regression may be occurring. Similar problems arise in the use of the other descriptive terms. In the pages that follow, the "transitional" or "developing" societies are described at greater length, but since the analytical categories for separating states on the basis of their level of development are as yet imprecise, no final judgment can be made as to the proper category into which the marginal states (those that have both many modern and pre-modern characteristics) should be placed.

[2] See Appendix for selected data on the developing states.

narrow ribbon for over 2,600 miles along the western coast of the continent, averaging only 110 miles in width.

The topography of these states is similarly diverse, ranging from the generally level terrain in a few states such as Uruguay to the largely mountainous states like Peru. Within many of these states, the terrain varies considerably, from broad coastal areas to high, rugged mountains. Deserts, swamps, rich valleys, and barren plateaus are features sometimes found within a single state. In Chile, for example, from the long seacoast the land rises rapidly to the mountains towering over 19,000 feet in the east. A harsh desert region in the north, in parts of which rain almost never falls, is juxtaposed with a fertile valley in the central part of the state. Similarly in Algeria, a fertile coastal region gives way to a high plateau and mountainous area beyond which the Sahara imposes its barriers to commerce, communications, and transportation. Most developing states lie in the tropics, but temperatures and rainfall vary greatly, depending upon the prevailing winds, mountain ranges, and other topographical features. In some areas, as in northern Brazil, the temperatures and rainfall combine to create an environment basically inhospitable to man, while in other areas in similar latitudes, such as the highlands of Kenya, they create an environment conducive to settlement and the exploitation of natural resources.

These natural resources, in turn, differ markedly among the states. In some the land is rich and fertile, as in much of Indonesia, while in others it is poor and unproductive, either because of natural conditions as in desert regions or because of the poor farming methods employed in so many areas. Mineral resources are similarly variable. Some states, such as Nigeria and Brazil, are known to possess large mineral deposits, while others, such as the Chad, have few apparent resources to exploit. While few states have, as yet, completed surveys of their mineral and other resources, it appears that many of them have some valuable resources that are not currently being exploited.

The diversity in size, topography, and resources among these states is matched by that of their peoples and cultures. There are, of course, many different "kinds" of Asians, Africans, and Latin Americans; they differ in such obvious ways as race, color, language, and culture. Included among the Asians are Chinese, Indians, Indonesians, Burmese, and other groups. In the Middle East reside Turks, Arabs, Jews, and some Negroes. The population of sub-Saharan Africa is composed of several indigenous African races, e.g., the Bushmen, Bantu, and Hottentots, along with nonnative groups including Asians, Arabs, and Europeans. In Latin America Indians, Negroes, *mestizos*, and "whites" constitute the principal groups. Within each of the major racial and ethnic groups there are, in addition, numerous divisions along cultural, linguistic, and tribal lines. Few states are racially or ethnically homogeneous;

in most of them are found several major groups and a number of linguistic and cultural minorities.

Politically, these states also differ widely in their formal institutions and processes. A very few, such as Saudi Arabia and Yemen, are still traditional oligarchies in which the hereditary ruler and a small group of princes govern with few restraints. In some others, e.g., Thailand, the powers of the traditional national elite have been circumscribed either by constitutional provisions that provide for popularly elected leaders, or by the emergence of strong modernizing groups such as the armed forces that can effectively restrain the traditional leadership group. Modern political institutions take several forms. States such as India have adopted a modified form of the British parliamentary system, replacing the hereditary monarchy with an elected president. Other states, particularly those in Latin America, have established a presidential form of government, more or less on the American model. Communist China's "parliamentary" form is an important innovation that follows the Soviet Union's format only in the most general terms. Government by the armed forces is found in many states. In some instances, constitutions have been formally suspended while the military leaders hold power "temporarily"; in others, the constitutions have been abrogated and plans are nominally being made for the writing of new ones.

Wide variations are also found in the duration of political independence enjoyed by these states. A few, like Thailand and Afghanistan, have never been completely dominated politically by Western states; though, in most cases, their full independence has been circumscribed from time to time by agreements into which they were coerced. Other states, however, have just recently achieved independence. Some of the most recent additions to the list of independent states include Guyana, Botswana, Lesotho, and Barbados, all former British colonies which attained their independence during 1966. Prior to independence, the new states were subjected to Western control as colonies, mandates, or protectorates, or through other formal arrangements. The early 1960's were particularly vibrant times for achieving independence in sub-Saharan Africa; rapidly—and sometimes without much preparation—the former colonies of France, Britain, and Belgium were released. This subcontinent that a decade ago was almost completely controlled by a few European states is now, with the principal exception of the Portuguese possessions of Angola and Mozambique, divided into over twenty-five independent states. Similarly, all major former colonies in Asia have achieved political independence since the end of World War II. In contrast, most states in Latin America attained their independence during the early decades of the nineteenth century.

Despite the many diverse elements, the developing states nevertheless possess some common characteristics and are confronted by some similar social, economic, and political problems. Compared with those in Western Europe and North America, these nations as a group are economically underdeveloped, far less literate, less socially integrated, and less politically stable. Nevertheless, wide variations exist among the developing states with respect to these characteristics.

Undoubtedly the best known characteristic of the developing states is their low level of economic development. Rarely does the gross national product provide an average per capita income in Asian or African societies exceeding $200 a year; frequently it is less than half that amount.[3] In India, the figure is $74; in Afghanistan, $72; in Lebanon, $153; and in Nigeria, $102. Although this figure tends to be significantly higher in most Latin American states, it seldom exceeds $500. These low figures reflect the fact that neither agricultural nor industrial production is high. The large majority of persons in most developing states are engaged in agriculture, fishing, or animal husbandry. The traditional methods employed in these occupations produce few surpluses; in some cases, production does not even provide subsistence for the population. Irrigation projects are primitive and wasteful, and the poor quality and inadequate use of fertilizers fail to replenish the depleted fertility of the soil. Few insecticides are used, and crop destruction by insect invasions or floods and droughts frequently makes the position of the peasant precarious. Herds are of poor quality, and grazing lands are often unable to sustain the animals in a satisfactory condition. Fishing equipment and techniques are primitive and are incapable of supporting large-scale commercial operations.

Dissatisfaction with current methods and levels of production and the resulting low standard of living is one of the principal characteristics of the "revolution of rising expectations." A widespread desire for economic development is evident throughout the underdeveloped world, and progress through industrialization and diversification has become virtually an article of faith. But although many states have devised plans that call for the development of heavy and medium industries, in only a few is there a significant industrial capacity as yet. Several large steel mills, cement plants, and textile mills have been constructed in a few states such as China and India, but in most Asian and African states the largest plants are usually those for the processing of raw materials in preparation for their export. Latin American states have, in general, achieved a higher level of industrialization. In Brazil, for example, automobile assembly and shipbuilding are undertaken, and in Mexico and Chile, among others, a number of medium size industries have been established. Light industries—manufacturing a variety of small consumer

---

[3] Per capita income figures are, of course, of limited utility since they do not take into account the relative purchasing power of the monetary unit, nor do they indicate the range and grouping of incomes within a state.

goods such as tools, utensils, and bicycles—are found in many developing states. For all of them, however, a substantial industrial complex represents an aspiration rather than a current reality. In many cases, the development of an industrial complex is dependent not only on the utilization of resources but also on the expansion of markets through trade (and schemes such as common markets) since the internal demand is too limited to sustain large-scale production. For many years to come, most states will have to rely on the major industrial powers to provide their heavy machinery requirements.

One factor that accounts for the intense drive to industrialize and diversify these economies is the present extraordinarily heavy reliance on the export of one crop or product. Oil, for example, accounts for 96 per cent of Libya's exports and 95 per cent of Venezuela's; coffee, for 90 per cent of Rwanda's; and peanuts, for 85 per cent of Gambia's. Frequently the primary export is that of a product for which world demand is fairly inflexible, a fact that causes drastic movements in market prices because of short-term fluctuations in supply, thus making a stable income from these exports difficult to maintain.

There are, however, many obstacles to economic development. In some cases, natural resources are inadequate, of poor quality, or not readily accessible. Adequate transportation and communication systems are lacking to handle the demands of a complex industrial society. Investment capital is usually in critically short supply. Even when resources and capital are available, the limited internal markets and the strong competition offered by the major industrial powers for world markets inhibit industrial development. In addition, there are severe shortages of trained and skilled personnel in the developing states to plan and operate an industrial complex. Further, the traditional organizational structures and cultural values in the society often impede economic development. Only gradually are the values, attitudes, and techniques that underlie and are associated with Western industrial societies beginning to emerge. Finally, the political instability of many governments disrupts planning and discourages private investment.

A further characteristic of the economic conditions in the developing states is the striking inequality in incomes and standards of living between the masses and the economic elite. While the masses are poor and in some cases acutely destitute, the elite, in contrast, are often remarkably wealthy. In Colombia, for example, over 40 per cent of the national wealth is controlled by 5 per cent of the population; in Brazil, over 60 per cent is held by less than 20 per cent of the population. The enormous wealth of some Asian families and Middle Eastern aristocrats contrasts sharply with the poverty of the masses in their societies. Those who possess such wealth have little in common with the masses; the two groups live in different worlds, each with its own distinctive manners, dress, values, and often language. In few of these societies is there a substantial economic middle class of businessmen, engineers, technicians, and skilled manual workers.

In most developing states, the masses, besides being poor, are also illiterate. In Senegal, for example, about 95 per cent of the population is illiterate, while in India the figure is 72 per cent and in Iran, 87 per cent. In some Asian and African states, considerable progress has been made in reducing the high level of illiteracy; in Burma, for example, the illiteracy rate is below 43 per cent. The illiteracy rate in most Latin American states has been substantially reduced, though in Bolivia the figure is still 69 per cent and in Haiti, 90 per cent. Contrasts within individual states are again marked. In many rural areas, schools are few or nonexistent. Even when available, the levels of instruction and attendance are poor. In the larger towns and cities, however, instruction is usually much better, and a far higher percentage of school-age children attend classes, often for a period of several years. The number of students who receive more than a primary education is still very small, and only a very few persons are able to attend colleges and universities. Those who do receive an advanced education, sometimes in European and American schools, frequently become the principal voices in society advocating modernization and reform.

Particularly in the new African and Asian states, this "Westernized" intellectual elite is frequently in a position to attempt to carry out its objectives since it constitutes the political elite as well. Whether civilian or military in composition, it is this small group that champions rapid social and economic changes. In some cases, this new intellectual elite, created largely through colonial policies of developing an indigenous civil service and military force, has been joined by the traditional political elite in its efforts to modernize society; in other cases, the traditional elite has sought to retain its privileges and prerogatives in time-honored ways, thus creating a major barrier to the policies and programs of the new political elite. Many of the intellectual elite were instrumental in the drive for political independence. Their positions of authority are based primarily on their ability to motivate and organize their followers in the pursuit of developmental goals, rather than on the traditional bases of authority, birth, and wealth. In most Latin American states, in contrast, the political elite is still drawn from the conservative socioeconomic "white" elite, reflecting the fundamentally different pattern of history in Latin American states in comparison with that of most Asian and African states.

Few organized groups exist to bridge the wide gap between the masses and the elite, whether traditional or "modernizing." Rarely are the peasant masses organized to promote their interests and, in many cases, neither are the limited commercial and laboring sectors of the society. Where industrialization is growing, trade unions and business organizations are emerging, but with few exceptions, these organizations are not yet large and politically powerful. Political parties, bureaucracies, and the armed forces provide the principal channels of communication and contact between the elite and the masses. Often the political parties are little more than personal followings of individual leaders, or else broad, comprehensive, nationalistic parties that represent "the general will." Increasingly, the armed forces have assumed a broad range of social, economic, and political functions in addition to their military duties. In Asia and Africa, the military, along with the bureaucracy, is often the principal institutionalized force supporting the "modernizing" elite.

A pronounced characteristic of many developing states—and one that frequently causes the progressive political elite some of its most difficult problems—is the lack of integration among the several cultural and ethnic groups comprising society. In some cases, these relatively autonomous, self-contained, self-sufficient groups have traditionally been hostile toward each other. Each group has its own deeply rooted traditions, values, organizations, lands, and occupations, and often its own language and religion. Frequently these groups are stratified within the state along social, economic, and political lines, further complicating the problem of nation-building.

A few examples illustrate the complex social pattern that exists in many developing states. In Indonesia, the population is divided into sixteen major ethnic groups, each of which occupies a fairly distinct region, speaks its own language or dialect, possesses its own traditional forms of social and political organization, and pursues somewhat different economic activities. Deep-seated differences exist between the Javanese and non-Javanese over social and political issues, with the latter continuing to press their demands for regional autonomy. Similarly, India's social structure is highly complex. Within its enormous population at least twelve major languages are spoken. Although 85 per cent of the population is Hindu, this religion includes a wide variety of sects and beliefs. It forms the basis for the rigid caste system which divides society into thousands of relatively small kinship groups, each with its own rather specific occupation and habits of speech, manners, and dress. Within the half million villages where 80 per cent of the people reside, these caste and kinship ties are particularly strong. The Muslim minority, about 10 per cent of the population, with its distinctively different religious beliefs and social structure, is largely unintegrated into Indian society. In many Asian states, Chinese and Indians form important, unintegrated minority groups. They are found primarily in the urban areas, where they maintain strong, cohesive communities. Engaging in business enterprises and the professions, they constitute alien economic and social groups, frequently disliked and distrusted, but often performing essential roles that would otherwise remain unfilled.

Intricate social patterns are also found in Africa. While in few states other than in Rhodesia and the Union of South Africa are there significant white minorities, the African population is nevertheless divided into many ethnic and cultural groups. In Ghana, three major groups, subdivided into over sixty tribal and lineage groups, can be identified. Five major languages and many dialects are spoken by these groups. Deep-seated animosities divide the various groups in some African states, as in Nigeria, the most populous state, where these divisions threaten to destroy the Nigerian federation. In addition to numerous tribal groups, Asians, Arabs, and Europeans form small but important ethnic groups in a few states, where they are particularly prominent in commercial enterprises and in the professions. These various groups are further divided by religious beliefs, as several native religions are practiced by the Africans, while the Asians and Arabs are primarily Muslims and the Europeans, Christian.

A complex social structure based upon race is also found in many Latin American states. Three distinct groups comprise the three separate classes: Indians, *mestizos*, and "whites." While these groups share a common religion, Roman Catholicism, they are divided in every other respect. Each class has its distinctive customs, language, and occupations. The Indians—and, where they exist in large numbers, the Negroes— occupy the lowest positions. They live apart from the other classes, occupying in particular the more inhospitable areas of the state. There they have established close-knit communities that preserve the traditional Indian customs and practices. Relegated to the most menial occupations and politically without power, they are only rarely able to obtain the education and cultural characteristics that permit them to move upward in the social order. The *mestizos*—those of mixed European and Indian ancestry—form a middle social and cultural group. The "whites" —the descendants of many European groups, Spanish, Portuguese, Irish, German, and others—form the social, economic, and political elite. Their European-based languages and culture, higher rate of literacy, wealth, and occupations form the basis of their dominant position in the social order. In several states they form a minority of the total population, but they own most of the land and control the economic and political sectors of society as well as the social.

The problem of integrating the several ethnic and cultural groups typically found in a developing state is compounded by the solidarity and cohesion of each individual group. Particularly in the rural areas, the basic social and political patterns of the group establish a stable, comprehensive set of personal relationships for its members, determining status, occupation, and values that together provide a sense of personal security. The primary identification and loyalty of the individual to his own immediate group rather than to the larger society has quite often been strengthened in the newly independent states as the different groups, no longer either protected or obstructed by the former colonial power, compete for positions of control. Most leaders confronted with the problem of integrating their societies have relied upon nationalistic appeals and the effects of education, a more complex, interdependent economy, and a higher standard of living. The process of integration is slow, delicate, and uncertain, however, and traditional loyalties and rivalries are not easily surmounted.

As this brief survey suggests, the study of transitional societies, their political systems, and the process of modernization must account for the great diversity of characteristics found in the African, Asian, and Latin American states. In addition to these widely varying characteristics, the different rates and nature of change occurring within the individual states must also be considered. In some cases, the indices of progress show little movement; in others, significant advances have been made, while in still others, regression has occurred. Since no single index of development is available, states may be making certain advances while simultaneously be moving backward along other dimensions of change. Thus, the search for patterns of change and the relationship of different types of change confronts the student of transitional societies with a challenging task. In the chapter that follows, the initial problem of devising a framework for analysis is considered.

SUGGESTED READINGS

Almond, Gabriel A., and Coleman, James S., eds., *The Politics of the Developing Areas.* Princeton, N. J., Princeton University Press, 1960.
Apter, David E., *The Politics of Modernization.* Chicago, University of Chicago Press, 1965.
Eisenstadt, S. N., *Modernization: Protest and Change.* Englewood Cliffs, N. J., Prentice-Hall, Inc., 1966.
Horowitz, Irving Louis, *Three Worlds of Development.* New York, Oxford University Press, 1966.
McCord, William, *The Springtime of Freedom.* New York, Oxford University Press, 1965.
Moyes, Adrian, and Hayter, Teresa, *World III: A Handbook on Developing Countries.* New York, The Macmillan Company, 1964.
Silvert, Kalman H., ed., *Expectant Peoples: Nationalism and Development.* New York, Random House, 1963.
von der Mehden, Fred R., *Politics of the Developing Nations.* Englewood Cliffs, N. J., Prentice-Hall, Inc., 1964.
Worsley, Peter, *The Third World.* Chicago, University of Chicago Press, 1964.

the study of political systems

The student of comparative politics is today confronted with many problems. Not only have many new states with their diverse cultures, ideologies, institutions, and processes been added to his universe during the past two decades, but significant changes have also been occurring within the discipline of political science concerning the methods of analyzing political systems. Traditionally, the study of comparative government focused upon the formal political institutions and processes of a limited number of major European states, in addition to those of the United States. A detailed description of the constitutional base of each of these governments and of the legal powers and relationships of institutions within them constituted the principal method of analysis. Although there was increasing concern for economic, social, psychological, and other factors and their relationship to politics, few attempts were made to analyze these relationships in a systematic manner. In particular, few concepts or analytical frameworks were available to political scientists to compare systematically similar aspects of politics among several political systems.

The reasons for the limited scope of political studies are not hard to identify. As major world powers, the European and North American states attracted the attention of those who sought to understand the reasons for their pre-eminent positions. More specifically, since the discipline of political science is itself of Western origin, it was only natural for political scientists to devote their primary attention to Western political systems, particularly those that dominated large portions of the world. Since these states were the major industrial powers, it was easy to assume that they were the most "advanced" political systems—if not, indeed, morally superior—and that the study of non-Western political systems had little to offer those interested in modern political institutions and processes. Even though there was increasing interest to develop more "scientific" methods of political analysis, the range of states to be studied remained limited to the major powers, all of which shared a common cultural base.

With the appearance of many new states in Asia and Africa after the war, however, and the widespread concern for their future in an unstable world, political scientists as well as other social scientists were challenged by the fascinating opportunities afforded them to observe the creation and evolution of many newly independent political systems. In addition to the growing interest in developing more scientific approaches for the analysis of politics, political scientists have in recent years been devoting much attention to the problems of devising comprehensive analytical frameworks for the study of politics on a universal basis. These problems are, of course, complex. Not only are there substantial differences in the formal organizations and processes of governments; there are also the wide variations in the levels of political development and the differences in the cultural, social, and economic characteristics of states that must be taken into account. Thus, the construction of a theoretical framework of analysis that can be systematically applied to the widely varying political systems found in Asia, Africa, Latin America, Europe, and North America looms as a most difficult task for political scientists.

In their search for an adequate conceptual framework, political scientists have had to re-examine the basic question, What *is* politics? Obviously, it is difficult to proceed with the construction of a framework for analysis until the subject matter itself is defined. What phenomena constitute politics in, for example, Ghana, Burma, Brazil, and the United States? What are the essential characteristics of a political act? A political system? Although different specific answers have been proposed to these questions, political scientists generally agree that politics involves the organization and exercise of authority within a society for the purposes of establishing and maintaining order, resolving differences between groups and individuals, and promoting common goals. These ends give rise to institutions and processes through which authority is exercised and decisions made on how to achieve the basic goals. The study of politics, then, is the study of the organization and base of authority and the means by which authoritative decisions for a society are made and enforced. However, considerable differences of opinion exist on the question of the proper boundaries delimiting political studies—for example, on the extent to which political scientists should incorporate social, economic, and other data into their analyses in order to encompass all factors that affect, even marginally, the political system. On the one hand, a narrow focus facilitates concentrated attention on a few aspects of politics. However, the tendency is then to focus on the

most obvious "political" elements, the formal, legal structures and processes of government. Such a focus can, of course, be quite misleading,
especially when applied to developing political systems. On the other
hand, while a broader, more inclusive approach may relate important
ancillary social, economic, and other phenomena to politics—and thereby
inject a dynamic element into the analysis of politics and change—
difficult problems arise in attempting to collect and organize such diverse data and relate it to the political processes.

The purpose of employing a systematic approach to the study of
politics is to enable the student to compile data on a political system in
such a manner that interrelationships of political variables are suggested. Hypothetical propositions relating these variables may then be
constructed, but before they can be asserted as explanatory theories they
need to be tested against the evidence from as many political systems as
possible. To compile the data systematically requires the development of
theoretical categories, which collectively constitute the framework for
analysis. The repeated use of these common categories for different
political systems will result in the modification of the initial hypotheses
until all variations in the interrelationships of the political data are
accounted for. When this has been accomplished, the hypotheses may be
said to be verified as explanatory theories. Predictions of trends and the
consequences of changes within the political variables are then possible.

Thus the essential problem is to construct the categories for the
collection of data. These categories must be both comprehensive, to
envelop all relevant data, and precise, to order this data in a manner
that suggests significant relationships. Since political systems perform
certain functions in a society, as outlined above, many of the categories
currently used in comparative political analysis are based upon these
common functions. Again, the problem is to define these functions in
such a manner that they can be stated in relatively few categories to
guide the selection and organization of the necessary data.

In the selections that follow, two approaches to the study of political
systems are described. Each approach attempts to provide a comprehensive framework for the systematic analysis of politics within a particular political system. Accurate comparisons of particular aspects of politics in several political systems will, it is hoped, be possible through the
use of the suggested analytical categories.[1]

Of course, the successful analysis of political systems requires more
than a logical, well-structured theoretical framework. The necessary
data must be obtained, and to the extent that it is not available, the
analysis of political systems must remain incomplete. In attempting to

[1] For additional examples of approaches to the study of comparative politics and
discussion of some problems, see the SUGGESTED READINGS at the end of the
chapter.

compile the necessary data on developing political systems, the student faces many obstacles. Frequently, much of the basic data he requires is unavailable or unreliable. In contrast to the wealth of government statistics and reports available in most European, the North American, and a few other states on social and economic conditions and trends, this type of information on developing states is often sparse, unsystematically compiled, outdated, or inaccurate. Reports of administrative agencies and government corporations are difficult to obtain and, even when available, are often incomplete or distorted. Official records of legislative debates and committee meetings may be available only in summary form, if at all, and court decisions are often unpublished or even unrecorded.

Similarly, relatively little non-official information is available in many states. Few professional groups or civic, social, or economic organizations exist that undertake their own studies of specific problems within their societies. The extensive social science research executed by European and American university faculty members is also rarely duplicated in the developing societies, both because higher education in these latter states has traditionally stressed the humanities, and because their universities and colleges lack the financial resources to underwrite many comprehensive, and often expensive, social studies. Furthermore, political science as a discipline is almost unknown in the educational systems of the developing states. Only a very limited number of trained native political scientists are available to undertake specialized political analyses of their own or other political institutions and processes. Neither are there large numbers of skilled political journalists to contribute their insights into policies and personalities in their political systems.

The many languages and dialects found in the developing areas create additional difficulties. Even though many leaders speak English or French, and many documents are issued in English translations, much important data is not readily available to those without proficiency in non-European languages. The English translations, moreover, often fail to convey the subtleties and nuances that are essential for precise meanings and measurements.

More basic than the language barrier is the psychological obstacle that confronts the student attempting to analyze the social and political systems in Asia and Africa, and to a lesser degree, in Latin America. The problem of defining and understanding unfamiliar cultures, values, and institutions is further complicated by the highly personal, informal, and undifferentiated nature of some political systems. For students accustomed to the pragmatic, rational approach to problems in European and American societies, the irrational and unscientific search for answers to social, economic, and political problems carried on in some societies is disconcerting and incomprehensible. Further complicating the problem of analysis is the social and cultural fragmentation found in some states. While the psychological barrier can probably never be fully overcome, it can, nevertheless, be lessened by thorough preparation and careful attention to details.[2]

The challenge confronting students of comparative politics is, then, two-fold. First, a conceptual framework must be constructed that will make possible simultaneous, systematic analyses of diverse Western and non-Western political systems. The concepts to be employed in these studies will have to be formulated in such a manner that they can be utilized regardless of the type of formal political institutions found in individual states. In addition, this framework must take account of variables formerly excluded in the traditional approach. These variables, in turn, must be related to each other in the form of testable hypotheses. Moreover, they should be stated in such a way that political systems can be viewed as in a state of constant evolutionary, and sometimes revolutionary, change.

Second, the framework of analysis will have to be carefully applied to individual political systems. As hypotheses are tested against the data compiled through empirical investigation, necessary modifications must be made in the initial formulation of the hypotheses. Through the interplay of theory and empirical observation, each affecting the other, a more comprehensive and accurate understanding of individual political systems, and of the differences and similarities among several such systems, emerges.

SUGGESTED READINGS

Almond, Gabriel A., and Powell, G. Bingham, Jr., *Comparative Politics: A Developmental Approach*. Boston, Little, Brown and Company, 1966.

Apter, David E., "A Comparative Method for the Study of Politics," *The American Journal of Sociology*, Vol. LXIV, No. 3 (November, 1958), 221–237.

Dahl, Robert A., *Modern Political Analysis*. Englewood Cliffs, N. J., Prentice-Hall, Inc., 1963.

Easton, David, *A Systems Analysis of Political Life*. New York, John Wiley & Sons, 1965.

Kuhn, Alfred, *The Study of Society: A Unified Approach*. Homewood, Ill., The Dorsey Press, Inc., 1963.

Macridis, Roy C., *The Study of Comparative Government*. Garden City, New York, Doubleday & Company, Inc., 1955.

Spiro, Herbert J., "Comparative Politics: A Comprehensive Approach," *The American Political Science Review*, Vol. LVI, No. 3 (September, 1962),577–595.

[2] The difficulties, as well as the rewards, of conducting research in the developing areas are considered in more detail in Robert E. Ward, *et al.*, *Studying Politics Abroad* (Boston, Little, Brown and Company, 1964).

Wiseman, Herbert V., *Political Systems: Some Sociological Approaches.* New York, Frederick A. Praeger, Inc., 1966.

Young, Roland, ed., *Approaches to the Study of Politics.* Evanston, Ill., Northwestern University Press, 1958.

᚛ᚹᚯ

1. AN APPROACH TO THE ANALYSIS OF POLITICAL SYSTEMS[*][†]

d a v i d   e a s t o n

I. SOME ATTRIBUTES OF POLITICAL SYSTEMS

✿   ✿   ✿   ✿   ✿

The study of politics is concerned with understanding how authoritative decisions are made and executed for a society. We can try to understand political life by viewing each of its aspects piecemeal. We can examine the operation of such institutions as political parties, interest groups, government, and voting; we can study the nature and consequences of such political practices as manipulation, propaganda, and violence; we can seek to reveal the structure within which these practices occur. By combining the results we can obtain a rough picture of what happens in any self-contained political unit.

In combining these results, however, there is already implicit the notion that each part of the larger political canvas does not stand alone but is related to each other part; or, to put it positively, that the

[*] Excerpts from "An Approach to the Analysis of Political Systems" by David Easton, *World Politics*, Vol. IX, No. 3 (April, 1957), pp. 383–399. By permission.
[†] In modified form, the substance of this article was presented to a meeting of the New England Political Science Association in May 1956 and to a special conference of the International Political Science Association held in Switzerland in September 1956.

operation of no one part can be fully understood without reference to the way in which the whole itself operates. I have suggested in my book, *The Political System*,[1] that it is valuable to adopt this implicit assumption as an articulate premise for research and to view political life as a system of interrelated activities. These activities derive their relatedness or systemic ties from the fact that they all more or less influence the way in which authoritative decisions are formulated and executed for a society.

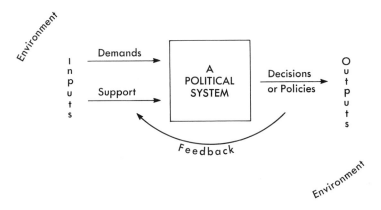

Once we begin to speak of political life as a system of activity, certain consequences follow for the way in which we can undertake to analyze the working of a system. The very idea of a system suggests that we can separate political life from the rest of social activity, at least for analytical purposes, and examine it as though for the moment it were a self-contained entity surrounded by, but clearly distinguishable from, the environment or setting in which it operates. In much the same way, astronomers consider the solar system a complex of events isolated for certain purposes from the rest of the universe.

Furthermore, if we hold the system of political actions as a unit before our mind's eye, as it were, we can see that what keeps the system going are inputs of various kinds. These inputs are converted by the processes of the system into outputs and these, in turn, have consequences both for the system and for the environment in which the system exists. The formula here is very simple but, as I hope to show, also very illuminating: inputs—political system or processes—outputs. These relationships are shown diagrammatically in Figure I. This diagram represents a very primitive "model"—to dignify it with a fashionable name—for approaching the study of political life.

[1] New York, 1953.

THE STUDY OF POLITICAL SYSTEMS

Political systems have certain properties because they are systems.[2] To present an over-all view of the whole approach, let me identify the major attributes, say a little about each, and then treat one of these properties at somewhat greater length, even though still inadequately.

(1) Properties of identification. To distinguish a political system from other social systems, we must be able to identify it by describing its fundamental units and establishing the boundaries that demarcate it from units outside the system.

(a) Units of a political system. The units are the elements of which we say a system is composed. In the case of a political system, they are political actions. Normally it is useful to look at these as they structure themselves in political roles and political groups.

(b) Boundaries. Some of the most significant questions with regard to the operation of political systems can be answered only if we bear in mind the obvious fact that a system does not exist in a vacuum. It is always immersed in a specific setting or environment. The way in which a system works will be in part a function of its response to the total social, biological, and physical environment.

The special problem with which we are confronted is how to distinguish systematically between a political system and its setting. Does it even make sense to say that a political system has a boundary dividing it from its setting? If so, how are we to identify the line of demarcation?

Without pausing to argue the matter, I would suggest that it is useful to conceive of a political system as having a boundary in the same sense as a physical system. The boundary of a political system is defined by all those actions more or less directly related to the making of binding decisions for a society; every social action that does not partake of this characteristic will be excluded from the system and thereby will automatically be viewed as an external variable in the environment.

(2) Inputs and outputs. Presumably, if we select political systems for special study, we do so because we believe that they have characteristically important consequences for society, namely, authoritative decisions. These consequences I shall call the outputs. If we judged that political systems did not have important outputs for society, we would probably not be interested in them.

Unless a system is approaching a state of entropy—and we can assume that this is not true of most political systems—it must have continuing inputs to keep it going. Without inputs the system can do no work; without outputs we cannot identify the work done by the system. The specific research tasks in this connection would be to identify the

[2] My conceptions relating to system theory have been enriched through my participation in the Staff Theory Seminar of the Mental Health Research Institute at the University of Michigan. There has been such thorough mingling of ideas in this Seminar that rather than try to trace paternity, I shall simply indicate my obligation to the collective efforts of the Seminar.

inputs and the forces that shape and change them, to trace the processes through which they are transformed into outputs, to describe the general conditions under which such processes can be maintained, and to establish the relationship between outputs and succeeding inputs of the system.

From this point of view, much light can be shed on the working of a political system if we take into account the fact that much of what happens within a system has its birth in the efforts of the members of the system to cope with the changing environment . . .

❖   ❖   ❖   ❖   ❖

(3) Differentiation within a system. As we shall see in a moment, from the environment come both energy to activate a system and information with regard to which the system uses this energy. In this way a system is able to do work. It has some sort of output that is different from the input that enters from the environment. We can take it as a useful hypothesis that if a political system is to perform some work for anything but a limited interval of time, a minimal amount of differentiation in its structure must occur. In fact, empirically it is impossible to find a significant political system in which the same units all perform the same activities at the same time. The members of a system engage in at least some minimal division of labor that provides a structure within which action takes place.

(4) Integration of a system. This fact of differentiation opens up a major area of inquiry with regard to political systems. Structural differentiation sets in motion forces that are potentially disintegrative in their results for the system. If two or more units are performing different kinds of activity at the same time, how are these activities to be brought into the minimal degree of articulation necessary if the members of the system are not to end up in utter disorganization with regard to the production of the outputs of interest to us? We can hypothesize that if a structured system is to maintain itself, it must provide mechanisms whereby its members are integrated or induced to cooperate in some minimal degree so that they can make authoritative decisions.

II. INPUTS: DEMANDS

Now that I have mentioned some major attributes of political systems that I suggest require special attention if we are to develop a generalized approach, I want to consider in greater detail the way in which an examination of inputs and outputs will shed some light on the working of these systems.

Among inputs of a political system there are two basic kinds: demands and support. These inputs give a political system its dynamic character. They furnish it both with the raw material or information that the system is called upon to process and with the energy to keep it going.

The reason why a political system emerges in a society at all—that is, why men engage in political activity—is that demands are being made by persons or groups in the society that cannot all be fully satisfied. In all societies one fact dominates political life: scarcity prevails with regard to most of the valued things. . . .

Systematic research would require us to address ourselves to several key questions with regard to these demands.

(1) How do demands arise and assume their particular character in a society? In answer to this question, we can point out that demands have their birth in two sectors of experience: either in the environment of a system or within the system itself. We shall call these the external and internal demands, respectively.

Let us look at the external demands first. I find it useful to see the environment not as an undifferentiated mass of events but rather as systems clearly distinguishable from one another and from the political system. In the environment we have such systems as the ecology, economy, culture, personality, social structure, and demography. Each of these constitutes a major set of variables in the setting that helps to shape the kind of demands entering a political system. For purposes of illustrating what I mean, I shall say a few words about culture.

The members of every society act within the framework of an ongoing culture that shapes their general goals, specific objectives, and the procedures that the members feel ought to be used. Every culture derives part of its unique quality from the fact that it emphasizes one or more special aspects of behavior and this strategic emphasis serves to differentiate it from other cultures with respect to the demands that it generates. As far as the mass of the people is concerned, some cultures, such as our own, are weighted heavily on the side of economic wants, success, privacy, leisure activity, and rational efficiency. Others, such as that of the Fox Indians, strive toward the maintenance of harmony, even if in the process the goals of efficiency and rationality may be sacrificed. Still others, such as the Kachins of highland Burma, stress the pursuit of power and prestige. The culture embodies the standards of value in a society and thereby marks out areas of potential conflict, if the valued things are in short supply relative to demand. The typical demands that will find their way into the political process will concern the matters in conflict that are labeled important by the culture. For this reason we cannot hope to understand the nature of the demands presenting themselves for political settlement unless we are ready to explore systematically and intensively their connection with the culture. And what I have said about culture applies, with suitable modifications, to other parts of the setting of a political system.

But not all demands originate or have their major locus in the environment. Important types stem from situations occurring within a political system itself. Typically, in every on-going system, demands may emerge for alterations in the political relationships of the members themselves, as the result of dissatisfaction stemming from these relationships. For example, in a political system based upon representation, in which equal representation is an important political norm, demands may arise for equalizing representation between urban and rural voting districts. Similarly, demands for changes in the process of recruitment of formal political leaders, for modifications of the way in which constitutions are amended, and the like may all be internally inspired demands.

✿   ✿   ✿   ✿   ✿

(2) How are demands transformed into issues? What determines whether a demand becomes a matter for serious political discussion or remains something to be resolved privately among the members of society? The occurrence of a demand, whether internal or external, does not thereby automatically convert it into a political *issue*. Many demands die at birth or linger on with the support of an insignificant fraction of the society and are never raised to the level of possible political decision. Others become issues, an issue being a demand that the members of a political system are prepared to deal with as a significant item for discussion through the recognized channels in the system.

✿   ✿   ✿   ✿   ✿

If we assume that political science is primarily concerned with the way in which authoritative decisions are made for a society, demands require special attention as a major type of input of political systems. I have suggested that demands influence the behavior of a system in a number of ways. They constitute a significant part of the material upon which the system operates. They are also one of the sources of change in political systems, since as the environment fluctuates it generates new types of demand-inputs for the system. Accordingly, without this attention to the origin and determinants of demands we would be at a loss to be able to treat rigorously not only the operation of a system at a moment of time but also its change over a specified interval. Both the statics and historical dynamics of a political system depend upon a detailed understanding of demands, particularly of the impact of the setting on them.

III. INPUTS: SUPPORT

Inputs of demands alone are not enough to keep a political system operating. They are only the raw material out of which finished products called decisions are manufactured. Energy in the form of actions or orientations promoting and resisting a political system, the demands arising in it, and the decisions issuing from it must also be put into the system to keep it running. This input I shall call support.[3] Without support, demands could not be satisfied or conflicts in goals composed. If demands are to be acted upon, the members of a system undertaking to pilot the demands through to their transformation into binding decisions and those who seek to influence the relevant processes in any way must be able to count on support from others in the system. Just how much support, from how many and which members of a political system, are separate and important questions that I shall touch on shortly.

What do we mean by support? We can say that A supports B either when A acts on behalf of or when he orients himself favorably toward B's goals, interests, and actions. Supportive behavior may thus be of two kinds. It may consist of actions promoting the goals, interests, and actions of another person. We may vote for a political candidate, or defend a decision by the highest court of the land. In these cases, support manifests itself through overt action.

On the other hand, supportive behavior may involve not external observable acts, but those internal forms of behavior we call orientations or states of mind. As I use the phrase, a supportive state of mind is a deep-seated set of attitudes or predispositions, or a readiness to act on behalf of some other person. It exists when we say that a man is loyal to his party, attached to democracy, or infused with patriotism. What such phrases as these have in common is the fact that they refer to a state of feelings on the part of a person. No overt action is involved at this level of description, although the implication is that the individual will pursue a course of action consistent with his attitudes. . . .

Supportive states of mind are vital inputs for the operation and maintenance of a political system. For example, it is often said that the struggle in the international sphere concerns mastery over men's minds.

---

[3] The concept support has been used by Talcott Parsons in an unpublished paper entitled "Reflections on the Two-Party System." I am pleased to note that in this article Professor Parsons also seems to be moving in the direction of input-output analysis of political problems, although the extent to which he uses other aspects of system theory is not clear to me.

To a certain extent this is true. If the members of a political system are deeply attached to a system or its ideals, the likelihood of their participating in either domestic or foreign politics in such a way as to undermine the system is reduced by a large factor. Presumably, even in the face of considerable provocation, ingrained supportive feelings of loyalty may be expected to prevail.

We shall need to identify the typical mechanisms through which supportive attitudes are inculcated and continuously reinforced within a political system. But our prior task is to specify and examine the political objects in relation to which support is extended.

(1) The Domain of Support

Support is fed into the political system in relation to three objects: the community, the regime, and the government. There must be convergence of attitude and opinion as well as some willingness to act with regard to each of these objects. Let us examine each in turn.

(a) The political community. No political system can continue to operate unless its members are willing to support the existence of a group that seeks to settle differences or promote decisions through peaceful action in common. The point is so obvious—being dealt with usually under the heading of the growth of national unity—that it may well be overlooked; and yet it is a premise upon which the continuation of any political system depends. . . .

☼   ☼   ☼   ☼   ☼

(b) The regime. Support for a second major part of a political system helps to supply the energy to keep the system running. This aspect of the system I shall call the regime. It consists of all those arrangements that regulate the way in which the demands put into the system are settled and the way in which decisions are put into effect. They are the so-called rules of the game, in the light of which actions by members of the system are legitimated and accepted by the bulk of the members as authoritative. Unless there is a minimum convergence of attitudes in support of these fundamental rules—the constitutional principles, as we call them in Western society—there would be insufficient harmony in the actions of the members of a system to meet the problems generated by their support of a political community. The fact of trying to settle demands in common means that there must be known principles governing the way in which resolutions of differences of claims are to take place.

THE STUDY OF POLITICAL SYSTEMS

(c) The government. If a political system is going to be able to handle the conflicting demands put into it, not only must the members of the system be prepared to support the settlement of these conflicts in common and possess some consensus with regard to the rules governing the mode of settlement; they must also be ready to support a government as it undertakes the concrete tasks involved in negotiating such settlements. When we come to the outputs of a system, we shall see the rewards that are available to a government for mobilizing support. At this point, I just wish to draw attention to this need on the part of a government for support if it is going to be able to make decisions with regard to demands. Of course, a government may elicit support in many ways: through persuasion, consent, or manipulation. It may also impose unsupported settlements of demands through threats of force. But it is a familiar axiom of political science that a government based upon force alone is not long for this world; it must buttress its position by inducing a favorable state of mind in its subjects through fair or foul means.

✿　✿　✿　✿　✿

(2) Quantity and Scope of Support

How much support needs to be put into a system and how many of its members need to contribute such support if the system is to be able to do the job of converting demands to decisions? No ready answer can be offered. The actual situation in each case would determine the amount and scope required. We can, however, visualize a number of situations that will be helpful in directing our attention to possible generalizations.

Under certain circumstances very few members need to support a system at any level. The members might be dull and apathetic, indifferent to the general operations of the system, its progress or decisions. In a loosely connected system such as India has had, this might well be the state of mind of by far the largest segment of the membership. Either in fact they have not been affected by national decisions or they have not perceived that they were so affected. They may have little sense of identification with the present regime and government and yet, with regard to the input of demands, the system may be able to act on the basis of the support offered by the known 3 per cent of the Western-oriented politicians and intellectuals who are politically active. In other words, we can have a small minority putting in quantitatively sufficient supportive energy to keep the system going. . . .

Alternatively, we may find that all the members of a system are putting in support, but the amount may be so low as to place one or all aspects of the system in jeopardy. Modern France is perhaps a classic illustration. . . .

* * * * *

IV. MECHANISMS OF SUPPORT

To this point I have suggested that no political system can yield the important outputs we call authoritative decisions unless, in addition to demands, support finds its way into the system. I have discussed the possible object to which support may be directed, and some problems with regard to the domain, quantity, and scope of support. We are now ready to turn to the main question raised by our attention to support as a crucial input: how do systems typically manage to maintain a steady flow of support? Without it a system will not absorb sufficient energy from its members to be able to convert demands to decisions.

In theory, there might be an infinite variety of means through which members could be induced to support a system; in practice, certain well-established classes of mechanisms are used. . . .

A society generates support for a political system in two ways: through outputs that meet the demands of the members of society; and through the processes of politicization. Let us look at outputs first.

(1) Outputs as a Mechanism of Support

An output of a political system, it will be recalled, is a political decision or policy. One of the major ways of strengthening the ties of the members to their system is through providing decisions that tend to satisfy the day-to-day demands of these members. Fundamentally this is the truth that lies in the aphorism that one can fool some of the people some of the time but not all of them all of the time. Without some minimal satisfaction of demands, the ardor of all but the most fanatical patriot is sure to cool. The outputs, consisting of political decisions, constitute a body of specific inducements for the members of a system to support that system.

Inducements of this kind may be positive or negative. Where negative, they threaten the members of the system with various kinds of sanctions ranging from a small monetary fine to physical detention, ostracism, or loss of life, as in our own system with regard to the case of legally defined treason. In every system support stems in part from fear of sanctions or compulsion; in autocratic systems the proportion of co-erced support is at a maximum. For want of space I shall confine myself to those cases where positive incentives loom largest.

Since the specific outputs of a system are policy decisions, it is upon the government that the final responsibility falls for matching or bal-ancing outputs of decisions against input of demand. But it is clear that to obtain the support of the members of a system through positive incentives, a government need not meet all the demands of even its most influential and ardent supporters. Most governments, or groups such as political parties that seek to control governments, succeed in building up a reserve of support. This reserve will carry the government along even though it offends its followers, so long as over the extended short run these followers perceive the particular government as one that is in general favorable to their interests. One form that this reserve support takes in Western society is that of party loyalty, since the party is the typical instrument in a mass industrialized society for mobilizing and maintaining support for a government. However, continuous lack of specific rewards through policy decisions ultimately leads to the danger that even the deepest party loyalty may be shaken.

✩ ✩ ✩ ✩ ✩

Thus a system need not meet *all the demands* of its members so long as it has stored up a reserve of support over the years. Nor need it satisfy even *some of the demands* of all its members. Just whose de-mands a system must seek to meet, how much of their demands, at what time, and under what conditions are questions for special research. We can say in advance that at least the demands of the most influential members require satisfaction. But this tells us little unless we know how to discover the influentials in a political system and how new sets of members rise to positions of influence.[4]

The critical significance of the decisions of governments for the support of the other two aspects of a system—namely, the political com-munity and the regime—is clear from what I have said above. Not all withdrawal of support from a government has consequences for the success or failure of a regime or community. But persistent inability of a government to produce satisfactory outputs for the members of a system may well lead to demands for changing of the regime or for dissolution of the political community. It is for this reason that the input-output balance is a vital mechanism in the life of a political system.

---

[4] See C. W. Mills, *The Power Elite*, New York, 1956.

(2) Politicization as a Mechanism of Support

It would be wrong to consider that the level of support available to a system is a function exclusively of the outputs in the form of either sanctions or rewards. If we did so conclude, we could scarcely account for the maintenance of numerous political systems in which satisfaction of demands has been manifestly low, in which public coercion is limited, and yet which have endured for epochs. Alternately, it might be difficult to explain how political systems could endure and yet manage to flout or thwart urgent demands, failing thereby to render sufficient *quid pro quo* for the input of support. The fact is that whatever reserve of support has been accumulated through past decisions is increased and reinforced by a complicated method for steadily manufacturing support through what I shall call the process of politicization. It is an awkward term, but nevertheless an appropriately descriptive one.

As each person grows up in a society, through a network of rewards and punishments the other members of society communicate to and instill in him the various institutionalized goals and norms of that society. This is well known in social research as the process of socialization. Through its operation a person learns to play his various social roles. Part of these goals and norms relate to what the society considers desirable in political life. The ways in which these political patterns are learned by the members of society constitute what I call the process of politicization. Through it a person learns to play his political roles, which include the absorption of the proper political attitudes.

*   *   *   *   *

The mechanism through which this learning takes place is of considerable significance in understanding how a political system generates and accumulates a strong reserve of support. Although we cannot pursue the details, we can mention a few of the relevant dimensions. In the first place, of course, the learning or politicization process does not stop at any particular period for the individual; it starts with the child and, in the light of our knowledge of learning, may have its deepest impact through the teen age. . . .

In the second place, the actual process of politicization at its most general level brings into operation a complex network of rewards and punishments. For adopting the correct political attitudes and performing

the right political acts, for conforming to the generally accepted interpretations of political goals, and for undertaking the institutionalized
obligations of a member of the given system, we are variously rewarded
or punished. For conforming we are made to feel worthy, wanted, and
respected and often obtain material advantages such as wealth, influence, improved opportunities. For deviating beyond the permissible
range, we are made to feel unworthy, rejected, dishonored, and often
suffer material losses.

This does not mean that the pattern of rewards and punishments is
by any means always effective; if it were, we would never have changed
from the Stone Age. A measure of non-conformity may at certain stages
in the life history of a political system itself become a respected norm.
Even where this is not the case, the most seductive rewards and the
severest punishments will never succeed in preventing some of the
members of a system from pursuing what they consider to be their
inextinguishable interests and from seeking, with varying degrees of
success, to change the goals and norms of the system. This is one of the
important sources of political change closely associated with changes in
the inputs of demands that are due to a changing environment. . . .

In the third place, the means used for communicating the goals and
norms to others tend to be repetitive in all societies. The various political myths, doctrines, and philosophies transmit to each generation a
particular interpretation of the goals and norms. The decisive links in
this chain of transmission are parents, siblings, peers, teachers, organizations, and social leaders, as well as physical symbols such as flags or
totems, ceremonies, and rituals freighted with political meaning.

These processes through which attachments to a political system
become built into the maturing member of a society I have lumped
together under the rubric of politicization. They illustrate the way in
which members of a system learn what is expected of them in political
life and how they ought to do what is expected of them. In this way they
acquire knowledge about their political roles and a desire to perform
them. In stable systems the support that accrues through these means
adds to the reservoir of support being accumulated on a day-to-day basis
through the outputs of decisions.[5] The support obtained through politicization tends to be relatively—although, as we have seen, not wholly—
independent of the vagaries of day-to-day outputs.

When the basic political attachments become deeply rooted or
institutionalized, we say that the system has become accepted as legitimate. Politicization therefore effectively sums up the way in which
legitimacy is created and transmitted in a political system. And it is an
empirical observation that in those instances where political systems

[5] In primitive systems, politicization, not outputs of decisions, is normally the chief
mechanism.

have survived the longest, support has been nourished by an ingrained belief in the legitimacy of the relevant governments and regimes.

༺✠༻

2. A FUNCTIONAL APPROACH TO COMPARATIVE POLITICS*

g a b r i e l   a.   a l m o n d

To find concepts and categories appropriate for the comparison of political systems differing radically in scale, structure, and culture—to say nothing of dealing adequately with the familiar phenomena of Western Europe—we have had to turn to sociological and anthropological theory. Some of the concepts we use . . . , such as *political system, political role, political culture, political structure,* and *political socialization,* have acquired a certain currency among scholars in the field. Perhaps their utility may be said to have been tested. The additional categories which we introduce here have had only a preliminary trial. . . .

It ought also to be pointed out that the search for new concepts reflected in these terms is not an *ad hoc* matter. It reflects an underlying drift toward a new and coherent way of thinking about and studying politics that is implied in such slogans as the "behavioral approach." This urge toward a new conceptual unity is suggested when we compare the new terms with the old. Thus, instead of the concept of the "state," limited as it is by legal and institutional meanings, we prefer "political system"; instead of "powers," which again is a legal concept in connotation, we are beginning to prefer "functions"; instead of "offices" (legal again), we prefer "roles"; instead of "institutions," which again directs us toward formal norms, "structures"; instead of "public opinion" and "citizenship training," formal and rational in meaning, we prefer "polit-

*   From "Introduction: A Functional Approach to Comparative Politics" by Gabriel A. Almond in Gabriel A. Almond and James S. Coleman, eds., *The Politics of the Developing Areas.* Reprinted by permission of the Princeton University Press. Copyright © 1960 by Princeton University Press. Selections from pp. 3–55.

ical culture" and "political socialization." We are not setting aside
public law and philosophy as disciplines, but simply telling them to
move over to make room for a growth in political theory that has been
long overdue.

✧   ✧   ✧   ✧   ✧

I. THE POLITICAL SYSTEM

If the concept of political system is to serve the purpose to which we
wish to put it—that is, separate out analytically the structures which
perform political functions in all societies regardless of scale, degree of
differentiation, and culture—we shall have to specify what we mean by
politics and the political system. . . .

✧   ✧   ✧   ✧   ✧

. . . What we propose is that the political system is that system of
interactions to be found in all independent societies which performs the
functions of integration and adaptation (both internally and vis-à-vis
other societies) by means of the employment, or threat of employment, of
more or less legitimate physical compulsion. The political system is the
legitimate, order-maintaining or transforming system in the society. We
use the term "more or less" to modify legitimacy because we do not
want to exclude from our definition political systems, like the totalitarian
ones, where the degree of legitimacy may be very much in doubt;
revolutionary systems, where the basis of legitimacy may be in process of
change; or non-Western systems, in which there may be more than one
legitimate system in operation. We use the term "physical compulsion"
since we believe that we can distinguish political systems from other
social systems only by such a specific definition, but this is by no means
the same thing as reducing politics to force. Legitimate force is the
thread that runs through the inputs and outputs of the political system,
giving it its special quality and salience and its coherence as a system. . . .

With the conceptions of input and output we have moved from the
definition of "political" to that of "system," for if by the "political" we
mean to separate out a certain set of interactions in a society in order to
relate it to other sets, by "system" we mean to attribute a particular set
of properties to these interactions. Among these properties are (1) comprehensiveness, (2) interdependence, and (3) existence of boundaries.
The criterion of comprehensiveness means that when we speak of the
political system we include all the interactions—inputs as well as outputs
—which affect the use or the threat of use of physical coercion. We mean
to include not just the structures based on law, like parliaments, execu-

tives, bureaucracies, and courts, or just the associational or formally organized units, like parties, interest groups, and media of communication, but *all of the structures in their political aspects*, including undifferentiated structures like kinship and lineage, status and caste groups, as well as anomic phenomena like riots, street demonstrations, and the like.

By "interdependence" we mean that a change in one subset of interactions (e.g., the electoral reforms of 1832 in England) produces changes in all the other subsets (e.g., the characteristics of the party system, the functions of parliament and cabinet, and so forth). . . .

By the existence of a boundary in the political system, we mean that there are points where other systems end and the political system begins. . . .

✿   ✿   ✿   ✿   ✿

II. THE COMMON PROPERTIES OF POLITICAL SYSTEMS

The Universe of Political Systems

✿   ✿   ✿   ✿   ✿

. . . What are the common properties of all political systems? What makes the Bergdama band and the United Kingdom members of the same universe? We would suggest that there are four characteristics which all political systems have in common, and in terms of which they may be compared.

1. First, all political systems, including the simplest ones, have political structure. In a sense it is correct to say that even the simplest societies have all of the types of political structure which are to be found in the most complex ones. They may be compared with one another according to the degree and form of structural specialization.

2. Second, the same functions are performed in all political systems, even though these functions may be performed with different frequencies, and by different kinds of structures. Comparisons may be made according to the frequency of the performance of the functions, the kinds of structures performing them, and the style of their performance.

3. Third, all political structure, no matter how specialized, whether it is found in primitive or in modern societies, is multifunctional. Political systems may be compared according to the degree of specificity of function in the structure; but the limiting case, while specialized, still involves substantial multifunctionality.

4. Fourth, all political systems are "mixed" systems in the cultural

sense. There are no "all-modern" cultures and structures, in the sense of rationality, and no all-primitive ones, in the sense of traditionality. They differ in the relative dominance of the one as against the other, and in the pattern of mixture of the two components.

The Universality of Political Structure

There is no such thing as a society which maintains internal and external order, which has no "political structure"—i.e., legitimate patterns of interaction by means of which this order is maintained. Furthermore, all the types of political structures which are to be found in the modern systems are to be found in the non-Western and primitive ones. The interactions, or the structures, may be occasional or intermittent. They may not be clearly visible, but to say that there are no structures would be to argue that the performance of the political function is random. . . .

. . . An adequate analysis of a political system must locate and characterize all of these functions, and not simply those performed by the specialized political structure. . . . The rule to follow which we suggest here is: If the functions are there, then the structures must be, even though we may find them tucked away, so to speak, in nooks and crannies of other social systems.

The Universality of the Political Functions

But if all the structures which are to be found in specialized Western systems are also to be found in the non-Western, we are able to locate them only if we ask the correct functional questions. . . .

✧   ✧   ✧   ✧   ✧

. . . The particular functional categories which we employ . . . were developed for the purpose of comparing political systems as whole systems; and particularly for comparing the modern Western ones with the transitional and traditional.

They were derived in a very simple way. The problem essentially was to ask a series of questions based on the distinctive political activities existing in Western complex systems. In other words, we derived our functional categories from the political systems in which structural specialization and functional differentiation have taken place to the greatest extent. Thus the functions performed by associational interest groups in Western systems led us to the question, "How are interests articulated in different political systems?" or the *interest articulation* function. The functions performed by political parties in Western political systems led us to the question, "How are articulated demands or interests aggregated or combined in different political systems?" or the *aggregative function*. The functions performed by specialized media of communication in Western political systems led us to the question, "How is political information communicated in different political systems?" or the *political communication function*. The existence in all political systems of methods of political recruitment and training led us to the question, "How are people recruited to and socialized into political roles and orientations in different political systems?" or the *recruitment* and *socialization function*. Finally, the three authoritative governmental functions, *rule-making, rule application,* and *rule adjudication,* are the old functions of "separation of powers," except that an effort has been made to free them of their structural overtones—rule-making rather than "legislation," rule application rather than "administration." Indeed, this taking over intact of the three functions of "separation of powers" reflects the political bias of this undertaking. It was the conviction of the collaborators in this study that the political functions rather than the governmental ones, the input functions rather than the output, would be most important in characterizing non-Western political systems, and in discriminating types and stages of political development among them.

Our functional categories therefore are as follows:

    A.   Input functions
        1. Political socialization and recruitment
        2. Interest articulation
        3. Interest aggregation
        4. Political communication
    B.   Output functions
        5. Rule-making
        6. Rule application
        7. Rule adjudication

✿   ✿   ✿   ✿   ✿

III. THE FUNCTIONS OF THE POLITICAL SYSTEM

Political Socialization and Recruitment

✿   ✿   ✿   ✿   ✿

What do we mean by the function of political socialization? We mean that all political systems tend to perpetuate their cultures and structures through time, and that they do this mainly by means of the socializing influences of the primary and secondary structures through which the young of the society pass in the process of maturation. We use the qualifier "mainly" deliberately, since political socialization, like learning in general, does not terminate at the point of maturation, however this is defined in different societies. It is continuous throughout life. . . .

✵　　✵　　✵　　✵　　✵

Political socialization is the process of induction into the political culture. Its end product is a set of attitudes—cognitions, value standards, and feelings—toward the political system, its various roles, and role incumbents. It also includes knowledge of, values affecting, and feelings toward the inputs of demands and claims into the system, and its authoritative outputs.

In comparing the political socialization function in different political systems, it becomes necessary to examine the structures which are involved in the function and the style of the socialization. . . .

✵　　✵　　✵　　✵　　✵

The analysis of the political socialization function in a particular society is basic to the whole field of political analysis, since it not only gives us insight into the pattern of political culture and subcultures in that society, but also locates for us in the socialization processes of the society the points where particular qualities and elements of the political culture are introduced, and the points in the society where these components are being sustained or modified. Furthermore, the study of political socialization and political culture is essential to the understanding of the other political functions. . . .

The relationship between the political socialization function and the *political recruitment function* is comparable to the relationship between Linton's "basic personality" and "status" or "role" personality.[1] All members of societies go through common socialization experiences. Differences in the political cultures of societies are introduced by differences in the political socialization processes in the subcultures of that society, and by differences in socialization into different status groups and roles.

The political recruitment function takes up where the general political socialization function leaves off. It recruits members of the society

[1] Ralph Linton, *The Cultural Background of Personality*. New York, 1945, pp. 125 ff.

out of particular subcultures—religious communities, statuses, classes, ethnic communities, and the like—and inducts them into the specialized roles of the political system, trains them in the appropriate skills, provides them with political cognitive maps, values, expectations, and affects.

In comparing the political recruitment function in different political systems, we have again to consider—as we did in the analysis of the political socialization function—the social and political structures which perform the function and the style of the performance. We have to examine in each political system the role of family, kinship, and lineage in recruitment to specialized political roles, status and caste, religious community, ethnic and linguistic origins, social class, schooling and training institutions. We have to examine the structures affecting specific induction patterns—political parties, election systems, bureaucratic examining systems, "in-role political socialization," and channels of recruitment and advancement within the political and authoritative governmental structures. . . .

Styles of political recruitment may be compared according to the way in which ascriptive and particularistic criteria combine with performance and universalistic criteria. Thus, in a modern Western political system, recruitment is affected both by ascriptive and by performance criteria. Kinship, friendship, "school ties," religious affiliation, and status qualities affect recruitment in various important ways, but the more thorough-going the political modernization, the more these ascriptive criteria are contained within or limited by achievement criteria— educational levels, performance levels on examinations, formal records of achievement in political roles, and the like. But the recruitment pattern is both structurally and culturally dualistic. Similarly, in the primitive or traditional political system the recruitment function is dualistic, but the achievement or performance criterion is less explicitly and generally applied. A chief or headman is selected because of his place in a lineage. He may be removed for poor performance according to either sacred or secular norms. He is replaced again by ascriptive criteria.

✧　✧　✧　✧　✧

Interest Articulation

Every political system has some way of articulating interests, claims, demands for political action. The function of interest articulation . . . is closely related to the political socialization function and the patterns of political culture produced by it. Among the input functions, interest articulation is of crucial importance since it occurs at the boundary of the political system. The particular structures which perform the articulation function and the style of their performance determine the character of the boundary between polity and society.

In characterizing the interest articulation function in a political system and in comparing it with that of other political systems, we have to discover first what kinds of structures perform the function and, second, the style of their performance. Four main types of structures may be involved in interest articulation: (1) institutional interest groups, (2) non-associational interest groups, (3) anomic interest groups, and (4) associational interest groups.

By institutional interest groups we have in mind phenomena occurring within such organizations as legislatures, political executives, armies, bureaucracies, churches, and the like. These are organizations which perform other social or political functions but which, as corporate bodies or through groups within them (such as legislative blocs, officer cliques, higher or lower clergy or religious orders, departments, skill groups, and ideological cliques in bureaucracies), may articulate their own interests or represent the interests of groups in the society.

By non-associational interests we have in mind kinship and lineage groups, ethnic, regional, religious, status and class groups which articulate interests informally, and intermittently, through individuals, cliques, family and religious heads, and the like. Examples might be the complaint of a tribal chief to a paramount chief about tributes or law enforcement affecting his lineage group; a request made by a landowner to a bureaucrat in a social club regarding the tariff on grains; or the complaint of an informal delegation from a linguistic group regarding language instruction in the schools.

The distinguishing characteristic of the institutional interest group is the fact that a formally organized body made up of professionally employed officials or employees, with another function, performs an interest articulation function, or constitutes a base of operations for a clique or subgroup which does. The distinguishing characteristic of the non-associational interest is that the structure of interest articulation is intermittent and often informal.

By anomic interest groups we mean more or less spontaneous breakthroughs into the political system from the society, such as riots and demonstrations. Their distinguishing characteristic is their relative structural and functional lability. We use the term "relative" advisedly, since riots and demonstrations may be deliberately organized and controlled. But even when organized and controlled they have the potentiality of exceeding limits and norms and disturbing or even changing the political system. Though they may begin as interest articulation structures, they may end up performing a recruitment function (i.e., transferring power from one group to another), a rule-making function (i.e., changing the constitution, enacting, revising, or rescinding statutes), a rule application function (i.e., freeing prisoners, rescinding a bureaucratic decision), a rule adjudication function (i.e., "trying" and lynching), an aggregative or a communication function (drawing other interest groups to it, or publicizing a protest).

Associational interest groups are the specialized structures of interest articulation—trade unions, organizations of businessmen or industrialists, ethnic associations, associations organized by religious denominations, civic groups, and the like. Their particular characteristics are explicit representation of the interests of a particular group, orderly procedures for the formulation of interests and demands, and transmission of these demands to other political structures such as political parties, legislatures, bureaucracies.

‡   ‡   ‡   ‡   ‡

The structure and style of interest articulation define the pattern of boundary maintenance between the polity and the society, and within the political system affect the boundaries between the various parts of the political system—parties, legislatures, bureaucracies, and courts. For example, a high incidence of anomic interest articulation will mean poor boundary maintenance between the society and the polity, frequent eruptions of unprocessed claims without controlled direction into the political system. It will affect boundary maintenance within the political system by performing aggregative, rule-making, rule application, and rule adjudication functions outside of appropriate channels and without benefit of appropriate process.

A high incidence of institutional interest articulation is also an indication of poor boundary maintenance between the polity and the society and within the political system. Thus the direct impingement of a church (or parts of a church) or of business corporations on the political system introduces raw or diffuse claims and demands difficult to process or aggregate with other inputs into the political system. Within the political system a high incidence of interest articulation by bureaucratic or military groups creates boundary difficulties among rule application, rule-making, articulative, and aggregative structures, and may indeed result in their atrophy. A high incidence of non-associational interest articulation—in other words, the performance of the interest articulation function intermittently by individuals, informal groups, or representatives of kinship or status groups, and so forth—similarly may represent poor boundary maintenance between the polity and the society. . . . Finally, a high incidence of associational interest articulation may indicate good boundary maintenance between society and polity and may contribute to such maintenance within the subsystems of the political system. Good boundary maintenance is attained by virtue of the regulatory role of associational interest groups in processing raw claims or interest articulations occurring elsewhere in the society and the political system, and directing them in an orderly way and in aggregable form through the party system, legislature, and bureaucracy.

✻　✻　✻　✻　✻

The Function of Aggregation

Every political system has some way of aggregating the interests, claims, and demands which have been articulated by the interest groups of the polity. Aggregation may be accomplished by means of the formulation of general policies in which interests are combined, accommodated, or otherwise taken account of, or by means of the recruitment of political personnel, more or less committed to a particular pattern of policy. The functions of articulation and aggregation overlap, just as do those of aggregation, recruitment, and rule-making. In certain political systems, such as the authoritarian and the primitive ones, the three functions of articulation, aggregation, and rule-making may be hardly differentiated from one another. In what appears to be a single act, a headman of a primitive society may read cues in his people, aggregate different cues and complaints, and issue an authoritative rule. We might say that he is intermittently interest articulator, aggregator, and rule-maker in the course of this process. . . .

The distinction between interest articulation and aggregation is a fluid one. The narrowest event of interest articulation initiated by a lineage head in a primitive political system, or the smallest constituent unit of a trade association, involves the aggregation of the claims of even smaller groups or of individuals or firms. Modern interest groups—particularly the "peak" associations—carry aggregation quite far, sometimes to the point of "speaking for" whole classes of the society—"labor," "agriculture," "business."

In our definition we reserve the term "aggregation" for the more inclusive levels of the combinatory processes, reserving the term "articulation" for the narrower expressions of interest. This is not the same thing as identifying interest articulation with "pressure groups" and aggregation with "political parties," though again in the developed modern systems these agencies have a distinctive and regulatory relation to these functions.

Actually the aggregative function may be performed within all of the subsystems of the political system—legislative bodies, political executives (cabinets, presidencies, kingships, chieftainships), bureaucracies, media of communication, party systems, interest groups of the various types. Parties, factions, blocs in legislatures; cliques or factions in political executives and bureaucracies; individual parties or party coalitions outside the legislature; and individual interest groups (in particular the civic or "general interest" groups) or *ad hoc* coalitions of interest groups —all perform an aggregative function, either by formulating alternative public policies or by supporting or advocating changes in political personnel.

But again it is the party system which is the distinctively modern structure of political aggregation and which in the modern, developed, democratic political system "regulates" or gives order to the performance of the aggregative function by the other structures. Without a party system the aggregative function may be performed covertly, diffusely, and particularistically, as in a political system such as Spain. . . .

. . . [P]arty systems are classified under four headings (1) authoritarian, (2) dominant non-authoritarian, (3) competitive two-party systems, and (4) competitive multiparty systems. Authoritarian party systems may in turn be classified into the totalitarian and authoritarian varieties. Totalitarian parties aggregate interests by means of the penetration of the social structure of the society and by the transmission and aggregation of demands and claims through the party structure. Overt interest articulation is permissible only at the lowest level of individual complaints against the lower-echelon authorities. Above this level, interest articulation and aggregation are latent or covert. . . .

Authoritarian parties . . . have some of the properties of totalitarian parties, except that the penetration of the party into the social structure is less complete and some interest groups are permitted to articulate demands overtly. . . .

Dominant non-authoritarian party systems are usually to be found in political systems where nationalist movements have been instrumental in attaining emancipation. Most of the significant interest groups, associational and non-associational, have joined in the nationalist movement around a common program of national independence. In the period following emancipation the nationalist party continues as the greatly dominant party, opposed in elections by relatively small left-wing or traditionalist and particularist movements. This type of party system is a formally free one, but the possibility of a coherent loyal opposition is lacking. Hence the dominant party is confronted by a complex problem of interest aggregation. . . .

The third type of party system is the competitive two-party system exemplified by the United Kingdom, the members of the old Commonwealth, and the United States. . . .

Multiparty systems may be divided into two classes—the so-called "working" multiparty systems of the Scandinavian area and the Low Countries, and the "immobilist" multiparty systems of France and Italy.

In the Scandinavian version of the multiparty system, some of the parties are broadly aggregative. . . . Secondly, the political culture is more homogeneous and fusional of secular and traditional elements. . . .

The characteristics of the "immobilist" type of multiparty system have been referred to in the discussion of the articulation function above. In comparison to the working multiparty system, with its relatively homogeneous political culture, the political socialization processes in countries such as France and Italy tend to produce a fragmented, isolative political culture, and as a consequence the relations between interest groups and parties are not of an instrumental bargaining kind. The boundaries between the articulative and aggregative functions are poorly maintained. . . .

We may also compare the performance of the aggregative function in different political systems in terms of its style. We may distinguish three different kinds of parties from this point of view: (1) secular, "pragmatic," bargaining parties; (2) absolute value-oriented, *Weltanschauung* or ideological parties; and (3) particularistic or traditional parties. The secular, pragmatic, bargaining type of party is instrumental and multivalue-oriented and its aggregative potential is relatively high. It is capable of generalized and adaptive programs intended to attract the maximum of interest support. . . .

The *Weltanschauung* or ideological party is absolute value-oriented and is usually revolutionary, reactionary, or oriented toward national independence or power. . . . [T]hey penetrate deeply into the society, almost replace all other social structures and, once securely rooted, are most difficult to dislodge by means short of violence.

The "particularistic" party is limited in its aggregative potential by being identified completely with the interests of a particular ethnic or religious group. . . .

❖   ❖   ❖   ❖   ❖

The Political Communication Function

All of the functions performed in the political system—political socialization and recruitment, interest articulation, interest aggregation, rule-making, rule application, and rule adjudication—are performed *by means of* communication. Parents, teachers, and priests, for example, impart political socialization through communication. Interest group leaders and representatives and party leaders perform their articulation and aggregation functions by communicating demands and policy recommendations. Legislators enact laws on the basis of information communicated to them and by communicating with one another and with other elements of the political system. In performing their functions, bureaucrats receive and analyze information from the society and from various parts of the polity. Similarly, the judicial process is carried on by means of communication.

At first thought, it might appear that there is no political communication function as such, that communication is an aspect of all of the other political functions. But a view such as this comes into conflict with the fact that in the modern political system differentiated media of communication have arisen which have developed a vocational ethics of "neutral" or objective communication. This ethics requires that the dissemination of information ought to be separated from the other political functions such as interest articulation, aggregation, and recruitment.

The separating-out of the communication function is not unique to modern political systems. . . . Primitive political systems have their drummers and runners, medieval towns had their criers, noblemen and kings their heralds. Even when there is no specialized political communicator, we can distinguish in the combined performance of, for example, the interest articulation and communication function the articulative event from the event of communicating the act of articulation. Thus a labor news medium may both advocate a trade union policy and communicate the content of that policy.

Failure to separate out the political communication function from the other political functions would deprive us of an essential tool necessary for distinguishing among political systems and characterizing their performance. It is not accidental that those political systems which have homogeneous political cultures and autonomous and differentiated structures of interest articulation and aggregation—the United Kingdom, the old Commonwealth, and the United States—also have to the greatest extent autonomous and differentiated media of communication. Nor is it accidental that the political systems with fragmented political cultures and relatively undifferentiated structures of interest articulation and aggregation—France and Italy, for example—also have a "press" which tends to be dominated by interest groups and political parties. The whole pattern of function in these political systems is affected by and tends to sustain a fragmented political culture. The control over the media of communication by parties and interest groups means that the audience for political communications is fragmented.

Thus it is essential in characterizing a political system to analyze the performance of the communication function. . . .

       ✿   ✿   ✿   ✿   ✿

But here, as in the treatment of the other functions, we have to avoid polarizations. The political communication networks of modern political systems are full of latent, diffuse, particularistic, and affective messages. . . .

In order to illustrate this mode of analysis of the political communication function, it may be useful to compare its performance in a modern Western system such as the United States with its performance in a transitional political system such as India. The comparison may be made in four respects: (1) the homogeneity of political information; (2) the mobility of information; (3) the volume of information; (4) the direction of the flow of information.

With respect to the homogeneity of political information, the point has already been made that the existence of autonomous and specialized media of communication and their penetration of the polity as a whole in modern Western political systems do not eliminate latent, diffuse, particularistic, and affective messages but only tend to afford opportunities throughout the political system for such messages to be couched in a manifest, specific, general, and instrumental language of politics. There is, in other words, a system whereby these messages are made manifest and homogeneous. . . . In contrast, in a transitional political system the messages in the communication network are heterogeneous. In the urban, relatively modern areas, specialized media of communication are to be found, but they tend to be organs of interest groups or political parties. Even in the cities, among the illiterate and uneducated elements of the urban population, the impact of the specialized media of communication is relatively limited. The illiterate and certainly the newly urbanized elements of the population tend to persist in a traditional, rural-type network of communication, with kinship, lineage, caste, and language groupings performing the political communication function intermittently, diffusely, and particularistically.

Although here too there are interpreters standing between the modernized and the non-modernized sectors of the urban populations, the problem of interpretation is much more difficult than in the modern Western system. The opinion leader in the United States receives information from the mass media and interprets it for his "opinion followers." These opinion followers tend to speak the same language, share the same values, and have cognitive maps similar to the ones conveyed in the mass media. The politician or interest group leader in an Indian urban area faces a far greater gap between the communication content of the literate modern sector of the Indian city and the illiterate and traditional sector. The gap is one of culture; it may include language in the specific sense, values, and cognitive maps differing radically in amount and specificity of information and in the range of political objects which they include. What has been said of the communication gap in the urban areas of a country like India is true to an even greater extent of connections between the urban and rural and village areas.

Here, the problem of interpretation is a massive one. The interpreter, whether he be a bureaucrat, interest group leader, or party leader, cannot readily find equivalents in language, values, and cognitive material to make an accurate translation. There is a genuine block in communication between the urban central and the rural and village periphery. No real penetration by communication is possible, and the audience of the polity consists of a loosely articulated congeries of subaudiences.

This takes us to the second major point of contrast between a modern Western and a transitional system of political communication—the mobility of information. In a modern Western system, neutral information flows freely throughout the polity, from the initiators of information into the neutral secondary media of communication, and into the capillaries of primary communication. In a transitional system, information circulates relatively freely in the urban areas, but never penetrates fully the diffuse and undifferentiated networks of the traditional and rural areas. Obstacles to mobility exist in both the input and the output process.

Third, in the modern Western system, the volume of political information passing through the communication network is far greater than in a transitional system. . . . The volume of flow in a transitional system is uneven. Much information remains covert and latent, and it is consequently difficult to make political estimates accurately and quickly.

Finally, there are important differences in the direction of the flow of information. The output of messages from the authoritative governmental structures in a transitional system tends to be far larger than the input of messages from the society. The government employs the mass media and operates through its own media as well. To be sure, governmental messages cannot be accurately transmitted to "tribesmen," "kinsmen," and "villagers." They may hear the messages over the radio, but they cannot register their meaning precisely. Nevertheless the messages get there physically. On the input side, much important information regarding the needs of the base and periphery of the society never gets explicated, and cannot therefore be fully taken account of by other elements in the political system.

✿   ✿   ✿   ✿   ✿

The Governmental Functions: Rule-Making, Rule Application, Rule Adjudication

. . . [In the analysis of developing areas], far greater stress . . . [must be] placed on the political functions than on the governmental. The primary reasons for this are the indeterminacy of the formal governmental structures in most of the non-Western areas, and the gross deviations in the performance of the governmental functions from the constitutional and legal norms. Most of these political systems either have had, have now, or aspire to constitutions which provide for legislatures, executives, and judiciaries. In the distribution of legal powers they follow either the British, the American, or the French model. But it is the exceptional case in which these institutions perform in any way corresponding to these norms. A careful examination of governmental structures and their formal powers would have yielded little of predictive value.

On the other hand, a careful examination of the political culture of these political systems, the factors making for change, the political socialization processes, patterns of recruitment into politics, and the characteristics of the infrastructure—interest groups, political parties, and media of communication—yield some insight into the directions and tempo of political change. . . .

In a recent paper Shils[2] classifies the "new states" of the non-Western world into five groups: (1) political democracies, (2) "tutelary" democracies, (3) modernizing oligarchies, (4) totalitarian oligarchies, and (5) traditional oligarchies. Although these are classes of *political systems*, they each imply a particular state of governmental structure.

The political democracies are those systems with functioning and relatively autonomous legislatures, executives, courts, and with differentiated and autonomous interest groups, political parties, and media of communication. In the non-Western areas, Japan, Turkey, Israel, and Chile are examples which approximate this type.

Tutelary democracies are political systems which have adopted both the formal norms of the democratic polity—universal suffrage, freedom of association, and of speech and publication—and the structural forms of democracy. In addition, the elites of these systems have the goal of democratizing their polities even though they may be unclear as to the requirements—in particular, the requirements in political infrastructure and function. In reality, as Shils points out, these systems are characterized by a concentration of power in the executive and the bureaucracy. The legislature tends to be relatively powerless, and the independence of the judiciary has not been fully attained. A country such as Ghana comes close to this model.

Modernizing oligarchies are political systems controlled by bureaucratic and/or army officer cliques in which democratic constitutions have been suspended or in which they do not exist. The goals of the elites may or may not include democratization. The modernizing impulse

---

[2] Edward Shils, "*Political Development in the New States*" (mimeographed paper prepared for the Committee on Comparative Politics, Social Science Research Council, 1959).

usually takes the form of a concern for efficiency and rationality, and an effort to eliminate corruption and traditionality. Modernizing oligarchies are usually strongly motivated toward economic development. The governmental structure of modernizing oligarchies concentrates powers in the hands of a clique of military officers or bureaucrats who are usually placed in control of the chief ministries. Turkey under Atatürk and contemporary Pakistan and the Sudan are examples of modernizing oligarchies.

Totalitarian oligarchy such as exists in North Korea and Viet Minh differs from modernizing oligarchy by the degree of penetration of the society by the polity, the degree of concentration of power in the ruling elite, and the tempo of social mobilization. There have been two types of totalitarianism—the Bolshevist and the traditionalist, such as Nazi Germany and Fascist Italy. Two criteria distinguish the Bolshevist version from the traditional version. National Socialism and Fascism left some autonomy to other institutions, such as the Church, economic interest groups, and kinship and status groups. In addition, its goals took the form of an extremely militant and charismatic nationalism. The Bolshevist version is more thoroughly penetrative of the society, and its goals are revolutionary and global.

Traditional oligarchy is usually monarchic and dynastic in form, based on custom rather than constitution or statute. The ruling elite and the bureaucracy are recruited on the basis of kinship or status. The central governmental institutions control local kinship, lineage, or territorial units only to a limited extent. The goals of the elite are primarily maintenance goals; the capacity and mechanisms for adaptation and change are present only to a limited extent. Nepal, Saudi Arabia, and Yemen are examples of traditional oligarchy.

✻　✻　✻　✻　✻

The most frequent types of political systems to be found in the non-Western areas are tutelary democracies and modernizing and traditionalistic oligarchies. From a functional point of view, the tutelary democracy tends to concentrate—to a far greater extent than is true of developed democracies—the rule-making function and the rule application function in the executive and the bureaucracy. Because of the rudimentary character of the party system, the interest group system, and the modern media of communication, the executive and the bureaucracy are far more dominant in the performance of the political functions than they are in developed democracies. Furthermore, the cultural dualism of the tutelary democracy is either "isolative" or "incorporative," rather than "fusional," in character. Nevertheless the elites of the tutelary democracies have in their goal system, more or less clearly spelled out, the functional properties of the modern differentiated, fusional political system, with its autonomies and its boundary maintenance pattern.

The modernizing oligarchies are characterized to an even greater extent by the concentration of functions in a ruling clique and in the bureaucracy, and by the absence of a competitive party system. The activities of associational interest groups, to the extent that they exist, are greatly limited, and the media of communication are controlled. But though the activities of interest groups are limited, there is an overt, pluralistic system of interest articulation in which local communities, informal status and lineage groups, and institutional groups take part. Like the tutelary democracy, the modernizing oligarchy is characterized by an incorporative or isolative dualism. Particularistic, diffuse, and ascriptive groups perform the political functions, along with groups that are characterized by "modern" styles although not necessarily penetrated by them.

The development of modern structure in traditionalistic oligarchies is defensive. Thus only the army, the police, and parts of the civil bureaucracy are rationalized in order to control or prevent modernizing tendencies in the society. Thus, while a modernizing oligarchy may use an authoritarian party as an instrument of mobilization and aggregation, this is less likely in a traditionalistic oligarchy where the aggregative, articulative, and communication functions are usually performed by the bureaucracy and/or the army, as well as by kinship or tribal units, status groups, and local units such as villages.

While there is justification for having underplayed the governmental structures in this study, their neglect in the development of the theory of the functions of the polity represents a serious shortcoming in the present analysis. The threefold classification of governmental or output functions into rule-making, rule application, and rule adjudication will not carry us very far in our efforts at precise comparison of the performance of political systems. . . .

3.   THE NON-WESTERN POLITICAL PROCESS*†

l u c i a n   w.   p y e

The purpose of this article is to outline some of the dominant and distinctive characteristics of the non-Western political process. In recent years, both the student of comparative politics and the field worker in the newly emergent and economically underdeveloped countries have found it helpful to think in terms of a general category of non-Western politics.[1]

There are, of course, great differences among the non-Western societies. Indeed, in the past, comparative analysis was impeded by an appreciation of the rich diversity in the cultural traditions and the historical circumstances of the Western impact; students and researchers found it necessary to concentrate on particular cultures, and as a consequence attention was generally directed to the unique features of each society. Recently, however, attempts to set forth some of the characteristics common to the political life of countries experiencing profound social change have stimulated fruitful discussions among specialists on the different non-Western regions as well as among general students of comparative politics.

For this discussion to continue, it is necessary for specialists on the different areas to advance, in the form of rather bold and unqualified statements, generalized models of the political process common in non-Western societies.[2] Then, by examining the ways in which particular

*   From "The Non-Western Political Process" by Lucian W. Pye, *The Journal of Politics*, Vol. XX, No. 3 (August, 1958), pp. 468–486. By permission of the publisher and the author.

†   This is a revised version of a paper presented at the annual meeting of the American Political Science Association on September 5–7, 1957.

[1]   For two excellent discussions of the implications for comparative politics of the current interest in non-Western political systems, see: Sigmund Neumann, "Comparative Politics: A Half-Century Appraisal," *Journal of Politics*, XIX (August, 1957), 269–290; and Dankwart A. Rustow, "New Horizons for Comparative Politics," *World Politics*, IX (July, 1957), 530–549.

[2]   The picture of the non-Western political process contained in the following pages was strongly influenced by: George McT. Kahin, Guy J. Pauker, and Lucian W. Pye, "Comparative Politics in Non-Western Countries," *American Political Science Review*, XLIX (December, 1955), 1022–41; Gabriel A. Almond, "Comparative Politi-

non-Western countries differ from the generalized models, it becomes possible to engage in significant comparative analysis.

1. *In non-Western societies the political sphere is not sharply differentiated from the spheres of social and personal relations.* Among the most powerful influences of the traditional order in any society in transition are those forces which impede the development of a distinct sphere of politics. In most non-Western societies, just as in traditional societies, the pattern of political relationships is largely determined by the pattern of social and personal relations. Power, prestige, and influence are based largely on social status. The political struggle tends to revolve around issues of prestige, influence, and even of personalities, and not primarily around questions of alternative courses of policy action.

The elite who dominate the national politics of most non-Western countries generally represent a remarkably homogeneous group in terms of educational experience and social background. Indeed, the path by which individuals are recruited into their political roles, where not dependent upon ascriptive considerations, is essentially an acculturation process. It is those who have become urbanized, have received the appropriate forms of education, and have demonstrated skill in establishing the necessary personal relations who are admitted to the ranks of the elite. . . .

At the village level it is even more difficult to distinguish a distinct political sphere. The social status of the individual and his personal ties largely determine his political behavior and the range of his influence. The lack of a clear political sphere in such communities places severe limits on the effectiveness of those who come from the outside to perform a political role. . . .

The fundamental framework of non-Western politics is a communal one, and all political behavior is strongly colored by considerations of communal identification. In the more conspicuous cases the larger communal groupings follow ethnic or religious lines. . . .

This essentially communal framework of politics makes it extremely difficult for ideas to command influence in themselves. The response to any advocate of a particular point of view tends to be attuned more to his social position than to the content of his views. Under these conditions it is inappropriate to conceive of an open market place where political ideas can freely compete on their own merits for support. Political discussion tends rather to assume the form of either intracommunal debate or one group justifying its position toward another.

The communal framework also sharply limits freedom in altering

cal Systems," *Journal of Politics,* XVIII (August, 1956), 391–409; Rustow, *op. cit.,* and also his *Politics and Westernization in the Near East,* Center of International Studies (Princeton, 1956).

political allegiances. Any change in political identification generally requires a change in one's social and personal relationships; conversely, any change in social relations tends to result in a change in political identification. . . .

2. *Political parties in non-Western societies tend to take on a world view and represent a way of life.* The lack of a clearly differentiated political sphere means that political associations or groups cannot be clearly oriented to a distinct political arena but tend to be oriented to some aspect of the communal framework of politics. In reflecting the communal base of politics, political parties tend to represent total ways of life. . . . Usually political parties represent some sub-society or simply the personality of a particularly influential individual.

Even secular parties devoted to achieving national sovereignty have tended to develop their own unique world views. Indeed, successful parties tend to become social movements. The indigenous basis for political parties is usually regional, ethnic, or religious groupings, all of which stress considerations not usually emphasized in Western secular politics. . . .

❉   ❉   ❉   ❉   ❉

3. *The political process in non-Western societies is characterized by a prevalence of cliques.* The lack of a distinct political sphere and the tendency for political parties to have a world view together provide a framework within which the most structured units of decision-making tend to be personal cliques. Although general considerations of social status determine the broad outlines of power and influence, the particular pattern of political relationships at any time is largely determined by decisions made at the personal level. This is the case because the social structure in non-Western societies is characterized by functionally diffuse relationships; individuals and groups do not have sharply defined and highly specific functions and thus do not represent specific interests that distinguish them from other groupings. . . . The pattern of personal associations provides one of the firmest guides for understanding and action within the political process. Personal cliques are likely to become the key units of decision-making in the political process of most non-Western societies.

❉   ❉   ❉   ❉   ❉

4. *The character of political loyalty in non-Western societies gives to the leadership of political groups a high degree of freedom in deter-*

mining matters of strategy and tactics. The communal framework of politics and the tendency for political parties to have world views means that political loyalty is governed more by a sense of identification with the concrete group than by identification with the professed policy goals of the group. The expectation is that the leaders will seek to maximize all the interests of all the members of the group and not just seek to advance particular policies or values.

✧   ✧   ✧   ✧   ✧

5. *Opposition parties and aspiring elites tend to appear as revolutionary movements in non-Western politics.* Since the current leadership in non-Western countries generally conceives of itself as seeking to effect changes in all aspects of life, and since all the political associations tend to have world views, any prospective change in national leadership is likely to seem to have revolutionary implications. . . .

In addition, the broad and diffuse interests of the ruling elites make it easy for them to maintain that they represent the interest of the entire nation. Those seeking power are thus often placed in the position of appearing to be, at best, obstructionists of progress and, at worst, enemies of the country. Competition is not between parties that represent different functional specific interests or between groups that claim greater administrative skills; rather, the struggle takes on some of the qualities of a conflict between differing ways of life.

This situation is important in explaining the failure of responsible opposition parties to develop in most non-Western countries. . . .

6. *The non-Western political process is characterized by a lack of integration among the participants, and this situation is a function of the lack of a unified communications system in the society.* In most non-Western societies there is not a single general political process that is the focus of most political activities throughout the population; rather, there are several distinct and nearly unrelated political processes. The most conspicuous division is that between the dominant national politics of the more urban elements and the more traditional village level of politics. The conflicts that are central to the one may hardly appear in the other.

Those who participate, for example, in the political life of the village are not an integral part of the national politics, since they can act without regard to developments at the central level. Possibly even more significant is the fact that at the village level all the various village groups have their separate and autonomous political processes.

This situation is a reflection of, and is reinforced by, the communication system common to non-Western societies, where the media of mass communication generally reach only to elements of the urban population and to those who participate in the national political process. The vast majority of the people participate only in the traditional word-of-mouth communication system. Even when the media of mass communications do reach the village, through readers of newspapers or owners of radios, there is almost no "feedback" from the village level. The radio talks *to* the villagers but does not talk *with* them. The views of the vast majority of the population are not reflected in the mass media. . . .

The lack of a unified communication system and the fact that the participants are not integrated into a common political process limit the types of political issues that can arise in non-Western societies. For example, although these are essentially agrarian societies in which industrial development is just beginning to take place, there has not yet appeared (in their politics) one of the issues basic to the history of Western politics: the clash between industry and agriculture, between town and countryside. . . .

7. *The non-Western political process is characterized by a high rate of recruitment of new elements to political roles.*[3] The spread of popular politics in traditional societies has meant a constant increase in the number of participants and the types of organizations involved in the political process. This development has been stimulated by the extraordinary rise in the urban population, which has greatly increased the number of people who have some understanding about, and feeling for, politics at the national level. A basic feature of the acculturation process which creates the sub-society of the elite is the development of attitudes common to urban life. It is generally out of the rapid urban growth that there emerge the aspiring elites who demand to be heard. In almost all non-Western societies, there is a distinct strata of urban dwellers who are excluded from direct participation in national politics but whose existence affects the behavior of the current elite.

☼   ☼   ☼   ☼   ☼

8. *The non-Western political process is characterized by sharp differences in the political orientation of the generations.* The process of social change in most non-Western societies results in a lack of continuity in the circumstances under which people are recruited to politics. Those who took part in the revolutionary movement against a colonial ruler are not necessarily regarded as indispensable leaders by the new generations; but their revolutionary role is still put forward as sufficient reason for their continued elite status. . . .

[3]   Kahin, Pauker, and Pye, *loc. cit.*, p. 1024.

THE STUDY OF POLITICAL SYSTEMS

This problem in non-Western societies is further complicated by demographic factors, for such societies are composed of rapidly growing populations that have a high birth rate. In Singapore, Malaya, and Burma, over half the population is under voting age, and the median age in most non-Western countries is in the low twenties. There is thus a constant pressure from the younger generation, whose demands for political influence conflict with the claims of current leaders who conceive of themselves as being still young and with many more years of active life ahead. In most of the newly independent countries, the initial tendency was for cabinet ministers and high officials to be in their thirties and forties, a condition which has colored the career expectations of the youth of succeeding generations, who now face frustration if they cannot achieve comparable status at the same age.

This telescoping of the generations has sharpened the clash of views so that intellectually there is an abnormal gap in political orientations, creating a potential for extreme reversal in policy, should the aspiring elites gain power. Ideas and symbols which are deeply felt by the current leaders, including those relating to the West, may have little meaning for a generation which has not experienced colonial rule.

9. *In non-Western societies there is little consensus as to the legitimate ends and means of political action.* The fundamental fact that non-Western societies are engrossed in a process of discontinuous social change precludes the possibility of a widely shared agreement as to the appropriate ends and means of political activities. In all the important non-Western countries, there are people who have assimilated Western culture to the point that their attitudes and concepts about politics differ little from those common in the West. At the other extreme there is the village peasant who has been little touched by Western influences. Living in different worlds, these individuals can hardly be expected to display a common approach toward political action.

The national leadership, recruited from people who have generally become highly urbanized, is in a position to set the standards for what may appear to be a widely shared consensus about politics. However, more often than not, this apparent national agreement is a reflection only of the distinct qualities of the elite sub-society. . . .

The lack of a distinct political sphere increases the difficulties in achieving agreement about the legitimate scope and forms of political activities. The setting is not one in which political issues are relatively isolated and thus easily communicated and discussed. Instead, a knowledge of national politics requires an intimate acquaintance with the total social life of the elite. The fact that loyalty to the particular group rather than support of general principles is the key to most political behavior strengthens the tendency toward a distinct and individual rather than a shared orientation towards politics.

The situation is further complicated by the fact that, since most of the groupings within the political process represent total ways of life, few are concerned with limited and specific interests. The functionally diffuse character of most groups means that each tends to have its own approaches to political action in terms of both ends and means. . . .

❈　❈　❈　❈　❈

10. *In non-Western societies the intensity and breadth of political discussion has little relationship to political decision-making.* Western observers are impressed with what they feel is a paradoxical situation in most non-Western countries: the masses seem to be apathetic toward political action and yet, considering the crude systems of communications, they are remarkably well informed about political events. Peasants and villagers often engage in lengthy discussions on matters related to the political world that lies outside their immediate lives, but they rarely seem prepared to translate the information they receive into action that might influence the course of national politics.

The villagers are often responding in the traditional manner to national politics. In most traditional societies, an important function of the elite was to provide entertainment and material for discussion for the common people; but discussions in villages and teashops could center on the activities of an official without creating the expectation that discussion should lead to action. . . .

A second explanation for this pattern of behavior is that one of the important factors in determining social status and prestige within the village or local community is often a command of information about the wider world; knowledge of developments in the sphere of national and even international politics has a value in itself. But skill in discussing political matters again does not raise any expectations of actual participation in the world of politics.

Finally, many of the common people in non-Western societies find it desirable to keep informed about political developments in order to be able to adapt their lives to any major changes. . . .

11. *In the non-Western political process there is a high degree of substitutability of roles.*[4] It seems that in non-Western societies most politically relevant roles are not clearly differentiated but have a functionally diffuse rather than a functionally specific character. For example, the civil bureaucracy is not usually limited to the role of a politically neutral instrument of public administration but may assume some of the functions of a political party or act as an interest group. Sometimes armies act as governments. Even within bureaucracies and governments, individuals may be formally called upon to perform several roles.

[4]　See Almond, *loc. cit.*, p. 30.

A shortage of competent personnel encourages such behavior either because one group may feel that the other is not performing its role in an effective manner or because the few skilled administrators are forced to take on concurrent assignments. However, the more fundamental reason for this phenomenon is that in societies just emerging from traditional status, it is not generally expected that any particular group or organization will limit itself to performing a clearly specified function. . . .

12. *In the non-Western political process there are relatively few explicitly organized interest groups with functionally specific roles.* Although there are often large numbers of informal associations in non-Western countries, such groups tend to adopt diffuse orientations that cover all phases of life in much the same manner as the political parties and cliques. It is the rare association that represents a limited and functionally specific interest. Organizations which in name and formal structure are modeled after Western interest groups, such as trade unions and chambers of commerce, generally do not have a clearly defined focus.

In many cases groups, such as trade unions and peasant associations that in form would appear to represent a specific interest, are in fact agents of the government or of a dominant party or movement. . . .

In situations where the associations are autonomous, the tendency is for them to act as protective associations and not as pressure groups. That is, their activities are concentrated on protecting their members from the consequences of governmental decisions and the political power of others. They do not seek to apply pressure openly on the government in order to influence positively the formation of public policy.

☼   ☼   ☼   ☼   ☼

13. *In the non-Western political process the national leadership must appeal to an undifferentiated public.* The lack of explicitly organized interest groups and the fact that not all participants are continuously represented in the political process deprive the national leadership of any readily available means for calculating the relative distribution of attitudes and values throughout the society. The national politician cannot easily determine the relative power of those in favor of a particular measure and those opposed; he cannot readily estimate the amount of effort needed to gain the support of the doubtful elements.

It is usually only within the circle of the elite or within the administrative structure that the national leaders can distinguish specific points of view and the relative backing that each commands. In turning to the population as a whole, the leaders find that they have few guides as to how the public may be divided over particular issues. . . .

The inability to speak to a differentiated public encourages a strong propensity toward skillful and highly emotional forms of political articulation on the part of non-Western leaders. Forced to reach for the broadest possible appeals, the political leader tends at times to concentrate heavily on nationalistic sentiments and to present himself as a representative of the nation as a whole rather than of particular interests within the society. This is one of the reasons why some leaders of non-Western countries are often seen paradoxically both as extreme nationalists and as men out of touch with the masses.

14. *The unstructured character of the non-Western political process encourages leaders to adopt more clearly defined positions on international issues than on domestic issues.* Confronted with an undifferentiated public, leaders of non-Western countries often find the international political process more clearly structured than the domestic political scene. Consequently, they can make more refined calculations as to the advantages in taking a definite position in world politics than they can in domestic politics. This situation not only encourages the leaders of some non-Western countries to seek a role in world politics that is out of proportion to their nation's power, but it also allows such leaders to concentrate more on international than on domestic affairs. It should also be noted that in adopting a supra-national role, the current leaders of non-Western countries can heighten the impression that their domestic opposition is an enemy of the national interest.

15. *In non-Western societies the affective or expressive aspect of politics tends to override the problem-solving or public-policy aspect of politics.* Traditional societies have generally developed to a very high order the affective and expressive aspects of politics. Pomp and ceremony are usually basic features of traditional politics, and those who are members of the ruling elite in such societies are generally expected to lead more interesting and exciting lives than those not involved in politics. In contrast, traditional societies have not usually emphasized politics as a means for solving social problems. Questions of policy in such societies are largely limited to providing certain minimum social and economic functions and maintaining the way of life of the elite.

✿ ✿ ✿ ✿ ✿

In part the stress on the affective or expressive aspect of politics is related to the fact that, in most non-Western countries, questions of personal loyalties and identification are recognized as providing the basic issues of politics and the bond between leader and follower is generally an emotional one. In fact, in many non-Western societies, it is considered highly improper and even immoral for people to make loyalty contingent upon their leaders' ability to solve problems of public policy.

In the many non-Western societies in which the problem of national integration is of central importance, the national leaders often feel they must emphasize the symbols and sentiments of national unity since substantive problems of policy may divide the people. . . .

16. *Charismatic leaders tend to prevail in non-Western politics.*[5] Max Weber, in highlighting the characteristics of charismatic authority, specifically related the emergence of charismatic personalities to situations in which the hold of tradition has been weakened. By implication, he suggested that societies experiencing cultural change provide an ideal setting for such leaders since a society in which there is confusion over values is more susceptible to a leader who conveys a sense of mission and appears to be God-sent.

The problem of political communication further reinforces the position of the charismatic leader. Since the population does not share the leadership's modes of reason or standards of judgment, it is difficult to communicate subtle points of view. Communication of emotions is not confronted with such barriers, especially if it is related to considerations of human character and personality. All groups within the population can feel confident of their abilities to judge the worth of a man for what he is, even though they cannot understand his mode of reasoning.

So long as a society has difficulties in communication, the charismatic leader possesses great advantage over his opponents, even though they may have greater ability in rational planning. However, the very lack of precision in the image that a charismatic leader casts, especially in relation to operational policy, does make it possible for opposition to develop as long as it does not directly challenge the leader's charisma. . . .

Charisma is likely to wear thin. A critical question in most non-Western societies that now have charismatic leaders is whether such leadership will in the meantime become institutionalized in the form of rational-legal practices. . . . The critical factor seems to be whether or not the leader encourages the development of functionally specific groups within the society that can genuinely represent particular interests.

17. *The non-Western political process operates largely without benefit of political "brokers."* In most non-Western societies there seems to be no institutionalized role for carrying out the tasks of, first, clarifying and delimiting the distribution of demands and interests within the population, and, next, engaging in the bargaining operation necessary to

[5]   Kahin, Pauker, and Pye, *loc. cit.*, p. 1025.

accommodate and maximize the satisfaction of those demands and interests in a fashion consistent with the requirements of public policy and administration. In other words, there are no political "brokers."

※　　※　　※　　※　　※

In most non-Western societies, the role of the political "broker" has been partially filled by those who perform a "mediator's" role, which consists largely of transmitting the views of the elite to the masses. Such "mediators" are people sufficiently acculturated to the elite society to understand its views but who still have contacts with the more traditional masses. In performing their role, they engage essentially in a public relations operation for the elite, and only to a marginal degree do they communicate to the elite the views of the public. They do not find it essential to identify and articulate the values of their public. Generally, since their influence depends upon their relations with the national leadership, they have not sought to develop an autonomous basis of power or to identify themselves with particular segments of the population as must the political "broker." As a consequence, they have not acted in a fashion that would stimulate the emergence of functionally specific interest groups.

transitional societies

The transition from traditional societies to modern nation-states involves many complex, interrelated changes in cultural values and attitudes, and in social, economic, and political institutions and processes. Some of these changes as they have been occurring in the developing states have been dramatic, obvious, and easily measured. Political independence has been secured by many African and Asian societies that a few years ago were generally regarded as unlikely to be ready for self-government for many decades. Constitutions have been written and modern political institutions formally established. In some states, urban areas have been growing rapidly, and new industries, including some heavy industries, are being established. Strenuous efforts have been made to expand educational facilities as rapidly as possible. Increasing numbers of students are being enrolled, and the high rates of illiteracy have been gradually, and in some cases rapidly, reduced. Per capita income has increased or decreased in response to economic and population growth rates. Death rates, particularly among infants and children, have sharply declined as improvements have been made in medical facilities, public health programs, and diets.

Many of the other changes that are occurring, however, are far more subtle and less readily measured. Changes in values, beliefs, and attitudes within societies are particularly difficult to measure with precision. Nevertheless, it is clear that alterations are occurring within the value and attitude patterns of transitional societies, accompanying changing conditions in the physical environment. In this interplay between values and objective conditions, either may reflect or stimulate changes in the other. More specifically, political values, attitudes, and expectations have also been undergoing various modifications. The national revolutions for political independence, for example, and the trying problems of creating nation-states have had their impact on political values as well as on political institutions. In addition, expectations of further changes in the social, economic, and political systems have injected a dynamic and often unstabilizing element into the political process of many societies.

As these changes take place, tensions and strains of varying intensity result within the fabric of traditional society. The traditional family structure, for example, with its values based upon a closely interwoven network of personal relationships is challenged when members of the family leave the rural village and move to the cities to work. Similarly, mass education has a disruptive effect on the traditional patterns of beliefs and authority. The increasing secularization of society also exacts its toll on traditional religious beliefs, even though ritualized practices may continue long after they have lost their primary meanings. Defenders of the traditional religions are confronted not only by the apathy of many who find little satisfaction in the ancient beliefs and practices, but also by a minority who view the traditional religions as definite obstacles to modernization. Further, the gradually changing economic structure of many societies causes shifts in the distribution of wealth and the realignment and strength of individuals and groups supporting or opposing various economic policies. And, in the political realm, changing social and economic conditions affect the bases of political power and the groups that compete for positions of influence and authority. The authority of conservative traditional leaders is challenged by those who have achieved popular acclaim for their radical programs and by those who have attained control over new instruments of power, such as modern military forces, bureaucracies, or economic institutions.

Of course, the contemporary bases from which development is proceeding vary greatly from society to society in Asia, Africa, and Latin America. The different problems these societies confront and the different policies they pursue reflect the variety of traditional bases from which they have evolved. In some states in general, and in most states in some particulars, this evolution has been exceedingly limited, and the contemporary society is much like the traditional. In a few cases, the pace and scope of changes have been rapidly transforming the traditional bases. Although significant differences may be identified between individual traditional societies, some commonly shared characteristics may also be noted. In general, a traditional society is characterized by its relatively limited economic base (primarily agricultural), a low level of technology, a lack of functionally specific institutions (such as separate religious and political authorities and institutions), a largely illiterate population, a low life expectancy, and a non-scientific, even mystical approach to the problems confronting it. The cultures of traditional societies reflect these characteristics. The family, tribe, or communal group, providing close personal relationships for its members, establishes the base from which values are derived, rather than the more abstract nation or state. A sense of fatalism often pervades these values, mirroring the inability to overcome natural forces that impede progress. Though some traditional societies have, in the past, attained a fairly high level of development of technology, and skills in art and literature, long periods of stagnation and decline interrupted continuous development.

The changes that have, historically, taken place in traditional societies were stimulated by many forces, both internal and external. The discovery of raw materials and the means to utilize them, changing patterns of economic production, and the development of an alphabet and a written language have provided the base for many changes. Contacts with other societies and cultures, whether through war, trade, travel, or communications have also been important prods for change. In particular, contacts with Western cultures have promoted many changes. In the process of "discovering" and then conquering much of the world through the exercise of their military, economic, technological, and organizational superiority, the European powers implanted in the traditional societies in Asia, Africa, and Latin America many Western ideas, values, skills, and institutions.

The pattern of contact with the West took different forms and had different consequences. In Latin America, the military victories by the Spanish and Portuguese forces over the indigenous Indian societies in the fifteenth and sixteenth centuries provided the base from which the colonial policies of the mother countries were executed. In the Caribbean islands, the native populations were completely exterminated: large numbers were killed in the course of military actions, and the rest succumbed to the diseases and harsh treatment of their European conquerors. Negro slaves were then imported to provide the working force for the Spanish landlords. Elsewhere in Latin America, the defeated Indians, saved from complete extermination through the intervention of the Catholic Church, were nevertheless reduced to a state of abject servility, forced to work on the land and in the mines whose ownership was claimed by the victors. The Spanish and, in Brazil, the Portuguese, having taken possession of the land and its resources, established themselves as the permanent social, political, and economic elite. They created large urban centers from which they administered the policies of exploitation as directed by the mother states. Gradually, a middle cultural group, the *mestizos*, emerged from the intermarriages of the Europeans and Indians. Sharp contrasts developed between each of the three classes with the Indians, *mestizos*, and "whites" each forming a distinct group in terms of social, political, and economic rights and opportunities. In the Caribbean islands, the Negroes and mulattos held positions corresponding to those of the Indians and *mestizos,* respectively. In the process of establishing their permanent settlements, the Spanish and Portuguese brought with them the entire paraphernalia of their cultures. Thus, after political independence was achieved by the settlers early in the nineteenth century, the patterns that had developed over three centuries of colonial rule were continued largely unchanged. For the indigenous Indian populations, the achievement of independence by the white settlers had little meaning, unlike the consequences of this act in almost all African and Asian societies, where the indigenous groups attained control of their governments; it merely involved a change from foreign to domestic "white" rule.

After a long period of political instability, economic stagnation, and little social change, most Latin American states are now in a phase of more rapid change. Increasing industrialization during the past quarter century has been accompanied by increasing urbanization, a higher standard of education to meet the needs of industrial development, a gradual weakening of the rigid class divisions as employment opportunities have grown, and the emergence of political groups capable of challenging the dominant positions of those whose power is based on land ownership. The traditionally conservative social and political attitudes of the Catholic Church and the support given to conservative leaders are also in a state of transition. While the values and institutions that characterized nineteenth century Latin American societies have not been destroyed, they are nevertheless being subjected to intensifying pressures from groups demanding more rapid modernization.

The manner in which the European powers—and much later the United States—penetrated and came to dominate the Asian and African societies was generally quite different from that in Latin America. In Asia, after the initial discoveries by European explorers in the fourteenth and fifteenth centuries, adventurers, missionaries, and traders arrived to provide the first sustained, though limited, contact. In the Philippines, Spanish rule (until 1898, when the islands were surrendered to the United States) produced a social and political pattern resembling that found in the Spanish colonies in Latin America. Elsewhere, however, the Spanish and Portuguese military forces were defeated by other European powers, and British and Dutch traders, whose activities initially had little impact on the native populations, became the principal agents of Western influence. With the establishment of the English East India Company in 1600 and the Dutch East India Company in 1602, the traditional societies were increasingly disrupted as these Companies, eager to protect and promote their economic functions, began to assume governmental functions as well. Various forms of indirect rule, in which the traditional elites were retained but forced to make concessions to the Companies, were employed to maintain order and control.

The activities of these Companies, along with those of the missionaries sent out to convert the native populations, increasingly involved the European governments more directly in Asian affairs. The Companies themselves were replaced by the Dutch and British governments in the late eighteenth and nineteenth centuries, respectively. Together with the French, who had gradually established control over Indochina in the second half of the nineteenth century, the British and Dutch exercised rule over most Asian societies. Both the dominant philosophies of the colonial powers and the nature of the societies over which they ruled differed significantly, however. The Dutch in Indonesia chose to rule indirectly through traditional native rulers. Subscribing to theories of cultural relativism, the Dutch encouraged the development of local cultures while retaining ultimate authority. The effect of this policy was to create two quite distinct spheres of authority and styles of life, the European and the native, with few persons or groups capable of bridging the two worlds. While the authority of the native rulers was gradually undermined as the Dutch increased the authority of the centralized administration, no clear patterns of authority integrating European and native values and institutions emerged from which development could proceed upon the achievement of independence.

The British, on the other hand, were much less inclined toward the paternalistic attitudes and policies of the Dutch. Their objective of establishing law and order, through which policies of economic liberalism could be pursued, led the British to employ both direct and indirect means of control. Where native rulers were strong, indirect rule was exercised; where weak, the British imposed their authority directly over the native societies. In either case, a centralized administration was created and the British legal system introduced. While both the economic policies and British law produced profound changes in the traditional order, British rule imparted a relatively unambiguous concept of government based upon representative political institutions, unlike Dutch rule which attempted to preserve traditional native political institutions.

In contrast to both the Dutch and the British, the French sought to assimilate the societies they ruled into French culture. Although a small group of Vietnamese were successfully assimilated, the bulk of the population retained its strong ties to the native cultures. The result was a fragmented social and political structure, with the Westernized Vietnamese attempting to exert authority over the unassimilated, tradition-oriented masses. The instability of this structure became apparent immediately upon the attainment of independence and the withdrawal of French military and administrative forces. A much different pattern resulted from American rule in the Philippines. By emphasizing the development of democratic parties, institutions, and processes in preparation for eventual independence, a much closer relationship between native political leaders and the people was encouraged. In addition, since independence was the goal, American policy deliberately promoted the development of the social and economic systems (as, for example, through mass education and local industry) considered necessary for a democratic state. These policies were only partially successful, however, in altering the social and economic structures created under Spanish rule, which resembled, in many respects, those found in Latin America. Thus, under the successive impact of Spanish and American rule, traditional Filipino societies were altered in ways significantly different from those ruled by other European powers.

The major Western impact on sub-Saharan Africa came much later than in Asia. Prior to 1885, contact had been limited and sporadic, resulting primarily from the slave trade. Only a few small areas had come under control of the European states, principally at the southern tip of the continent. In 1885, however, the European powers at the Congress of Berlin laid the ground rules governing the division of the continent, and soon Britain, France, Belgium, Portugal, Spain, and, later, Germany established their control over all African societies except Ethiopia, though frequently it was more nominal than truly effective. In the scramble for colonies, boundary lines were drawn and agreed upon that bore little relationship to the cultural and ethnic patterns of the native populations. In a few areas, as in Kenya and Rhodesia, large numbers of Europeans arrived to found permanent white settlements, establishing within these areas a privileged social, economic, and political class.

Imposed upon the radically different traditional African systems were the equally varied colonial policies of the European powers. As in Asia, both direct and indirect forms of rule were utilized. While the British employed several forms of indirect rule in their colonies, the French favored direct rule with the objective of assimilating and incorporating their colonies into a French Union. Belgium, while a colonial power, also ruled directly, as do Spain and Portugal today, but only Portugal shares the French objective of assimilation, though its policies to attain that goal are much different from the French ones. These several forms of rule were, of course, modified at different times by the colonial powers, as was also true in Asia. In general, the British policy of indirect rule produced only gradual changes initially in the traditional African societies. Limited, but slowly expanding educational, employment, and political opportunities were afforded before World War II. After the war, with the sharply increasing demands for independence, the British expanded these opportunities while also establishing political institutions in which the Africans increasingly participated. In the process, the position of the traditional political elites on whom the British had earlier relied was undermined. On the other hand, indirect rule had the effect of encouraging the individual tribal groupings to retain their sense of identity. The preservation of tribal identity led, in turn, to the demands for federal forms of government and in some cases to separatist movements within the newly independent states. In those colonies where large European settlements were established, difficult problems were encountered in creating independent states in which Africans would have a substantial or controlling voice.

The French policy of assimilation had the potentiality for the greatest disruption of the traditional order, since if it were to succeed, substantial changes in traditional values and patterns of authority would be required. As in French Indochina, a small group of Africans successfully made the transition; for the masses, however, the transition was only partial because of both deep-seated resentment toward or disinterest in the assimilation policy and the unwillingness or inability of the French to provide adequate educational, economic, and political opportunities to make the policy successful. Belgium's paternalistic policies, in contrast, were not designed to effectuate a full and rapid Europeanization of their colony. Slow, controlled changes in preparation for independence in the distant future were considered desirable. For example, while a primary education was gradually made available to large numbers of natives, no higher educational institutions were established or education in foreign universities permitted until the 1950's. Similarly, only the lowest levels of the civil service were open until shortly before independence was granted. Plantations and small industries were established to promote economic development, but in all fields of activity, the higher positions were retained almost exclusively for Europeans, which left the Congolese critically short of managerial and political skills at the time independence was attained. Little of this gradual preparation for future independence is found in the contemporary Spanish and Portuguese paternalistic policies, however. Few educational, economic, or political opportunities are made available under the harsh and repressive policies of these colonial powers. Even though the Portuguese assert that individual assimilation of the Africans is the goal, equal status and opportunities with their European counterparts are not available to the assimilated Portuguese Africans, unlike the assimilated French Africans. The repressive policies of Spain and Portugal, augmented by the widespread use of various forms of coercion, have so far enabled them to maintain control of their colonies in spite of growing demands for independence.

In both Asia and sub-Saharan Africa, colonial rule resulted in many basic changes in the traditional societies. Although the colonial policies of the several European powers varied in many important details, in general they (1) brought together within a single colony cultural and ethnic groups that had previously not been politically united, (2) established rationalized bureaucratic structures, staffed at least in the lower ranks by native personnel, (3) created legal systems based on European values and codes, (4) established armed forces and police units partially manned by natives and equipped with some modern weapons, (5) introduced a monetary system patterned after those in Europe and provided for standardized taxes, and (6) created a Western-style, secular educational system.

The impact of many colonial policies was, however, usually felt directly by only a relatively small number of persons. At the rural village level and among groups in the isolated interior regions, the changes introduced by the colonial powers were much less immediately and intensively realized. Yet even at the local level, the forces set in motion by the colonial powers were sufficient over time to disrupt traditional patterns of authority, economic production, and cultural values. In general, the small group of native leaders who were trained within the framework of colonial rule have been determined to carry the modernizing process down to the local level. These Western-trained elites, often coming from the ranks of the bureaucracies and the armed forces, were usually the principal groups in the nationalist movements leading to independence. They demanded for themselves and their peoples those very rights that the colonial powers themselves claim to prize: political independence and its attendant freedom to make their own choices in all areas of social and economic policy. Having achieved independence, these leaders have been attempting to speed and shape the processes of modernization throughout their societies.

In contrast to the relatively recent contact between the European powers and the sub-Saharan African societies, resulting almost immediately in the subjugation of the latter to the former, a long period of contact between the European and Middle Eastern societies preceded the establishment of formal European control. The contributions of ancient societies in the Middle East to Western civilization are, of course, well known. During the past several centuries, however, the economic and political development of the Middle Eastern societies has lagged far behind that in Europe. The once powerful Middle Eastern empires had disintegrated under the impact of domestic strife, foreign attack, and economic stagnation (the latter complicated by the lack of resources, especially arable land). Although a common faith, the Islamic, bound the societies together, political authority was highly fragmented. In an effort to reverse their fortunes in order to compete more successfully in the modern world, some rulers of the Middle Eastern societies have, since the eighteenth century, attempted to incorporate and utilize selected features of European technology and organizational forms. Bureaucracies and military forces were organized along the lines of their European counterparts. Inevitably, other European ideas and values, particularly those concerning nationalism, were injected into the traditional societies by those Western-trained army officers and civil servants charged with constructing modern military machines and administrative institutions. Thus, the goals and some of the processes of modernization were well established in some Middle Eastern societies before European control was directly imposed.

Prior to the late nineteenth century, few European colonies were established in the Middle East. Not until after World War I, when a number of territories such as Syria, Iraq, and Lebanon were designated as mandates of Britain and France, was European control asserted over most of the Middle East except Turkey, Iran, and Saudi Arabia. Yet in neither the colonies, such as Tunisia or Morocco, nor in the mandated territories was European power exercised to the same degree as in the Asian or sub-Saharan colonies. While the control was sufficient to disrupt native political authority, it rarely brought significant benefits of colonialism in the form of stable governments or auxiliary services, such as improved standards of health, education, or transportation and communications networks. Consequently, the legacy of this short period of imperial rule, with its uneven pattern of penetration and control, has been one of bitterness and disillusionment on both sides. The bitterness existing between the Arab states on the one hand, and Britain, France, and the United States on the other, was sharply intensified by the establishment, under auspices of a British mandate, of the state of Israel in 1948, and the struggle over the Suez Canal that culminated in a short war in 1956. Although the Arab-Israeli war in 1967 did not involve the American or European states directly, the crisis led to the rupturing of diplomatic relations by several Arab states with the United States on grounds of the latter's support for Israel.

While many of the changes occurring within the transitional states thus stem quite clearly from the impact of colonial rule, other forces only partially related to colonialism are also helping to reshape traditional societies. As in the case of Latin America, the rapid urbanization taking place in many Asian and some African states is a manifestation of several forces, in addition to that of the colonial policy of establishing cities as administrative and trading centers. Under the pressure of population growth and the surplus of labor in the rural areas, many people are moving to the cities in search of industrial employment and a standard of living unobtainable in the countryside. This search is frequently frustrated, given the limited industrialization that has yet occurred. Nevertheless, the process of urbanization has been a major factor promoting changes in the traditional societies. The movement to the cities tends to undermine the traditional values and personal relationships characteristic of rural societies. Since this movement is often proceeding without an industrial base to supply work for all those seeking it, most cities contain a substantial group of persons who are unemployed or underemployed. Their frustrations in not being able to obtain employment and a satisfactory standard of living have on numerous occasions been translated into political action in the form of demonstrations and riots. To a degree unparalleled in Europe and North America, political activity in the developing states centers in the urban areas where the modernizing elite and the restless urban masses dominate the national political processes.

The rapid population growth in both the urban centers and the rural areas, with all its implications for economic and political development, is caused primarily by a sharp decline in infant mortality rates and increasing longevity rather than by an increase in the birth rate. In addition, better medical, sanitary, and public health facilities and practices have reduced the incidence of disease and have contributed to better care for the sick and injured, further reducing the death rate.

Accelerating the changes in traditional societies is the spread of education. As larger numbers of persons become educated, particularly to more advanced levels, traditional values come under increasingly critical examination. Education has become a principal determinant of the modernizing elite, and the requirements of a modern, industrialized state force emphasis to be placed upon the development of a modern, secular educational system. Contributing to the spread of ideas are the mass communications media. Motion pictures, radio, and printed materials bring new ideas and methods to people in the remotest areas as well as to those already involved in the modernization process.

External pressures similarly promote the evolution of traditional societies. To compete in the modern world requires the substantial revision of traditional values and methods of production. Surplus goods must be produced for sale abroad to obtain the necessary exchange for the payment of imported goods. Since the defense of the state no longer rests directly in the hands of the former colonial power, modern military forces must be established and adequately equipped. In many of these societies, the military has become a principal agency for modernization. Strong feelings of nationalism and an uncertain relationship with other states have led to heavy appropriations for defense, including modern, complex weaponry. Supporting skills, industries, and communication and transportation networks are required to make the military forces effective. In addition, the military serves as a modernizing agency through its programs of basic education and advanced technical training.

Under the impact of these various forces, some societies are undergoing a period of rapid transformation. A sense of urgency is apparent among the modernizing elite as they seek to move their societies to a position that will enable them to compete successfully in the modern world. Even where this sense of urgency is much less obvious, as in some Latin American states, demands for modernization are increasingly voiced by segments of society who are unwilling to accept present conditions and who believe that their own positions can be improved.

The "revolution of rising expectations" thus inevitably involves substantial changes in the traditional order. Whether the ways and means to realize these expectations can be discovered remains, at present, the unanswerable question.

SUGGESTED READINGS

Barnett, H. G., *Innovation: The Basis of Cultural Change*. New York, McGraw-Hill Book Company, Inc., 1953.

Easton, Stewart C., *The Rise and Fall of Western Colonialism*. New York, Frederick A. Praeger, Inc., 1964.

Emerson, Rupert, *From Empire to Nation*. Cambridge, Mass., Harvard University Press, 1960.

———, and Kilson, Martin, eds., *The Political Awakening of Africa*. Englewood Cliffs, N. J., Prentice-Hall, Inc., 1965.

Hagen, Everett E., *On the Theory of Social Change*. Homewood, Ill., The Dorsey Press, Inc., 1962.

Lerner, Daniel, *The Passing of Traditional Society*. New York, The Free Press of Glencoe, 1958.

Millikan, Max F., and Blackmer, Donald L. M., eds., *The Emerging Nations*. Boston, Little, Brown and Company, 1961.

Zinkin, Maurice, *Asia and the West*. New York, Institute of Pacific Relations, International Secretariat, 1953.

⟨∽∾⟩

4. THE EMERGING NATIONS*

edited by max f. millikan and donald l. m. blackmer

The nature of the transitional process which we are considering here—and which American policy confronts in many parts of the world—takes its start from the character of the traditional societies that are in the

* From *The Emerging Nations: Their Growth and United States Policy*, edited by Max F. Millikan and Donald L. M. Blackmer. Copyright © 1961, Massachusetts Institute of Technology. Reprinted by permission of the publishers, Little, Brown and Company (Inc.). Selections from pp. 3–17.

process of being superseded. We begin, therefore, by sketching briefly the major features of traditional societies.

These were societies with hereditary hierarchical rule, living under the sway of customs rather than of law. Their economies were static and remained at the same level of limited technology and low income from one generation to the next. Even though some ancient societies exhibited high proficiency in certain directions, they should be termed traditional since they were incapable of generating a regular flow of inventions and innovations and of moving into a phase of sustained economic growth. Before the appearance of the modern scientific attitude and of advances in basic scientific knowledge, no society could produce a continuing flow of new technology. It followed from this limitation that the bulk of men's economic activity was taken up in acquiring food. Typically, at least 75 per cent and often more of the working force in traditional societies was in agriculture. History offers us a wide range of such societies. Some were relatively primitive tribes living within a narrow region, on a self-sufficient base, with tribal rather than territorial political and economic organization, and tenuously connected if at all with other tribes and regions. In parts of Africa and in some areas elsewhere we can still find such isolated and primitive forms of social, political, and economic organization.

Other traditional societies have been made up of loosely organized regions, with fairly elaborate structures of political and social organization and quite sophisticated agricultural techniques, but weak or nonexistent central governments. Medieval Europe, for example, could be described in some such terms, as well as India before the arrival of the European colonial powers.

But some traditional societies were very substantial empires with quite powerful centralized governments, manipulating a corps of civil servants and a military establishment, capable of collecting taxes and maintaining public works over large areas, capable of conquering and administering other regions and of generating a framework for elaborate patterns of trade and even significant industrial development. The Roman and Mayan Empires were such elaborate traditional organizations, as were certain of the Chinese dynasties at the peak of their effectiveness and some of the Middle Eastern empires at various stages of history.

Nor were these societies all primitive intellectually. Some of them, such as the Greek and Chinese, developed philosophy and the arts to levels hardly since surpassed. Societies of the Near East developed the modern alphabet and the number tools on which modern achievements in mathematics are built. In traditional societies of the West there evolved the concept of monotheism, and then Christianity; in India, Buddhism.

The history of traditional societies, and notably of those that had reasonably strong centralized governments, was not static. In times of peace, more acreage was cultivated, trade expanded, the population increased; the government collected taxes efficiently, maintained the irrigation works, and enlarged the opportunities for commerce. The nation extended its boundaries and learned how to administer a large empire. Colonization of distant areas occurred. But then change would come to a halt, and governmental administration would begin to disintegrate; the society would break down. The immediate causes of collapse were various—population pressure, war, disintegration of central rule, and so on. But behind these varied events lay one common circumstance: the society had encountered a new condition to which it could not adapt. Old patterns of behavior persisted even though new circumstances required changed behavior, and the society ceased to function well enough to prevent disaster.

It followed from the preponderant role of agriculture that the ownership and control of land was a decisive factor in social prestige and, usually, in political influence. In some places the bulk of the land was owned by a relatively small number of nobles and the king, and worked by peasants who stood in a feudal, hierarchical relationship to the owners. This condition still exists, for example, in parts of the Middle East. In other countries landownership was quite widely spread, as it was in China, resulting in an endless struggle by the peasants to acquire more land, to establish an economic position relatively independent of the luck of the harvests, and thus to rise in the society. In many of the African tribes, land was owned communally, with no concept of individual tenure and thus little incentive for systematic investment in improvements.

In traditional societies, face-to-face relationships were extremely important, as were the ties to family and clan. Men tended to be bound together and to be valued by one another in terms of such intimate connections rather than because of their ability to perform specific functional tasks. It was very rarely that the average person had dealings with anyone he did not know quite well. Social, political, and even economic relations with strangers were seen as neither necessary nor desirable. Hence human intercourse, which in modern societies would be guided by functional considerations of economic benefit, political advantage, technical exchange, and the like, were in traditional societies much more influenced by codes of friendship, family and tribal loyalty, and hierarchical status.

Although traditional societies sometimes provided a channel for able men of the lower economic classes to rise in power and prestige (often through the civil service and the military establishment), there was a tendency for people to assume that the status of their children and grandchildren would be similar to that of their parents and grand-parents. A kind of long-run fatalism pervaded traditional societies de-spite the ebb and flow of family fortunes and despite the slow evolution of the society as a whole.

The cultural and religious life of traditional societies, and the values they elevated, varied widely. Generally, however, they formed a co-herent pattern, giving men a reasonably orderly rationale for the rela-tively stable round of life they faced, at whatever level in the society they found themselves. They provided a set of relationships of men to one another and to the world about them which gave them a degree of security in facing their appointed destiny within the traditional struc-ture.

✿   ✿   ✿   ✿   ✿

DISEQUILIBRIUM WITHIN TRADITIONAL SOCIETIES

That change in traditional societies is not determined solely by the impact of the West is clear from the comparative history of India, Indo-nesia, China, and Japan. The English were well established in India and the Dutch in Indonesia by the middle of the sixteenth century, and channels for the introduction of Western skills and ideas were far more readily available than in China or Japan. Next in degree of contact with the West was China, where the powers established trading beach-heads at the important ports and carried on trade with the interior of the country. Japan had the least contact of all, for it ejected Westerners during the first half of the seventeenth century, except for a tiny colony of Dutch traders who were suffered to remain at Deshima Bay at the far tip of the main island. What little contact there was with the West was deliberately permitted to flow through the tiny Deshima Bay funnel. Yet of the four countries mentioned, Japan gave increasing evidence of modernization between 1800 and 1850 and was undergoing rapid change by the last quarter of the nineteenth century, almost three quarters of a century before any of the others.

Clearly factors other than contact with the West were at work within some traditional societies to produce men, institutions, and atti-tudes conducive to change. . . .

In some societies, for example, the requirements of conducting war led the central government to enlarge the military caste. . . . War also increased the requirements for credit and trade, tending to elevate somewhat the status of moneylenders and of those who managed do-mestic and foreign commerce—men whose formal place in the traditional hierarchy was usually low. In those traditional societies which assumed imperial responsibility, the management of empire itself strengthened the role and status of the civil servant and the technician.

It appears that a traditional society turned the more readily to modernization if there was any articulate group of men in it with reason to be unhappy about their position. Feeling aggrieved, already questioning the values and attitudes of the traditional society, they were psychologically prepared to accept new ways of life as a means of proving their worth and gaining self-satisfaction, status, and prestige. . . .

✧　　✧　　✧　　✧　　✧

In Colombia the Spanish conquerors inhabited three high valleys which are the sites of the four main present cities of Colombia. In two of these valleys they developed landed estates and became landed gentry or cattlemen. In the third, Antioquia, because the land was less suitable and because other activities were more attractive, they did not. During the eighteenth and nineteenth centuries, as the historical literature of the time shows, the gentry of the other two valleys looked down on the Antioqueños because they too had not become gentry, and the Antioqueños resented this attitude. Today it is the Antioqueños who are spearheading economic and political modernization throughout Colombia.

In India successive waves of migration over several millennia have resulted in the existence of a number of social groups who even today are very conscious of their historical differences from each other. It is probably significant that much of the effective modern business activity to date in India has been initiated by several of the minority social groups—the Parsis, the Marwari, and others.

Thus social tensions may lead to the rejection of traditional attitudes by certain groups, who turn to new activities which may restore their prestige and sense of achievement. Indeed, it is virtually never the social group in control of a traditional society that leads the way to modernization. That group, which finds the traditional social order satisfactory, virtually always resists change, even if the society is threatened from without and change is necessary to resist that threat.

But this social and psychological dynamic need not, by itself, lead disaffected groups to engage in new sorts of economic activities. Modernization must first become a realistic alternative. Only when new ideas and ways of doing things are introduced from more advanced societies will the possibilities of economic change be perceived as real.

THE IMPACT OF MORE ADVANCED SOCIETIES

The initial impact of a comparatively modernized society on a traditional society most commonly took the form of, or was followed by, occupation and the setting up of colonial administrations, actions that had revolutionary effects on the traditional society in two ways.

First, in pursuit of its own interests (and often, too, in response to an impulse to spread the values and advantages of modern civilization) the colonial power executed specific policies which directly affected the economic, social, political, and cultural life of the traditional society. Ports, docks, roads, and, in some places, railroads were built. These were usually designed primarily for the economic or military advantage of the colonial power; but they had wider effects in creating national markets, commercializing agriculture, helping cities to grow, and bringing backward areas into contact with elements of modern life. Forms of central administration and centralized tax systems were usually set up. Some colonials were drawn into the economic and administrative activities necessary to execute the purposes of the colonial power. Some modern goods and services were diffused, altering the conception of the level of life that men could regard as attainable. To at least a few colonials the opportunity for a Western education was opened. Perhaps most important, the colonial power often introduced the traditional society to the Western tradition of law, to some version of those rules and procedures for the dispensation of justice which transcend and limit the powers of the individuals who exercise political authority.

In short, it was of the nature of the colonial experience that at every level of life it brought the traditional society into contact with some degree of modernization.

The character and extent of the contact with modernization varied with the concept of colonial rule that each power brought to its various colonies. In India, for example, the British made special efforts to train men for both the civil service and the army: the Moslems on the whole opted for military training, the Hindus for the civil service, reflecting in that choice underlying differences in the culture of the two groups in the Indian peninsula. In Burma, on the other hand, the British did relatively little to train either soldiers or civil servants. The French, in their empire, made great efforts to bring a thin top layer of the indigenous leaders as fully as possible into French cultural, intellectual, and political life. The Belgians in the Congo concentrated, for economic reasons, on literacy and vocational training for the lower levels of the labor force and did nothing to prepare an elite for leadership. The Dutch in Indonesia and the Portuguese in East Africa by and large adopted policies designed to limit the extent and the pace of modernization.

But however colonial policy might vary, colonialism nevertheless had one universal direct effect: it disrupted the static traditional societies. In establishing their own control the colonial administrators destroyed the existing power structure. In varying degrees they cast aside the traditional political and administrative system, substituting their own. They often treated the traditional religion with scorn and profaned what had been held holy. They violated many customary and revered human and property rights by introducing Western ideas of law and contract which in the light of traditional morals often must have seemed as wrong to the indigenous people as the Soviet doctrine of the supremacy of the state over the individual seems to the West. In these and other ways the cohesion and integrity of the traditional social and political system were violated.

The second effect of colonialism was indirect but perhaps even more profound than the direct infusion of modern elements. As an increasing number of men in the colonial society became acquainted with the methods and ideas of the West, they reacted against the human and collective humiliation that inevitably accompanied colonial rule; and they sought independence. . . .

Colonial rule was not, however, the only form of intrusion that helped unhinge traditional societies. The defeat of the traditional society in war against a more advanced power often played an important role. This was so, for example, in Germany after the Napoleonic occupation; in Russia after the Crimean War; in Japan after its imposed opening to trade by the West in the shadow of modern naval cannon; in Turkey after the First World War; in China after the defeats by the British in the 1840's and by the Japanese in the 1890's. The demonstration that the traditional form of organization was incapable of maintaining the physical integrity of the nation tended to lower the prestige of the traditional rulers, their values, and their institutions, and it tended to strengthen the hand of those groups in the traditional society—soldiers, intellectuals, men of commerce, civil servants, lesser nobility—who for various, often differing reasons were already interested in making the social changes necessary to increase their own power and the strength and prestige of their society.

     ✽   ✽   ✽   ✽   ✽

The Western example can cause other inner conflicts. After independence, the desire for power and dignity, combined with the recognition of industrialization as a symbol of the power of the West, often provides a powerful emotional stimulus to the desire for industrialization; but it does not inculcate a corresponding desire to live the kinds of lives, perform the kinds of functions, and maintain the kinds of relationships with other individuals that are necessary for industrialization. The fruits of industrialization are urgently desired; the social and psychological changes which go with it may still be unwelcome.

In the countryside, the influence of the West has in several ways stimulated an intense desire by the peasant for land reform. . . .

. . . The point to be made here is that, wherever for any reason landlessness or land scarcity has existed, the spread of egalitarian ideas from the West has given the peasant an increased feeling that something could be done about it and has intensified the demand for land reform. From the French Revolution, through the Taiping Rebellion in China and the Russian Revolution, down to the pressure for land reform in contemporary Egypt and Iran, this has been true.

❖　❖　❖　❖　❖

The introduction of Western ideas has also had profound effects on traditional societies. Among the new ideas were the Western notions that all men stood equal before the law, that they should have equal opportunity to develop their talents, and that policies should be determined and political leadership selected on a universal suffrage basis. In addition to encountering democratic concepts, many of the new intellectuals from the old societies have been exposed during their formative years in the West to Marxist and other socialist theories. These have often had a great appeal because they purport to explain the forces at work in societies in the process of modernization. The theory of the class struggle, Lenin's theory of imperialism, and Communist doctrine on the organization of revolutionary movements have gained considerable currency and influence, and have helped generate dissatisfaction with traditional attitudes and values. Although the traditional societies or those early in the modernization process did not necessarily desire to install modern democratic processes, the infusion of new ideas sometimes led to strong movements toward increased popular participation in the political process—a revolutionary violation of the customs of traditional rule.

5. SOURCES OF CULTURAL STRAIN*

d a v i d   e.   a p t e r

Cultural strain may derive from family division, religious division, anti-traditionalism, urban migration, ethnic competitiveness, racial compart-mentalization, economic discrimination, reliance on political solutions, or any combination of these factors. They are all potential sources of cleavage and social tension, for they mirror fundamental differences in outlook and belief from which most new nations suffer in an extreme form. Indeed, the most distinguishing characteristic of new nations is the great range of divergencies incorporated by the casual lines drawn by the colonial political cartographers in another day.

FAMILY DIVISION

Divisions within the family result in wider impacts upon personality than is the case with other, more ordinary, primary and secondary social groupings. The family is endowed with high solidary and affectual qualities. These qualities make the family a key agency of socialization. Basic divisions in the family, which arise from widespread lack of consensus in society at large, reflect themselves in a failing of the family to create stable roles and images of propriety, right conduct, and social responsibility.

Where the family can no longer perform the role of a basic orienting device, those molecules of stability which the family normally represents are themselves diminished. . . . Socialization is weakened when its function is shifted to other primary and secondary organizations. Political groups, clubs, schools and universities, and work associations can absorb only some of the socialization burden. The chief reason, however, that the family can do the socialization job so well is that the internal-

* From "Introduction" to Chapter IX, "Non-Western Government and Politics," pp. 650–654, by David E. Apter. Reprinted with permission of The Free Press from *Comparative Politics* edited by Harry Eckstein and David E. Apter. Copyright © 1963 by The Free Press of Glencoe, a division of The Macmillan Company.

ization of certain fundamental norms of right and propriety depends upon natural affection and the need for familial approval and makes the socialization process ultimately possible.

In contrast, secondary groupings cannot provide the emotional gratifications that lie behind socialization, unless they take on familial qualities. A political party, having personalized leadership, may be one alternative to the family in the socialization process, if the family becomes a scene of conflict and malintegration. Another alternative is a separatist religious movement. Either way, challenges to the scope of authority in the family make the task of social control by external means, political and social, much more difficult.

Family conflicts are not simply limited to socialization. They appear in conflicts over division of sexual roles—a common difficulty in Moslem countries, for example, and even worse where part of a country follows Moslem practice while another part does not.

Conflicts in the family are, of course, for the most part between generations. The younger elements are often in spiritual rebellion, not simply against their parents, but against what their parents represent in lost opportunity, acceptance of the past, and lack of vision. Indeed, there is much in common between the younger generations in new nations and second-generation Americans. Embarrassment over a way of life that is increasingly regarded as socially marginal is common in both cases.

Of course, the family continues to play a mediating role in all new nations. . . . Typically, however, as the family consists of traditionally oriented members, it will contain conflicts over tradition, ancestral religious factors, land, and the allocation of responsibilities. Where the family is pitched between traditionalism and modernity, it may involve other strains such as that between husband and wife, particularly if the former is better educated than the latter (a common occurrence because of the colonial practice of giving greater educational and occupational opportunities to men).

Whatever their source, conflicts in the family arouse and promote fundamental emotional disequilibrium, which has the effect of increasing hostility between members of a society, adding to the psychological intensity of all other cleavages and conflicts in a society. Most new nations have been traditionally "family centered." When the importance of the family diminishes, all other aspects of social life are profoundly affected.

RELIGIOUS DIVISION

In most new nations there was a close and intimate connection between traditional religious practices and beliefs and the pre-colonial political systems. The colonial period was not only a point of entry for new and alien religious forms, but also involved the secularization of authority. Systems in which the legitimacy of government had in the past relied upon religious myths and beliefs were thus governed by colonial regimes whose claims to rule were based, first, on superior power, second, upon superior institutions, and third, upon efficiency and welfare. Independent governments coming into office may find that the withdrawal of the Europeans involves a sudden resurgence of traditional religious practice that may result in open religious conflicts, some of which had always smouldered under the surface, although others might be quite new. Meanwhile, the new governments try to incorporate a new system of political legitimacy that itself is not entirely dissimilar to religion. New gods are substituted for old ones, to be worshiped in the name of reason and modernity.

This religious aspect of nationhood is extremely important. The very symbol of nationhood and independence is birth, the supreme act of creativity. Such creative acts are endowed with a special mystical appeal. Inevitably the establishment of political legitimacy and the more usual conflicts over religion are intimately connected, especially as in many new nations we find a rebirth of religion through political ideals, often indeed in the name of modernity, secularism, and socialism.

Thus, the problem of religious division extends far beyond the competition between major religious groupings—Moslem, Hindu, Christian—and far beyond ordinary variations in values. The classic conflicts in the West, between the spiritual and secular spheres of life, is not what is at stake here, but rather competing spiritualities; the values of government and leadership, moral proprieties of state action—all these are involved in the religious sphere, no less than what we generally think of as religious matters. It is no accident that the language of nationalism is often the language of religious usage, and the "political kingdom" is both a claim to secular authority, and an ecclesiastical allusion, the one reinforcing the other.

ANTITRADITIONALISM

Closely related to the problem of religious division, the problem of traditionalism lies athwart religious change. We can distinguish several different factors here. First, a good many old issues that were of political origin tend to renew themselves when seen as a fight over custom. These in turn may give meaning to a parochial society that itself has not yet accepted the idea of a larger polity or citizenship. Clan conflicts, arguments over custom, and the like all help to make the continuation of traditional life appear as the fundamental reality, with some modern forms and institutions regarded as more extraneous. Hostages to fortune, traditionalists have been badly used by contemporary political leaders. In Ghana or Eastern Nigeria, for example, traditionalists are viewed with dislike. The Accra Conference of December, 1958, branded "tribalism" as feudal and reactionary. The traditionalists, on the other hand, seek to preserve their power by absorbing "modernity" where possible. Sometimes they are extremely successful in this attempt, as has been shown by the political achievements of the Northern Nigerians or the Kabaka's government in Buganda.

Occasionally a new form of traditionalism appears. This is the traditionalism of the "establishment" versus the politicians. The more usual case of this occurs where the army or the civil service reflects the emphasis on a rational and efficient polity reminiscent of the colonial period. Often fed up with what becomes viewed as political vagrancy, the establishment sees the nation dissipating its energies and resources on inane political battles and steps in, just as, in a previous day, colonial officers would have done to insure "normalcy." This has happened in Burma, where, after restoring order and cleaning up the towns, the army turned the responsibilities for running the state back to the politicians. In Pakistan and the Sudan, where similar situations have occurred, there are few signs that the army is about to restore the politicians. In contrast, in Ghana the clash has resulted in threats by the politicians to "politicize" the civil service, that is, to introduce a spoils system.

      ✿   ✿   ✿   ✿   ✿

URBAN MIGRATION

The migration of rural people to towns always creates uncertainty. Consider the rural person who decides to leave the intimacy of his surroundings, the warmth of the hearth, and the security of ascertainable career prospects. He knows that the town is exciting, that his kinsmen will help him, and that the rhythm of life will be very different from that which he has known. His is the classic problem of the rural person becoming a townsman—a subject of a very large literature, both scientific and literary. But in new nations this is a particularly complex process. For one thing, there is rarely a sharp division between the rural and the urban area. Many cities in new nations have tightly enclosed rural centers, almost self-contained villages, existing within the town itself, organized around occupational and ethnic clusters. Stubborn differences in outlook and attitude may continue to prevail within the city, without its usual effects of atomization and homogenization. Indeed, many cities in new nations are dormitories for migrant populations rather than urban settlements in a real sense.

At the same time, this is a generational problem. Kinship and religious ties do tend to loosen in cities. Heterogeneous relationships between social groups are inevitable as children are thrown together in schools and as industry and commercial penetration make the town a center of economic and social dynamism. Where loyalties are being robbed of their particularism, the tendency is towards the opposite extreme, particularly among the young—toward atomism, separatism, and personal independence. This is the milieu which produces the political "street urchin," the broker, and the political entrepreneur. They find ready-made political groups in those protective associations, churches, trade unions, and tribal societies, which are characteristic of cities in new nations. Local urban followings propel them into national politics. The effect of town politics is a corrupting one, primarily because towns provide so many opportunities to politicians, with few requirements of accountability. Rarely are the dormitory towns bearers of culture, although they may give rise to senior social elites who are profoundly aware of their self-importance (as well as objects of envy and often fear).

Characteristically the towns in new nations have not experienced a sharp break between rural and urban life, but rather a blending of one into the other. . . .

✧   ✧   ✧   ✧   ✧

ETHNIC COMPETITIVENESS

Too often the ethnic factor is regarded as a somewhat romantic figment of the past, its passing viewed with regret, but what is termed "ethnicity" is not simply of residual interest—a quaint and historical antecedent in a new nation. Quite the contrary: ethnic formation is another form of nationhood. The still remaining primary attachment of many in new nations is not to the polity of the modern state, but to the polity of the ethnic group. Such ethnic attachments do not wither away with the formation of a national state. As a result many new countries experience bitter conflict between ethnic groups that challenges the new politics in demands for federal political arrangements and other claims to autonomy.

Where ethnicity is strong, few institutions can be immune to its effects. In the case of Indonesia, for example, it has proved most difficult to create a civil service free from ethnic conflict. Such conflict has manifested itself in political party affiliations of administrators, and brought competitive party politics inside the administration. A similar situation prevails in parts of former French Africa.

RACIAL COMPARTMENTALIZATION

The problem of racial compartmentalization is most acute in those societies which have a substantial proportion of *white* settlers. Where there are other minority groups in important economic or social positions, such as the Chinese in Thailand, Sarawak, or Malaya, the problems have usually not been acute unless activated from "outside," as, for example, the recent effort of the Chinese government to exhort the Chinese community in Indonesia to resist relocation schemes favored by the Indonesian government.

Racial compartmentalization exists in any society where racial groups have a very high number of transactions within the racial group and very few outside the group. Thus, in South Africa, Kenya, or Southern Rhodesia, a European can live a full life without coming into contact with Africans or Asians except under highly regularized and, in a sense, "ritualized" ways. . . .

How to build a plural society is one problem posed by racial compartmentalization. How to prevent racial conflict from becoming class conflict is another. Where race, culture, and class combine in racial compartmentalization, the outlook for violence and turbulence becomes pronounced. We have only to regard South Africa to see this.[1]

The greatest difficulty with racial compartmentalization is that, once created, the nature of the relationship between the races becomes hardened and fixed so that any alteration of it is tantamount to a social revolution. Under such circumstances any increase in the transactions between racial communities only helps to confirm each in its prejudices.

Commonplace in Western studies of race relations is the idea that as members come to know one another their prejudices slowly begin to give way. Unfortunately this is not the case in plural societies. There is a difference between a racial *group* and a racial *community*. Once a community is built on grounds of race, it repels or tries to render impotent any threats to the stereotyped basis of its conceptions. For a racial *community* cannot dismiss race as trivial or irrelevant if it wishes to maintain its exclusiveness. Under such circumstances, increased contact between *communities* simply means greater prejudice. . . .

ECONOMIC DISCRIMINATION

Economic discrimination tends to carry over its effects long after it is removed. It becomes part of the heritage of nationalists who, explain-

[1] Europeans amount to 21 per cent of the population in South Africa. See *State of the Union*, Economic, Financial and Statistical Year Book for South Africa, Capetown, Culemborg, 1957, p. 37.

ing backwardness as a consequence of Western exploitation, see in their country's inability to "catch up" with the West an extension of an earlier process. We have always tended, however, to regard economic discrimination as something practiced by Europeans against Africans or Asians, whether in the form of large expatriate firms or in the practices of colonialism, including debarment of native peoples from participation in the economy in all but the most subservient positions. This still goes on to some degree in many areas, but by and large both "social welfare colonialism" of the postwar period and effective organization by nationalists have made these forms of discrimination less significant, except in plural societies.

There is some danger that the nationalism of the 1940's, mainly Marxian in its overtones, should result in a reverse kind of economic discrimination. For example, it is quite possible that attitudes toward private investment, resulting from a previous period of aggressive capitalism, should lead politicians to deny any useful role to private investors. By so doing, they can easily make the burden for planning and state enterprise too great. . . .

Another reason that private enterprise is denigrated in new nations is related to the informal and unplanned manner of doing business that is the historical way of the West. When they were protected and controlled by strong colonial oligarchs with a commitment to service and efficiency under the later periods of social welfare colonialism, the colonial territories were in some measure safeguarded against the inroads of uncontrolled commerce. After independence the situation is radically different. . . .

✿   ✿   ✿   ✿   ✿

EMPHASIS ON POLITICAL SOLUTIONS

It is characteristic of new nations that, having won their freedom through political action and having taken over from civil service oligarchies responsible for the major activities of social life and welfare, they should continue to view progress in purely political terms. Politics is at once a major means of social mobility and a source of power and prestige. Thus, government tends to become omnivorous. Indeed, in most new nations government depletes the intellectual resources of regions, towns, and villages, drawing men of ability towards the center and then pushing a few reluctant administrators outward again to handle administrative tasks.

Politics becomes itself society rather than only a part of it. This trend is a most important source of strain in new states, for it causes all social matters to become political. Education, development, and religion all become evaluated in political terms. Planners, politicians, and administrators begin to live by the competitive practices of power rather than an image of public well-being. There is great danger of the public itself being viewed as the greatest of all obstacles, and tension between rulers and ruled becomes acute. Most new nations are democracies and believe in majority rule; but, as Panikkar points out, the right of the majority to exact obedience runs into grave difficulties. The difficulties of new nations stem from the very factors we have been discussing and, if fundamental enough, lead politicians to prefer forms of government other than majority rule.[2]

⟨∽∾∾⟩

6. SOCIAL CHANGE IN AFRICA[*]

l. p. m a i r

Whatever judgments may be passed on the aims and methods of colonial rule in Africa, the historical fact is that it set in motion processes of change which African leaders themselves now wish to carry farther. The techniques of production evolved in the industrial revolution were extended to Africa by what has been through the greater part of history the principal method of disseminating superior techniques, the extension of political control. Of course most of the people who were concerned in the process were not primarily interested in the benefits which would accrue to Africans, though a few were. One could argue for ever, and for ever inconclusively, such questions as who got undue advantage out of it, whether economic development 'really makes people happier', and so forth. The wider the field over which such questions are asked, the more impossible it becomes to strike a balance. The fact which is relevant to the situation today is that Africans, in rejecting their European rulers,

[2] See K. M. Panikkar, *The Afro-Asian States and Their Problems* (London, Allen & Unwin, 1959), p. 19.

[*] From "Social Change in Africa" by L. P. Mair, *International Affairs*, Vol. XXXVI, No. 4 (October, 1960), pp. 447–456. By permission of the publisher and the author.

have not sought to reject the techniques of production and of government which those rulers brought to Africa, but, on the contrary, to assert
African control over them. *Négritude* emphatically does not mean a
return to the mode of life of a century ago.

To a superficial observer changes in mode of life are measured by
what can immediately be seen. . . . But it is the kind of change in social
relationships of which these are the signs that interests the student of
society. The process through which Africa is passing can be summarized
as a process of change from small-scale to large-scale organization, economic and political.

        ❁   ❁   ❁   ❁   ❁

What I want to consider is the effect on African society of this
widening of the scale of social relationships. It has resulted in an im-
mense redistribution of population, which is most conspicuous in the
great industrial and commercial centres, but can also be seen in immigration to the limited areas of land that are suitable for growing profitable export crops, such as the coffee lands of East Africa or the cocoa
forest area along the Gulf of Guinea. This physical movement is obvious.
Along with it goes the movement from status to contract, to use Maine's
classic phrase: from reliance on the co-operation of kin and neighbours
to the impersonal cash nexus. The change has not gone nearly as far in
the rural as it has in the urban areas, but it is in progress there too. It is
seen both in a new attitude towards rights over land and in the employment of wage-labour by Africans. Old and new values mix uneasily in
both these fields.

Land, once the cherished, inalienable patrimony of a kin group, is
becoming a negotiable good. Cocoa farms and cotton land are sold for
cash or sometimes rack-rented. But few, if any, Africans will deliberately
divest themselves of all claim to land. It is not yet just one among many
possible sources of income, but has an almost mystical significance, as
well as the social significance carried over from the days of subsistence
agriculture, when those who had no rights over land had to become
dependants, or clients, of those with land to spare. This intense desire to
have rights in some land, no matter how little, may disappoint the hopes
of those who see the key to economic development in making all land
freely negotiable.

The interesting fact about the employees of African farmers is that
they are invariably immigrants to the areas where they are working. In
Ghana they come from the Northern Territories, in Uganda from
Ruanda or Tanganyika, or else from the less fertile parts of the Protec-
torate itself. The explanation that some peoples 'think they are above

work' is superficial. Everyone, everywhere, who can buy a machine or pay another person to do his hard manual labour for him, does so. But in a small closed society in which the relationship of employer and labourer has never previously existed, people do not spontaneously enter into it. Such contracts can only be made with outsiders. This fact, however, gives rise to delicate political situations. The immigrants may seek to obtain full membership of the new community, in particular the right to settle on the land, and this is usually opposed by the sons of the soil, as it is for example on the cotton land around Lake Victoria.

○　○　○　○　○

In the last twenty years urban populations in Africa have increased at an enormous rate. Housing has not kept pace with the influx, and all the social problems of the slum have appeared. In those towns which owe their existence to the European 'presence', attempts have been made to control immigration, though only the Union still tries to maintain that Africans ought not to be more than temporary sojourners in its cities. In town the African is dependent for subsistence on a contract with an employer, and for physical security not on tribal authorities but on national laws, enforced by State police. He is plunged right into the world of impersonal cash transactions. He may be able to have wife and children with him—this depends on municipal housing policies—but he can no longer live as a member of a community of a hundred or more all bound by the ties of kinship and recognizing obligations of mutual assistance. . . .

Nevertheless, it is clearly in the towns that modern African society must come into being. It is there that members of the many traditional small-scale societies are brought into constant contact, and do organize themselves in wider associations, as we see in the development of political parties, trade unions, new religions, and even pan-African movements.

To a student of society one of the most interesting aspects of the new urban populations is the interplay of the old ties, based on locality, language, and the recognition, in the chief, of a common political head and symbol of unity, and the new ones based on common interests in the new situation. Both in Nigeria and in Ghana the urban associations of which we hear most are locally based—bodies such as the Ibo improvement unions which assist newcomers from their own home area, raise money for the education of bright boys from home, and at elections, local and general, may be more interested in the home town than in their place of work.

Inevitably the immigrants to urban areas cluster in groups which have language and customs in common and in which the immigrants have kin and personal friends. Little conscious effort is made by anyone in authority to create wider communities; some municipal housing authorities have supposed that all that was needed would be to refuse to delineate 'tribal' areas in new estates. Yet the new common interests of urban dwellers do lead them to submerge tribal divisions in other forms of association.

Trade unions flourish in Nigeria, where under 5 per cent of the population is employed in wage-labour, and indeed throughout West Africa, as well as in the really industrial environment of the copper-belt. A recent study made there shows how, although tribal divisions have by no means lost their meaning, they do not prevent combination on a wider scale where there is a clear community of interest.[1] Competitors for leadership may appeal to tribal sentiment; dissatisfied sections may explain the failure of the union to achieve the results hoped for by the argument that the officials care only for their own tribesmen. But the detached observer can see the development of an urban society as this is generally understood, in which solidarity and opposition are expressions of economic interest and class structure, and no longer primarily of ethnic origin.

The new religions do not seem in practice to have a widely unifying effect, although their doctrines sometimes proclaim the appearance of a prophet sent by God expressly to be the saviour of all Africans. Typically they have expressed disillusionment with Christianity as it has been presented by missionaries—a religion which makes promises to all the children of God, but in practice appears to be no more than the supernatural source of Western domination. African churches have appeared in many places, each with its own Messiah, a man who has lived quite recently. . . .

Unfortunately it is only in the urban areas that the unifying forces of the modern economic and political system have their full effect; and it is characteristic of those African territories which have already attained independence, or are closest to it, that they are still very largely rural. An exception should be made perhaps for the ex-Belgian Congo with its great mining industries; but these industries do not weld together the populations of all its enormous area, but rather form points around which divisions crystallize.

Of course it is above all in the political field that the contradictions between the wide and the narrow outlook are most apparent. These contradictions result in a condition which could be called political immaturity in a very different sense from that normally implied by the term. It is not a question of understanding techniques of administration

[1] A. L. Epstein, *Politics in an Urban African Community* (Manchester University Press, 1958).

or of accepting constitutional conventions. It is rather that in the African territories the major political issues are questions which the older nations are presumed to have either settled or learned to put up with. Reporters who deplore the absence of programmes and policies in pre-independence elections are wrong in supposing that the only alternative is competition between personalities. Every personality has a following, and the characteristic of this following is that it is a local one. To some extent this results inevitably from the language barriers that divide the African peoples. A leader should be able to speak directly to his followers; where he cannot do this he can only rely on emotive slogans, and such slogans are provided more readily by opposition to colonial rule than by the issues which arise after independence. . . .

'Freedom' in Africa does not mean primarily civil liberties; it means not having to obey somebody you think of as an outsider, and once the most conspicuous outsiders, the expatriates, withdraw, small political units with common traditions begin to look uneasily at their neighbours (with whom they may share a tradition of mutual hostility). These attitudes are identical in essence with the territorial or pan-African nationalisms which command the sympathy of the liberal-minded. They are the nationalisms of the people who still belong to the small-scale society. Their existence presents serious problems for the new States. But they will never be eliminated by homilies about the pettiness of parochialism. People's ideas are necessarily limited to the world of their experience.

The fears of minorities and their demands for greater autonomy are by no means peculiar to Africa or to the newly emerging States. They have appeared in one form or another in every nation, but the older nations have settled by now into moulds which they are not likely to crack. In West Africa, as things stand at present, Ghana and Nigeria illustrate the alternative ways of dealing with minorities—by suppressing them and by seeking to allay their fears. The contrast may merely reflect the fact that Ghana became independent earlier; the Colonial Office wrote a Constitution for Ghana which provided some degree of regional autonomy, but this did not last long. Dr Nkrumah's centralizing policy has culminated in his republic, which gives no recognition to minority groups. Moreover, the recent referendum showed a surprisingly large favourable vote in the minority areas, though of course the Opposition have accused the Government party of intimidation.

                                                     ◦   ◦   ◦   ◦   ◦

In Africa local solidarity is the stronger because so many of the small local groups of which we are speaking have been until recently autonomous political units, each headed and symbolized by its own chief. British administrators are now being taken to task for having recognized these chiefs, a policy which was indubitably in line with popular sentiment at the time of its inception. Critics of this policy have never made it quite clear what alternative they would have preferred. It is true, and is well known, that French administration did not give much administrative responsibility to traditional rulers, but it is less well known that traditional rulers in the French-speaking territories retained considerable political influence, and in some were only formally 'abolished' by the newly created representative assemblies. It is fair, however, to admit that the most conspicuous divisions in these territories comprise wider areas than those associated with individual chiefs.

Except in such cases as Northern Nigeria, Western Uganda, and Basutoland, where rulers do still rule, chiefs are rapidly losing all governmental and administrative functions. This is inevitable in the modern large-scale world; the sphere of authority of the great majority of African chiefs is too small to be any longer meaningful, and the Belgian policy of grouping chiefdoms together and promoting one chief to be paramount had the same disadvantages as the creation of elected councils embracing several traditional units, and no obvious advantages. The same might be said of the Tanganyika federations of native authorities. The present position of most African chiefs is unhappy. In terms of the needs of modern government they are an anachronism. In the eyes of nationalist politicians they have sided with the enemy by accepting responsibility under colonial rule. They are 'reactionary' not in the sense that they themselves are obstructing the modernization of their countries (though they may be), but in the sense that they incarnate the old order in the eyes of the many people who are still more at home in the old order than in the new. Ghanaian fishermen still think, if the catch is not good, that this is because the chief can no longer afford to perform the necessary rituals.

The changes which African societies are going through are not in essence different from those which European societies have experienced as the mass of their populations ceased to be peasants and craftsmen and became agricultural labourers and machine-minders. What makes the changes in Africa so striking is their speed. As one reads the history of the eighteenth century, the seventeenth, the sixteenth, and even farther back, one can find parallels with contemporary events on that continent. The existence, right up to the time of industrialization, of such tiny political units makes a contrast with other parts of the world that have only recently been industrialized. But the most striking contrast between the experience of Africa and the history of Europe lies in the fact that from mediaeval times the rulers of Europe have been able to command the services of literate persons in sufficient numbers to meet the needs of administration as these have been conceived at any given time; and there has been a gradation rather than a gulf in outlook and mode of life between literate and illiterate.

In Africa the gulf is real and deep. The top people are those who have been educated in schools giving instruction in the language of the metropolitan Power. Not all of them have had secondary education; only a few have had more. From them come the politicians, the professional men, the civil servants and technicians. As the colonial governments saw independence approaching, they have done what they could to increase opportunities for professional, particularly technical, training, and some of the large firms have introduced training schemes for their employees. But the difficulty of adequately staffing the public services and industry without recourse to 'expatriates' is everywhere considerable. The new élite are the people whose mode of life is thoroughly Westernized as far as externals are concerned, who live in brick or cement houses and own cars and refrigerators, and they are the source of nationalist leadership and political ideas.

✧　✧　✧　✧　✧

In effect, the political system, although now it is manned by Africans, has been superimposed from outside on the smaller-scale polities that existed before it, and many of the values which it is supposed to represent have not emerged from any local searching of hearts. It is indeed recognized that democracy involves elections, but delicate considerations such as the genuine freedom of the vote, not to mention the tolerance of the majority for the minority, are not apt to be taken very seriously. It is worth recalling that during the greater part of the period of colonial rule government was neither subject to democratic checks nor required to guarantee civil liberties. Nevertheless, it is not my impression that when African politicians take a cavalier line towards democratic procedures they are deliberately imitating their colonial predecessors. Rather, they look on party politics as a battle in the literal sense, and they fight it both in invoking and by breaking the law.

Since the unity of the new States is so precarious, it may well be that their rulers cannot at present afford that tolerance of opposition which is the ideal of representative democracy. It is even possible that a more ruthlesss programme of technical re-organization than colonial governments have attempted is the only way to save the agricultural resources of Africa from destruction. The crucial problem for the new governments seems likely to be how to be authoritarian enough to maintain stability and carry through their modernizing policies, and yet not so obviously oppressive as to provoke active or passive resistance.

7. MODERNIZING STYLES OF LIFE: A THEORY*

d a n i e l   l e r n e r

1. THE MOBILE PERSONALITY: EMPATHY

People in the Western culture have become habituated to the sense of change and attuned to its various rhythms. Many generations ago, in the West, ordinary men found themselves unbound from their native soil and relatively free to move. Once they actually moved in large numbers, from farms to flats and from fields to factories, they became intimate with the idea of change by direct experience.[1] This bore little resemblance to the migrant or crusading hordes of yore, driven by war or famine. This was movement by individuals, each having made a personal choice to seek elsewhere his own version of a better life.

Physical mobility so experienced naturally entrained social mobility, and gradually there grew institutions appropriate to the process. Those who gained heavily by changing their address soon wanted a convenient bank in the neighborhood to secure their treasure; also a law-and-police force to guard the neighborhood against disorder and devaluation; also a voice in prescribing standards of behavior for others.[2] So came into operation a "system" of bourgeois values that embraced social change as normal. Rules of the game had to be worked out for adjudicating conflicts over the direction and rate of change. Who was to gain, how, and how much? As the profits to be gained from mobility became evident to all, conflicts over access to the channels of opportunity became sharper. The process can be traced through the evolution of Western property and tax laws, whose major tendency is to protect the "haves" without disqualifying the "have-nots."[3] It was by protecting

---

* Reprinted with permission of The Free Press from *The Passing of Traditional Society* by Daniel Lerner. Copyright 1958 by The Free Press, a Corporation. Selections from pp. 47–60.

[1] See autobiographical literature of human migration, especially W. I. Thomas and F. Znaniecki, *The Polish Peasant in Europe and America*, v. 5 (1927).

[2] Robert Park, *Human Communities* (1952).

[3] S. Ratner, *American Taxation, Its History As A Social Force in Democracy* (1942).

every man's *opportunity* to gain that the modern West turned decisively in the direction of social mobility.

Social institutions founded on voluntary participation by mobile individuals required a new array of skills and a new test of merit. Every person, according to the new democratic theory, was equally entitled to acquire the skills needed for shaping his own "future" in the Great Society. The vigorous controversy over public education that agitated the eighteenth century produced a net affirmation of equal opportunity. In every Western country the verdict was pronounced that education should be freely available to all who wanted it, and in some countries whether they wanted it or not. Thus the idea spread that personal mobility is itself a first-order value; the sense grew that social morality is essentially the ethics of social change. A man is what he may become; a society is its potential. These notions passed out of the realm of debate into the Western law and mores.

A mobile society has to encourage rationality, for the calculus of choice shapes individual behavior and conditions its rewards. People come to see the social future as manipulable rather than ordained and their personal prospects in terms of achievement rather than heritage. Rationality is purposive: ways of thinking and acting are instruments of intention (not articles of faith); men succeed or fail by the test of what they accomplish (not what they worship). So, whereas traditional man tended to reject innovation by saying "It has never been thus," the contemporary Westerner is more likely to ask "Does it work?" and try the new way without further ado.

The psychic gap between these two postures is vast. It took much interweaving through time, between ways of doing and ways of thinking, before men could work out a style of daily living with change that felt consistent and seamless. The experience of mobility through successive generations gradually evolved participant lifeways which feel "normal" today. Indeed, while past centuries established the public practices of the mobile society, it has been the work of the twentieth century to diffuse widely a *mobile sensibility* so adaptive to change that rearrangement of the self-system is its distinctive mode.

The mobile personality can be described in objective and technical fashion. . . . The mobile person is distinguished by a high capacity for identification with new aspects of his environment; he comes equipped with the mechanisms needed to incorporate new demands upon himself that arise outside of his habitual experience. These mechanisms for enlarging a man's identity operate in two ways. *Projection* facilitates identification by assigning to the object certain preferred attributes of the self—others are "incorporated" because they are like me. (Distantiation or negative identification, in the Freudian sense, results when one projects onto others certain disliked attributes of the self.) *Introjection* enlarges identity by attributing to the self certain desirable attributes of the object—others are "incorporated" because I am like them or want to be like them. We shall use the word *empathy* as shorthand for both these mechanisms. . . .

We are interested in empathy as the inner mechanism which enables newly mobile persons to *operate efficiently* in a changing world. Empathy, to simplify the matter, is the capacity to see oneself in the other fellow's situation. This is an indispensable skill for people moving out of traditional settings. Ability to empathize may make all the difference, for example, when the newly mobile persons are villagers who grew up knowing all the extant individuals, roles and relationships in their environment. Outside his village or tribe, each must meet new individuals, recognize new roles, and learn new relationships involving himself. . . . Our interest is to clarify the process whereby the high empathizer tends to become also the cash customer, the radio listener, the voter.[4]

It is a major hypothesis of this study that high empathic capacity is the predominant personal style only in modern society, which is distinctively industrial, urban, literate and *participant*. Traditional society is nonparticipant—it deploys people by kinship into communities isolated from each other and from a center; without an urban-rural division of labor, it develops few needs requiring economic interdependence; lacking the bonds of interdependence, people's horizons are limited by locale and their decisions involve only other *known* people in *known* situations. Hence, there is no need for a transpersonal common doctrine formulated in terms of shared secondary symbols—a national "ideology" which enables persons unknown to each other to engage in political controversy or achieve "consensus" by comparing their opinions. Modern society is participant in that it functions by "consensus"—individuals making personal decisions on public issues must concur often enough with other individuals they do not know to make possible a stable common governance. Among the marks of this historic achievement in social organization, which we call Participant Society, are that most people go through school, read newspapers, receive cash payments in jobs they are legally free to change, buy goods for cash in an open market, vote in elections which actually decide among competing candidates, and express opinions on many matters which are not their personal business.

Especially important, for the Participant Style, is the enormous proportion of people who are expected to "have opinions" on public matters—and the corollary expectation of these people that their opinions

---

[4] This formulation approaches the typology on American society developed by David Riesman in *The Lonely Crowd* (1950). Cf. my article "Comfort and Fun: Morality in a Nice Society," *The American Scholar* (Spring 1958).

will matter. It is this subtly complicated structure of reciprocal expectation which sustains widespread empathy. . . .

. . . The model of behavior developed by modern society is characterized by empathy, a high capacity for rearranging the self-system on short notice. Whereas the isolate communities of traditional society functioned well on the basis of a highly constrictive personality, the interdependent sectors of modern society require widespread participation. This in turn requires an expansive and adaptive self-system, ready to incorporate new roles and to identify personal values with public issues. This is why modernization of any society has involved the great characterological transformation we call psychic mobility. The latent statistical assertion involved here is this: In modern society *more* individuals exhibit *higher* empathic capacity than in any previous society.

As history has not been written in these terms, we were obliged to organize our own forays into historical data to establish a traceline on the evolution of the participant society and the mobile personality. We restrain our account of these forays to some main lines which lead directly to the problem in hand.

2. THE MOBILITY MULTIPLIER: MASS MEDIA

The historic increase of psychic mobility begins with the expansion of physical travel. Historians conventionally date the modern era from the Age of Exploration. . . . This was an initial phase in the modern expansion of human communication. Gradually the technical means of transporting live bodies improved and physical displacement became an experience lived through by millions of plain folk earlier bounden to some ancestral spot. Geographical mobility became, in this phase, the usual vehicle of social mobility. It remained for a later time to make vivid that each mobile soma of the earlier epoch housed a psyche, and to reconstruct transatlantic history in terms of psychic mobility. . . .

The expansion of psychic mobility means that more people now command greater skill in imagining themselves as strange persons in strange situations, places and times than did people in any previous historical epoch. In our time, indeed, the spread of empathy around the world is accelerating. The earlier increase of physical experience through transportation has been multiplied by the spread of *mediated* experience through mass communication. A generation before Columbus sailed to the New World, Gutenberg activated his printing press. . . .

Radio, film and television climax the evolution set into motion by Gutenberg. The mass media opened to the large masses of mankind the infinite *vicarious* universe. Many more millions of persons in the word were to be affected directly, and perhaps more profoundly, by the communication media than by the transportation agencies. By obviating the physical displacement of travel, the media accented the psychic displacement of vicarious experience. For the imaginary universe not only involves more people, but it involves them in a different order of experience. There is a world of difference, we know, between "armchair travel" and actually "being there." What is the difference?

Physical experience of a new environment affronts the sensibility with new perceptions in their complex "natural" setting. The traveler in a strange land perceives simultaneously climate and clothing, body builds and skin textures, gait and speech, feeding and hygiene, work and play—in short, the ensemble of manners and morals that make a "way of life." A usual consequence for the traveler is that the "pattern of culture" among the strangers becomes confused, diverging from his prior stereotype of it and from his preferred model of reality.

Vicarious experience occurs in quite different conditions. Instead of the complexities that attend a "natural" environment, mediated experience exhibits the simplicity of "artificial" settings contrived by the creative communicator. Thus, while the traveler is apt to become bewildered by the profusion of strange sights and sounds, the receiver of communications is likely to be enjoying a composed and orchestrated version of the new reality. He has the benefit of more facile perception of the new experience as a "whole," with the concomitant advantage (which is sometimes illusory) of facile comprehension. The stimuli of perception, which shape understanding, have been simplified.

✧　✧　✧　✧　✧

Thus the mass media, by simplifying *perception* (what we "see") while greatly complicating *response* (what we "do"), have been great teachers of interior manipulation. They disciplined Western man in those empathic skills which spell modernity. They also portrayed for him the roles he might confront and elucidated the opinions he might need. Their continuing spread in our century is performing a similar function on a world scale. The Middle East already shows the marks of this historic encounter. As a young bureaucrat in Iran put it: "The movies are like a teacher to us, who tells us what to do and what not." . . .

3. THE "SYSTEM" OF MODERNITY[5]

A second proposition of this large historical order derives from the observation that modern media systems have flourished only in societies

[5]   For a fuller discussion of the material in this section, see my paper "Communication Systems and Social Systems: A Statistical Exploration in History and Policy," *Behavioral Science* II (October 1957), pp. 266–275.

that are modern by other tests. That is, the media spread psychic mobility most efficiently among peoples who have achieved in some measure the antecedent conditions of geographic and social mobility. The converse of this proposition is also true: no modern society functions efficiently without a developed system of mass media. Our historical forays indicate that the conditions which define modernity form an interlocking "system." They grow conjointly, in the normal situation, or they become stunted severally.

It seems clear that people who live together in a common polity will develop patterned ways of distributing *information* along with other commodities. It is less obvious that these information flows will interact with the distribution of power, wealth, status at so many points as to form a system—and, moreover, a system so tightly interwoven that institutional variation in one sector will be accompanied by regular and determinate variation in the other sectors. Yet, just this degree of interaction between communication and social systems is what our historical exploration suggests.

We differentiated two historical systems of public communication, Oral and Media, according to the paradigm: Who says what to whom and how? On these four variables of source, content, audience, channel the ideal types differ as follows:

	Media Systems	Oral Systems
Channel	Broadcast (mediated)	Personal (face-to-face)
Audience	Heterogeneous (mass)	Primary (groups)
Content	Descriptive (news)	Prescriptive (rules)
Source	Professional (skill)	Hierarchical (status)

In media systems, the main flow of public information is operated by a corps of professional communicators, selected according to skill criteria, whose job it is to transmit mainly descriptive messages ("news") through impersonal media (print, radio, film) to relatively undifferentiated mass audiences. In oral systems, public information usually emanates from sources authorized to speak by their place in the social hierarchy, i.e., by status rather than skill criteria. Its contents are typically prescriptive rather than descriptive; news is less salient than "rules" which specify correct behavior toward imminent events directly involving the larger population, such as tax collections and labor drafts. . . . Even these prescriptive messages are normally transmitted via face-to-face oral channels (or via such point-to-point equivalents as letters) to the primary groups of kinship, worship, work and play.

Naturally, few societies in the world today give a perfect fit to either of these idealized sets of paired comparisons. . . . As we move around the world, subjecting our ideal types to empirical data, various elements in the patterns begin to shift. Most countries are in some phase of transition from one system to the other.

But two observations appear to hold for all countries, regardless of continent, culture, or creed. First the *direction* of change is always from oral to media system (no known case exhibiting change in the reverse direction). Secondly, the *degree* of change toward media system appears to correlate significantly with changes in other key sectors of the social system. If these observations are correct, then we are dealing with a "secular trend" of social change that is global in scope. What we have been calling the Western model of modernization is operating on a global scale. Moreover, since this means that other important changes must regularly accompany the development of a media system, there is some point in the frequent references to a "world communication revolution." We here consider the more moderate proposition that a communication system is both index and agent of change in a total social system. This avoids the genetic problem of causality, about which we can only speculate, in order to stress correlational hypotheses which can be tested. On this view, once the modernizing process is started, chicken and egg in fact "cause" each other to develop.

о   о   о   о   о

Having . . . established high pairwise correlations between urbanization-literacy and literacy-media participation, with critical optima for joint growth in each pair, we are in a position to suggest an interpretation in terms of historical phasing. The secular evolution of a participant society appears to involve a regular sequence of three phases. Urbanization comes first, for cities alone have developed the complex of skills and resources which characterize the modern industrial economy. Within this urban matrix develop both of the attributes which distinguish the next two phases—literacy and media growth. There is a close reciprocal relationship between these, for the literate develop the media which in turn spread literacy. But, historically, literacy performs the key function in the second phase. The capacity to read, at first acquired by relatively few people, equips them to perform the varied tasks required in the modernizing society. Not until the third phase, when the elaborate technology of industrial development is fairly well advanced, does a society begin to produce newspapers, radio networks, and motion pictures on a massive scale. This, in turn, accelerates the spread of literacy. Out of this interaction develop those institutions of participation (e.g., voting) which we find in all advanced modern societies. For countries in transition today, these high correlations suggest that literacy and media participation may be considered as a supply-and-demand reciprocal in a communication market whose locus, at least in its historical inception, can only be urban.

political ideologies

One of the more striking characteristics of politics in the developing areas is the attempt by many leaders to fashion and articulate a comprehensive political ideology. Some leaders, such as Léopold Senghor, Mao Tse-tung, and Fidel Castro, have achieved world prominence through the vigorous exposition of their ideas. Confronted by extraordinarily complex social, political, and economic problems, many leaders of the developing states have sought to rally and mobilize the intellectual and emotional forces of their followers through an appeal to a blueprint for modernization. To induce the commitment of necessary human and material resources for development, specific plans are systematically and often emotionally related to an overall conception of the ultimate society the leaders hope to achieve.

As in other matters, considerable variation is found among the developing societies and their leaders in the extent to which a more or less integrated doctrine of social change has been formulated as well as in the importance of ideological considerations in policy-making. Among the more conservative elites in many Latin American and some Asian and African states, the fundamental beliefs and values upon which policies are predicated remain oriented toward the maintenance of traditional privileges and institutions. Few dramatic social, economic, or political changes are proposed or supported by these elites, though in some cases they are being increasingly challenged by counter-elites who demand more rapid and far-reaching changes in the traditional order. On the other hand, some radical revolutionary leaders, impatient with gradual, pragmatic changes, have formulated elaborate ideologies to guide and justify their actions designed to reconstruct their societies as rapidly as possible. These leaders seek to generate such enthusiasm for and dedication to their goals that suffering and hardship, if required,

101

will willingly be borne and tolerated during the transitional period. Between these extreme positions of the conservative (or reactionary) and the radical leaders are many others whose approaches to the problems of modernization are, while vigorous, more pragmatic and less encumbered with rigid ideological considerations.

Ideologies can perform several important functions in states that seek and are undergoing rapid change. As we have seen, many of the developing states are confronted by the difficult problems that arise from their social fragmentation and the disintegration of the old order. As the traditional bases of personal identification are being eroded, an ideology may provide an important psychological and emotional base from which individuals can derive meaning and significance for their own participation in a changing society. Thus an ideology provides a framework within which the individual may orient himself to others in an emotionally satisfying manner. In sharing with others in the pursuit of common goals, individuals develop relationships and loyalties with each other which help to fill the voids created by the disruption of the traditional order. The establishment of broad, common goals may also serve to bridge the deep social and ethnic divisions within the society, thereby promoting national unity. In addition, by encouraging a common perspective on societal goals and problems, an ideology helps to legitimize authority. In many cases, the legitimacy of governments in the developing states is weak and in doubt, resulting from the serious divisions of opinion within society concerning the proper bases and structures of political authority. To the extent that leaders can obtain general acceptance of the goals postulated in their ideologies, the legitimacy of their own personal authority and that of the political institutions within the state is enhanced. In short, an ideology that is increasingly accepted performs the vital function of building common beliefs and attitudes among the political elite and masses, uniting the different groups within society in the pursuit of shared goals. The utility of a comprehensive, explicit ideology is, then, greater in most transitional societies than in either more traditional or more modern ones where, in both cases, a higher level of consensus on existing values, institutions, and processes is likely to be found. A major problem confronting leaders of transitional societies is to develop and maintain, in a period of rapid change, consensus on both objectives and the means to achieve them, and an ideology can help to perform this essential function.

Despite important variations in the specific doctrines and the emphases given them, the ideologies articulated by the leaders of the developing nations are all founded on a general idea which, while commonplace to persons in American or European societies, is often revolutionary in the context of the history and present level of development of the transitional states. That basic idea asserts that a better life *is* possible for individuals and groups than the one provided by the traditional order. This better life is conceived in terms of a higher standard of living, the dignity and equality of the nation and state, and the full self-determination by the state of its internal and international affairs. To achieve these goals, fundamental changes are assumed to be required throughout the social, political, and economic systems within the state. On the question of how to achieve these goals, different leaders provide different specific answers. Nevertheless, certain general themes are commonly stressed.

Of the several principal themes comprising the "ideology of modernization and development," that of nationalism is the most pervasive and perhaps persuasive. In addition, there is usually a commitment to the doctrines and values of socialism and democracy, though both of these doctrines are interpreted in several ways. These three themes are woven together into different patterns by the leaders of the developing states.[1] The individual patterns vary, in part, because of different historical experiences, perceptions of the present conditions and problems of society, and aspirations for the future. Particular variations also arise from the cultural, religious, and social characteristics of the individual societies as well as from the personalities of the individual leaders.

The emotional and intellectual commitment to development and modernization exhibited by many leaders of the developing states cannot be understood apart from their perception of the nature and consequences of political domination and economic exploitation by the major powers over the past several hundred years. Even in the Latin American states, which have been politically independent for over a century, a strong reaction arises from the fear that their economic independence is or can be easily impaired. For most African and Asian leaders, of course, the impact of colonialization and economic imperialism has been much more recent and encompassing. As these leaders perceive the recent history of their societies, the colonial powers drained enormous wealth from their areas while giving little in return. While the major powers improved their own standards of living and enjoyed the benefits of mass education, high standards of health, and political freedom, the exploited areas languished in poverty, disease, and ignorance. In seeking raw materials and markets for their expanding industries and economies, the major powers established political and economic controls from which there seemed no escape. The economies of the underdeveloped areas were frequently made dependent on one or a very few exports, subject to the vicissitudes of world market prices for these raw materials. Through their controls, the colonial powers forced the underdeveloped

---

[1] See the useful compilation of statements in Paul E. Sigmund, Jr., ed., *The Ideologies of the Developing Nations*, rev. ed. (New York, Frederick A. Praeger, Inc., Publishers, 1967).

areas to purchase their finished products with little opportunity to bargain for lower prices. Even the United States, which never possessed extensive colonial holdings, does not escape this harsh criticism. Its gunboat diplomacy and its sanction and support of the exploitative policies pursued by private American firms in Latin America are seen as only a variation—perhaps more subtle, and for that reason more dangerous—of the basic principles of colonial domination and exploitation which were more openly employed by European powers. As a major industrial power, the United States, like its European counterparts, could exercise great influence over the prices paid for the exports of the developing states as well as affect their economies directly through its investments.

This interpretation of colonial relationships obviously has much in common with the classical Marxist-Leninist analysis of imperialism. Indeed, many of these leaders acknowledge the influence of Marx and Lenin on their thinking, though few call themselves Marxists. The importance of the present leaders' interpretation of history is that it produces ambiguous, complex, and sometimes contradictory attitudes toward the present conditions of their societies, the manner in which change should take place, and relationships among sovereign states. On the one hand, these leaders admire the scientific achievements of the technologically advanced societies, even if they are former colonial powers. On the other hand, their interpretation of history stirs feelings of deep resentment and distrust of the advanced societies which, they believe, achieved their superiority largely as a consequence of their exploitative policies, and which today and in the future may employ their superiority in devious ways to perpetuate their dominant power. Further, this interpretation of history may distort the perception of the nature and causes of present-day problems. By emphasizing the evils arising from colonial policies, fundamental causes indigenous to the society tend to be overlooked or blurred.

To prevent the policies of exploitation and subjugation from continuing, much more than political independence is required, these leaders assert. What is further required is the development of a strong, unified, stable, respected, and prosperous society. This position can be attained through the development of a diversified economy, a broad industrial base, a mass educational system, modern transportation and communication facilities—in short, all the accoutrements of a modern, industrialized society. Only in this way can the full political and economic independence of the state be assured. The problem confronting these leaders is how this desired state of affairs can be achieved.

The first requirement on the road to modernization, according to these leaders, is the achievement of political power. Whether this takes the form of an independence movement against a colonial power or the overthrow of an existing conservative or reactionary government (such as accomplished by Castro's overthrow of Batista in Cuba), the fundamental need is to obtain control of the authoritative instruments of the state. In many areas in Asia and Africa, the present leaders have been faced with two tasks: first, securing political independence from a major European power, and second, establishing the political framework for the nation-state through which the instruments of power could be exercised. In some cases, protracted conflict preceded the attainment of independence; in others, the colonial power seemed almost eager to shed its control. Particularly in the former cases, leaders of the independence movement vigorously espoused the doctrine of nationalism as a rallying call. National self-determination was asserted as a fundamental right, and appeals for support were directed to leaders of those states, such as the United States, that historically have supported this concept. This nationalism, however, as John Kautsky indicates below, differs from the classical European type in that it seeks to erect independent states where none existed before and is not usually founded upon a common language or nationality. In many areas of Asia and Africa, it is not clear just what constitutes the nation that is to be independent or how far the principle of self-determination is to be carried out. In general, the boundaries established by the colonial powers have been retained as the geographic bases of the new states. Yet the several attempts to create larger political unions, such as the unsuccessful Mali Federation in Africa, are indicative of the problem of deciding what groups are to comprise the nation-state. In other cases, leaders of some newly independent states find themselves confronted by groups demanding the same rights to national self-determination that have just been successfully employed against the former colonial power. In Burma, for example, the Karens, a large ethnic minority, have repeatedly sought to establish their own autonomous state.

The development of a common feeling of identification with and loyalty to the geographically defined state remains a major problem in many areas. National leaders are attempting to replace the present primary loyalties of the masses to their individual ethnic and cultural groups with new primary loyalties toward the state. A variety of approaches are used in these attempts to create a feeling of nationalism centering upon the state. Leaders try, for example, to resurrect, preserve, and reinvigorate those traditional loyalties that are compatible with the new loyalty to the state. Local and regional heroes become national heroes, the songs of individual ethnic groups are nationalized, and new symbols that utilize traditional elements are created, such as flags and mottoes. More importantly, programs of national development from which all groups may derive benefits are designed and executed. "Enemies" of the state and its developmental schemes—frequently the former colonial powers—are sometimes created or identified; to overcome these enemies, whether internal or external, leaders may attempt to rally their followers through emotionally charged campaigns to protect the state and its progress. Nationalism is also encouraged through education and the mass communications media when those unique features of national society—its history, symbols, geography, religion, and so on—are stressed.

The creation of nationalistic feelings is considered fundamental to the implementation of developmental policies. *National* development is impeded if local groups cannot cooperate; their disputes and attempts to promote their own interests at the expense of the larger community disrupt national progress. A strong feeling of nationalism inspires a commitment to the larger community and a willingness to work for the promotion of the welfare of the nation and state. Nationalism thus provides an essential psychological base on which the successful execution of national developmental programs must in large part rest. Since nationalism also helps to legitimize the authority of those who plan and enforce these policies, great stress is placed upon developing positive attitudes toward the state and its leaders. Intensive propaganda campaigns are undertaken to promote and intensify feelings of national unity. Many speeches are devoted to a discussion of the state and its achievements and the need to maintain national solidarity, both for purposes of internal development and in order to play a significant role in international affairs. The result is that in most states some progress has been made in creating a sense of nationhood among the various groups within the individual states. Yet the traditional primary identifications with the ethnic, tribal, or other more limited group have by no means disappeared among wide segments of many populations, nor are they likely to be obliterated for many years to come.

A second widely shared doctrine in the ideology of development and modernization is that of socialism. With few exceptions, primarily in some of the Latin American states, the Philippines, and Malaysia, the present leaders of the developing states maintain that the goal of social justice is most readily and properly attained through the active intervention of the state in a broad range of social and economic affairs of the society. The specific economic and social principles to which they subscribe, however, vary considerably, ranging from those expounded in Communist China and Cuba to those in Chile and India. Typically, the doctrine of socialism has little rigidity; it is commonly developed on the basis of broad principles and shaped and modified as practical problems of development are confronted. Social justice is to be achieved through policies that, while diminishing the traditionally great gap separating the economic and social elite from the poor and illiterate masses, will raise the general standard of living and thus provide greater social and economic equality and opportunity for all persons. Much importance is usually attached to comprehensive central planning by the governments as the means to achieve the most efficient utilization of the often limited resources available for development. While the developmental plans differ in their specific provisions for state ownership or control of land, industry, transportation and communication facilities, and other businesses, extensive public ownership is commonly provided for and justified in terms of the social as well as the economic benefits to be derived by the society as a whole. In addition to developing the economy of the state directly, the plans also provide for the establishment and extension of educational, medical, and other facilities necessary to raise the standard of living.

Laissez-faire capitalism is rejected by many leaders on both intellectual and moral grounds. They believe that the competitive aspects of capitalism are wasteful of human and natural resources, that development through capitalism is slow and inefficient, and that capitalism promotes undesirable social and economic divisions within a society. If the gaps between the rich and the poor within their societies, and between the rich and the poor nations, are to be narrowed quickly, the more leisurely pace of capitalism must be replaced by planned, orderly development. These leaders argue that to attempt to develop a complex industrial economy from their agrarian base through capitalism would result in widening the division between their states and the industrial giants. Here the Soviet example of economic development is suggestive of the speed with which a backward society can achieve a high level of economic development through careful, comprehensive planning. Such planning can utilize and exploit the scientific discoveries and the technology created by capitalism for the rapid transformation of the economy.

At the same time that socialism is regarded as more efficient, it is also viewed as being morally superior to capitalism. By eliminating or substantially restraining the profit motive, leaders seek to avoid the harsh, divisive, and exploitative aspects of capitalism, and the creation of an economic and social elite at the expense of the masses. Socialism is also regarded as conducive to national unity in that the economic policies to be pursued ignore ethnic and cultural differences within the state. Through central planning and control of the economy, all groups within the society can be afforded greater opportunities for their social development.

While often highly critical of capitalism, most leaders also reject the economic and social policies advocated by the communists. Though the rapid industrialization of the Soviet Union elicits admiration, criticisms are leveled against the ruthless regimentation of workers and the agricultural collectivization that accompanied it. The leaders of the developing states regard their humanistic socialism as morally superior to materialistic communism, which, they assert, has so little concern for other than material values. These leaders believe that they can fashion a program of rapid economic development without the more extreme social consequences of human suffering and loss of dignity and freedom that occurred in the Soviet Union. Yet the fact that the Soviet Union possessed no colonies and did not pursue economic policies that openly exploited the developing areas makes the criticisms of Soviet policies less emotional and intense than those directed against capitalism and capitalist states.

For many leaders, the doctrines of socialism and democracy are inseparably interwoven. The social and economic equality promoted by socialism is equated with the political equality inherent in democracy. Nevertheless, just as the concept of socialism is variously interpreted, so is the concept of democracy. Of course, few leaders today, no matter how conservative or liberal, claim to be other than democratic. Similarly, most states are designated as democracies, at least by their own leaders. Political systems as widely divergent as Communist China, Uruguay, and Ethiopia proclaim that democracy is practiced in their societies. Obviously, the term itself has achieved almost universal acceptance. But the component principles within the concept range over a wide spectrum of fundamental rights and privileges, responsibilities and duties, and organizational structures and political processes.

As with the social and economic doctrines to which these leaders generally subscribe, political doctrines are designed to perform two related roles: they are to contribute to the unification of society and to its overall development and modernization. A principal theme in all the various interpretations of democracy is that national unity is promoted by mass political participation. By involving the masses in national politics, the leaders hope to foster a feeling of identification and participation, and thus to override social and economic cleavages within the society. As political solidarity is achieved, the legitimacy of the state, and the government and its policies, is strengthened. Strong governments are considered essential if the goals of modernization and development are to be achieved. To formulate and execute the broad social and economic plans that will transform society, vigorous leadership and strong institutional structures are required; these, in turn, are to be supported by an increasing consensus on the direction society is to take.

Two major interpretations of democracy may be identified in the developing states. Stemming from these different interpretations, different political frameworks in these states have been constructed in terms of institutions, processes, and rights and liberties.

Some leaders assert that national unity and strong, progressive, and responsible governments are best promoted by an interpretation of democracy that emphasizes individual rather than collective rights and duties. Democracy, from this point of view, is based upon the right of every individual freely to express himself and to organize with others for the promotion of particular interests and policies. Democracy is the framework within which these competing views contend for acceptance. Through free debate and discussion, compromises emerge, forming the foundation upon which national unity is built. National unity, in turn, supports stable governments that are endowed with a high degree of legitimacy and capable of exercising direction and control of the society. Consequently, the institutions of government should be constructed to promote the achievement of compromise. The role of the opposition must be respected. Free elections should be held periodically to enable the people to express themselves, selecting their choices from competing programs and candidates. Political parties are necessary to provide the organizational structure through which candidates and programs compete for popular acceptance. An independent judiciary is essential for the protection of political freedoms and rights as well as for the impartial administration of justice. Some leaders advocate additional checks upon the concentration of powers, such as a federal structure for the state, a separation of executive and legislative powers, and a politically neutral civil service.

A fundamentally different interpretation of democracy is presented by some other leaders. In its more extreme form, this interpretation asserts that national unity and development are attainable only through the disciplined subordination of individual interests, the absolute supremacy of a single political party, and a strong, highly centralized government. Only one general will exists, not a multiplicity of competing interests, and those who do not support the general will either lack an adequate understanding of it or purposely deviate from it in order to promote their own selfish interests. The former can be educated into an awareness of the popular will, while the latter must be suppressed. Since only one general interest exists, only one political party is required and permitted to express it. This party encompasses all specific interests within society, from which the general interest arises. Decisions within the party are reached by defining the general will and subordinating specific interests to it. Once decisions are reached, there can be no further dispute since the general will must always be obeyed. Further, since the party represents the general will, it is superior to the state and government. The state is but an important institutional framework for the execution of the general will as determined by the party. Consequently, governmental institutions are to be organized to provide efficient expression of the general will; they are not intended to promote compromise or restrain authority. Thus, no loyal opposition is conceivable, nor is an independent judiciary or a neutral civil service. Efficiency in the implementation of the general will is the standard by which the organization of the government is judged.

Many variations of these two conflicting interpretations of democracy may be found in the developing states, both in theory and in practice. The authoritarian interpretation is often modified by several practices, such as the creation of a mass, rather than an elite, political party, in which large numbers of individuals participate in a meaningful way in determining the general will. On the other hand, the liberal interpretation is sometimes modified by a denial of voting rights to substantial segments of the population, or the legislature, as representative of diverse interests, is effectively subordinated by a strong executive. Yet, whatever the interpretation, the idea of mass political participation is today almost everywhere accepted. Leaders have found that this aspect of democracy can be a potent instrument in mobilizing national unity and in promoting those attitudes necessary for the further development of the social and economic revolutions occurring in their societies.

Included in many ideologies is the additional doctrine of nonalignment in international affairs. This doctrine, especially prominent in Asia and Africa, is based on the assumption that too close an alignment with one of the major power blocs is detrimental to political and economic independence and self-determination. The view is advanced that the developing states are devising important and morally superior alternatives to those foreign and domestic policies pursued by the great power blocs. A close alignment with either bloc, it is feared, will corrupt the development of these policies. Nonalignment does not imply noninvolvement in international affairs, however, and many of the developing states play a prominent role in world politics. But they seek to play this role outside the orbit of the great power blocs, mobilizing among themselves a level of power and moral influence the great powers must heed. Greater prestige—an important consideration for many leaders—is assumed to accrue to those who successfully pursue an independent foreign policy rather than to those who follow closely the leadership of a great power.

The spokesmen for the "revolution of rising expectations" have thus sought to construct and justify a program for revolutionary change. They are simultaneously appalled by conditions within their own societies and stimulated by the possibilities of rapid change. But the changes that they regard as essential will not, they claim, come about through the slow, evolutionary processes that have enabled the present noncommunist industrial powers to attain their positions. Only through the careful planning and execution of comprehensive developmental schemes can significant advances now be made, they assert. Even among the more conservative national leaders there is generally a commitment to industrialization and modernization, though many of them hope that this can be accomplished with relatively little disturbance of the present social order. Their position is challenged, however, by those counter-elites who propose to undertake a far more inclusive revolution which, in the name of justice and equality, will reshape the entire social order.

SUGGESTED READINGS

Abraham, W. E., *The Mind of Africa.* Chicago, University of Chicago Press, 1962.

Apter, David E., ed., *Ideology and Discontent.* New York, The Free Press of Glencoe, 1964.

Binder, Leonard, *The Ideological Revolution in the Middle East.* New York, John Wiley & Sons, Inc., 1964.

Brecher, Michael, *Nehru, A Political Biography.* London, Oxford University Press, 1959.

Burns, Edward M., *Ideas in Conflict: The Political Theories of the Contemporary World.* New York, W. W. Norton & Company, Inc., 1960.

Castro, Fidel, *History Will Absolve Me.* New York, Lyle Stuart, 1961.

Davis, Harold E., *Latin American Social Thought Since Independence.* Washington, D. C., University Press of Washington, 1961.

Duffy, James, and Manners, Robert A., eds., *Africa Speaks.* Princeton, N. J., D. Van Nostrand Company, Inc., 1961.

Friedland, William H., and Rosberg, Carl G., Jr., eds., *African Socialism.* Stanford, Calif., Published for the Hoover Institution on War, Revolution, and Peace by Stanford University Press, 1964.

Griffith, Samuel B., ed., *Mao Tse-tung on Guerrilla Warfare.* New York, Frederick A. Praeger, Inc., 1961.

Jack, Homer A., ed., *The Gandhi Reader.* Bloomington, Ind., Indiana University Press, 1956.

Nkrumah, Kwame, *I Speak of Freedom: A Statement of African Ideology.* New York, Frederick A. Praeger, Inc., 1961.

Senghor, Léopold Sédar, *On African Socialism,* translated by Mercer Cook. New York, Frederick A. Praeger, Inc., 1964.

Sigmund, Paul, Jr., ed., *The Ideologies of the Developing Nations,* rev. ed. New York, Frederick A. Praeger, Inc., 1967.

Snyder, Louis L., ed., *The Dynamics of Nationalism.* Princeton, N. J., D. Van Nostrand Company, Inc., 1964.

8. NATIONALISM*

j o h n h. k a u t s k y

N A T I O N A L I S M   A P A R T   F R O M   N A T I O N A L I T Y

The concept of nationalism has taken its meaning from the "national" consciousness which began to grow in France with the Revolution, and from the movements that completely changed the map of Central and Eastern Europe during the following century and a half. Nationalism may be defined from this European experience as an ideology and a movement striving to unite all people who speak a single language, and who share the various cultural characteristics transmitted by that language, in a single independent state and in loyalty to a single government conducted in the people's language. A looser and less meaningful connotation of the word nationalism has also been widespread, which would seem to define it merely as the loyalty and emotional attachment of a population, regardless of its language, to an existing government and state. In this sense, one can refer to Soviet, Swiss, Belgian, and American nationalism, though all of these countries include inhabitants of different language and cultural backgrounds and the languages spoken by at least some of them are also the languages of other countries.

When we now turn to a consideration of what is generally referred to as nationalism in the underdeveloped areas, it becomes clear immediately that we are confronted with a phenomenon quite different from European nationalism. While it might therefore have been preferable to avoid the use of the term with reference to underdeveloped countries altogether, this would be futile in view of its adoption on all sides. We can only hope that the use of a single term to designate the two phenomena will not obscure the differences between them, that an easy assumption that the "nationalism" of underdeveloped countries must be like the "nationalism" of Europe will not obstruct recognition of the quite different forces producing it.

Neither of the two definitions of nationalism we derived from Euro-

---

* From "Nationalism" in John H. Kautsky, *Political Change in Underdeveloped Countries* (New York, John Wiley & Sons, Inc., 1962), pp. 32–39. By permission.

pean experience can account for the nationalism of underdeveloped areas. It seeks to create new independent states and governments where there were none before. This is clearly a nationalism different from one that may be defined as loyalty to an already existing state and government (although, once independent states do exist, this kind of nationalism may well emerge in underdeveloped countries, too). However, the nationalism that did create new states in Europe also proves to be irrelevant for the explanation of nationalism in underdeveloped countries, for in Europe the language or nationality factor was, as we saw, a key element in its growth. . . .

Being economically backward, the underdeveloped countries have not yet been subject (or were not until very recently) to the economic and political integration that created the pressure for the adoption of a single language in large areas of Europe. Nor, as we have seen, can there be in non-industrialized societies sufficiently widespread participation in politics to provide any large proportion of the population with the loyalty to "their" government that was essential to the growth of European nationalism. Typically, the more backward a country is economically, the more languages or dialects are spoken in a given area or by a given number of people. . . .

In most underdeveloped countries, the existence of numerous languages inhibits communication among the population. Thus, the Chinese do not, in effect, speak a single Chinese language, but several mutually incomprehensible dialects.[1] Even more clearly, there is no such thing as a single Indian or Indonesian language. Some ten or twelve major languages and hundreds of minor tongues and local dialects are spoken in India. Some thirty languages are spoken in the Republic of Indonesia, many of them totally unrelated to each other. In territories in which commerce and communications are not even so highly developed as in these three major Asian countries and which have not, like these countries, been united under a single government for centuries, many more languages may be in use. Thus, in Nigeria a population of approximately 34,000,000 speaks roughly 250 different languages, a situation that is not unusual in much of Africa and among the tribes in the interior of Southeast Asia and Latin America. In Australian-ruled Papua and New Guinea, perhaps the most backward area in the world, 1,750,000 natives speak 500 different languages and dialects, no one language being used by more than 50,000 and some by only 300.

In spite of the fact that most underdeveloped countries are inhabited by numerous "nationalities," i.e., language and culture groups, their

---

[1] The Chinese merely share a single system of writing which, being ideographic, is not bound to any particular language, and is, at any rate, not available to the great bulk of the population. Their intellectuals can communicate in a single language, the Peking dialect of Mandarin Chinese, which serves roughly the same function as Latin in medieval Europe.

nationalists have virtually nowhere sought to change the boundaries of their new states to conform to language lines. . . . [I]t is striking that existing boundaries have remained intact as colony after colony has become independent in recent years and already independent countries, too, have undergone nationalist revolutions. Countries including many language and culture groups, like most African and Asian ones, have not split up and those taking in only part of a single language group, like the Arab ones in the Near East and North Africa, have . . . not united. The colonial boundaries which have thus persisted beyond the attainment of political independence, like the boundaries of older independent under-developed countries, were in virtually all cases drawn without any regard to language or cultural divisions among the natives. They chiefly reflected the political and economic requirements of the colonial powers, or of earlier conquerors, as in China, Turkey, and Latin America. Whatever it may be, then, nationalism in underdeveloped countries—if it does not aim at changing these boundaries—cannot be a movement seeking to unite all people speaking a particular language under a single independent government.[2]

Only after nationalism has been produced chiefly by other factors, is an attempt sometimes made by Western-trained intellectuals to introduce the language and cultural element into it. The artificial resurrection of the Irish language may be a case in point. So is the pan-Arab movement insofar as it is not a mere tool of the nationalist movements of individual Arab states. The continuing failure of Arab unification would seem to indicate that these nationalist movements are in any case a good deal more powerful than pan-Arabism. More significant is the attempt of the Chinese Communist regime, itself a continuation of earlier Kuomintang policy, to impose a single language (that of the Peking region) and a simplified system of writing on all of China, a policy required, and facilitated, by the rapid economic and political integration of that area. Similar in nature, though not in the methods used to attain it, is the goal of the Indian government to spread the use of Hindi to all of India.

        ✣   ✣   ✣   ✣   ✣

Even in India and China, as well as in Ireland and the Arab countries, the desire to make all people under one government speak

[2] On the relationship of nationalism to existing colonial boundaries, see Rupert Emerson, "Nationalism and Political Development," *The Journal of Politics*, XXII, No. 1 (February 1960), 3–28, an article offering many insights into the nature of nationalism in underdeveloped countries. See also William Bascom, "Obstacles to Self-Government," *The Annals of the American Academy of Political and Social Science*, vol. 306 (July 1956), 62–70; C. E. Carrington, "Frontiers in Africa," *International Affairs*, XXXVI, No. 4 (October 1960), 424–439; and E. R. Leach, "The Frontiers of 'Burma'," *Comparative Studies in Society and History*, III, No. 1 (October 1960), 49–67.

one language (or to give a new autonomous government to those speak-ing one language) was not among the original motivations underlying the nationalist movement. In most underdeveloped countries no such desire has to this day appeared at all. If the origins of nationalism have nothing to do with nationality, i.e., with a common language and cul-ture, nor with loyalty to an existing independent government, for there is none, then what is nationalism?

Nationalism in underdeveloped countries appears to have in com-mon with European nationalism the desire of people to be rid of alien rulers and to have their own government, and it is probably for this reason that it has been labeled nationalism. In fact, the matter is not so simple, even if we leave aside the point, made at greater length earlier, that in underdeveloped countries, until modernization progresses, most people have no desires with reference to the central government at all, and they do not play any active role in politics. Apart from that, the words "alien" and "own" as just used, however, assume what is yet to be proved, that there is a collectivity of people, somehow defined by a common element other than a language, who share "their" nationalism. Why does a community in the South of India regard a prime minister from the North more as their "own" ruler than a viceroy from Britain? Why does one tribe in the Congo think of a government dominated by another tribe as less "alien" than a government of Belgians? In terms of language differences, these questions cannot be answered.

In some underdeveloped countries, notably Moslem ones, a religion and other cultural characteristics shared by all the natives regardless of their language, but different from those of their colonial rulers, may have been a common element around which their nationalism could have grown. But in many underdeveloped countries there are vast religious and cultural differences among the natives who nevertheless produced a single nationalist movement. And not infrequently, such movements are led by Christian natives who share their religion with their colonial rulers, whom they oppose, rather than with the great majority of the natives whom they claim to represent.

A more important element of unity setting the nationalists apart from their colonial rulers may be race, i.e., physical (as distinguished from cultural) characteristics. Some underdeveloped countries are in-habited by people of more than one race, however, and yet, in the Sudan, a European remains more "alien" to an Arab than a Negro, in Bolivia a "North-American" is more alien to a white nationalist than an Indian, in Cuba the "Yanqui" is regarded by nationalists as the enemy of both whites and Negroes. Sometimes certain unity among the natives has been created by Europeans or Americans who set themselves apart by discriminatory practices directed against all natives or "colored" people regardless of their particular race. The racial factor, then, is undoubtedly an important element in an explanation of nationalist unity in some underdeveloped countries, particularly where all natives are of a single nonwhite race and where it appears as a reaction to racial discrimination by whites. But not everywhere is this the case. There is no clear racial distinction between the European and the native inhabitants of North Africa nor is there between the English and the Irish or between some Americans and some Mexicans or Cubans.

NATIONALISM AS ANTI-COLONIALISM

In the absence of a common language, culture, religion, or race, what is it, then, that provides the focus for the unity among politically conscious elements from all strata of the population that is as characteristic of nationalist movements in underdeveloped countries as of European nationalist movements? Speaking of underdeveloped countries in general, there would seem to be no positive factor at all, but rather the dislike of a common enemy, the colonial power. Since nationalism is based on opposition to the colonial government, it is quite understandable that each colony's nationalist movement should operate within the existing boundaries and should not aim at a change in these boundaries. Thus, Indonesian nationalism is directed at the acquisition of Western New Guinea, because it is ruled by the Netherlands, the former colonial power in Indonesia, but makes no active claims to British-ruled Northern Borneo and Sarawak or Portuguese Timor, even though these are geographically, ethnically, and culturally much closer to Indonesia than Western New Guinea is. That the boundaries of a colony may cut across language and cultural lines is irrelevant; what matters is that they define the very purpose of the movement, anti-colonialism, and a change in them would therefore undermine the power of the movement and its leaders. Hence the general ineffectiveness of unification movements among former colonies, and the opposition by nationalists to movements of secession (as in Indonesia and the Congo), which are regarded as anti-nationalist, i.e., inspired by the colonial power.

However, nationalist movements are not confined to territories that are or were until recently administered by foreign powers as colonies, like India and most of Africa. Quite similar movements have appeared in independent underdeveloped countries like Turkey, China, and Mexico and, more recently, Egypt, Iraq, and Cuba. Unless they are virtually inaccessible, underdeveloped countries almost by necessity stand economically in a colonial relationship to industrial countries, in which the former serve as suppliers of raw materials (often made available by cheap native labor) and sometimes as markets for the industries of the latter. Anti-colonialism, then, must here be understood as opposition not merely to colonialism narrowly defined but also to a colonial economic status.

It is opposition to colonialism so defined and to those natives who benefit from the colonial relationship that constitutes nationalism in underdeveloped countries.[3] As such, nationalism can unite not only people of quite different language and cultural background, but also, interestingly, people of all the major economic and social classes, even though it is directed against certain economic policies. To be sure, in underdeveloped countries, as in Europe, many have been opposed and many indifferent to nationalism. Remarkable unity across social class lines has nevertheless been attained by nationalism. This is probably even more marked in underdeveloped countries than it was in Europe, where first the aristocracy and later important strata among the intellectuals and industrial labor proved to be anti-nationalist. The social tensions which modernization and industrialization produce everywhere and which in Europe were necessarily turned inward, resulting in conflicts dividing societies, are, in underdeveloped countries, largely turned outward. Instead of blaming each other for the difficulties growing out of modernization, the various social strata all blame the colonial power, the result being, not internal conflict, but that internal unity of anti-colonialism which is the basis of nationalism in underdeveloped countries.

---

[3] An impressive attempt to generalize about the nature of nationalism in Asia and Africa, providing both a wealth of data and much thoughtful interpretation, is Rupert Emerson, *From Empire to Nation* (Cambridge, Mass.: Harvard University Press, 1960). For excellent detailed studies of the bases of nationalism in two underdeveloped areas, see James S. Coleman, *Nigeria: Background to Nationalism* (Los Angeles and Berkeley: University of California Press, 1958) and some of the articles in Walter Z. Laqueur, ed., *The Middle East in Transition* (New York: Frederick A. Praeger, 1958).

9. NATIONALISM, LATIN AMERICA'S PREDOMINANT IDEOLOGY[*]

r o b e r t   j.   a l e x a n d e r

The predominant ideology of Latin America for the last generation has been nationalism. Within this broad nationalist movement there has existed great variety. There have been those who are democratic and those who are totalitarian, and there have been other kinds of variety as well.

Latin America has produced some original contributions to the ideology of nationalism. Long before it was a world-wide problem, important Latin American spokesmen developed a platform for the nationalistic aspirations of people of the "underdeveloped" countries.

However, the advent of the regime led by Fidel Castro, and the direction which it has taken since the end of 1959, perhaps presages the end of the predominance of nationalism. It raises for the first time on a major scale the world-wide ideological dichotomy presented by the struggle between the Soviet Union and the United States.

❖   ❖   ❖   ❖   ❖

CHARACTERISTICS OF LATIN AMERICAN NATIONALISM

Latin American nationalism has some particular characteristics which, though they may not be entirely peculiar to it, are certainly associated with the area. In the first place, nationalism in the area tends to be as much Latin American as it is strictly Argentine, Chilean, or Peruvian. There has been surprisingly little growth of animosity between one Latin American country and another as a result of the development of widespread nationalism in the nations of the area. There is a broad feeling of solidarity among the people of the Latin American countries.

[*] From "Nationalism, Latin America's Predominant Ideology" by Robert J. Alexander, *Journal of International Affairs*, Vol. XV, No. 2 (1961), pp. 108–114. Reprinted by permission.

Another characteristic of Latin American nationalism is that it has tended to be negative as well as positive. It has not only consisted of a heightened love of and militancy on behalf of one's own country, but also strong animosity toward some other outside country. . . .

Unfortunately, but understandably, the principal butt of the ire of Latin American nationalists in recent decades has been the United States. This has been due to a variety of causes: the overwhelming predominance which this country has tended to have over the whole hemisphere; the history of our military interventions between 1900 and the 1930's; resentment against behavior of many U.S. firms in the area; U.S. government policies of backing dictatorships since World War II; inadequate United States aid to the economic growth of the area.

NATIONAL REVOLUTIONARY IDEOLOGY

One branch of Latin American nationalists may be called the National Revolutionaries. Since World War II they have been the most significant nationalist element in the area, though they have been challenged by others, and these challenges are gaining force today.

Much of the attention of the National Revolutionaries has been concentrated on economic matters. They have stressed the need for obtaining "economic independence" and on reducing the influence of foreign firms and foreign nations in their nations' economies. They have written widely on these questions and have developed pretty well-defined ideas on the subject.

Fundamentally, the National Revolutionaries have sought to put the national economies of their countries in the hands of their own people. This objective they have sought to obtain through the achievement of more diversified economies, and through the limitation of the role of foreign investment in these economies.

The program for diversification of their economies has relied very heavily on industrialization. The National Revolutionaries have felt that the ability of their countries to obtain the necessary textiles and clothing, processed foodstuffs, pharmaceuticals, and cement should not depend absolutely on their ability to import these goods. This ability has in turn depended on the possibility of exporting the one or two raw materials or foodstuffs on which their foreign trade has absolutely depended. Finally, the National Revolutionaries point out that their countries have little power to control either the demand or the prices of their export products, a fact which goes far to explain the dependence of their economies on foreign countries.

Hence the National Revolutionaries have strenuously supported the fomenting of industry. To this end, they have backed positive action to build up this branch of their national economies, as well as extending considerable protection through tariffs, exchange controls and other measures.

The second aspect of the economic nationalism of the National Revolutionaries has been limitation of the role of foreign investment in their countries. They realize the usefulness of private foreign investment, though they do not wish foreign firms to dominate their economies.

There is a widespread feeling that foreign investment should no longer be permitted in the "infrastructure" of the Latin American economies. Thus, since World War II, there has been widespread expropriation or purchase of foreign firms operating in electricity, gas and other public utilities. The same thing has occurred in the field of railroads and civil air lines. This whole trend has been demonstrated recently by the amendment of the Mexican constitution to forbid in the future, any foreign firm in the public utility field.

The National Revolutionaries have also developed policies with regard to the exploitation of mineral and petroleum resources. A minority of opinion in the National Revolutionary ranks has favored nationalization of these resources. However, more characteristic is the position of President Romulo Betancourt of Venezuela with regard to the iron and oil resources of his country. He argues that it is in Venezuela's best interest in the short run to continue to permit the foreign oil companies to exploit Venezuela's petroleum, but assuring that the Venezuelans receive the largest possible return. Furthermore, this return must be invested as intensively as possible to strengthen the economy for the day when the oil resources have been exhausted. Finally, he has established a national oil firm, which will slowly move in to take over the control of the industry as the foreign oil companies' existing concessions expire.

In pushing this program of economic nationalism and growth, the National Revolutionaries have not been particularly concerned with the ideological question summed up in the dichotomy of "socialism vs. capitalism." They have not generally judged in ideological terms the utility of using the state or private interests in the development of a particular part of the economy. The important factor has been efficient development or how best to bring a particular part of the economy under national, as opposed to foreign, control.

This aspect of Latin American nationalism has often been misunderstood in the United States. The extensive intervention of the State in economic affairs in Latin American economies, particularly in those countries in which the National Revolutionaries have considerable influence, is generally not due to ideological predilections. Or perhaps, one may say that it is due to nationalist ideological predilections, not to the strength of "Communism" or even "Socialism" in these countries.

Another aspect of the ideological bent of the National Revolutionaries is their desire to achieve a greater degree of political independence from the Great Powers, particularly the United States. This desire finds concrete expression in votes in the United Nations, as well as the assumption of an independent role in the Organization of American States.

However, the desire for political independence does not resolve itself into blind or dogmatic opposition to the United States for its own sake. Quite to the contrary, the National Revolutionaries basically side with the United States in the world struggle. Furthermore, they are akin to the United States in their fundamental belief in political democracy. Thus, it might be said that the National Revolutionaries combine two ideological strains—nationalism and political democracy.

THE CHALLENGE OF THE JACOBIN LEFT

The advent of the Castro regime has dramatized a basic challenge to the National Revolutionary version of nationalism in Latin America. But it has gone further, and has introduced for the first time on a major scale the ideological struggle which has existed generally in the world for a decade and a half between the Communist version of totalitarianism on the one hand, and democracy on the other.

Fidel's basic challenge to the National Revolutionaries was first stated at the end of 1959 in more or less the following terms: it is impossible to have a fundamental social revolution in a Latin American country, and follow a truly nationalist policy through political democracy and with the tolerance of the United States. On the contrary, these objectives can be achieved only through a totalitarian dictatorship and alignment with the Soviet Union.

More than a decade ago, Juan Peron presented the same challenge to the National Revolutionaries. He decried democracy as a fraud and for most of his career was violently anti-United States. The only reason he didn't align his regime more closely with the Soviet Union was that the Soviet Union was not yet ready to play a big role in American Hemisphere affairs.

For approximately a year, the Castro regime continued to act on this challenge. However, since the beginning of 1961 the Cuban government has gone on from this original position, to take a new tack. It has increasingly indicated its ideological as well as tactical association with the Soviet Union. After the ill-fated "invasion" by anti-Castro exiles in April 1961, Castro went so far as to proclaim that his regime was "the first Socialist revolutionary regime" in the American hemisphere, indicating in the context of his discourse that his interpretation of the word "socialist" coincided with that of the USSR.

This evolution of the Castro regime raises for the first time in a serious way the question of the Marxist–Leninist–Stalinist ideology as an indigenous element in the Latin American political picture. This represents the most serious challenge to the nationalist ideology which has faced the National Revolutionaries since their appearance on the scene a quarter of a century or more ago.

Whether the National Revolutionaries are able to meet this challenge effectively depends on two factors. First is their ability to govern effectively in those countries—Venezuela, Colombia, Bolivia, etc.—and put their social and nationalist program into effect. The second factor is the support which the United States will or will not give to the National Revolutionaries.

OTHER IDEOLOGIES

The fact that nationalism and Jacobin totalitarianism are the principal ideologies in Latin America does not indicate that there are no other ideological influences operating in the area. However, others are either of little current importance, or are generally associated with one or the other of the major ideological currents which we have discussed.

Thus, in the past the European Liberal philosophy was of considerable importance in many of the Latin American countries. However, in recent decades it has tended to be submerged. Many of the present-day Liberals are supporters of a nationalism akin to that of the National Revolutionaries.

Democratic Socialism, such as developed in Europe in the last quarter of the 19th Century, also has had some importance in several of the Latin American countries. However, although there are still Socialist parties in about a dozen Latin American countries, they are not of major importance today except in Chile and Ecuador. Most of the Socialist parties have aligned themselves with the Jacobin Left which we have described, while a minority is in the nationalist camp in alliance with the National Revolutionaries.

The orthodox Communists, and their Trotskyite offshoot, have also been active in Latin America. There is a Communist party today in every Latin American country, but in only one or two are they currently a factor of first rank importance. They have completely thrown in their lot with the Jacobin Left.

Finally, there are the Christian Democrats. Parties of this type have appeared in a dozen Latin American countries in recent decades, particularly since World War II. Although they differ on many points from the

National Revolutionaries, in the broader struggle they are aligned with the National Revolutionaries.

ᏻᎳᎳᏹ

10. *COMMUNISM AND NATIONALISM IN TROPICAL AFRICA**

w a l t e r z. l a q u e u r

Communism in 1961 means different things to different people. Afro-Communism as it now emerges has not very much in common with the theories of Karl Marx, not even in the modified form in which they have been applied in politically and economically backward countries. Afro-Communism represents above all a means of gaining political power for a small group of intellectuals. In foreign policy its protagonists stand for close collaboration with the Soviet bloc and/or China. On the domestic scene it implies agrarian reform, frequently a foreign trade monopoly and central planning, a one-party dictatorship and the gradual indoctrination of the population with some kind of official ideology. It hardly needs to be demonstrated that such revolutionary technique may be very efficient both in gaining power and in maintaining it; of this China will serve as an example. But it is equally obvious that the net result is a system that has very little in common with Marxism as it was originally conceived. It is in effect a new political phenomenon that can be only partly explained by reference to developments in the past, or in other parts of the world.

Clearly Afro-Communism cannot be equated with Communism as known in Russia or the West, but there are also important differences between Afro-Communism and Communism in Asia. The leaders of the

* From "Communism and Nationalism in Tropical Africa" by Walter Z. Laqueur, *Foreign Affairs*, Vol. XXXIX, No. 4 (July, 1961), pp. 612–618. Excerpted by special permission from *Foreign Affairs*, July 1961. Copyright by the Council on Foreign Relations, Inc., New York.

Chinese, Korean or Indonesian parties were closely connected with the Comintern or Cominform for decades; they have had a thorough training in the essentials of Leninism, they have acquired the specific mental make-up of leading members of a very powerful sect, and they subject themselves to party discipline and "proletarian internationalism." In short, leaders like Mao or Ho Chi-Minh modelled themselves on the "ideal type" of the Russian Bolshevik of the 1920s.

The representatives of Afro-Communism, on the other hand, belong to a much younger generation. They grew up at a time when Communism had become much more powerful, but its ideological and psychological impact much lighter—and when various centers of Communist power had come into being. Their familiarity with the theory of Marxism-Leninism is often superficial, restricted in most cases to some knowledge of its more practical aspects such as political organization and planning, and of course a nodding acquaintance with the Leninist theory of imperialism. These are not the strong and silent heroes who had to fight for many years in conditions of illegality. Independence and power came to them on the whole rather easily; as in Guinea, they sometimes received it on a platter. Their beliefs are, in short, less deeply rooted and they are very unlike the intransigent "Old Bolsheviks" with their iron discipline and their unending ideological squabbles. The rudimentary political training they have received may give them an advantage over their political rivals and competitors, but it does not make them Communists in the sense of the word accepted in the West; at most they are Communists of a new type. This is not to split theoretical hairs or to stick unduly to ideological niceties; it has important and far-reaching implications.

It means, for instance, that nationalism, Pan-Africanism and even racialism play an important part in the attitude of these leaders. In Moscow their *nationalisme communisant* is regarded with great indulgence as a transitional phenomenon that will in due time give way to the real thing. (No such tolerance is shown to Tito, an old Comrade who ought to know better.) But it is highly doubtful whether this "transitional phenomenon" will really end as the Communists expect. The Afro-Communists have their own ideas about what ought to be done in their continent, and they are not overawed by the authority of Lenin or the experience of Communist régimes outside Africa.[1] They regard themselves as the founding members of a new third group, the African ex-Colonial International; "People of the Colonies Unite," Kwame Nkrumah wrote in one of his articles.

The name of a half-forgotten precursor of this ex-Colonial Communism, Sultan Galiev, has frequently been mentioned in recent years in

---

[1] As Sékou Touré once put it, discussing dialectical materialism: "Philosophy does not interest us. We have enough concrete tasks." Sékou Touré, *Texte des Interviews accordées aux Représentants de la Presse.* Conakry, 1959, p. 108.

this context. He was a Soviet leader of Tatar origin, at one time Stalin's deputy as Commissar of Nationalities. He was expelled for "nationalist deviations" and disappeared in the purges. His theories were, briefly, that Marxism had been mistaken in concentrating its hopes on the industrialized people of the West rather than the colonial peoples of the East, who are progressive, in as much as they constitute the proletarian nations on the world scale. Since all classes in these countries had been subjected to Western rule and exploitation, the class struggle there is of much less importance. His ideas culminated in an appeal for the establishment of a new Colonial International. On some points Sultan Galiev went even farther, as in his demand for the establishment of the dictatorship of the ex-colonial peoples over the metropolitan nations.

Some of Sultan Galiev's basic notions are now generally accepted throughout Asia and Africa; to a certain extent they have even superseded the Leninist theory of imperialism, though Lenin is remembered and the name of Sultan Galiev forgotten. There is abundant evidence that the Communists are perfectly aware of the dangers involved. Commenting on the general attitude of some of his compatriots, M. Achufusi, an African Communist now teaching in East Germany, recently wrote: "Their experience in the capitalist world has strengthened the Africans in their belief that world political problems have a racial character. . . . They think that Africa is the proletariat while Europe constitutes the bourgeoisie. They demand a specific African philosophy and ideology in order to liberate the Africans spiritually. . . . They equate the workers of Europe with the exploiters and thus violate the canon of proletarian internationalism. . . . Such a trend leads to playing down the class conflicts inside Africa." [2]

Afro-Communism is taking only its first steps, and predictions about its future developments are probably premature. In view of the conflict of ambition and interest between its leaders, it seems rather doubtful whether any unity of action will be achieved in the near future. What can be stated now with near certainty is that, though strongly influenced by some tenets of Soviet ideology, Afro-Communism is showing marked political independence. This does not make it more friendly toward the West. But it is not willing to take orders from the East either; its apparent ambition is to emerge as an independent factor in world politics.

I I

The observations made so far apply in varying degree to most supporters of Communism in Africa. But supporters of Communism in Africa are a very heterogeneous group—among them left-wing nationalist

[2] *Geschichte und Geschichtsbild Afrikas*, (East) Berlin, 1960, p. 222.

elements and orthodox Communists, with the great majority somewhere in between. It is doubtful whether much significance should be attributed to vaguely pro-Communist declarations made from time to time by leading nationalists. Most African political parties are in favor of some form of socialist planning, all are anti-imperialist, and traces of the Leninist theory of imperialism can be recognized in their views. This hardly makes them Communists, for the theory has in the past and present found many adherents (including Chiang Kai-shek) both in Asia and Europe, in circles otherwise very much opposed to Leninism. Such leaders may frequently follow the Soviet lead in the United Nations or participate in conferences convened by Communist-front organizations, but a closer analysis usually shows that they are radical nationalist rather than Communist in character.

○   ○   ○   ○   ○

. . . There are other dividing lines between orthodox Leninists and the Afro-Communists. Many of the latter hold strong opinions about the central role of the African intellectuals as the pioneers and leaders of the national liberation movement; the orthodox Communists, on the other hand, disparage the role of the intelligentsia. But the central issue on which opinions widely diverge is the question of the specific character of Africa. The Leninists do not deny the existence of peculiarities in the historical development and present state of Africa, but they maintain that all the basic tenets of Marxism-Leninism are applicable in Africa and that to disregard them would lead to dangerous nationalist deviations. The Afro-Communists, on the other hand, are much more selective in their approval of Leninist theory; while borrowing with much enthusiasm some of the tenets of this body of doctrine, they have emphatically rejected others. Some of their more sophisticated spokesmen who have read the young Marx consider Communism in Europe the natural reaction against a society in which the individual has been alienated, in which money is the supreme good, and in which spiritual values count for little if anything. Africa, in their view, is different; it may be economically backward but it is not a society with its values in process of disintegration; it still has a human richness, warmth and spontaneity sadly lacking in both West and East. These convictions are shared by a majority of African intellectuals and incidentally by quite a number of White missionaries who have called for the "Bantuization of Christianity." On the cultural level these convictions have given rise to the concept of *négritude;* on the political level they have found their reflection in the movement of Pan-Africanism.

Orthodox Leninists are bound to reject both *négritude* and Pan-

Africanism as romantic petty-bourgeois nationalist deviations. They try to do so with the maximum of tact, for they realize clearly that this rejection brings them into conflict with the great majority of African political leaders and intellectuals, who all share these views to some degree. For obvious tactical reasons, the orthodox Communists want to prevent a split with the Afro-Communists, but in the long run they cannot afford to compromise, for without clearly defining their own views they cannot hope to make much headway in the future. They face a dilemma which they probably will not be able to resolve, for the prevailing political climate is overwhelmingly in favor of nationalism and Pan-Africanism. The situation in this respect is not dissimilar to the state of affairs in the Middle East a few years ago. The Arab Communists tried very hard to evade, or at any rate to delay, a head-on clash with Pan-Arabism as represented by President Nasser. It is doubtful whether orthodox African Communists will be more successful in postponing the outbreak of what seems otherwise an inevitable conflict.

11. *THE APPEAL OF COMMUNISM TO THE UNDERDEVELOPED PEOPLES*[*]

m o r r i s   w a t n i c k

Fortunately, there is no need to trace out the tortuous course of the careers of the various Communist parties in the backward areas of the world in order to gain some appreciation of the extent and intensity of their indigenous appeal. For purposes of this discussion we can confine ourselves to China, India, and the area of Southeast Asia, where they have had their greatest successes to date. Despite the blunders and ineptitudes which marked their initial grand play in China in 1924–27, ending in almost complete disaster for their most promising single

[*] From "The Appeal of Communism to the Underdeveloped Peoples" by Morris Watnick. Reprinted from *The Progress of Underdeveloped Areas* edited by Bert F. Hoselitz by permission of The University of Chicago Press. Copyright 1952 by The University of Chicago. Selections from pp. 152–171.

party organization in these areas, they have emerged today as a political magnitude of the first order, boasting a seasoned leadership, a core of trained cadres, and a mass following recruited mainly from the peasant masses of the region. It is the purpose of the remarks which follow to indicate the nature of the Communist appeal to the peoples of these areas and to suggest some of the sociological factors which have made that appeal so effective.

It was once the wont of certain Continental writers, preoccupied with the problem of imperialism, to refer to the peoples who form the subject of our deliberations as the "history-less" peoples. Better than the Europa-centric term, "underdeveloped peoples," it delineates in bold relief all the distinctive features which went to make up the scheme of their social existence: their parochial isolation, the fixity of their social structure, their tradition-bound resistance to change, their static subsistence economies, and the essential repetitiveness and uneventfulness of their self-contained cycle of collective activities. With a prescience which has not always received its due, these theorists of imperialism also called the right tune in predicting that the isolated careers of these archaic societies would rapidly draw to a close under the impact of economic and social forces set in motion by industrial capitalism and that these history-less peoples would before long be thrust onto the arena of world politics, impelled by a nascent nationalism born of contact with the West and nurtured by a swelling resentment against the exactions of its imperialism.[1]

The final result of this process is unfolding today with a disconcerting force and speed in almost all the backward regions of the world. We can see its culmination most clearly among the classic exemplaries of history-less peoples in China, India, and the regions of Southeast Asia where the political and economic predominance of western Europe is being successfully challenged by forces unmistakably traceable to the forced absorption of these societies into the stream of world history. Their internal cohesiveness, largely centered on self-sufficient village economies, has been disrupted by enforced contact with the West, giving way to a network of commercialized money transactions in which the strategic incidence of economic activity has shifted from subsistence agriculture to plantation production of raw materials and foodstuffs for the world market. Their economies thus took on a distorted character which rendered the material well-being of the native populations peculiarly subject to the cyclical fluctuations of the world market. All this, coupled with rapid population increases which the existing state of primitive technique, available area of cultivation, and customary alloca-

---

[1] For typical discussions see Otto Bauer, *Die Nationalitätenfrage und die Social-demokratie* (Vienna, 1907), pp. 494–97 *et passim;* Rudolf Hilferding, *Das Finanz-kapital* (Vienna, 1910; Berlin, 1947), p. 441.

tion of soil could not adjust to the requirements of maximum output, has conspired to create widespread rural indebtedness, abuses of plantation and tenant labor, and other excrescences traditionally associated with the prevalence of a raw commercial and financial capitalism superimposed on a predominantly agricultural economy.[2]

Given the fact that the new economic dispensation in these regions was fashioned under the aegis if not active encouragement of the Western imperialisms, it should occasion no surprise that these regions, particularly Southeast Asia, have seen the efflorescence of a distinctive type of nationalism, especially after the debacle of Western rule during the second World War, differing in many crucial respects from the historical evolution of nationalism as experienced by western Europe. Indeed, the employment of a term like "nationalism" with all its peculiarly Western connotations to describe what is going on in Southeast Asia today is in a sense deceptive precisely because it diverts our attention from some of the distinctive attributes of native sentiment which set it apart from the nineteenth-century manifestations of nationalism in Europe. It is, moreover, a particularly inappropriate characterization because it inhibits a full appreciation of the potency of the Communist appeal among the populations of these regions. Historically, nationalism in western Europe has flourished with the burgeoning of an industrial technology, the urbanization of the population, the growth of a self-conscious middle class and an industrial proletariat, the spread of literacy, and the multiplication of media of mass communication. Now it is one of the distinctive features of the movements of revolt in Southeast Asia today that they lack any of these marks of Western nationalism. The indigenous "nationalism" of Southeast Asia today, lacking any of these props, nevertheless derives its peculiar potency from a universal reaction of personalized resentment against the economic exploitation of foreign powers. Whether all the economic and social dislocations of this region are directly attributable in refined analytic terms to Western rule is quite beside the point. The simple and crucial datum which we must take as the point of orientation in all our thinking is that to the mind of the masses of indigenous peoples they do stem from this common source. . . . The distinctive and novel aspect of the native movements of Southeast Asia . . . is that they represent a mass collective gesture of rejection of a system of imposed economic and social controls which is compelled by historic circumstances to take the form of a nationalist movement of liberation from foreign rule.[3]

---

[2] For an excellent analysis of the economic impact of the West on the rural economies of Southeast Asia, where the results are most clearly apparent today, see Erich Jacoby, *Agrarian Unrest in Southeast Asia* (New York, 1949).

[3] Bauer (*op. cit.*, pp. 262–63) has given the classic formulation of this relationship in his analysis of the problem of national conflicts in the old Austro-Hungarian Empire which showed some formal resemblance to the situation in the backward

POLITICAL IDEOLOGIES

It is this distinctive coalescence of two sources of resentment which offers the Communist parties the opportunities they lack elsewhere to any comparable degree. The two-dimensional direction of native resentment lends itself ideally to Communist appeal and manipulation for the simple reason that Communists can successfully portray Soviet Russia both as a symbol of resistance to political imperialism imposed from without as well as a model of self-directed and rapid industrialization undertaken from within.[4] This twin appeal gains added strength from the multinational composition of the U.S.S.R., which enables indigenous Communists of Southeast Asia to confront their audience with the glaring disparity between the possibilities of ethnic equality and the actualities of Western arrogance and discrimination. Communist propaganda has accordingly exploited this theme in almost all important policy pronouncements directed to the people of Asia.[5]

With the victory of the Chinese Communists, the incidence of these appeals has perceptibly shifted the symbolism of successful resistance and internal reconstruction from Russia to China, which is now being held up as a model for emulation by the other areas of Southeast Asia.[6] The shift is not without its tactical and propaganda value, since the adjacent region of Southeast Asia is now regarded as the "main battlefront of the world democratic camp against the forces of reaction and imperialism."[7] Success in this case carries its own rewards beyond the frontiers of China itself, for it is altogether probable that Mao Tse-tung will take his place alongside Lenin and Stalin as a font of revolutionary sagacity for these movements in India and Southeast Asia.[8]

regions today. The resemblance was superficial, however, since the lines of conflict were far less clearly drawn in Austria-Hungary, especially as regards professional and intellectual groups.

[4] It is noteworthy that variations of both types of Communist propaganda have also been attempted in western Europe in the last three years. The Marshall Plan, for example, has been presented to Europeans as an attempt on the part of the United States to impose its political rule over the Continent and to throttle its industries, without, however, carrying the conviction it enjoys in Asia.

[5] See the report of L. Soloviev at the Congress of Asian and Australasian Trade Unions at Peking, November 19, 1949, in *World Trade Union Movement* (organ of the WFTU), No. 8 (December, 1949), pp. 25–27. Also cf. "Manifesto to All Working People of Asia and Australasia," *ibid.*, pp. 43–46.

[6] "Mighty Advance of National Liberation Movements in Colonial and Dependent Countries," *For a Lasting Peace, for a People's Democracy!* (organ of the Cominform), January 27, 1950; cf. speech by Liu Shao-chi at the Trade Union Conference of Asian and Australasian countries, Peking, 1949, *World Trade Union Movement*, No. 8 (December, 1949), pp. 12–15.

[7] R. Palme Dutt, "Right Wing Social Democrats in the Service of Imperialism," *For a Lasting Peace, for a People's Democracy!* November 1, 1948, p. 6.

[8] See statement of Ho Chi Minh's newly constituted Laodong party, which "pledges itself to follow the heroic example of the Communist party of China, to learn the Mao Tse-tung concept which has been leading the peoples of China and Asia on the road to independence and democracy" (Viet-Nam News Agency, English Morse to Southeast Asia, March 21, 1951). Likewise, the ruling body of the Indian Communist party fell into line with the general trend by declaring its adherence to Mao's strategy (*Crossroads* [Bombay], March 10, 1950).

Unfortunately, recent discussions of the Communist movement in Asia have done more to obscure than to clarify the nature and direction of its appeal to the indigenous populations. All too frequently, the tendency has been to fall back on the blanket formula that Communists have sought to identify themselves with local nationalism and demands for agrarian reform. We have already seen that their identification with nascent nationalism, if such it must be called, derives its peculiar strength from certain of its unique qualities. It is no less important to an appreciation of the problem to recognize that the Communist appeal does not by mere virtue of this process of identification acquire the same uniform access to all sectors of the population. Indeed, the most striking and disconcerting feature of much of the propaganda appeal emanating both from Moscow, Peking, and other centers is that it is not, and in the nature of the case cannot be, designed for peasant or worker consumption. The appeal of communism as such in these areas is first and foremost an appeal which finds lodgment with indigenous professional and intellectual groups. Its identification with native nationalism and demands for land reform turns out to be, when carefully scrutinized, not so much a direct appeal to specific peasant grievances, powerful though its actual results may be, as it is an identification with the more generalized, highly conscious, and sharply oriented outlook of the native intelligentsia.[9]

Given the entire range of sociological and economic forces at work in these areas, the very logic and terms of the Communist appeal must of necessity filter through to the peasant masses by first becoming the stock in trade of the intellectual and professional groups. To revert to the terminology suggested at the outset of this paper, we may say that, by and large, it is the old history-less style of social existence which still claims the loyalty and outlook of the bulk of the indigenous populations. It is still the old village community which serves as the center of peasant and worker aspirations, and, if they have taken to arms, it is because European rule has destroyed the old securities and values without replacing them by new ones.[10] Without leadership and organization, their

[9] Failure to appreciate the true direction of the Communist appeal in these areas frequently causes some observers to commit the mistake of minimizing its effectiveness. Thus, Mr. Richard Deverall, the AF of L representative in these areas and an otherwise very perceptive student of the subject, ventures the opinion that Communist propaganda in these areas is mere "rubbish" because it is for the most part couched in terms which hold no interest for the masses, having meaning only for intellectuals (see his "Helping Asia's Workers," *American Federationist*, September, 1951, p. 16). Mr. Deverall's account of the nature of Communist propaganda is quite accurate, but, if the thesis presented above is a valid estimate of the current situation in Asia, he has not drawn the conclusion which follows from the evidence.

[10] In most backward areas the tie to the countryside is still apparent in the tendency of laborers engaged in industry and mining periodically to drift back to the village (W. E. Moore, "Primitives and Peasants in Industry," *Social Research*, XV, No. 1 [March, 1948], 49–63). See also the observations of Soetan Sjahrir in his *Out of Exile*, trans. C. Wolf (New York, 1949), pp. 74–75, concerning the mental outlook

unrest would be without direction and certainly without much chance for success, quickly dissipating itself in spontaneous outbursts against individual landowners and achieving no lasting goals. Whatever else it may be that we are facing in Southeast Asia today, it certainly does not resemble the classic uprisings of peasant *Jacquerie* but a highly organized and well-integrated movement, with a leadership that has transcended the immediate urgencies of its mass following and can plan ahead in terms of long-range perspectives.

That leadership is supplied by the new indigenous intelligentsia. It is from this group that native Communist and non-Communist movements alike recruit their top leadership as well as the intermediate layers of cadres, for, of all the groups which make up the populations of these areas, it is the intelligentsia alone (taking the term in its broadest sense) that boasts an ideological horizon which transcends the historyless values of the bulk of the population and makes it the logical recruiting ground for the leadership of political movements. For this, it can thank the formal schooling and intellectual stimulus provided by the West, which not only brought such a group into existence but also—and this is crucial—condemned large sections of that intelligentsia to a form of *déclassé* existence from the very beginnings of its career. The new intelligentsia was in large measure consigned by the imperial system to hover uneasily between a native social base which could not find accommodation for its skills and ambitions and the superimposed imperial structure which reserved the best places for aliens. There were, of course, considerable variations and differences in the various areas of Southeast Asia—India, for example, did succeed in absorbing a good many of its professionally trained native sons—but, by and large, the picture is one of a rootless intellectual proletariat possessing no real economic base in an independent native middle class. The tendency in all these areas, moreover, has been to train technicians, lawyers, and other groups of professional workers in numbers far out of proportion to the absorptive capacity of the social structures of the home areas, even if more of the higher posts in industry and administration were thrown open to native talent. In any case, those who did find such employment were frozen in minor posts, the most coveted positions going to Europeans.[11]

of the masses in these regions. This fact was not lost on the leaders of the Communist movement. In the 1928 resolution on colonial strategy the Sixth Comintern Congress noted that the proletariat "still have one foot in the village," a fact which it recognized as a barrier to the development of proletarian class consciousness (see *International Press Correspondence* [Vienna], VIII, No. 88 [December 12, 1928], 1670).

[11] Some interesting data on this score for Indonesia are offered by J. M. van der Kroef's "Economic Origins of Indonesian Nationalism," in *South Asia in the World Today*, ed. Phillips Talbot (Chicago, 1950), pp. 188–93, and his "Social Conflicts

But if these groups could not be integrated into the social structure of these dependent areas, the same does not hold true of their acclimatization to the cross-currents of political doctrine. Western education exposed many of them to the various schools of social thought contending for influence in Europe, and from these they distilled the lessons which seemed to offer the best hope for their native communities. Western capitalism was necessarily excluded from their range of choices if for no other reason than that its linkage with imperialist rule over their own societies debarred it from their hierarchy of values. The anticapitalist animus is common to the intellectual spokesmen of these areas, whatever their specific political allegiance or orientation may be.[12] Nor does it appear that any populist variety of Gandhiism, with its strong attachment to the values of a static subsistence economy, has won any considerable following among these intellectual groups. . . .

We can now appreciate the enormous initial advantage which was thus offered the Communist movements in these backward areas. The Russian Revolution of 1917 and the subsequent course of planned industrialization could not but fail to impress native intellectuals as offering a model pattern of action by which they could retrieve their communities from precapitalist isolation and backwardness without paying the price of continued foreign exploitation. . . .

. . . The Communist parties of these underdeveloped areas of Asia were from their very beginnings initiated, led by, and predominantly recruited from (prior to their conversion into mass organizations as has been the case in China after 1949) native intellectual groups. Though this vital sociological clue to the nature of the Communist appeal in the colonial areas has not received the recognition it deserves, amid the general preoccupation with the theme of Communist appeals to the peasantry, its implication was perfectly plain to the leaders of the Comintern. . . .

The fact that this did not accord with the *idée fixe* of this and all other Comintern pronouncements that leadership of colonial revolutionary movements is properly a function of the industrial urban workers should in no way blind us to the fact which Comintern leadership was realistic enough to acknowledge, namely, that membership of these

and Minority Aspirations in Indonesia," *American Journal of Sociology*, March, 1950, pp. 453–56. Cf. L. Mills (ed.), *New World of Southeast Asia* (Minneapolis, 1949), pp. 293–95.

[12] For a typical rejection of the capitalist solution coming from anti-Communist sources see D. R. Gadgil, "Economic Prospect for India," *Pacific Affairs*, XXII (June, 1949), 115–29; Sjahrir, *op. cit.*, pp. 161–62; and the remarks of H. Shastri, of the Indian Trade Union Congress at the Asian Regional Conference of the International Labor Office, Ceylon, January 16–27, 1950, *Record of Proceedings* (Geneva, 1951), p. 112. Cf. van der Kroef's article, "Social Conflicts and Minority Aspirations in Indonesia," *op. cit.*, pp. 455–56, and J. F. Normano, *Asia between Two World Wars* (New York, 1944), pp. 83–87.

Communist parties is heavily weighted in favor of the intelligentsia. One may, in fact, go one step further and say that, in accepting the predominance of the "colonial" intelligentsia, the Comintern was closer to the genus of Leninist doctrine than were any of its indorsements of the leadership role of the urban proletariat. No other group in these areas but the intelligentsia could be expected to undertake the transformation of the social structure under forced draft and in a predetermined direction and thus fulfil the main self-assigned historical mission of Leninism.[13]

If we bear this key factor in mind, it throws a new light on the nature of the grip which Communists exercise on the political movements of these areas. . . . As matters stand today, the intellectuals are the sole group in these areas which can infuse these raw social materials of agrarian discontent, etc., with the organization and leadership necessary for their success. And it is largely this group which has acted as the marriage broker between the international Communist movement and the manifestations of indigenous revolt.

☼   ☼   ☼   ☼   ☼

As matters stand, then, the organization and leadership of Communist parties in colonial areas do not accord with their accepted doctrinal precepts. For over a generation now it has been a standard item of doctrine, reiterated again and again, that the leadership of these parties must rest with the industrial working class.[14] The realities of the situation in these areas have not been very obliging to this formula, though it still occupies its customary niche in all their pronouncements. From the standpoint of their own strategic imperatives and long-term objective, however, the Communist parties of these areas have not hesitated to draw the necessary practical conclusions. They have acquiesced in the primacy of the intellectuals in the movement because the acceptance of any alternative leadership coming from the ranks of the peasantry or the industrial workers (assuming the possibility of such leadership) would entail the sacrifice of the prime objectives of the party—viz., the seizure

[13] Though cognizant of the role of the intellectuals in the Chinese party, Benjamin Schwartz's illuminating study, *Chinese Communism and the Rise of Mao* (Cambridge, 1951), falls short of an appreciation of its significance by focusing attention on a purely strategic problem—Mao's peasant-oriented movement—and concluding from this that Mao's ideology represents a radical break with classical Leninism.

[14] See, e.g., "The Revolutionary Movement in Colonies and Semi-colonies; Resolution of the Sixth Congress of the Communist International" (adopted September 1, 1928), *International Press Correspondence*, VIII (1928), 1670–72 *et passim;* and Mao's pamphlet, *The Chinese Revolution and the Communist Party of China*, pp. 15–16.

of power and the launching of a long-range plan for internal planning and reconstruction. . . .

❊   ❊   ❊   ❊   ❊

If we discern the central driving force of communism in the under-developed areas to be its appeal to a considerable number of the in-digenous intelligentsia, we are also in a position to reassess the meaning and changes of its mass appeal, most notably its program of land redis-tribution. To no inconsiderable extent, much of the confusion which attends thinking and discourse on the subject in this country can be traced to a widespread impression still current that the Communist movement in underdeveloped areas owes its success to the fact that it is finely attuned to the most urgent and insistent "land hunger" of millions of the poorest peasants living on a submarginal level of existence. There is just enough historical truth in this impression to make it a plausible explanation of Communist strength. It is unquestionably true that the mass base of the Communist parties in Southeast Asia can be accounted for by the almost universal prevalence of local agrarian unrest which thus constitutes the necessary precondition for the activities of the Com-munists. But if—as is not infrequently done—this is offered as the crucially strategic element in the complex of circumstances which have served the cause of the Communist parties, we are once again confronted with the old confusion of necessary with sufficient causes.[15] For there is no intrinsic reason which compels the ground swell of agrarian discontent to favor the fortunes of the Communist parties—unless that discontent can be channeled and directed in predetermined fashion by the inter-vention of a native social group capable of giving organized shape to its various amorphous and diffused manifestations. If the foregoing analysis has any merit, the balance of the sociological picture in these areas will have to be redressed in our thinking to give greater weight to the Communist-oriented intelligentsia and to its role as the prime mover of the native Communist movements.

❊   ❊   ❊   ❊   ❊

. . . Without the active intervention of a Communist-oriented intel-ligentsia, a large-scale peasant movement in China as well as in the region of Southeast Asia, if successful, would not go beyond agrarian

---

[15] An otherwise excellent discussion by Miss Barbara Ward verges on this error, especially in its opening remarks. See her article in the *New York Times Magazine*, March 25, 1951.

reform pure and simple. The end goal would be Sun Yat-sen's and Stambulisky's rather than Lenin's, given the essentially static and conservative temper of the bulk of the peasant populations. As matters stand now, however, the schedule of agrarian reform under Communist sponsorship has definitely been subordinated to the long-range perspectives of industrialization with a program of collectivization in store for the future when conditions are more favorable to its success.[16] Accordingly, the imperatives of the "New Democracy" require a shift in the main incidence of Communist appeal to secure for the regime a base of support more in accord with its long-range plans.

The shift is equally apparent in the industrial field, where attempts are being made to enlist the support of the "national bourgeoisie" during an indefinite transition period pending the introduction of "genuine" socialism. The present program envisions a form of limited state-sponsored and state-regulated capitalist enterprise to promote the process of industrialization,[17] and the attractions now being employed to enlist entrepreneurial co-operation are strangely reminiscent of the "infant-industry" argument so familiar in "imperialist" countries.[18]

☼   ☼   ☼   ☼   ☼

To say, then, that the Communist program in the underdeveloped areas of Asia is designed purely and simply as an appeal to the poorest and landless sections of the peasant population is to indulge in an oversimplification of the facts. The Communist appeal is rather a complicated function of the total interplay of political forces in these areas and has therefore tended to shift both in direction and in content with the degree of influence and political power exercised by the Communist parties. The only constant element among all these changes has been the abiding appeal of the Communist system to certain sections of the intelligentsia. Whether the new dispensation of the appeal can be expected to evoke the same degree of sympathetic response from the "national bourgeoisie" and the more prosperous peasantry as the discarded slogan of outright land confiscation had for the impoverished peasants is open to considerable doubt. The avowed transitional charac-

[16]   Mao Tse-tung, *On the Present Situation and Our Tasks* (East China Liberation Publishers, 1946); see also remarks of Liu Shao-chi in *People's China*, July 16, 1950.
[17]   See, e.g., Mao Tse-tung, *On People's Democratic Rule*, p. 12, and the text of the "Common Program of the People's Political Consultative Conference of 1949" included as an appendix to Mao's speech, esp. p. 19.
[18]   Wu Min, "Industry of People's China Grows," *For a Lasting Peace, for a People's Democracy!* November 17, 1950, p. 4. This outright nationalistic appeal to the interests of domestic business groups is also plainly apparent in the latest draft program of the Indian Communist party (see *For a Lasting Peace, for a People's Democracy!* May 11, 1951, p. 3).

ter of the program of the "People's Democracy" is alone sufficient to rob these appeals of any sustained response. It does not require any high degree of political sophistication on the part of the "national bourgeoisie," for example, to realize that a full measure of co-operation with a Communist-controlled regime would only serve to hasten its own extinction. How seriously such a withdrawal of support would affect the fortunes of a Communist regime would depend to a crucial extent on the speed with which it could find a substitute support in newly evolved social groups with a vested stake in its continued existence. . . .

12. ARAB SOCIALISM*

g o r d o n   h.   t o r r e y
a n d   j o h n   f.   d e v l i n

The socialism of the Arab states in the mid-century is a movement of protest—protest against the concentration of political and economic power in the hands of a small ruling class. It is directed against a system which the socialists believe existed to benefit only that class, against privilege and excessive wealth. The post-Ottoman generation of political leaders in Egypt, Iraq, Syria and to a lesser extent in the smaller Arab states, conducted themselves in such fashion as to make the emergence of revolutionary movements virtually certain. . . .

✿   ✿   ✿   ✿   ✿

Since Ba'thist doctrine is the oldest coherent socialist doctrine in the Arab world, it deserves primary consideration. Gamal Abdel Nasser's "Arab Socialism," while not a direct outgrowth and adaptation of Ba'thist ideology, is very similar in its economic and social theories, and these are the only manifestations of socialism which have general influ-

* From "Arab Socialism" by Gordon H. Torrey and John F. Devlin, *Journal of International Affairs*, Vol. XIX, No. 1 (1965), pp. 47–53. Reprinted by permission.

ence in the Arab world. Ba'thism is an ideology, much of which is yet to be put into effect despite the establishment of Ba'thist governments in Iraq and Syria; Nasser's "Arab Socialism," is a series of specific moves undertaken to revolutionize the economy and social structure of Egypt. The intriguing attempt by Ben Bella's revolutionary regime to achieve a synthesis of Marxism and Islam remains confined to Algeria. The other socialist movements, such as the National Democratic Party in Iraq and the People's Socialist Party in Lebanon, have had relatively little influence even in their own countries.

Bourgeois in origin and composition, nationalist in outlook, strongarmed in action, the Ba'th is a party of paradox and contrast. It dates from 1943, when Michel Aflaq and Salah-al-Din Bitar, Damascus schoolteachers and earlier colleagues at the Sorbonne, founded the Arab Resurrection (Ba'th) Movement. . . . By the latter part of 1945, the Ba'thists were calling themselves a party, and in mid-summer 1946 they brought out the first issue of the Party newspaper, *Al-Ba'th*. Then in April 1947, some two hundred of the Party faithful gathered for a three day conference—the Party's first—to debate and approve the Ba'th Constitution. Following this conference, the Party entered national politics . . .

✧   ✧   ✧   ✧   ✧

The basis of the Ba'th's appeal is embodied in the Party Constitution. This document is not a blueprint for action or a set of rules by which the Party should function, but rather a picture of what the Ba'th views as the good society.[1] This Constitution has never been amended; the only difference between the first version, printed in Syria in 1947, and later reprints is the addition of the word *ishtirāki* (socialist) to the title at the time of the 1953 Hawrani Socialist-Ba'th merger. The word "socialist," however, occurs frequently in the document itself and is found in the earliest party literature.

This Constitution envisions a united Arab society encompassing all Arabs from Morocco to Iraq, in which social justice will prevail and political liberalism will persuade the people to choose the Ba'th path. The goal of a just and equitable society, in which extremes of wealth and poverty do not exist, is a cardinal one for the Ba'th—and for Nasser as well. The Ba'th Constitution, for example, calls for the redistribution of land holdings among the citizens on a just basis (Art. 27), for the nationalization of utilities and large industries (Art. 29), for sweeping

---

[1] An English translation of the Constitution is available in the *Middle East Journal*, Vol. xiii, No. 2, Spring 1959, pp. 195–200; the Arabic text in *Nidal al-Ba'th*, Beirut, Dar al-Talia, 1963, Vol. I, pp. 172–81.

guarantees of wages, working conditions and old age insurance (Art. 40), for complete free medical care (Art. 39) and for free compulsory education through the secondary level (Arts. 45 & 46). The Constitution is explicit in saying that "the educational policy of the party aims at creating a new Arab generation faithful to the unity of its nation and the perpetuity of its mission." [2]

There is a second facet of the Ba'thist future which is even more important than its aim of social justice; this is Arab nationalism. The Constitution and the extensive writings of Aflaq and other Ba'thists devote considerable attention to what is called, for lack of a more precise term, "Arabness." "The Arab nation is distinguished by its merits [which are] revealed in its successive rebirths; it is noted for its abundant vitality and creative ability and its capacity for renewal and rebirth." [3] "Arab nationalism for the Ba'th is a self-evident fact which is established without the need for argument or struggle . . . for this reason there is no need to argue whether we are Arabs or not, but it is necessary that we determine and establish [what] Arabism [is] at the present. . . ." [4]

These two aspects of Ba'thist ideology, socialism and Arab nationalism, are inseparable. Aflaq views social progress and a better life for the Arab people as springing directly from a strong and united Arab nation. For him, the classic international socialism of nineteenth century Europe is not suited to the Arab world. Aflaq puts forth his reasoning on this point in an article written in 1946.[5] Western socialism was perfectly correct in taking the form it did because "socialism in the West was forced to stand up not only against capitalism but also against nationalism, which protected capitalism, against religion, which defended it, and against every concept which called for conservatism and the sanctification of the past." [6] The Arab nation, however, lacks the freedom and sovereignty which the Western nations possessed. Every Arab nationalist—for it must be remembered that Aflaq saw his doctrine as applying to the entire Arab-speaking world—should recognize that socialism is the most useful means to revive his nation. Hence, "there is neither incompatibility nor contradiction nor war between nationalists and socialists." [7] "The Arab nationalists are the socialists." [8]

[2] Ba'th Constitution, preambulatory paragraph to that part entitled "The Educational and Instructional Policy of the Party," *Nidal*, I, p. 180.
[3] Ba'th Constitution, Basic Principles, *Nidal*, I, p. 173.
[4] Michel Aflaq, "Arab Nationalism and the Nationalist Theory," *Fi Sabil al-Ba'th*, Beirut, Dar al-Tali'ah, 1959, p. 211. *Fi Sabil al-Ba'th* (On the Road to Resurrection) is a collection of Aflaq's writings. It was first issued in 1953, revised and enlarged in 1959 and a version with considerable new material was published in 1963. All references are to the 1963 edition unless otherwise specified.
[5] "The Features of Arab Socialism," *Fi Sabil al-Ba'th*, pp. 200–8.
[6] *Ibid.*, p. 202.
[7] "The Features of Arab Socialism," *Fi Sabil al-Ba'th*, p. 204.
[8] *Idem.*

Communism, too, is a system unsuited to the Arab world, a position Aflaq reiterates many times in his writings. Aflaq spells out a number of theoretical and practical differences between Ba'th socialism and communist socialism.[9] Communism explains the evolution of society in economic terms only; it does not give due weight to the individual; it does not recognize the right to private property.[10] Perhaps most significant to Aflaq, and to his young nationalist, anti-colonial supporters, communism is deceitful because it seeks to tie "the Arab destiny to the destiny of another state, namely Russia."[11] A great point of difference lies in Aflaq's rejection of the Marxist view of the class struggle. For him, too, there is a class struggle, but it is the struggle between the Arab people, on one hand, and everyone who is hostile to them, on the other. These hostile elements may, however, include Arab capitalists, feudalists and politicians who support the division of the Arab nation, as well as others who cooperate with imperialism.[12] Aflaq's class battle is between the Arabs and their enemies, not simply one between the proletariat and the capitalist exploiters.

o   o   o   o   o

In positive terms, then, Ba'th socialism is for the Arabs—for all Arabs but only for Arabs. It has no expansionist aims other than to liberate those areas of the Arab homeland presently under foreign domination.[13] Aflaq is quite specific in stating his belief that "our socialism" can only be realized completely in one united Arab state. This theme is repeated elsewhere in Ba'thist literature. Independence and unity are pre-requisites for the socialist society he believes the Arabs must build. The theme is constant in Aflaq's own writings, in the columns of the party newspaper, in the stream of statements, pronouncements and anathemas which have flowed from the party's leaders.

Thus, Ba'th socialism is distinguished from Marxian communism by its rejection of the class struggle[14] and from classic western socialism by its espousal of insular nationalism. The resurrection of the Arab nation is the chief aim of the Ba'th Party. From this resurrection is to flow all the necessary elements to make this nation great and powerful. This is not a

[9] In *Fi Sabil al-Ba'th*, "Our Position Regarding the Communist Theory" (1944), pp. 195–99, and "Between our Socialism, Communism, and National Socialism" (1950), pp. 209–13.
[10] *Ibid.*, pp. 210–11.
[11] *Ibid.*, p. 212.
[12] *Ibid.*, p. 223, "Our View of Capitalism and the Class Struggle."
[13] Party Constitution, Art. 7.
[14] There are other differences as well; the Ba'th ignores religion, for example, but is not actively hostile to it.

question of merely restoring past glories; "the present experience of the Arab nation is the first and greatest value of this [Arab] nationalism, for it is richer and more valuable than all the stages through which our nation has lived in the past." [15] The Ba'thist mission (risālah khālidah) is to carry out the vitalization of the Arab world and to build a new society.

This nationalist theme is the basis of Ba'thist ideology. It has been a theme with appeal for the young, educated, urban Arab; in many respects it runs parallel to the nationalist ideas propagated by other Arab intellectual leadership. . . .

13. *NEW CONCEPTS OF DEMOCRACY IN SOUTHERN ASIA*[*]

m a r g u e r i t e j. f i s h e r

Since the end of the second world war, . . . certain Asian theorists or leaders, recognizing the incompatibility of Western-style democratic institutions and traditional Asian cultures, have sought to evolve new versions of democracy, both in theory and practice. Their objective has been to construct a new concept of democracy, perhaps unacceptable to the Western oriented, but nevertheless rooted in Asian cultural patterns and the realities of Asian life. These new concepts of democracy are characterized by a number of features in common, including the repudiation of Western-style parliamentary government as too remote and complicated to be comprehended by the masses of the people. Political parties, in particular, are condemned as disruptive forces which destroy the unity needed for national development. The new theories recognize

[15] *Fi Sabil al-Ba'th* (1959), p. 212.
[*] From "New Concepts of Democracy in Southern Asia" by Marguerite J. Fisher, *Western Political Quarterly*, Vol. XV, No. 4 (December, 1962), pp. 626–636. By permission of the University of Utah, copyright owners.

the fact that the majority of Asians, psychologically as well as physically, are restricted to the local societal level. Hence attention is focused on the local or village community and the value of the small group. Social cohesion, unity and cooperation rather than competition are stressed as imperative needs. The amelioration of social and economic conditions is assigned a more important position than "politics." In all these new concepts runs the argument that Asian democratic institutions, to be successful, must have roots in Asian history and tradition.

I N D I A

✿   ✿   ✿   ✿   ✿

Jayaprakash Narayan

Probably the most significant voice raised in India today on behalf of an Indian rather than Western-style democratic government is that of Jayaprakash Narayan, founder and former leader of the Socialist party. In his youth he was a confirmed Marxist. After participating in Gandhi's civil disobedience movement Jayaprakash Narayan went to the United States, studying at several different universities and supporting himself by working in various odd jobs. On his return to India he helped to organize the Congress Socialist party, the forerunner of the present PSP (Praja Socialist party). He broke with the Communists in 1940 and came increasingly under the influence of Gandhi. During the early years of independence Jayaprakash Narayan was regarded as the likeliest successor to Nehru. In 1954, however, he announced his renunciation of active politics and his resignation as leader of the Praja Socialist party. He declared his intention to devote his life to the *Bhoodan Yagna* [gift-of-land] movement and similar activities outside of regular political channels for the realization of Gandhian ideals of *Sarvodaya* [service to all]. Not the Western alternatives of parliamentary socialism or communism, he decided, but only the principles of Gandhi could effect a sufficient revolution in the lives and values of the Indian masses.

The *Sarvodaya* pattern of society, Jayaprakash Narayan asserted, could never be constructed by legislation from New Delhi. There must be a far more fundamental change, "change at the root." Even though progress had been made by the Indian government in such areas as the community development program, the concept of social organization, he declared, remained the same as that of the atomized society of the West. In 1959 he published his theory of a democratic system for India in a book entitled *A Plea for Reconstruction of Indian Polity*.[1] His purpose in this document, he stated, was to search for "forms of social life, particularly of political life, that would assure the preservation of human values . . . and my approach has been non-partisan and non-sectarian."[2]

It is questionable, according to Jayaprakash Narayan, "if democrats of all times and climes, social idealists and thinkers, the spirit of man itself, will ever remain satisfied with the current Western definition of democracy. Already . . . all these elements have combined . . . to demand a more satisfying participating democracy. Indeed, it is my firm belief that the extent to which democracy becomes truly participative, to that extent would the onrush of totalitarianism be stemmed and even rolled back." The atomistic and statistical democracy of the West "is based on a negation of the social nature of man and the true nature of human society," conceiving of society as an "inorganic mass of separate grains of individuals."[3]

The evidence "from Cairo to Djakarta indicates that Asian peoples are having second thoughts, and are seeking to find better forms than parliamentary democracy to express and embody their democratic aspirations."[4] The author devotes a whole chapter to the faults of Western parliamentary democracy, listing such points as: governments elected by universal suffrage under the party system are commonly representative of a minority of the voters; present-day mass elections manipulated by the super media of communication "represent far less the electorate than the forces and interests behind the parties and the propaganda machines";[5] demagogy is inevitable with the need to "catch" votes by any methods; there is an inherent trend toward centralism, a "central state of overwhelming power and resources and the individual voter reduced to abject helplessness"[6] by an ever-increasing autocracy of bureaucracy; the political parties become centralized organizations in which the people have only "fictional" control, while small caucuses of politicians decide all matters of importance; the political parties create dissensions and divisions when unity is the greatest need; and finally, elections create unnecessary passions and excitement, stimulate demagogy, and necessitate fabulous expenditures.

The remedy will never be found in the strong centralized state, the author declares. The concentration of economic power in the hands of a central state, even under democratic conditions, will result in the

---

[1]   Wardha (Bombay State), Sarva Seva Sangh Prakashan.
[2]   *Ibid.*, p. ii.
[3]   *Ibid.*, p. 35.
[4]   *Ibid.*, p. 36.
[5]   *Ibid.*, p. 49.
[6]   *Ibid.*, p. 50.

"thwarting and limiting of political democracy itself." [7] Thus the Western welfare state threatens to enslave man as does totalitarianism. State socialism as found in the Soviet Union offers the worst example of the ruthless power of centralized state bureaucracy, said Jayaprakash Narayan, confessing that he had watched the Soviet experiment "with anguish."

In reconstructing Indian democracy, according to the author, one of the main objectives must be *social integration.* "Man is alone and bored; he is 'organization man,' he is man ordered about and manipulated by forces beyond his ken and control—irrespective of whether it is a 'democracy' or dictatorship." [8] The first necessity is to "put man in touch with man, so that they may live together in meaningful, understandable, controllable relationships. In short, *the problem is to re-create the human community.*" [9] There must be sharing, fellowship, identity of interest, a feeling of unity in the midst of diversity, and voluntary participation by all the people in community affairs. Only then will the "social nature of man and the great humanist ideals of modern civilization find fulfillment." [10]

New forms of Indian democracy must be based on the ancient "social genius of India" and its "organically, self-determining communal life." [11] It is a question of an ancient country finding its lost soul again. Political reconstruction must be founded upon the local democracies of past centuries, "the village councils, the town committees, the trades and artisans' guilds of old." [12] Unless life in India is again organized on the basis of self-determining and mutually coordinating and integrating communities, democracy will "remain distantly removed from the life of the people." [13] Like the author of the *Gandhian Constitution for Free India,* Jayaprakash Narayan devotes considerable space to the historic village *panchayats* on the ground that they are "pivotal not only for the regeneration of Indian polity but for the regeneration of Indian society as a whole." [14]

The author then turns to the subject of appropriate formal structures of government. The highest political institution of the local community is to be the General Assembly, the *Gram Sabha,* in which all adults are members. The Council or *Panchayat* should be chosen by general consensus in the *Sabha.* Each *panchayat* will function through subcommittees charged with different responsibilities. If the people can-

[7]   *Ibid.,* p. 9.
[8]   *Ibid.,* p. 37.
[9]   *Ibid.*
[10]   *Ibid.,* p. 38.
[11]   *Ibid.,* p. 19.
[12]   *Ibid.,* p. 13.
[13]   *Ibid.,* p. 23.
[14]   *Ibid.,* p. 30.

not come to a general consensus in the selection of their officials, then the alternative method should be by drawing lots.

Neighboring local or primary communities, in turn, are to be joined together to build a regional community. Each primary community

. . . might be able to provide for a primary school, primary health services, small irrigation works like wells and village banks, and village industries. But a number of primary communities must cooperate together in order to provide for a higher school, an indoor hospital, a power-station and servicing centre, larger industries, larger irrigation works, etc. Thus the regional community comes into existence by an organic process of growth.[15]

The regional community, however, must be an integral community in itself. It is not a superior or higher body that "can control or interfere with the internal administration of the primary communities. *Each* in its sphere is equally sovereign." [16]

The hierarchical structure erected upon the foundations of the village community, as sketched by Jayaprakash Narayan, is similar to the one outlined by Shriman Narayan Agarwal in the *Gandhian Constitution for Free India*. Above the regional community are larger communities, the district, provincial, and finally the National Community, each with functions and responsibilities appropriate to its area. There is no scope "for political parties to play any role in this process." [17] Such a communitarian society alone can guarantee the ideal participating democracy in which the individual "will be able to save himself from the fate of 'robotism' to which modern civilization has condemned him and find freedom and self-significance as a member of the community." [18]

In the economic area the communitarian society must be so organized that "human needs are satisfied as near home as possible," first in the primary community and then in the higher levels.[19] Each expanding area of community would then be as self-sufficient as possible, and every economic institution would be "integrated with the community to which it territorially belongs." [20] Thus, . . . planning would be facilitated on each level.

❖   ❖   ❖   ❖   ❖

THE PHILIPPINES

As early as 1940 President Manuel Quezon of the Philippines challenged his countrymen to discard one of the "fetishes" of democracy,

[15]   *Ibid.,* p. 42.
[16]   *Ibid.,* p. 43.
[17]   *Ibid.,* p. 77.
[18]   *Ibid.,* p. 44.
[19]   *Ibid.,* p. 56.
[20]   *Ibid.,* p. 57.

"the discarded theory that democracy cannot exist without political parties." [21] In a speech delivered by Quezon to the students of the University of the Philippines on July 16, 1940, there was recurring stress on unity, cooperation, and strong national leadership, and denunciation of partisan strife and obstructionism as inimical to true democracy and the economic and social development of the Philippines. Quezon declared:

In the very nature of things the struggle for power between contending political parties creates partisan spirit, and partisan spirit is incompatible with good government. . . . It is party politics that causes inefficiency in government; it is party opposition that causes delay in the execution of needed reforms; it is party spirit that weakens the government and makes it incapable of facing difficult situations. . . . This concept of the need of a majority and minority party is as wrong as saying that, in order that a home may be governed well, it is necessary that there should be a division, that there should be fighting all the time in the family. A nation is like a family, multiplied a thousandfold, and just as it is impossible for a family to be happy or to make progress when there is division among its members . . . so it is impossible for a nation to grow strong and accomplish great ends if the people are always divided, if they are taught to believe that patriotism means division.[22]

Impressed by Manuel Quezon's plea for a different system of democracy, Dr. Ricardo Pascual, head of the Department of Philosophy at the University of the Philippines, devoted his time to an amplification of the theories presented by President Quezon. In a book entitled *Partyless Democracy*, Dr. Pascual advanced a thesis holding that the "next stage in the development of democratic concepts and ideas is inevitably the 'partyless democracy.'" [23] Dr. Pascual begins his argument with a warning that democracy is on trial, not only in the Philippines but in the other new nations of Asia. Much is expected of democracy in the creation of a better way of life for millions of Asian peoples. But the failure to bridge this "wide gap between promise and accomplishment is the source of disgust and reckless swerving to the opposite extreme in the form of reaction." [24] Before popular disillusionment becomes too deep, warns Dr. Pascual, the processes of democratic government must be made more efficient. In this matter the Filipinos must "do their own thinking" and should not blindly copy the great democracies of the West.

Dr. Pascual then proceeds to challenge the Western thesis that political parties are necessary to a liberal political regime. His point of

[21]   Address of His Excellency Manuel L. Quezon, President of the Philippines. Manila, Bureau of Printing, 1940.
[22]   *Ibid.*
[23]   Ricardo R. Pascual, *Partyless Democracy* (Quezon City: University of the Philippines, 1952), p. viii.
[24]   *Ibid.*, p. 7.

view will encounter strong resistance, he warns, because it runs contrary to the classical line of thought on democracy. He examines various Western arguments for the necessity of the party system and rejects them as inappropriate for the needs and conditions of Filipino society. A scheme of democracy must be constructed, he asserts, in which:

> The *opinion* of the *genuine public*, that is, the *genuine public opinion*, is a *compromise opinion* of the *different elements* of a Democracy, not a *triumphant opinion* of the *majority* at the *vanquishment of the minority*. The scheme of Democracy which will carry out this ideal will be one which is not different from the type of organic unity, harmony, and process of a living organism. Biologists tell us that a living organism is the example of composite organization, of mutual participation, of synthetic harmony, of unity in diversity to speak in paradox. But this kind of ideal Democracy . . . is really impractical in the politics of the party system.[25]

Partyless democracy, maintains Dr. Pascual, would be an "organic social polity." In general, the various qualities of a partyless democracy will depend upon the "peculiar necessities of the country in which it is intended to be practiced; but all of them will do away with division, dissension, schism, competition, narrow vested interest, partisanship." [26] In the Western party system, on the other hand, "political parties are still in conflict, in competition, in struggle with one another in much the same way that in the pre-party era the individuals were in conflict, in competition, in struggle with one another. . . . When will Democracy learn to substitute cooperation, organization and mutual help for competition, group struggle, and selfish exploitation?" [27]

Furthermore, contends Dr. Pascual, the greatest need of the Philippines as well as other Asian nations is social justice. "The promotion of the social interest requires cooperation, not division, mutual cooperative mass action, not individual, competitive intrigues, the mustering of all forces toward the production of the social good, not the pitting of individuals against their fellow men. In this sense the partyless system . . . is the means for consummating the ideal of social justice." [28]

But how will partyless democracy work in practice? What structural design and organizational pattern will it assume? Dr. Pascual advocates a legislature based upon functional or occupational representation. First of all, the representatives in the Congress must

> . . . come from groups of people but let these groups be determined not by geographical division but by occupations or professions. . . . Let not any geographical division interfere in this occupational grouping. This means that the delegates, let us say, of the farmers, are delegates of all the farmers in the

---

25 *Ibid.*, p. 48.
26 *Ibid.*, pp. 119–20.
27 *Ibid.*, pp. 53–54.
28 *Ibid.*, p. 128.

Philippines. In this way we shall *practice unity* among the members of the group of farmers and *not simply dream about it.* This practice shall hold with all occupational groups. Each group shall be bound by the common interest inherent among the members of such group.[29]

The different groups are to be represented in Congress in proportion to their actual members in the nation, but with a stated maximum number of representatives. Whereas proportional representation should be followed in the lower house of Congress, in the Senate each occupational group should have an equal representation. Because the welfare of each occupation is mutually dependent upon the welfare of every other occupation, maintains Dr. Pascual, there would be less reason for competition. The representatives of each group will be elected at large, and only by members of their own group. Thus farmers would not be competing against fishermen because "their candidates are not competing for the same votes." [30] In this system there will be "greater unity among people pursuing the same trade or occupation. . . . The feeling of self-sufficiency within a group which will contribute to the seclusion and aloofness of that group, and hence to the creation of sectionalism, will not be found in each of the occupational groups . . . since each occupation is not independent of others in the scheme of social life." [31] Furthermore, the division of the electorate into occupational groups, according to Dr. Pascual, would encourage and accelerate long-range programs of social legislation, one of the greatest needs of Asian societies. National planning, too, would be facilitated. Under the new system "each occupational group would naturally endeavor to make lasting plans regarding its future." [32]

The author's arguments on behalf of functional representation are reminiscent of those advanced by various European writers of the late nineteenth and early twentieth centuries. But they assume new significance in that they are aimed in Dr. Pascual's book at the solution of problems felt to be characteristic of the new Asian nations.

[29]   *Ibid.,* pp. 167–68.
[30]   *Ibid.,* p. 172.
[31]   *Ibid.,* p. 176.
[32]   *Ibid.,* p. 181.

political systems

To the student of politics familiar with the basic stability of political institutions and processes in the American and European states, politics in the developing states is frequently baffling and incomprehensible. So often the political process in these states appears to be one of futility, disorder, and impending—if not actual—chaos. Constitutions are proclaimed, only to be ignored or suspended, civilian governments are overthrown and replaced by military juntas, federations are created and then quickly collapse, individual and collective acts of violence occur—everywhere, it sometimes seems, the developing states are in constant turmoil, unable to resolve the basic problem of establishing stable and effective governments. Yet these events, frequent as they may seem, are the type that capture the headlines; much less frequently noticed are the steady strides taken by some states toward the goals of modernization and effective mass participation in the political process. Less frequently noticed too is the gradual collapse into lethargy and stagnation that overtakes some of the others when they fail to maintain the dynamic forces essential for modernization. A summary of the principal characteristics of developing political systems may suggest the reasons for both the more dramatic cases of instability and disorder and the less publicized cases of slower, more evolutionary changes.

The analysis of developing political systems may usefully begin with a consideration of the political attitudes and values of the populace, which to a large extent determine the stability of political institutions and the efficiency and effectiveness of the decision-making process. In most developing states, the political value system is more highly fragmented than in most European or American states. Traditional values and beliefs remain firmly entrenched and continue to be supported by large numbers of persons, particularly those in rural areas. These persons accept the legitimacy of, and give their primary allegiance to, the tribal and communal leaders who exercise their authority through traditional institutions and processes. In contrast, an often much smaller number of persons adhere to values characteristic of Western political systems: a secular nation-state, political equality, universal suffrage, popularly elected political leaders, an independent judiciary, and an impartial, professional civil service, among others. The political values of a third, and usually increasingly large, group of persons are in a state of transition. Individuals in this group have begun to cast off as unsatisfactory the traditional values of their forefathers, but they have not as yet fully accepted the secular, egalitarian principles underlying Western political beliefs. Their primary loyalties are uncertain and ambivalent. While they may be attracted by the political values the modernizing leaders are attempting to inculcate in their followers, traditional values also exert a strong pull. Their support for the state and its political system is tenuous and qualified, the degree of legitimacy accorded the government fluctuating with its successes and failures.

In many of these states, the development of a broad consensus on political institutions and processes is further impeded by the inability or unwillingness of the different ethnic, tribal, or other major groups to reach agreement. Jealous of their own cultures and patterns of organization, they are often fearful that their own interests are not being adequately protected and promoted. In some cases, this fear has led to secessionist movements and the attempt to establish separate states for the dissident groups. Even in those cases where the controversies between these groups have not resulted in this extreme threat to the integrity of the state, the hostile attitudes of these groups toward each other may nevertheless impose severe strains upon the political system.

The developing political systems must also contend with the tensions arising from the changing social and economic conditions in society. Many states are now moving through the initial phases of industrialization, shifting from an almost exclusively agrarian to a more mixed economic base. In contrast to the relatively stable social and economic systems that existed in their traditional societies, the developing states are now confronted with the complex problems resulting from their attempts to modernize rapidly. As new methods of production, channels of communication, and patterns of authority are established, the traditional social fabric is often subjected to intense pressures. Since the governments in the developing states have commonly assumed a direct and active role in promoting modernization, they become the focal point of criticism from those individuals and groups adversely affected by the impact of modernization. As many of these governments, including both individual leaders and the institutional framework, have not achieved a high degree of stability and popular support, their capacity to withstand the shocks of social and economic change is limited.

Contributing to the instability of the developing political systems are the significant changes that have been occurring in the composition of political elites and in the bases from which political power is exercised. The political elite in any society consists of both the individual leaders and the groups or classes (from which the individual leaders typically come) who exercise significant influence in political decision-making. While changes in the political elite structure are most apparent in many of the new Asian and African states, alterations in this structure are also evident in many of the Latin American states. In only a few cases, such as Ethiopia and Saudi Arabia, has the traditional elite been able to preserve its dominant position largely intact to the present.

In many developing states, the traditional elite has been largely supplanted at the national level by the "new" elite. Nevertheless, the traditional elite still remains important, particularly at the local and regional levels. This elite is composed mainly of religious leaders, landowners, and hereditary rulers. The relative political power of these groups is declining for a number of reasons. In the case of the religious leaders, the increasing secularization of society is corroding their power. As an increasing number of social issues become disentangled from religious considerations, individuals (particularly in the urban centers) seek the guidance of religious leaders less and less frequently. In the villages and rural areas, however, the religious elite continues to exert its influence in every aspect of the lives of individuals and the community. The principal exceptions to the general decline of religious influence in national politics are found in those Latin American states where the Catholic Church is represented directly in the government, in some of the Middle Eastern and Asian states where Muslim religious leaders exert great authority, and in a few Asian states where Buddhist monks are politically active.

The traditional authority of hereditary chiefs, princes, and local notables has also declined as centralized governments and their bureaucracies have increasingly assumed decision-making power for the society. These traditional leaders have often been vigorously opposed to policies of modernization since the execution of these policies threatens to destroy their traditional base of authority. Despite their opposition, nationalist leaders have frequently had to retain this group of traditional leaders because of the considerable prestige and power they exercise at the local level. In few states do hereditary chiefs and princes exert significant power directly in the national governments, though their political power at the local and regional levels must often be taken into account in the formulation of national policies. With few exceptions, such as Jordan, Iran, Saudi Arabia, and Ethiopia, monarchies and royal families have been overthrown or their powers severely circumscribed.

The traditional authority of the landed aristocracy is also increasingly being undermined. The principal causes for their decline are the land reform programs that are breaking up the large estates in many states and the increasing industrialization and urbanization that result in the creation of a new urban middle class and new centers of financial power. Again, as with the other types of traditional elites, it is at the local level where the large landowners remain most influential. In some South American and Middle Eastern states, however, the landed aristocracy still holds considerable power at the national level also. This condition is not found in many African and Asian states, since a landed aristocracy was never created; ownership of large estates by aristocratic families was not a common feature of their societies.

The "new" elite that now possesses dominant power at the national level in almost all of the new states in Asia and Africa differs from the traditional elite in its nationalism, secularism, commitment to social and economic reform, and orientation to Western culture and values (though this last point is frequently denied). It is this elite that usually led the nationalist struggle for independence. This elite, composed of both civilian and military leaders, is far less dependent on traditional religious and economic institutions for its political power than on its intellectual and organizational skills. Although its members are not drawn from as definable a group or class as are the traditional elites, most of the "new" elite share a middle or upper-middle class background, possess a Western education, and reside in major urban areas. As is evident, this elite lacks the deeply rooted ties with the tradition-oriented masses that the traditional elites possess. Its relationships with the masses are established primarily through the bureaucracy, the armed forces, political parties, and strong individual personalities who can spark broad, popular support for themselves and their programs. This personal leadership, so prominent in many of the new states, is of course difficult to institutionalize. While a number of leaders have been able to attain a high level of personal popularity, support for the national government and its institutions has often remained markedly low. In states where this "new" modernizing, Westernized elite does not control the national government, as in some of the Latin American and Middle Eastern states, it nevertheless is often increasing its strength as more and more persons join reformist groups and movements.

The organization and articulation of interests in developing political systems take place through several types of groups. In most developing states, interests organized around traditional loyalties to ethnic, tribal, regional, linguistic, class, and religious groups are important forces. These groups, often highly cohesive in their social organization and in their political outlook and demands, articulate a broad range of social and economic interests considered necessary to protect and advance the welfare of the group. Seldom are these groups formally organized for political action since the traditional ties provide the necessary solidarity for effective identification and communication between the leaders and the members of the group. The comprehensive, integrated demands these groups make on the national political leaders frequently obstruct the formulation and implementation of specific developmental policies.

The political importance of individual associational groups (labor, business, professional, landlord, peasant, and others)—and of these groups collectively—varies significantly from state to state. In a few states, these groups are relatively numerous, well-organized, and politically influential; in most states, however, their importance is greatly overshadowed by the traditional groups and by groups such as the bureaucracy and the armed forces. Nowhere are the peasants very well organized, despite some attempts to establish organizations to represent their interests. The efforts of labor leaders to organize them are obstructed both by the traditional conservatism of the peasants and by their economic dependency on their landlords or money-lenders. Lacking alternative skills and strongly rooted in their communities, peasants are generally unwilling to risk the consequences of organizing in opposition to their landlords' commands. Even where the peasants own their small plots of land individually, they have rarely organized effectively for political action. Largely illiterate, often heavily in debt, and politically unsophisticated, they usually follow the leadership of the traditional rural elite.

Labor unions in a number of states, organized in industries, services, and on plantations, have begun to achieve a voice in the shaping of labor legislation, wage policy, and other programs of interest to them. In many cases, however, the unions have been incorporated into political parties whose programs include other objectives as well. As a result, the specific interests of the unions are often subordinated to the more general objectives of the parties. Business and landlord groups are often not as formally organized for political action as are labor unions. Several reasons account for this fact. In the first place, the number of individuals is smaller, and informal contacts are often sufficient to decide upon a course of action. Second, the landlords are on the defensive in many states, and the modernizing elite is often intolerant of organized landlord pressure. Third, many of the business enterprises and commercial activities in some states are controlled by aliens—for example, Indians in East Africa, Chinese in Southeast Asia, and American and British in Latin America—who find it expedient to avoid overt political activity in order to preserve their economic opportunities. In some states, since many of the basic industries and the transportation and communications systems are owned and operated by the state, the growth of a large, powerful, private industrial and business elite is largely foreclosed. Despite these limiting factors, business organizations such as chambers of commerce are increasing in number and strength in many states as industrial and business growth takes place.

Professional organizations representing lawyers, teachers, doctors, and military officers, among others, often exert political influence greatly disproportionate to their small memberships. Since the members of these organizations possess many of the technical skills required for modernization, political leaders of the modernizing states frequently look to them for advice and aid in planning the developmental programs. Student organizations are often some of the better organized and more politically active groups in these states. As part of the small but politically significant intelligentsia, students are in many instances leading exponents of change. Their restlessness over current conditions provides an advantageous psychological orientation for political organizers. Though their numbers are relatively small, student bodies are usually concentrated in the capital cities where their demonstrations and other forms of political activity produce the greatest effect.

In the majority of developing countries, particularly in those where associational interest groups are weakest, institutional interest groups— the armed forces, bureaucracies, and in some instances, religious groups —play a predominant role in the articulation of political interests. For both the modernizing elite and the traditional elite (in the oligarchic states), the armed forces and bureaucracies, with their instruments of control and sources of information, constitute principal agencies not only for the maintenance of law and order, but also for the formulation and implementation of social and economic policies. In many of the states, the present centralized, powerful bureaucracies were initially established by the colonial powers which recruited, at least into the lower levels of the civil services, some of the most able and talented persons in the indigenous populations. These Western-trained administrators are now engaged in the comprehensive planning that characterizes most of the developing states. Through their network of departments and agencies, the bureaucracies are also responsible for the administration of many policies and programs: tax collection, transportation and communications, education, land reform, resource surveys, industrial development, and many more.

The armed forces are similarly in a position to exert significant political influence. Many military officers have, like the administrators, received a Western education and are committed to programs of modernization. In addition to their defense functions, the armed forces are commonly engaged in a variety of non-defense and defense-related activities. They are often responsible, for example, for the construction of roads, communications facilities, and irrigation projects. They may also have broad educational responsibilities, teaching basic skills such as reading and writing in addition to specific military skills. As one of the few well-organized, disciplined, and progressive institutions in these states, the armed forces are often indispensable for the successful execution of policies necessary for modernization.

However, the same attributes that make the military forces a most useful agency for modernization also make them a potential—and often actual—threat to civilian control. As has been demonstrated recently and repeatedly in Asia and Africa, the military leadership may become impatient with the pace or direction of policy, or with the alleged inefficiency or corruption of the civilian leadership. The military may then itself assume political control of the government. Usually the military leaders assert that their control is only to be temporary; once the conditions leading to their intervention have been rectified, competent civilian leaders will again be permitted to assume control. Rarely, however, have military leaders been as willing to release their control as they have been to assume it.

The military *coups* so frequently staged in some Latin American states are usually of a different nature and have different purposes than those that occur in Asia and Africa. In general, the struggles for political supremacy reflect either interservice rivalries or personal and factional disputes. The tradition of military leaders in political office is well established in many Latin American states, and while issues of corruption, dictatorial practices, and violations of constitutional provisions may be involved, personal and service rivalries rather than the general direction of public policy seem to account for more of the *coups* than in Asia and Africa. As part of the traditional aristocracy, the military in Latin America has tended to be a conservative, rather than progressive, political force.

For the very large majority of persons in transitional societies, concern for or involvement in national politics is still minimal. Although elections may infrequently activate the tradition-oriented peasant masses and others of low socioeconomic status, their interest in and understanding of national politics and policies is restricted by their high level of illiteracy, the day-to-day struggle for subsistence, the relative isolation of the villages, and the traditional cultural patterns that restrict the participation of peasants, women, and other groups in deference to the political elites. Few of the devices common to developed societies for the gathering and dissemination of information are available. Newspapers are few and have limited numbers of readers. "Letters to the editor" columns, critical editorials, and public opinion polls that in Western societies provide some indication of support for or opposition to government policies are frequently unknown. Many of the major presses are controlled or dominated by the government, as are the other means of communication, radio, television, telephone, and telegraph. Few official or unofficial advisory committees exist to provide the government with information, and public hearings conducted by government officials are seldom a prominent part of the process of consultation. In short, few organizations or other channels of communication exist to bridge the gap between the modernizing elite and the mass population.

The most important nongovernmental organization—and sometimes this distinction is difficult to maintain—that partially fills this void is the political party. It is difficult, however, to state generalizations concerning the party systems in these states since such wide variations exist in their organizational structure, their specific programs, and the social bases from which they draw their support. In the more traditional authoritarian states such as Ethiopia and Saudi Arabia, organizations with any of the usual characteristics of political parties cannot be said to exist. In these states, the rulers have effectively prevented the organization of political parties; cliques, factions, and personal groups without organizational structures provide the principal links between the rulers and the politically active segments of society. At the other extreme, in a few states well organized political parties exist which aggregate many specific interests and compete for power in a manner familiar to the student of American or European politics. Between these extremes are found a variety of party systems. In some states, such as Pakistan and Thailand, parties may exist in name, but because of military rule they are ineffectual. In a number of other states, particularly in Africa, only one officially designated mass party is permitted to function. Still another type of party system may be found in states such as Mexico where one party has long been dominant, though other parties may enjoy a marginal existence, often at the discretion of the major party.

A broad distinction may be drawn between Latin America, on the one hand, and Asia and Africa, on the other, for purposes of specifying the major characteristics of political parties in these areas. In Latin America, national politics in most states remains the preserve of the upper classes—the "whites"—to the virtual exclusion of the *mestizos*, Indians, and Negroes. Membership in the political parties is thus usually confined to persons of the upper classes. Many of these parties are essentially the personal followings of particularly strong leaders, with relatively little organizational structure or program except that propounded by the leader. Such parties are highly dependent upon the personal political fortunes of the leaders. When a leader is successful, the party prospers and enjoys the spoils of victory; when he is defeated or overthrown, the party has little capacity for survival unless the leader can remain politically active. These personalistic parties have long been a prominent feature of Latin American politics. They have been headed by ruthless military or civilian dictators as well as by paternalistic, benevolent leaders. Increasingly, however, these *caudillo* parties are being challenged by parties that, while still often confined to the upper classes, are more permanently organized and present programs of broad social and economic principles. These parties, such as the Socialist, Communist, and Aprista, are less dependent upon individual leadership than on organizational structure and the popular appeal of their programs.

Political parties in Asia and Africa are distinguishable from those in Latin America in several major respects. They are, of course, usually of more recent origin. They reflect too the impact of the revolutionary movements that have in many cases so recently led to the creation of independent states. In addition, they more frequently possess a more or less elaborate program of modernization, an orientation that tends to shape the organizational structure of these parties along lines other than those that generally characterize Latin American parties.

In the preindependence period, a number of groups, sometimes distinguished with the name party, were in existence. These groups and parties were composed almost exclusively of the Western-oriented minority; they were neither mass organizations nor did they commonly possess and support broad political programs. Depending upon the colonial policies, some groups cooperated with the colonialists while others found it advantageous to oppose them. As feelings of nationalism grew, some of these "parties" broadened their organizational base and became mass movements. While controversies over the timing and direction of the revolution often divided these groups and parties, in general they were able to cooperate in the interests of securing independence. Once independence was achieved, however, the unifying element of the nationalist movement receded, and controversies broke out over the policies to be pursued in the drive for modernization. Although some of the parties that now exist are still primarily the personal followings of the strong leaders, others, such as the Congress Party in India, have achieved a relatively high level of permanent organization.

As noted in the previous chapter, many leaders in the African and Asian states reject the idea of competitive political parties, arguing that they are both divisive when tolerated and unnecessary in fact, since one mass party can and must embody the general will. The tendency toward the establishment of authoritarian, one-party systems is pronounced in these areas. Yet the authoritarianism that is promoted differs from that usually found in Latin America, with the exception of Cuba. Whereas the traditional authoritarianism in Latin America is conservative or even reactionary, seeking to perpetuate the privileges of the upper-class ruling elite, the authoritarianism in Africa and Asia is revolutionary, attempting to build broad support among the masses for the purpose of economic development and social reform. Thus the leaders of most Asian and African parties have attempted to organize and activate the mass populations in their societies for purposes of modernization, though they are frequently thwarted by the elements of traditionalism that still characterize their societies. In most Latin American states, in contrast, the major political parties have not striven for this mass participation. The issues that divide them are principally those of upper-class privileges, including the power of the Catholic Church and the landed aristocracy, rather than those relating to the pace of modernization.

In addition to political parties, one element of most modern states that has found almost universal acceptance in the developing states is that of a written constitution. In addition to provisions establishing the institutions of government and their powers, these constitutions commonly provide an elaborate statement of individual rights and duties and the goals of public policy. The structure of the national government as provided for in most Latin American constitutions follows that of the United States. A presidential system, rather than a parliamentary, has been uniformly adopted, and in a few states, such as Mexico and Argentina, a federal system has been created. In many of the new African and Asian states, the formal governmental institutions were initially patterned after those of the former colonial power. Several reasons account for this development. First, of course, is the fact that the leaders were most familiar with the constitutional framework of the colonial power, many of them having been educated in Europe, in the schools of the colonial power. Second, the colonial administrators often openly and strongly encouraged the new leaders to adopt the colonial power's institutional framework, believing it to be, quite naturally, superior to any other form. An important third reason was that, for the Westernized elite in the former colonies, these institutions represented part of the package of modernization they so ardently desired to attain. To modify substantially the institutional forms and practices appeared to them an admission of having achieved less than full equality with the West.

Formal institutions and processes can be far more readily adopted, however, than can the underlying attitudes, values, and other characteristics of another society that enable institutions to perform in a certain manner. Thus, the formal institutions established at the time of independence quickly broke down in some states and were replaced by others considered more compatible with the characteristics and requirements of the society. In Pakistan, for example, the Constitution of 1956 (which had taken nine years to frame) was abrogated in 1958. President Ayub Khan, justifying this action, asserted that the Pakistani leaders were initially provided with a system "totally unsuited to the temper and climate of the country." Similarly in other states in Africa and Asia, fundamental changes in the constitutional provisions relating to the structure and powers of the national government were effected in the years immediately following independence. In many cases, these changes were directed toward the strengthening of executive leadership, the presidential form of government replacing the parliamentary form that had been initially established.

However modern and efficient the institutional arrangements may appear, decision-making in transitional societies is often slow and inefficient. Leaders intent on achieving rapid changes are burdened with the numerous and complex problems of planning and implementing their revolutionary programs. Lacking adequate aides, and often disinclined to delegate authority, they assume many routine tasks in addition to those of basic planning. Further, traditional practices commonly intermingle with the new, resulting in a political process that often appears irrational and chaotic to foreign observers. In many Asian and African states, for example, the decision-making process is often slowed since unanimous or near-unanimous agreement must be achieved before policies can be announced. Decisions based upon formal votes, in which the members of the minority can be identified, are regarded as less desirable than those based upon unanimous consent. Again, in many Asian bureaucracies, few decisions can be made at the lower levels. Most problems that arise are passed on to high-ranking officials for decisions, since lower echelon bureaucrats are reluctant to make judgments that might be reversed, causing them to "lose face" with their contemporaries. Recourse to astrology is common in many of these societies before important decisions can be made. In 1964, for example, the Prime Minister of Ceylon delayed the decision to dissolve Parliament and hold new elections until the official astrologers could be consulted for the auspicious date of dissolution.

Whatever the specific format of governmental institutions that characterize a state's political system, the dominant position of the executive is a feature common throughout the developing areas. Rarely do legislatures pose formidable obstacles to the exercise of executive authority or its control of the decision-making process. Indeed, in few states in the world other than in the United States does the legislative body possess a largely independent capacity to participate in the process of enacting legislation. Nor, in most of the developing states, is there a strong tradition of judicial independence capable of disallowing and voiding the acts and decisions of the executive. Not only do the constitutions of most states grant broad powers of authority and control to the executive —including the power, in many countries, to declare a state of emergency and to rule by decree—but there is also a long tradition of executive-bureaucratic domination of the government that is deeply rooted in the values and customs of the societies. The traditional pattern of deference to the ruler, whether traditional or modern, and the expectation that strong leadership will be exercised, even in an arbitrary manner, further reinforce the constitutional prerogatives the executive enjoys. In those cases where only one party is legally permitted, or where one party is clearly dominant in the society, executive power is further enhanced by the controls exercised by and through the party apparatus.

Even with strong executive leadership, however, the probability of soon developing stable political systems in the transitional states is not high, as recent history demonstrates. The dual quests for stability and modernization are frequently incompatible. In the clash of traditional and modern groups and their values, the political systems of the developing states will continue to be subjected to intense pressures. Whether the developing states can successfully resolve their manifold problems must, at present, remain an open question. While the pessimist may point to the chaos and confusion in many states, the gradual progress being recorded in states such as Mexico and Malaysia in resolving their problems must not be ignored.

SUGGESTED READINGS

Adu, A. L., *The Civil Service in New African States.* New York, Frederick A. Praeger, Inc., 1965.

Alderfer, Harold F., *Local Government in Developing Countries.* New York, McGraw-Hill Book Company, Inc., 1964.

Anderson, James N. E., ed., *Changing Law in Developing Countries.* New York, Frederick A. Praeger, Inc., 1963.

Bayley, David H., *Public Liberties in the New States.* Chicago, Rand McNally & Company, 1964.

Coleman, James S., and Rosberg, Carl G., Jr., eds., *Political Parties and National Integration in Tropical Africa.* Berkeley, Calif., University of California Press, 1964.

Finer, S. E., *The Man on Horseback: The Role of the Military in Politics.* New York, Frederick A. Praeger, Inc., 1962.

Gutteridge, William, *Military Institutions and Power in the New States.* New York, Frederick A. Praeger, Inc., 1965.

Haddad, George M., *Revolution and Military Rule in the Middle East.* New York, R. Speller, 1965.

Halpern, Manfred, *The Politics of Social Change in the Middle East and North Africa.* Princeton, N. J., Princeton University Press, 1963.

Johnson, John J., *The Military and Society in Latin America.* Stanford, Calif., Stanford University Press, 1964.

————, ed., *The Role of the Military in Underdeveloped Countries.* Princeton, N. J., Princeton University Press, 1962.

Kautsky, John H., ed., *Political Change in Underdeveloped Countries: Nationalism and Communism.* New York, John Wiley & Sons, Inc., 1962.

Kuper, Hilda, and Kuper, Leo, *African Law: Adaptation and Development.* Berkeley, Calif., University of California Press, 1965.

LaPalombara, Joseph, ed., *Bureaucracy and Political Development.* Princeton, N. J., Princeton University Press, 1963.

————, and Weiner, Myron, eds., *Political Parties and Political Develop-ment*. Princeton, N. J., Princeton University Press, 1966.

Lieuwen, Edwin, *Generals vs. Presidents: Neomilitarism in Latin America*. New York, Frederick A. Praeger, Inc., 1964.

Lipset, Seymour M., and Solari, Aldo, eds., *Elites in Latin America*. New York, Oxford University Press, 1967.

Martz, John D., ed., *The Dynamics of Change in Latin American Politics*. Englewood Cliffs, N. J., Prentice-Hall, Inc., 1965.

Millen, Bruce H., *The Political Role of Labor in Developing Countries*. Washington, D. C., The Brookings Institution, 1963.

Prest, Alan R., *Public Finance in Underdeveloped Countries*. New York, Frederick A. Praeger, Inc., 1963.

Riggs, Fred W., *Administration in Developing Countries: The Theory of Prismatic Society*. Boston, Houghton Mifflin Company, 1964.

Smith, T. E., *Elections in Developing Countries*. London, Macmillan & Co. Ltd., 1960.

Weiner, Myron, *The Politics of Scarcity*. Chicago, University of Chicago Press, 1962.

⟨⟩

A. Political Leadership

14. THE RISE AND ROLE OF CHARISMATIC LEADERS[*]

ann ruth willner
and dorothy willner

Max Weber adapted the term *charisma* [1] from the vocabulary of early Christianity to denote one of three types of authority in his now classic classification of authority on the basis of claims to legitimacy. He distin-guished among (1) traditional authority, whose claim is based on "an

[*] From "The Rise and Role of Charismatic Leaders" by Ann Ruth Willner and Dorothy Willner, *New Nations: The Problem of Political Development, The Annals*, Vol. 358 (March, 1965), pp. 78–88. By permission of the publisher and the authors.

[1] The term is of Greek origin, meaning "gift," and was originally identified as a "gift of grace" or a divinely inspired calling to service, office or leadership.

established belief in the sanctity of immemorial traditions," (2) rational or legal authority, grounded on the belief in the legality of rules and in the right of those holding authoritative positions by virtue of those rules to issue commands, and (3) charismatic or personal authority, resting on "devotion to the specific sanctity, heroism, or exemplary character of an individual person, and of the normative pattern or order revealed by him." [2]

Of these types—and it must be emphasized that they are "ideal types" or abstractions—charismatic authority, according to Weber, differs from the other two in being unstable, even if recurrent, and tending to be transformed into one of the other two types. [3] While elements of charismatic authority may be present in all forms of leadership, [4] the predominantly charismatic leader is distinguished from other leaders by his capacity to inspire and sustain loyalty and devotion to him personally, apart from his office or status. He is regarded as possessing supernatural or extraordinary powers given to few to have. Whether in military prowess, religious zeal, therapeutic skill, heroism, or in some other dimension, he looms "larger than life." He is imbued with a sense of mission, felt as divinely inspired, which he communicates to his followers. He lives not as other men. Nor does he lead in expected ways by recognized rules. He breaks precedents and creates new ones and so is revolutionary. He seems to flourish in times of disturbance and distress. [5]

❖ ❖ ❖ ❖ ❖

NEW STATES AND THE EMERGENCE OF CHARISMATIC LEADERSHIP

❖ ❖ ❖ ❖ ❖

Charismatic leadership seems to flourish today particularly in the newer states that were formerly under colonial rule. Their very attain-

[2] Max Weber, *The Theory of Social and Economic Organization*, ed. by Talcott Parsons (New York: Oxford University Press, 1947), p. 328.

[3] This notion of transformation or "routinization" has led to criticism that Weber uses the concept of charisma ambiguously, that is, on the one hand as a characteristic of certain classes of people in certain situations, on the other as a more general quality that can be transmitted to and identified with institutions such as the family and the office; see *Ibid.*, p. 75 and Carl J. Friedrich, "Political Leadership and the Problem of Charismatic Power," *The Journal of Politics*, 23 (February 1961), p. 13. Such criticism overlooks the possibility that during the course of charismatic leadership, a transfer can be effected of aspects of the belief induced by the leader toward another object, especially if designated by him.

[4] Authority is here defined as the sanctioned basis for the exercise of a leadership role, whereas leadership refers to the individual seen as capable of exercising the role for the situation in which direction is called for.

[5] Weber, *op. cit.*, pp. 358–362; also H. H. Gerth and C. Wright Mills, *From Max Weber: Essays in Sociology* (New York: Oxford University Press, 1946), pp. 245–250.

ment of independence generally signified that the old order had broken down and the supports that sustained it had disappeared or were rapidly being weakened. We might more correctly distinguish two "old" orders in postcolonial countries: (1) the precolonial traditional system, many of whose elements survived during colonial rule and (2) the colonial system, a close approximation of Weber's rational-legal type, which was superimposed upon but did not completely efface the traditional system. Particularly under the "indirect rule" type of colonial regime, much of traditional belief and observance, political as well as socioeconomic, existed beneath the order imported from and imposed by the metropolitan country and in the more rural areas side-by-side with it.

The basis of traditional authority, however, was eroded by colonialism and indigenous nationalism, and the basis of legal authority was undermined by indigenous nationalism. Traditional authority, whether exercised through kingship and dominant caste, chieftainship and special lineage, or whichever of the many and varied institutions found in the many traditional societies, had been part of and based upon indigenous patterns of social organization, land tenure, economic activity, and other elements of a relatively integrated social system. Traditional social systems tended to disintegrate or be transformed under the impact of institutions imposed by the colonial power. Concomitantly, traditional prescriptions and procedures for the selection of rulers, for the control of conflict and the settlement of disputes, and for the maintenance of what had been considered appropriate relations between rulers and ruled were modified and in varying degrees displaced by colonial systems of authority. Even where colonial administrations supported or tolerated some maintenance of traditional authority, this was restricted to traditional contexts.

The attitude that traditional authority systems were inadequate to cope with the urban and industrial institutions introduced into colonies by Europeans was transmitted to and absorbed by the native elites educated in accordance with European standards and values and recruited into the colonial bureaucracies and business organizations. Nationalist intellectuals among the native elites also came to deprecate their own traditions, seeing them as weaknesses which had made colonialism possible and which were used by their colonial rulers to keep them in subjection.

※　※　※　※　※

In retrospect, it is clear why one of the major difficulties faced by leaders of successful national independence movements as they sought to establish their own governmental systems was the lack of respect for impersonal legal authority based on rational norms. For in successfully having discredited the colonial rulers and their works, they also unwittingly discredited the rule of law introduced by the colonial powers. However, the certainty of the traditional order had already been shattered during the colonial period. Thus there were no longer clear-cut and generally acceptable norms for the legitimacy of authority and the mode of its exercise. Their absence created the need for leadership that could serve as a bridge between the discredited past and the uncertain future. A climate of uncertainty and unpredictability is therefore a breeding ground for the emergence of charismatic leadership.

SOURCES AND VALIDATION OF CHARISMA

Having indicated the conditions propitious for the emergence of charismatic leadership, we now describe how it comes into existence and what sustains it. . . .

The process, broadly stated, is one of interaction between the leader and his followers. In the course of this interaction the leader transmits, and the followers accept, his presentation of himself as their predestined leader, his definitions of their world as it is and as it ought to be, and his conviction of his mission and their duty to reshape it. In actuality, the process is more complicated, involving several groups of followers and several stages of validation. There is the small group of the "elect" or "disciples," the initial elite whom the leader first inspires or who throw up from among themselves one who can inspire others. There is the public at large which, in turn, can be divided into those of predominantly traditional orientation and those oriented toward a newer order. In the societies with which we are concerned, further divisions may exist along ethnic, tribal, religious, regional, and linguistic lines. The point to be made is that the nationally significant charismatic leader can command the loyalty of all or most of these groups.

To understand how he can do so, it seems advisable to distinguish two levels on which his appeal is communicated and responded to. The first level is that of special grievance and special interest of each group; its significance is probably greatest during the stage in which the charismatic leader mobilizes the population in opposition to a prevailing order and in assertion of the possibility of a new order. In the situations of transition with which we deal, this stage is that of opposition to the rule of a colonial power.

Changes during the colonial period resulted in losses and uncertainties for many groups in the colonized population. Traditional agrarian land rights were interfered with, and unfamiliar forms of taxation were imposed on peasants. The monetary gains of those pushed or pulled out of their traditional agricultural, pastoral, or handicrafts occupations to become plantation and industrial workers may have been more than offset by the problems of adapting to unfamiliar environments. Traditional merchants and traders often lost out to the competition of imported manufactures. Traditional ruling groups may have given outward obedience to colonial overlords who allowed them to retain their titles and some vestiges of their past powers, but often resented their loss of real power. Those who gained from the new opportunities generated by the colonial system—and there were many—chafed at the limits placed upon their continued advancement. Native embryonic capitalists could not easily compete on equal terms with European businesses backed by the facilities of the metropolitan country. Native officials of the governmental and business bureaucracies often felt themselves unfairly excluded from the high-level posts. The intellectuals, especially those who were trained at European universities, became bitter at the disparity between the expectations aroused by their education and the blocks that appeared in the way of maximizing this education. For all of these groups, the colonial system was or could be made to appear the cause of their grievance.

While the attraction exercised by the charismatic leader can, in part, be attributed to his ability to focus and channel diverse grievances and interests in a common appeal, unifying a segmented population in pursuit of a common goal, this explanation is insufficient to account for the acceptance of a given leader. Nor does it tell us how a leader maintains charisma in the conditions of uncertainty and fractionalization following the attainment of the goal of independence.

To turn to a deeper level, we suggest that the charisma of a leader is bound up with and, indeed, may even depend upon his becoming assimilated, in the thought and feelings of a populace, to its sacred figures, divine beings, or heroes. Their actions and the context of these actions, recounted in myth, express the fundamental values of a culture, including its basic categories for organizing experience and trying to resolve basic cultural and human dilemmas.

❖   ❖   ❖   ❖   ❖

We wish to suggest that recent events in a people's politics, particularly those marking a major transition or extraordinary occurrence in public life, can become endowed with the quality of myth if they fit or can be fitted into the pattern of a traditional myth or body of myths. Furthermore, insofar as myths can be regarded as charters for action, validating ritual and moral acts,[6] or, indeed, any culturally prescribed behavior, the assimilation of a historical event to the pattern of traditional myth or of a given individual to a mythic figure endows the event or individual with the aura or sanction of the myth itself.

[6] Bronislaw Malinowski, "Myth in Primitive Psychology," *Magic, Science and Religion* (Boston: Beacon Press, 1948), pp. 96–108.

POLITICAL SYSTEMS

The charismatic leader, we suggest, is able to communicate to his followers a sense of continuity between himself and his mission and their legendary heroes and their missions. Since "a myth remains the same as long as it is felt as such,"[7] he and his claims are legitimated by his ability to draw on himself the mantle of myth. How a particular leader does this can be considered his strategy of "cultural management,"[8] in part conscious and deliberate, in part probably unconscious and intuitive.

The particular strategies of individual charismatic leaders are a subject for empirical investigation.[9] Elements of such strategies might be broken down into such categories as: rhetoric employed in speeches, including rhythm;[10] use of simile and metaphor and allusions[10] to myth and history; use of gesture and movement; employment of ritual and ceremony; manner of dealing with felt doubt and opposition; and mode of handling crises. While this list can be refined and extended, it suggests some of the categories in terms of which the charismatic appeal of leaders can be analyzed.

It should be stressed that the elements of behavior indicated by such categories vary from culture to culture. This, of course, would be true of the behavior of any leader, charismatic or not, who seeks to mobilize popular support. Specific to the charismatic leader, according to our theory, is the role of myth in validating his authority. His appeal, therefore, can best be understood by reference to the body of myth in a given culture that his strategy taps and manipulates, and the actions and values associated with and sanctioned by these myths.[11] In brief, the charismatic leader is charismatic because, in the breakdown of other means of legitimizing authority, he is able to evoke and associate with himself the sacred symbols of his culture.

✿　✿　✿　✿　✿

[7] Claude Lévi-Strauss, "The Structural Study of Myth," *The Journal of American Folklore*, Vol. 68 (October–December 1955), p. 435.
[8] See Lloyd A. Fallers, "Ideology and Culture in Uganda Nationalism," *American Anthropology*, Vol. 63 (August 1961), pp. 677–678 and McKim Marriott, "Cultural Policy in New States," in *Old Society and New States* (New York, 1963), p. 29.
[9] We deliberately refrain from giving concrete examples of strategies here; for, as is suggested below, to make meaningful the illustration of even a single strategy of a single leader would require an elaboration of the myths and values of his culture which lack of space prohibits.
[10] For example, it might be worth examining the frequency of Biblical allusions in the speeches of FDR, such as the reference in his first inaugural address to driving the money-changers out of the temple, and the extent to which his rhetoric paralleled the cadences of the St. James Bible. Similarly, it would be interesting to compare the rhythmic patterns of the speeches of Nkrumah and other African leaders with the predominant drum and dance rhythms of their societies.
[11] See Malinowski, *op. cit.*

We do not, however, suggest or wish to imply that a charismatic leader either achieves power or retains it on the basis of charisma alone. Charismatic appeal provides the source of and legitimates his authority. Other supports may be needed and are frequently employed to gain and maintain power, especially when charismatic appeal begins to decline.[12]

CHARISMATIC LEADERSHIP AND THE DILEMMAS OF DEVELOPMENT

As we have earlier indicated, the mission of the charismatic leader in the societies with which we deal is twofold, incorporating two distinct, although somewhat overlapping,[13] stages. The first is the destruction of the old order; the second, which might be termed "political development," is the building of the promised new and better order.

Political development, whether considered as a goal or as a process, can be viewed in the context of new countries as encompassing two distinct goals or processes. One is that of achieving and maintaining an autonomous and viable state or political community that can be recognized as such by, and participate with, other states in the international political community. The second is that of gaining and maintaining central government capacity to manage technological modernization and cope with its socioeconomic concomitants.[14]

These goals or processes are not necessarily synonymous or complementary, as is often assumed. While they may be interrelated and interdependent in some respects, they can be antipathetic and incompatible in others. What appear to be rational policies pursued in support of one goal may only serve to inhibit or prevent the attainment of the other.

Many new countries cannot begin either form of development at the point where their predecessors left off. In the first place, they start with less internal cohesion than existed in the same territories under colonial

[12] As David Apter points out in *Ghana in Transition* (New York: Atheneum, 1963), pp. 328–29, charisma can decline in favor of secular authority or, as he found in Ghana, as a result of conflict with traditional authority.

[13] These stages may overlap in several ways. The formation of a political unit that can gain external recognition can take place while the struggle against the old order continues. For some leaders, such as those of Indonesia and the United Arab Republic, the old order is not extinct, despite political independence, as long as former rulers retain ownership or control of important segments of the new country's economy.

[14] We use technological modernization rather than a more inclusive concept of modernization, not only because technological advance is the core of other forms, but because there are universally accepted and non-ethnocentric criteria to define and measure technological change. This leaves open the types of social, economic, and cultural systems which are or can be compatible with the development of a modern technology.

control or during nationalist mobilization against it. The very tactics of nationalist mobilization confront the new governments with new sets of expectations and conditions, limiting the alternatives open to it.

As recent Asian and African history has demonstrated, the preindependence solidarity forged in the common struggle of diverse groups against their common ruler does not long survive the departure of that ruler. The vision of a single nation submerged under colonial control fades before the reality of competitive subsocieties, each of which tends to view independence as a mandate to reassert its traditional heritage and strengthen its claims against those of other groups.

No longer can the conflicting interests and ambitions of different ethnic groups and, cross-cutting these, the different economic segments of the population be merged in the single overriding goal of freedom. Now they are couched in the concrete terms of more land and lower taxes for peasants, higher wages for workers, subsidies for small businessmen, boosts in status and salary for bureaucrats, or whatever particular benefits people had sought or been led to expect as the immediate and inevitable fruits of successful anticolonialism.

Moreover, nationalist leaders were committed to representative government, whether through personal conviction or because explicit adherence to democracy in its Western institutional forms was the implicit condition of American support for their cause. Soon new parliaments, parties, unions, and associations provide new forums to articulate expectations and arouse new aspirations.[15] Rival contenders for ethnic, regional, and national roles of intermediate political leadership press upon the central government the rival claims of those they lead.

But the already hard-pressed new governments have less capacity to provide even the expected services than had their colonial counterparts. This is not merely a matter of limited financial resources or unanticipated needs to rehabilitate refugees and reconstruct installations destroyed by military action. The replacement of skilled administrators and technicians by less trained or unskilled ones, especially where nationalist zeal and political reliability are the major criteria of appointment,[16] means that preindependence norms of governmental performance are difficult to restore, much less improve upon to meet the new aspirations. In this respect, India perhaps suffered least and the Congo most.

[15] In place of the conventional concept of *demand*, we prefer to distinguish between *expectation* and *aspiration* which are differently derived and have different potential for violence when frustrated. Expectations constitute claims made on the basis of prevailing norms whose satisfaction is felt as owed by right; aspirations are hopes of future gains not previously enjoyed which are seen as desirable but not necessarily due one. Whereas unrealized aspirations result in disappointment, frustrated expectations produce an often intolerable sense of deprivation.

[16] The provision of government jobs to the disciples and their followers may be seen as booty distribution, noted by Weber as one of the means of support of charismatic leaders.

At almost any stage of planning policies and programs or implementing them, dilemmas multiply and internal conflict increases. Basic dilemmas over how to allocate scarce resources as between long-run investment goals and short-run consumption requirements and between projects stimulating industrial growth and those needed to maintain levels of employment [17] are further complicated by struggles over the distribution of the available pie.[18] Satisfaction of one set of claims, even in terms of national developmental goals rather than particularistic ones, produces, at minimum, accusations of favoritism leveled against the central government and counter-claims from those feeling themselves disadvantaged. At maximum, it produces large-scale violence and even overt insurrection.

The charismatic leader can conceivably use his appeal to integrate the state and to create strong central government institutions to modernize the society, that is, to further development in both senses of the term as defined earlier. But the extent to which he can focus simultaneously on both will depend on the particular conditions and resistances in his society.[19] In circumstances of acute subgroup competition, many national modernization goals weaken or tend to be shelved. Of necessity, the leader concentrates his charisma on holding together a potentially fragmenting country. Priority is given to maintaining and unifying the state or gaining some semblance of solidarity whatever the cost.

In a society fissioned by parochial identifications and particularistic goals, the charismatic leader may be the single symbol of unity surmounting the diversity and the primary means of creating consensus on objectives. To the many who need some tangible referent for a loyalty still somewhat beyond their comprehension, he is the visible embodiment of the nation come into being. And to those confused by the loosening of familiar ties and the profusion of new groups and activities claiming their attention, he provides the reassurance that links them with the old and sanctions the new.

✻   ✻   ✻   ✻   ✻

[17] For fuller treatment of this and preceding points, see B. F. Hoselitz and A. R. Willner, "Economic Development, Political Strategies, and American Aid," in M. A. Kaplan, *The Revolution in World Politics* (New York: John Wiley & Sons, 1963), pp. 357–71.

[18] Even the implementation of a universal goal, such as education, can provoke dissent and conflict. The advantages of a single language of instruction that will also serve as a unifying force has often been countered by demands for education in the local languages. The very groups who have requested vernacular schools, after gaining their objectives, may often exhibit resentment when their members do not easily have access to posts and occupations that demand fluency in the dominant national language.

[19] This has been far more possible in India, Israel, and the United Arab Republic than in Indonesia or Ghana.

The charismatic leader can be seen as a double-visaged Janus, projecting himself on the one hand as the omniscient repository of ancient wisdom and on the other as the new man of the people, not only leading them toward, but sharing with them, the trials of revolutionary renewal.[20] . . .

Of major significance in the creation of a national identity can be the use by the charismatic leader of the international stage. Part of the sense of self derives from the measurement of self against others and much of the feeling of strength comes from the awareness of one's impact on others. The presence and prominence of their leaders in distant capitals and exerting obvious influence on international conferences, spelled out to their peoples through all the media of mass communication, give the latter a sense of national identity and pride.

There is another way in which charismatic leaders tend to have an impact on the international stage which often annoys and outrages the leaders and peoples of more established countries. This is the constant raising of such issues as cryptocolonialism, "disguised" imperialism, and perceived foreign "interference." These may strike outside observers as unwarranted and dangerous shadow battles. But they, too, serve the function of maintaining internal cohesion. . . .

While charismatic leadership may contribute in many ways to the consolidation of the state, its exercise may also delay the kind of institutionalization and continuity of authority needed for concrete tasks of development. The charismatic leader may become trapped by his own symbols and substitute symbolic action as ends instead of means. Viewing himself as the indispensable prop of his country's existence and the only one in whose hands its destiny can be trusted, he may treat constructive criticism as treason. Those surrounding him may do little more than echo him and vie for his favor while awaiting his demise and hoping for the mantle to descend on themselves. Charismatic leadership does not provide for orderly succession. In its absence the crisis of succession may undo much that was built up and conserved.

ᏨᏇᏇ

---

[20] This double-projection is frequent in the speeches of Sukarno and can also be found in some of Nasser's statements.

15. *THE INTELLECTUALS IN THE POLITICAL DEVELOPMENT OF THE NEW STATES*[*][†]

e d w a r d   s h i l s

I . THE POLITICAL SIGNIFICANCE
OF INTELLECTUALS
IN UNDERDEVELOPED COUNTRIES

The gestation, birth, and continuing life of the new states of Asia and Africa, through all their vicissitudes, are in large measure the work of intellectuals. In no state-formations in all of human history have intellectuals played such a role as they have in these events of the present century.

○   ○   ○   ○   ○

The prominence of intellectuals in the politics of the new states of Asia and Africa arises in part from the special affinity which exists between the modern intellectual orientation and the practice of revolutionary or unconstitutional politics, of politics which are uncivil in their nature. But even in the small space allotted to civil politics before the new states' acquisition of sovereignty and in its larger area since then, intellectuals have had a prominent position. They have not had to share their political role to the usual extent with the other participants in the building and ruling of states.

It was the intellectuals on whom, in the first instance, devolved the task of contending for their nations' right to exist, even to the extent of promulgating the very idea of the nation. The erosion of the conscience and self-confidence of the colonial powers was in considerable measure

[*]   Excerpts from "The Intellectuals in the Political Development of the New States" by Edward Shils, *World Politics*, Vol. XII, No. 3 (April, 1960), pp. 329–354. By permission.

[†]   This article is a revised version of a paper presented at a conference on political modernization held under the auspices of the Committee on Comparative Politics of the Social Science Research Council at Dobbs Ferry in June 1959.

the product of agitational movements under intellectual leadership. The impregnation of their fellow-countrymen with some incipient sense of nationality and of national self-esteem was to a large extent the achievement of intellectuals, both secular and religious. The intellectuals have created the political life of the underdeveloped countries; they have been its instigators, its leaders, and its executants. Until Gandhi's emergence at the end of the First World War, they were its main followers as well, but this changed when the nationalist movement began to arouse the sentiments of the mass of the population.

One of the reasons for the political pre-eminence of the intellectuals of the underdeveloped countries is a negative one. There was practically no one else. In so many of the colonial countries, the princely dynasties were in decay, their powers and their capacities withered, even before the foreigners appeared. . . .

Moreover, there was generally no military force either to fight against the foreign ruler once he was established or to supply the educated personnel for a modern political movement.[1] There was no military officer class except for a few subalterns in the jealously guarded army of the foreign ruler. There were many professional soldiers, but they were non-commissioned officers and other ranks and had no political interest whatsoever. The movement instigated in 1881 by the Egyptian Colonel Ahmed Orabi Pasha[2] had no counterparts until the tremors and tribulations of independence began to be felt. There was no profession of politics which men entered early, usually from some other profession, and remained in until final and crushing defeat or the end of their lives. There were very few merchants and industrialists who out of civic and "material" interest took a part in politics on a full or part-time scale—although many of them contributed substantially to the financial support of the nationalist and even the revolutionary movements. Prudence and the narrowness of their concerns kept businessmen out of politics. The "foreignness" of many business enterprisers in underdeveloped countries has further diminished the significance of this class as a reservoir of political personnel. There was and there still is scarcely any endogenous trade union movement which produces its own leaders from within the laboring class, and there have been practically none of those self-educated workingmen who helped to give an intellectual tone to the European and American socialist and revolutionary movements in their early years. There was no citizenry, no reservoir of civility, to provide not only the audience and following of politics but the personnel of

---

[1] The practitioners of the guerrilla warfare and terrorism which have been carried on in various parts of Asia and Africa against the European rulers have always included a significant admixture of intellectuals.

[2] It was, in any case, more of a protest against unsatisfactory service conditions than a political movement.

middle and higher leadership. In short, if politics were to exist at all in underdeveloped countries under colonial rule, they had to be the politics of the intellectuals.

The intellectuals did not, however, enter into the political sphere merely because other sections of the population forswore or abdicated their responsibilities. They entered because they had a special calling from within, a positive impetus from without.

II. THE INTELLECTUAL CLASS IN UNDERDEVELOPED COUNTRIES

What Is an Intellectual? We deal here with the modern intellectuals of the new states—not with traditional intellectuals. Whom do we regard as modern intellectuals in the new states? The answer, in a first approximation, is: all persons with an *advanced modern education*[3] and the intellectual concerns and skills ordinarily associated with it. . . .

In the new states, and in colonies which are shortly to achieve independence, the intellectuals are those persons who have become modern not by immersing themselves in the ways of modern commerce or administration, but by being exposed to the set course of modern intellectual culture in a college or university. . . . The possession of a *modern intellectual culture* is vital because it carries with it a partial transformation of the self and a changed relationship to the authority of the dead and the living.

The Occupational Structure of the Intellectuals: The professions of the intellectuals in underdeveloped countries are civil service, journalism, law, teaching (particularly college and university, but also secondary-school teaching), and medicine. These are the professions in which intellectuals are to be found and which require either intellectual certification or intellectual skill. (There are other professions with simi-

---

[3] This definition is ceasing to be adequate because the extension of opportunities for higher education is changing the composition and outlook of the group of persons who have availed themselves of these opportunities. Furthermore, the increase of those with an advanced technical or scientific and specialized education is creating a body of persons whose interests are narrower than their predecessors' in their own countries, and whose contact with the humanistic and political tradition of the hitherto prevailing higher education is becoming more attenuated. They themselves will not merely be different from the conventional political intellectuals of the colonial or recently colonial countries, but will also less frequently identify themselves as "intellectuals." This will make a considerable difference. In this respect, the underdeveloped countries will begin to approximate the more advanced countries.

This definition is not intended to deny the existence of a class of traditional intellectuals, largely religious in their concerns. Nor does it seek to obscure the influence of traditional intellectuals in political life (like the Muslim Brotherhood, the Darul Islam, etc.) or of traditional ideas on modern intellectuals.

lar qualifications of certification and skill, such as engineering and accounting, which have usually been regarded as marginal to the circle
within which the intellectuals dwell.)

The occupational structure which intellectuals enter in the underdeveloped countries is notably different from that of the more advanced
countries. The occupational distribution of the intellectuals in underdeveloped countries is a function of the level of economic development
and of their having only recently been colonial territories. Because they
were impoverished countries, they lacked a fully differentiated middle
class. They lacked and still lack a stratum of authors who could live from
the sale of their literary products.[4] They have only a very meager class
of technical intellectuals (electrical engineers, technologists, industrial
chemists, statisticians, accountants). They have lacked the higher levels
of scientific and humanistic personnel, the physicists, biologists, geneti-
cists, historians, and philosophers who carry on the intellectual work
which is the specific manifestation of the modern intellectual outlook.[5]

They lacked nearly all of these latter professions under colonial
conditions, and most of the underdeveloped countries still lack most of
them today under conditions of independence. In the colonial era, they
lacked them because poverty and the absence of a significant development of industry prevented the emergence of demand for technical
intellectuals, because illiteracy prevented the emergence of a market for
literary products, and because the higher levels of modern intellectual
creation and enquiry received no indigenous impulse and were too
costly for poor countries to maintain. As a result, persons trained in
those subjects found little opportunity for employment in their own
country, and few therefore attempted to acquire these skills.[6]

Under colonial conditions, the underdeveloped countries lacked the
effective demand which permits a modern intellectual class, in its full
variety, to come into existence. Persons who acquired intellectual qualifications had only a few markets for their skills. The higher civil service
was by all odds the most attractive of these, but opportunities were
restricted because it was small in size and the posts were mainly pre-
empted by foreigners. . . .

[4] By very rough methods I estimated that there might be as many as one hundred
professional literary men in India who are able to maintain themselves by their
writings. The Director of the *Sahitya Akademi* thinks that there are only about fifty.
Think then of the size of this stratum in Ghana, Nigeria, Egypt, or the Sudan!

[5] India is a very partial exception. It is practically alone in its possession of a large
corps of intellectuals, a fair number of whom work at a very high level. This is partly
a function of the much longer period that modern intellectual life has existed in
India. The British stayed longer in India and exercised greater influence there than
any other European power did in its colonial territory, and as a result many more
modern intellectual institutions came into being.

[6] There are other important reasons, growing out of the culture of these countries,
which precluded interest in these fields. We do not deal with them here since our
interest lies primarily in the political sphere.

Journalism, as a result of generally widespread illiteracy, was a stunted growth and provided only a few opportunities. . . .

The medical profession was kept small by the costliness of the course of study, the absence of an effective demand for medical services, and the preemption of much of the senior level of the medical service by the government and its consequent reservation for foreigners.

Teaching at its lower levels was unattractive to intellectuals because it involved living in villages away from the lights and interests of the larger towns, and because it was extremely unremunerative. Nor were there many opportunities in it. On the secondary and higher levels, opportunities were also meager. . . .

The Legal Profession: For these reasons, many of the intellectually gifted and interested who also had to gain their own livelihood entered the course of legal study and then the practice of the profession of the law. Entry to the legal profession was not restricted on ethnic grounds, the course of study was short and inexpensive and could be easily undertaken. There was, moreover, a considerable effective demand for legal services.

✧　✧　✧　✧　✧

. . . The law schools were therefore able to attract throngs of students. Once the legal qualification had been obtained, the young lawyer went into the nether regions of the bar, where he had much time for other interests. The leisure time of the young lawyer was a fertile field in which much political activity grew.

This existence of a stratum of underemployed young lawyers was made possible by their kinship connections. The aspirants to the intellectual professions in the underdeveloped countries almost always came from the more prosperous sections of society. They were the sons of chiefs, noblemen, and landowners, of ministers and officials of territories in which indirect rule existed, and of civil servants and teachers in countries under direct rule. In some countries, they occasionally came from prosperous mercantile families, though seldom in large numbers.

✧　✧　✧　✧　✧

Students: No consideration of the intellectual class in underdeveloped countries can disregard the university students. In advanced countries, students are not regarded as *ex officio* intellectuals; in underdeveloped countries, they are. Students in modern colleges and universities in underdeveloped countries have been treated as part of the intellectual class—or at least were before independence—and they have regarded themselves as such. . . .

The student enjoyed double favor in the eyes of his fellow-countryman. As one of the tiny minority gaining a modern education, he was becoming qualified for a respected, secure, and well-paid position close to the center of society, as a civil servant, teacher, or lawyer. As a bearer of the spirit of revolt against the foreign ruler, he gained the admiration and confidence of those of his seniors who were imbued with the national idea.

✧ ✧ ✧ ✧ ✧

The Unemployed Intellectual: In most underdeveloped countries during the colonial period, the unemployed intellectual was always a worry to the foreign rulers and to constitutional politicians, and a grievance of the leaders of the independence movement. He still remains a problem in the underdeveloped countries which have had a higher educational system for some length of time and which are not rapidly expanding their governmental staffs. In Ghana or Nigeria, there is a shortage of intellectuals and all graduates can find posts; in Pakistan, which inherited only a very small part of the higher educational system of British India, the government has tried to restrict entrance to the universities, especially in "arts" subjects. In India and Egypt, however, despite rapid expansion of opportunities for the employment of intellectuals in government, there has been a more than proportionate expansion in the number of university graduates and the problem remains as acute as ever.

Yet the difficulty is not so much "intellectual unemployment" as under- and mal-employment. Most of the graduates, sooner or later, do find posts of one sort or another, but they are not posts which conform with expectations. They are ill-paid, unsatisfying in status and tenure, and leave their incumbents in the state of restlessness which they experienced as students.

III. THE POLITICAL OUTLOOK OF THE INTELLECTUALS

Intense Politicization: The nature of the political movements which preceded independence and the indigenous traditions of the underdeveloped countries both forced political life into charismatic channels. Charismatic politics demand the utmost from their devotees.

When the intellectuals of the colonial countries were ready to engage in politics at all, they were willing to give everything to them.

Politics became the be-all and end-all of their existence. Those who were not restrained by fear of the loss of their posts in government schools and colleges or by the material and psychological advantages of their jobs became highly politicized. . . .

The high degree of political involvement of the intellectual in underdeveloped countries is a complex phenomenon. It has a threefold root. The primary source is a deep preoccupation with authority. Even though he seeks and seems actually to break away from the authority of the powerful traditions in which he was brought up, the intellectual of underdeveloped countries, still more than his confrere in more advanced countries, retains the need for incorporation into some self-transcending, authoritative entity. Indeed, the greater his struggle for emancipation from the traditional collectivity, the greater his need for incorporation into a new, alternative collectivity. Intense politicization meets this need. The second source of political involvement is the scarcity of opportunities to acquire an even temporary sense of vocational achievement; there have been few counterattractions to the appeal of charismatic politics. Finally, there has been a deficient tradition of civility in the underdeveloped countries which affects the intellectuals as much as it does the non-intellectuals. . . .

✧   ✧   ✧   ✧   ✧

Nationalism: The nationalism of the intellectuals usually made its first appearance alone, free from the complications of socialist and populist ideas. Only in those underdeveloped countries where the nationalist movement has come more lately on the scene has it been involved in other ideological currents which are not necessarily integral to it.

The nationalism of the intellectuals of the underdeveloped countries emerged at a time when there was little sense of nationality among the peoples whose nationality the intellectuals were proclaiming. Its first impetus seems to have come from a deepening of the feeling of distance between ruler and ruled, arising from the spatial and ethnic remoteness of the foreign rulers, and the dissolution of the particularistic tie which holds ethnically homogeneous rulers and ruled together. The identification of oneself as a subject of an unloved (however feared and respected) ruler with others who shared that subjection was one phase of the process. The discovery of the glories of the past, of cultural traditions, was usually but not always an action, *ex post facto*, which legitimated the claims asserted on behalf of that newly imagined collectivity.[7]

The assimilation of modern culture, which, historically, was a foreign culture, was an essential element in this process. . . . It was nei-

---

[7] The stirrings of religious reform and the effort to rehabilitate the dignity of the traditional religious culture became political only when there was an alliance of religious leaders with a politicized modern intelligentsia.

ther a simple attachment to their indigenous culture nor a concretely experienced love of their fellow-countrymen which made the intellectuals so fervently nationalistic. These would have presupposed a prior sense of affinity, which for many reasons was lacking and often still is. In fact, however, "fellow-countrymen" became so to the modern intellectuals primarily by virtue of their common differentiation from the foreign ruler. Fierce resentment against the powerful, fear-inspiring foreign ruler was probably a much more significant factor than either a sense of affinity or a conscious appreciation of the traditional culture.

The resentment of the modern intellectual grew from several seeds: one of the most important was the derogation implied in the barrier against entry into or advancement in the civil service. The other, closely related to this, was the feeling of injury from insults, experienced or heard about, explicit or implicit, which the foreign rulers and their businessmen fellow-nationals inflicted on the indigenous modern intellectuals. . . .

. . . Nationalism of an extremely assertive sort was an effort to find self-respect, and to overcome the inferiority of the self in the face of the superiority of the culture and power of the foreign metropolis.

It was therefore logical that prior to independence the politics of the intellectuals, once the movement for constitutional reform had waned, should have been concerned with one end above all others: national independence. . . .

The socialistic and the populistic elements in the politics of the intellectuals of underdeveloped countries are secondary to and derivative from their nationalistic preoccupations and aspirations. Economic policies have their legitimation in their capacity to raise the country on the scale of the nations of the world. The populace is transfigured in order to demonstrate the uniqueness of its "collective personality." The ancient culture is exhumed and renewed in order to demonstrate, especially to those who once denied it, the high value of the nation. Foreign policy is primarily a policy of "public relations" designed not, as in the advanced countries, to sustain the security of the state or enhance its power among other states, but to improve the reputation of the nation, to make others heed its voice, to make them pay attention to it and to respect it. The "world," the "imperialist world," remains very much on the minds of the intellectuals of the new states. It remains the audience and the jury of the accomplishments of the nation which the intellectuals have done so much to create.

✿   ✿   ✿   ✿   ✿

Incivility: Although the intellectuals of the underdeveloped countries have created the idea of the nation within their own countries, they have not been able to create a nation. They are themselves the victim of that condition, since nationalism does not necessarily become citizenship. Membership in a nation which is sovereign entails a sense of affinity with the other human beings who make up the nation. It entails a sense of "partness" in a whole, a sense of sharing a common substance. This feeling of being part of the whole is the basis of a sense of concern for its well-being, and a sense of responsibility to it and for it. It transcends ineluctable divisions, softening them and rendering them tolerable to civil order, regarding them as less significant than the underlying community of those who form the nation. In political life, these dispositions form the virtue of civility.

Civility has hitherto not been one of the major features of the politicized intelligentsia of the underdeveloped countries. An intense politicization is difficult to bring into harmony with civility. Intense politicization is accompanied by the conviction that only those who share one's principles and positions are wholly legitimate members of the polity and that those who do not share them are separated by a steep barrier. The governing party in many sovereign underdeveloped states, and those intellectuals who make it up or are associated with it, tend to believe that those who are in opposition are separated from them by fundamental and irreconcilable differences. They feel that they *are* the state and the nation, and that those who do not go along with them are not just political rivals but *total* enemies. The sentiments of the opposition are, *mutatis mutandis,* scarcely different. These are the fruits of intense politicization.

⟨∿∿⟩

16. THE AFRO-ASIAN ELITES*

s h l o m o   a v i n e r i

THE ORIGINS OF THE ÉLITE

With rare exceptions, no historical élite led the national liberation movements. The Indian Rajahs and the African tribal chieftains were

* From "Afro-Asia and the Western Political Tradition" by Shlomo Avineri, *Parliamentary Affairs,* Vol. XV, No. 1 (Winter, 1961–62), pp. 60–65. By permission.

mostly the staunchest supporters of British rule, which, though diminishing their authority, did however formalize, institutionalize, stabilize and guarantee it with a measure of safety and permanency hitherto unknown.

Similarly, neither did the spiritual élites lead the way in the struggle against foreign rule. Partly out of social motives, partly out of the lack of any tradition of a political philosophy of action in the East, we find such élites, as the Hindu Brahmins or the Muslim Ullemah comparatively acquiescent to European domination.

The Marxist version, sometimes rather naively held by Western observers quite far from Marxism themselves, suggests, on evidence drawn from European experience, that the nationalist movements were led by the local emergent bourgeoisie: the national bourgeoisie, so runs this explanation, finds its interests conflicting with the dominant rule of foreign capitalism and imperialism and turns against it, though, originally, it had its beginnings in the very impact of Western capital on the local economy.

Like much of the purely mechanistic vulgarization of Marxism, this is rather far from being an adequate explanation of actual conditions in any Afro-Asian country. One has only to look at India, Egypt or Ghana—examples chosen at random—to be convinced how utterly nonsensical such an explanation is. The local economic interests were committed to foreign investments and markets and virtually dreaded national independence, and their behaviour during the last years of colonial rule amply attests to their commitment. Moreover, due to historical reasons, economic-capitalistic activity in most countries has been in the hands of ethnic or religious minorities: Parsees in India, Chinese in Indonesia, Greeks, Turks, Copts and Jews in Egypt, Arabs in Ghana and Arabs and Indians in East Africa, and so on. Those minorities felt far more secure under foreign rule than under a local nationalist government.

If neither the traditional élites, nor the new economic élites led the nationalist movements—by whom were they actually led?

The answer is, perhaps, one of the most fascinating chapters in the annals of the history of *education:* for the nationalist leaders came neither from ancient, oriental traditional palaces nor from restless expanding economic business enterprises: they came from the European schools.

For one of the institutions transferred from the West to the colonies was the Western educational system, and the Indian case can be cited as an ideal type of this development.

The motives for having English education for Indians are mixed, and ultimately not very relevant to our inquiry. They are a curious blend of utilitarian motives—Britain needed educated Indians in order to run the country, and the Hindu Ashram or the Muslim Madrasah did not provide the right kind of education for this purpose. On the other hand, there was always the missionary streak in its secular version—so evident in Macaulay who was responsible for introducing this system into India—of the White Man's Burden.

✿   ✿   ✿   ✿   ✿

Thus out of a utilitarian calculus and a secular version of missionary zeal—a typical English blend—India and other territories (and the same goes for French colonies) received a modified version of the Victorian educational system, from public school to collegiate universities.

But here something went, dialectically if one may say so, wrong. The impact of a Western liberal education on a society which itself was miles apart from Victorian England was far different from what both the utilitarian and the benevolent promoters of this education ever dreamed.

THE TRICKS OF DISPLACED EDUCATION

English liberal education could be summarized as an institutionalized attempt at creating a platonic élite in a self-governing community. The much truncated idea of a well educated gentleman, politically and financially independent, who is well adapted to play a leading role in politics and finance, administration and military service, seems to have well adapted itself to the needs of a society on the Victorian model.

It became virtually a disaster in a society which was as different from Victorian England as any society could conceivably be. The young Indian graduates, steeped in free discussion and feeling their sense of power and superiority ingrained in their education, found themselves in a world in which they were destined, because of the fact of colonialism, to play institutionalized second and third fiddle, never attaining the commanding heights for which their education prepared them. The young bright graduate, reared to be statesman and financier, M.P. and minister, found himself as a subaltern clerk, subordinate to an Englishman who himself sometimes lacked those very qualities.

Because the content of their education had been geared to Western political ideas, because Locke and Mill (or Rousseau) figured prominently in the syllabi of Madras or Jaipur, as they did in Oxford and Cambridge, this educational success seemed to be the very undoing of the colonial rule itself. The history of men like Nehru (Harrow and Trinity, Cambridge), Nkrumah (Lincoln University, Pennsylvania, University of Pennsylvania and London School of Economics), Ho Chi-Minh and Ferhat Abbas (Sorbonne) and scores of others attests to this.

These graduates, imbibing their liberal and democratic ideas from their Western education, turned their personal and ideological frustration and sense of being betrayed against their conquerors and educators. The call for civil rights, self-government, representative government, social security, self-determination, autonomy and ultimately sovereignty —this call had to be termed in the European political jargon *because the local political tradition did not contain those ideas.* Therefore countries which did not educate their colonial people—like the Portuguese—did not supply them with the weapon against colonialism itself, and subsequently those territories were late in making their claim for independence. No other reason can explain how the mighty British and French empires collapsed, whereas Lisbon still holds its possessions.

This, uncomfortable as it is, must be faced, as must another major factor: the liberal-democratic norms were themselves a limitation on the effectiveness of the repressive measures against nationalism. Colonialism has never been militarily defeated. Its defeat was always political, politics being the art of the possible, and because England and France were themselves liberal and democratic countries, certain modes of behaviour were politically impossible for them.

Though there has always been in the West two political codes, and the London policeman and the commissioner in a jungle district did not strictly adhere to the same rules, the "internal" code necessarily kept the "colonial" in check. As the colonial power always introduced the Rule of Law, it had to fight nationalism with its hands tied behind its back. Nationalist leaders might be brought to trial—and acquitted, and it has to be borne in mind that with the bitter exception of Ireland, Britain did not execute *leaders* of nationalist movements: those people who were executed were people who committed acts of violence which would be normally dealt with quite severely, though not always punished by death. From the strictly crude utilitarian point of view, England could have been more successful if it had allowed itself to be more brutal, but this was largely out of the question: technically, the leadership of the national movements could have been executed: politically this was out of the question, and therefore a Commonwealth Prime Ministers' Conference looks nowadays like a reunion of ex-inmates of H.M. prisons. Atrocities like Camp Hola did occur: but they were the exception, not the rule, and the West's reaction was always a strong feeling of guilt. A Budapest was inconceivable.

This is due to the fact that Western political institutions make it difficult for any government to ignore certain standards of behaviour in the colonial territories: parliamentary questions, press comment in the metropolis and the dependency itself, etc. have an impact on any government which rules by consent and majority. The British Government was genuinely concerned about the possibility of Gandhi starving himself to death: it needs more than one's usual stretch of imagination to conceive the Soviet government having been unduly troubled by a similar move by, say, Imre Nagy.

This moral limitation, which countries like Portugal (themselves dictatorships) do not experience, cannot be brushed away, as this morality is institutionalized in the parliamentary system, and ultimately you pay for transgressing too many of its rules with your office. Only an authoritarian state can be utterly ruthless, and thus more "efficient" with its colonial policy, and here we come to the paradox of imperialism itself, which is bound to be self-destructive.

. . . Without any need to turn to obscure historiosophy one can safely say that as much as imperialism was the outcome of capitalism, so was it its downfall.

Thus, paradoxically, the victory of Gandhi and Nkrumah, Ho Chi-Minh and Bourguiba and—ultimately—Ferhat Abbas cannot by any means be construed as a victory of "Asia" or "Africa" over a decadent "Europe": the people who won the battle were educated by Europe, and their political ideas were derived from European political philosophy and history. *It was a victory of European ideas over European politics and economics.*

⟨∿∿∿⟩

17. ARMIES IN THE PROCESS OF POLITICAL MODERNIZATION*

l u c i a n   w.   p y e

THE ARMY AS A MODERN ORGANIZATION

In large measure the story of the underdeveloped countries is one of countless efforts to create organizations by which resources can be

---

* From "Armies in the Process of Political Modernization" by Lucian W. Pye in John J. Johnson, ed., *The Role of the Military in Underdeveloped Countries.* Reprinted by permission of the Princeton University Press. Copyright © 1962 by The RAND Corporation. Selections from pp. 73–85.

effectively mobilized for achieving new objectives. This is the problem of establishing organizations that, as rationalized structures, are capable of relating means to ends. . . .

Needless to say, there are not many bright spots in this history, and it is open to question as to who has been the more tragically heroic or comically futile: the Westerners struggling to establish their organizations in traditional societies, or the nationalist politician and the indigenous administrator endeavoring to create a semblance of order out of chaos. On balance, the attempts to establish military organizations seem to have been noticeably the most successful.

It would be wrong to underestimate the patient care that has gone into developing and training colonial armies, and in the newly independent countries the military have been treated relatively generously in the allocation of scarce resources. But in comparison to the efforts that have been expended in developing, say, civil administration and political parties, it still seems that modern armies are somewhat easier to create in transitional societies than are most other forms of modern social structures. The significant fact for our consideration is that the armies created by colonial administration and by the newly emergent countries have been consistently among the most modernized institutions in their societies. . . .

It would take us too far afield to explore the relative advantages military leaders have in seeking to establish armies in transitional societies. We need only note that there is a paradoxical relationship between ritualized and rationalized modes of behavior that may account for the ease with which people still close to a traditional order adapt themselves to military life. Viewed from one perspective, a military establishment comes as close as any human organization can to the ideal type for an industrialized and secularized enterprise. Yet from another point of view, the great stress placed on professionalism and the extremely explicit standards for individual behavior make the military appear to be a more sacred than secular institution. If discipline is needed to minimize random and unpredictable behavior, it is also consonant with all the demands that custom and ritual make in the most tradition-bound organization.

For these reasons, and for others related to the hierarchic nature of the organization, the division between traditional and rationally oriented behavior is not very great within armies.[1] Indeed, in any army there is always a struggle going on between tradition and reason. His-

---

[1] It is significant that the most common weaknesses of civil bureaucracies in the new countries—like exaggerating the importance of procedure to the point of ritualizing the routine, and the lack of initiative and of a pragmatic and experimental outlook—are not as serious drawbacks to smooth functioning of military establishment. On the contrary, the very qualities that have hobbled civil administration in these countries have given strength and rigidity to their military establishments.

torically, during periods of little change in the state of military technology the tendency has been for the nonrational characteristics to become dominant.[2] Given this inherent conflict in any military organization the question arises as to why the forces of custom and ritual do not readily dominate the armies of the newly emergent countries, and so cause them to oppose the forces of change. In societies where traditional habits of mind are still strong one might expect the military to be strongly conservative. Such was largely the case in the West during the preindustrial period. By contrast, in most of the newly emergent countries armies have tended to emphasize a rational outlook and to champion responsible change and national development.

This state of affairs is largely explained by the extent to which the armies in these countries have been influenced by contemporary Western military technology. In particular, nearly all of the new countries have taken the World War II type of army as their model.[3] In so doing they have undertaken to create a form of organization that is typical of and peculiar to the most highly industrialized civilization yet known. Indeed, modern armies are essentially industrial-type entities. Thus the armies of the new countries are instinct with the spirit of rapid technological development.

The fact that these new armies in preindustrial societies are modeled after industrial-based organizations has many implications for their political roles. One of their characteristics is particularly significant: the specialization that modern armies demand in skills and functions is only distantly related to the command of violence. There has generally been a tremendous increase in the number of officers assigned to staff functions as contrasted with line commands. As the armies have striven to approximate their ideal models they have had to establish all manner of specialized organizations and departments that require skills that are either in short supply or nonexistent in their societies. . . . Consequently, numbers of the more intelligent and ambitious officers have had to be trained in industrial skills more advanced than those common to the civilian economy.

The high proportion of officers assigned to staff functions means that large numbers of officers are forced to look outside their society for their models. The fact that army leaders, particularly the younger and more ambitious, generally come from those trained in staff positions

[2] The classic discussion of the spirit of militarism as contrasted with the rational military mind is Alfred Vagts, A History of Militarism: Romance and Realities of a Profession, New York, 1937.
[3] World War II was in itself a decisive event in the birth of many of these countries and, of course, the availability of large quantities of surplus equipment and arms made it realistic to aspire to a modernized army. American military aid has contributed to making the military the most modernized element in not only recipient countries, but also in neighboring countries which have felt the need to keep up with technological advances.

means that they are extremely sensitive to the needs of modernization and technological advancement. This kind of sensitivity bears little relationship to the command of physical violence and tests of human endurance—in short, to the martial spirit as we customarily think of it. In consequence the officers often find that they are spiritually in tune with the intellectuals, students, and those other elements in society most anxious to become a part of the modern world. They may have little in common with the vast majority of the men they must command. In this respect the gap between the officer class and the troops, once largely a matter of social and economic class (as it still is to some degree), has now been widened by differences in the degree of acculturation to modern life.

It should be noted that these revolutionary changes in military life have significantly influenced the status of the military profession in different societies and hence have had an interesting effect on relative national power. Cultures that looked down on the military at an earlier stage of technology now accord high prestige to the same profession as it has raised its technology. . . .

Above all else, however, the revolution in military technology has caused the army leaders of the newly emergent countries to be extremely sensitive to the extent to which their countries are economically and technologically underdeveloped. Called upon to perform roles basic to advanced societies, the more politically conscious officers can hardly avoid being aware of the need for substantial changes in their own societies.

It might seem that those occupying positions in other modern-type organizations in underdeveloped societies would also feel much the same need for change. To whatever extent this may be so, three distinctive features of armies seem to make them somewhat more dynamic in demanding changes.

First of all, armies by nature are rival institutions in the sense that their ultimate function is the test of one against the other. All other organizations operate within the context of their own society; although their initial inspiration may have come from abroad, their primary focus is on internal developments. The civil bureaucracy, for example, can, and indeed has to, deal with its domestic problems with little regard for what other bureaucracies in other countries are doing. The soldier, however, is constantly called upon to look abroad and to compare his organization with foreign ones. He thus has a greater awareness of international standards and a greater sensitivity to weaknesses in his own society.

Second, armies for all their concern with rationality and becoming highly efficient machines are relatively immune to pragmatic tests of efficiency on a day-to-day basis. Armies are created for future contingencies, and in many underdeveloped countries these contingencies have never had to be faced. . . . Other modernized organizations in underdeveloped societies have to cope with more immediate and day-to-day problems; hence they must constantly adjust themselves to local conditions. They cannot adhere as rigidly as armies can to their Western prototypes. . . .

Finally, armies always stand at some distance from their civilian societies and are even expected to have ways of their own, including attitudes and judgments, that are remote if not completely apart from those of civilian life. Thus again armies of the newly emergent countries can feel somewhat divorced from the realities of a transitional society and focus more on the standards common to the more industrialized world. In consequence they are often unaware of the difficulties inherent in modernizing other segments of their society. Within their tradition all problems can be overcome if the right orders are given.

ARMIES AS MODERNIZING AGENTS

So much for the army as one of the more modernized of the authoritative agencies of government in transitional societies. When we consider it as a modernizing force for the whole of society, we move into a less clearly defined area where the number of relevant considerations becomes much greater and where we are likely to find greater differences from country to country. . . .

In all societies it is recognized that armies must make those who enter them into the image of the good soldier. The underdeveloped society adds a new dimension: the good soldier is also to some degree a modernized man. Thus it is that the armies in the newly emergent countries come to play key roles in the process by which traditional ways give way to more Westernized ideas and practices. The very fact that the recruit must break his ties and associations with civilian life and adjust to the more impersonal world of the army tends to emphasize the fundamental nature of this process, which involves the movement out of the particularistic relationships of traditional life and into the more impersonal and universalistic relationships of an industrialized society.

Army training is thus consistent with the direction taken by the basic process of acculturation in traditional societies. Within the army, however, the rate of acculturation is greatly accelerated. This fact contributes to the tendency of army officers to underestimate the difficulties of changing the civilian society.

Probably the most significant feature of the acculturation process as it takes place under the auspices of the army is that it provides a relatively high degree of psychological security. The experience of breaking from the known and relatively sheltered world of tradition and moving into the more unknown modern world is generally an extremely traumatic one. In contrast to the villager who is caught up in the process of being urbanized, the young army recruit from the village has the more sheltered, the more gradual introduction into the modern world. It is hardly necessary to point out the disturbing fact that the urbanization process as it has taken place in most Asian, African, and Latin-American societies has generally tended to produce a highly restless, insecure population. . . . In contrast, those who are exposed to a more technologically advanced way of life in the army find that they must make major adjustments, but that these adjustments are all treated explicitly and openly. In the army one can see what is likely to happen in terms of one's training and one's future. This is not the case in the city.

It should also be noted that the acculturative process in the army often tends to be more thorough and of a broader scope than the urbanization process. In all the main Asian cities there are those who still follow many of the habits and practices of the village. . . .

It should also be noted that the acculturative process in the army tends to be focused on acquiring technical skills that are of particular value for economic development. Just as the army represents an industrialized organization, so must those who have been trained within it learn skills and habits of mind which would be of value in other industrial organizations. . . . Army veterans in India have played an important role not only in lower-level industrial jobs, but also in managerial positions. In Malaya and the Philippines the army has been the main instrument for training people in operating and maintaining motor vehicles and other forms of machinery.

Politically the most significant feature of the process of acculturation within the army is that it usually provides some form of training in citizenship. Recruits with traditional backgrounds must learn about a new world in which they are identified with a larger political self. They learn that they stand in some definite relationship to a national community. In this sense the army experience tends to be a politicizing experience. . . .

☆　☆　☆　☆　☆

Because the army represents one of the most effective channels for upward social mobility, military-inspired nationalism often encompasses a host of personalized emotions and sentiments about civilian society. Invariably the men, and sometimes even the officers, come from extremely humble circumstances, and it is only within the army that they are first introduced to the possibility of systematically advancing themselves. In transitional societies, where people's station in life is still largely determined by birth and by chance opportunities, powerful reactions usually follow from placing people in a position where they can recognize a definite and predictable relationship between effort and reward. The practice of giving advancement on merit can encourage people, first, to see the army as a just organization deserving of their loyalties, and then possibly, to demand that the same form of justice reign throughout their society.

Those who do move up to positions of greater respect and power through the army may often carry with them hostilities toward those with greater advantages and authority in civilian society. The tendency of the military to question whether the civilian elite achieved their station by merit adds another conflict to civil-military relations in most underdeveloped countries. More often than not the military show these feelings by seeking to make national loyalty and personal sacrifice the crucial test of national leadership.

The relationship between armies and civilian leaders varies, of course, according to the circumstances of historic development. . . . Broadly speaking, however, it is helpful to distinguish three different general categories of such relationships.

There are first those patterns of development in which the military stand out because in a disrupted society they represent the only effectively organized element capable of competing for political power and formulating public policy. This situation is most likely to exist when the traditional political order, but not necessarily the traditional social order, has been violently disrupted and it becomes necessary to set up representative institutions before any of the other modern-type political organizations have been firmly established. . . .

A second category includes those countries where the military, while formally espousing the development of democracy, actually monopolizes the political arena and forces any emerging civilian elite to concentrate on economic and social activities. In many ways this arrangement is reminiscent of the Belgian variety of colonialism. At present, the most outstanding example of this form of rule is Thailand.

A third major category, which is probably the largest, consists of those countries in which the organization and structures essential to democratic government exist but have not been able to function effectively. The process of modernization has been retarded to such a point that the army, as the most modernized organization in the society, has assumed an administrative role and taken over control. In these cases there is a sense of failure in the country, and the military are viewed as possible saviors.

B. *Political Groups, Parties, and Elections*

18. TRADE UNIONISM IN AFRICA AS A FACTOR IN NATION BUILDING*

j o h n   r i d d e l l

THE GROWTH OF TRADE UNIONS IN AFRICA

. . . [T]rade unionism was a foreign implantation on African soil. It started under the era of colonialism, and although that chapter is now rapidly drawing to a close it has left some imprints which will not easily be effaced. The first trade unions were brought to Africa by European settlers—in South Africa and the Rhodesias—and were naturally patterned on those which they knew in their homelands; in the case of South Africa they were sometimes set up even as branches of British unions. French officials did the same in the west and central African colonies, as well as in North Africa, and the organic ties of these unions to the metropolitan French centres remained unchanged virtually to the end of the colonial period.

Later, when the indigenous African workers began to organise towards the end of the twenties, they not unnaturally copied these metropolitan models; in the British territories this tendency received a further impetus when the Secretary of State for the Colonies, Sidney Webb, sent a memorandum to all colonial governors in 1931 urging the introduction of legislation to give a legal basis to trade unions and to provide for their compulsory registration. Labour departments were set up in most British colonies before the outbreak of the second world war, and from 1940 onwards experienced British trade unionists were appointed to advise on the formation of trade unions. In 1937 a French decree granted recognition to trade unions in overseas territories, but membership was so hedged round with restrictions that they were virtually open only to Europeans. Full trade union freedom for the French overseas territories came, in practice as well as in theory, only with the adoption of the Overseas Labour Code in 1952.

° From "Trade Unionism in Africa as a Factor in Nation Building" by John Riddell, *Civilisations*, Vol. XII, No. 1 (1962), pp. 28–36. By permission.

TRADE UNIONISM IN AFRICA AS A FACTOR IN NATION BUILDING

✿   ✿   ✿   ✿   ✿

IMPEDIMENTS TO TRADE UNION GROWTH

The legal obstacles to the growth of indigenous trade unions . . . were removed in the French possessions south of the Sahara in 1945, although they persisted in Morocco until 1955, and in the Congo in 1957. In the British territories legal obstacles in the strict sense of the word disappeared well before the first world war, except in South Africa. This does not mean that the trade unions in all African countries have not had serious difficulties of a practical and administrative nature to surmount.

The first and most obvious difficulty is the general economic, social and cultural backwardness of the continent as a whole. So long as subsistence agriculture remains the main economic basis of any country there is clearly little scope for the growth of trade unions in the normally accepted sense of that term; in all African countries, the first unions grew up among public service and transport workers. The absence of a real economic base [1] for a strong trade union movement has not, of course, diminished the appetite of the labour 'élite' to have one; and this is a factor, no less real for being psychological in nature, which cannot be ignored. It has however led to the failure of not a few attempts to build movements from the top, without a solid basis of local cadres capable of at least keeping elementary accounts and records. Administrative provisions, such as compulsory registration and the furnishing of annual returns, while no doubt introduced with the best of motives, have also in some cases acted as a brake on the growth of trade unions in conditions of semi-literacy.

In general however the most serious obstacles to the growth of trade unions in African countries have arisen, not so much from economic, cultural or administrative causes as from political difficulties. While they assumed their most acute and spectacular form in the colonial era, these difficulties have often persisted in a modified form in the newly independent states. The relations of trade unions to governments and political parties, both before and after independence, therefore merit closer examination.

TRADE UNIONS, GOVERNMENTS AND POLITICAL PARTIES

As in all colonial countries, the trade unions of Africa became involved in the struggle for independence at a fairly early stage. While

[1] The latest available UN statistics (1958) put the total population of Africa at about 195 million, while wage and salary earners may be estimated from I.L.O. and other sources at about 9 million.

the intellectual 'élite' may have provided the political leadership, it was the unions which furnished the shock troops whenever violent clashes with colonial governments became inevitable. Unlike India, where middle-class intellectuals produced the leadership not only for the nationalist political movement but also for the trade unions (and, in fact, largely continue to do so), where in effect the trade unions were created as a labour front of the nationalist movement, in Africa the unions joined this movement in their own right and indeed sometimes provided the political leadership themselves. There is nothing very remarkable about this; it simply stems from the relative weakness or even complete absence of an indigenous bourgeoisie in most African countries south of the Sahara. Nevertheless, it is a factor which is bound to have, and indeed in some cases has already had, important effects on the political balance of forces after independence.

The situation was somewhat different in North Africa, where the native intelligentsia was far more developed. There the nationalist parties undoubtedly inspired the creation of national trade union movements. Soon after the achievement of independence, however, there took place a polarisation of forces in the Moroccan nationalist party, the Istiqlal, which . . . led to a split in that party and to the formation of a splinter trade union centre; the *Union Marocaine du Travail* now forms the backbone of the opposition party, the *Union Nationale des Forces Populaires*, which is committed to a policy of radical social reform. One effect of this split on the U.M.T. has been that it has frequently been subject to official interference in the course of its legitimate trade union activities, and has twice had to appeal for the intervention of the International Confederation of Free Trade Unions. In Tunisia, a similar split threatened in 1956 when the *Union Générale Tunisienne du Travail* adopted a programme entailing structural changes in the economy, which clashed with the more pragmatic approach of the Neo-Destour Party. For a time the U.G.T.T. was actually split, but thanks to the statesmanship of President Bourguiba the integrity of the party was maintained. The final outcome was that the former general secretary of the U.G.T.T., Ahmed Ben Salah, joined the government, while the leadership of the labour organisation passed to a man who had sprung from the ranks of the workers, Ahmed Tlili.

It would be extremely rash to attempt any forecast of possible similar developments in the independent Algeria which now seems on the point of emerging after seven years of blood and tears. What can be said for certain is that the *Union Générale des Travailleurs Algériens*, whose members have borne the brunt of the struggle, has a programme of radical social reform very similar to those of the U.M.T. and the U.G.T.T. Whether that programme will in some form or other become government policy, as in Tunisia, or whether it is destined to form the platform of a future opposition, as in Morocco, is a question which only the future can answer.

In French-speaking Africa south of the Sahara the position is far too complex to attempt to describe it here in any detail. The salient fact is that, in face of the highly centralised, presidential types of government which have generally emerged, the trade union movement has so far been too disunited to be able to exert the influence which it might otherwise expect to enjoy. The tragedy is that the grounds of dissension, when not purely personal, have related mostly to ideological and religious differences which have little or no bearing on the economic and social problems facing these countries. It is to be hoped that the continental unity recently achieved at the Dakar conference . . . between free and democratic unions of varying outlook from all parts of Africa may eventually be translated into practice at the national level too. The monolithic unity which apparently characterises the trade unions of Guinea—and of Ghana, too, for that matter—is more illusory than real, having been imposed by the ruling party. Revealing gaps were torn in this façade recently in both countries by widespread strike movements which the national trade union centres were unable to control and which were suppressed only by drastic police measures.

As for the other English-speaking West African countries, the situation in Nigeria is rather similar to that in the French speaking: lack of unity has deprived an otherwise strong movement of much of its potential influence. It is interesting to note that the federal government itself took the initiative in seeking to effect a reconciliation some months ago, but this failed owing to the insistence of the Nigerian Trade Union Congress faction on disaffiliation from international organisations as a prior condition.[2] Sierra Leone is probably unique in West Africa as the only country which has managed to keep a united trade union movement from the outset.

It could be that one of the reasons for the general lack of unity in the movements of both English- and French-speaking West Africa is that independence has been achieved there in the main by peaceful means and that the centrifugal tendencies inherent in any democratic society have consequently had full play. Whatever the reasons, the long-term test of the maturity of the African trade union movement will be its ability to achieve unity on a democratic basis and without recourse to totalitarian methods: a dictum which is equally valid, of course, for some highly developed European countries.

In the British territories of East and Central Africa the trade unions have, as elsewhere, been closely associated with national independence

[2] How serious this condition was may be judged from the fact that, when it was posed, several N.T.U.C. leaders had just returned from a World Federation of Trade Unions world congress in Moscow.

movements from an early stage in their existence. Although in no terri-tory were the unions ever banned as such, many of their leaders and active members fell foul of the authorities, and normal activities were brought to a halt indirectly through the operation of emergency regula-tions in times of exceptional tension. This was the case in Kenya during the Mau Mau uprising which started in 1952, and in Nyasaland and the Rhodesias in 1959 during the agitation against the Central African Federation, which was, and still is, considered by the African national-ists in those territories as a device for perpetuating colonial rule. Other-wise relations were as amicable as might be expected between govern-ments and trade unions which were eager not only to secure substantial wage rises for their members (many of whom happened to be govern-ment employees), but also to take over the functions of government itself at the earliest convenient opportunity. As for the latter ambition the British government from about 1959 onwards did not go out of its way actively to discourage it; on the contrary, it appointed trade union leaders to some of the commissions and conferences set up to formulate recommendations on the terms and timing of self-government and inde-pendence.[3] And in the first East African territory to achieve self-government, Tanganyika, the general secretary of the Tanganyika Fed-eration of Labour, Rashidi Kawawa, was appointed minister for local government and housing in 1960, and later deputy prime minister; shortly after the achievement of full independence at the end of last year, he replaced Julius Nyerere as prime minister.

⟨✿⟩

[3] The late Lawrence Katilungu, then president of the Northern Rhodesian TUC and of its African Mineworkers' Union was a member of the Monckton Commission on the future of Central African Federation; Tom Mboya, general secretary of the Kenya Federation of Labour is a member of the present London constitutional conference on the future of Kenya (March 1962).

19.   *THE NEW MIDDLE CLASS**

m a n f r e d   h a l p e r n

In our unproductive search for middle classes in underdeveloped areas, the fault has been in our expectations. We have taken too parochial a view of the structure of the middle class. A study of both Western and non-Western historical experience suggests that the British and American middle classes, which have commonly been considered prototypes, were actually special cases. Moreover, with the growing scope and scale of modern enterprises and institutions, the majority of the middle class even in the United States and Great Britain is no longer composed of men whose independence is rooted in their possession of productive private property. Bureaucratic organization has become the characteristic structure of business (or charity or trade unions) no less than of government, and the majority of the middle class is now salaried. They may be managers, administrators, teachers, engineers, journalists, scientists, lawyers, or army officers. A similar salaried middle class constitutes the most active political, social, and economic sector from Morocco to Pakistan.

Leadership in all areas of Middle Eastern life is increasingly being seized by a class of men inspired by non-traditional knowledge, and it is being clustered around a core of salaried civilian and military politicians, organizers, administrators, and experts.[1] In its style of life, however, this new middle class differs from its counterpart in the industrialized states. The Middle East moved into the modern administrative age before it reached the machine age. Its salaried middle class attained

---

* From Manfred Halpern, *The Politics of Social Change in the Middle East and North Africa*, pp. 51–67. Reprinted by permission of the Princeton University Press. Copyright © 1963 by The RAND Corporation.

[1] For example, when Tunisia became independent in 1956 under the leadership of the Neo-Destour Party, a party controlled almost entirely by the new middle class, the election for a Constituent Assembly rewarded this class in the following way: To fill 98 seats, the country voted for 18 teachers and professors, 15 lawyers, 11 civil servants, 5 doctors, 4 pharmacists, 2 journalists, 2 commercial employees, 1 engineer, 1 appraiser, 5 workers, 17 farmers, and 17 businessmen and contractors. By contrast, every Middle Eastern parliament prior to 1950, except that of Turkey, contained a majority of landowners and a minority of professional men and industrialists.

power before it attained assurance of status, order, security, or prosperity. In the Middle East, the salaried new middle class therefore uses its power not to defend order and property but to create them—a revolutionary task that is being undertaken so far without any final commitment to any particular system of institutions.

This new salaried class is impelled by a driving interest in ideas, action, and careers. It is not merely interested in ideas: its members are not exclusively intellectuals, and, being new to the realm of modern ideas and eager for action and careers, they may not be intellectuals at all. Neither are they interested only in action that enhances their power: they also share a common commitment to the fashioning of opportunities and institutions that will provide careers open to all who have skills. This involves them in actions quite novel to their society, and hence also distinguishes them from previous politicians. They are not concerned merely with safe careers. They know that, without new ideas and new actions dealing with the backwardness and conflicts of their society, careers will not open or remain secure. The men of this new class are therefore committed ideologically to nationalism and social reform.

Obviously, there is also a part of the new middle class that has neither deep convictions nor understanding. In contrast to the dominant strata of its class, this segment excludes itself from the process of making political choices, and hence does not alter the present analysis. It is also true that some members of the new middle class are interested only in ideas (hence inspire and clarify, or merely stand by), only in action (hence rise spectacularly and fall), or only in safe careers (hence merely serve). Among the last, clerks especially compose the largest yet relatively most passive segment of the new middle class. Our analysis focuses on men interested in ideas, action, and careers because such a description fits the most influential core of this group.

There are also opportunists among them but, by now, of two different kinds which are often confused by those who are taken advantage of. There is the politician who, largely for the sake of satisfying the aspirations of his new middle class constituency and so also staying in power, takes advantage of whatever opportunities may offer, east or west, at home or abroad. There is also the free-floating opportunist—Stendhal's novels describe him very well for a period in French history when values and institutions were similarly in doubt—who represents no one but himself, but represents himself exceedingly well, being loyal only to the art of survival. Some sell their skills as political brokers; some come close to selling their country. In the twentieth century it has become essential, however, to be able to distinguish between those, however perverse they may appear, who are out to gain greater elbowroom for the new middle class they represent and those, however smooth, who also make deals because they can fashion no connections unless they continually sell themselves.

In the Middle East, this salaried new middle class assumes a far more important role than the local property-owning middle class. Although the latter is about as numerous as that portion of the new middle class which is actually employed,[2] it has far less power than the salaried group. Neither in capital, organization, nor skills do the merchants and middlemen control anything comparable to that power which can be mustered by the machinery of the state and hence utilized by the new salaried class. In this part of the world, no other institutions can mobilize as much power and capital as those of the state. By controlling the state in such a strategic historical period, this new salaried class has the capabilities to lead the quest for the status, power, and prosperity of middle-class existence by ushering in the machine age.[3]

In the West, a variety of organizational structures and devices—both governmental and private—have gradually made individual entrepreneurship a rare commodity. Stock companies, subsidies, insurance, tariffs, as well as large governmental, business, and union bureaucracies have served, among other things, to reduce individual risk and enlarge institutional predictability. The pressures that make for organization and organization men are much more desperate in the Middle East. In most of the countries of this region, there are few important jobs in the modern sector of the economy available outside the large organizations and institutions that constitute, or are guided by, government. Those who cannot get into them or cannot hold on to them usually count for little, and often cannot make a living. For most there is little hope for safety or prosperity in separate personal endeavors. Indeed, more organization is urgently needed for aggregating separate interests, bargaining among them, and executing a common will.

[2] In this analysis, the term "new middle class" excludes the property owning middle class. However, it includes both those who are now drawing salaries and a far larger group—a "would-be new middle class" which resembles this class in every respect except that it is unemployed. The "would-be" salariat is discussed in greater detail in the next section of this chapter.

❖   ❖   ❖   ❖   ❖

[3] The present work is not the first to notice the emergence of this new class in underdeveloped areas. Professor T. Cuyler Young, drawing in part on his experiences as Political Attaché at the American Embassy in Tehran during 1951–1952, was the first to publish an analysis of the role of the new middle class in the Middle East in "The Social Support of Current Iranian Policy," *Middle East Journal*, Spring 1952, pp. 125–143. Professor John J. Johnson was the first to suggest that in Latin America "the urban middle groups are vitally, if not decisively, important in an area where one still commonly hears and reads that there is no middle class to speak of [and] where, in the view of traditional scholarship, individuals hold the center of the stage." (*Political Change in Latin America: The Emergence of the Middle Sectors*, Stanford, 1958, pp. vii–ix.)

❖   ❖   ❖   ❖   ❖

POLITICAL SYSTEMS

The intelligentsia, that is, those with knowledge or awareness to see that a social and political revolution is in progress, form the largest and politically most active component of the new middle class. But they are not the only component of this class. Some members of this new class are already middle class in their pattern of consumption but still searching for ideas (hence new in a society once sure of its truths). Others are interested only in ideas about means and not, like the intelligentsia, also about ends, and the concern for truth of the intellectuals does not interest them. The intelligentsia, however, is the predominant force of this class, in part because its knowledge inescapably exposes the weakness or irrelevance of tradition. . . .

○   ○   ○   ○   ○

In the Middle East (as in other rapidly changing, underdeveloped societies) the new intelligentsia acts in behalf of the older ruling classes only until it is strong enough to win control of the government. When this occurs, however, the intelligentsia no longer remains socially unattached but acts in the interests of the new middle class of which it is an integral part. It cannot preserve the privileges of the older ruling classes if it hopes to propel any Middle Eastern country into the modern age. Similarly, it cannot offer the immediate rewards sought by workers and peasants, because its plans for the modernization of the country call for mobilization of the underlying population for new roles and productive sacrifices.

In the Middle East, . . . the new middle class springs largely, though not exclusively, from groups that had not hitherto been important, and hence had more reason and less deadweight to take advantage of new knowledge and skills. . . .

○   ○   ○   ○   ○

Unlike the traditional elite of landowners and trading bourgeoisie or the tradition-bound artisans or peasants, it is . . . the first class in the Middle East that is wholly the product of the transition to the modern age. Unlike the emergent new generation of peasants and urban workers, it is already powerful and self-conscious enough to undertake the task of remolding society.

The new middle class has been able to act as a separate and independent force because: (1) prior to its seizure of power, it is freer than any other class from traditional bonds and preconceptions, and better equipped to manipulate armies and voluntary organizations as revolutionary political instruments; (2) once it controls the machinery of a modernizing state, it possesses a power base superior to that which any other class in the Middle East can muster on the basis of prestige, property, or physical force; (3) it is numerically one of the largest groups within the modern sector of society; (4) it is, so far, more obviously cohesive, more self-conscious, and better trained than any other class; (5) its political, economic, and social actions, in so far as they come to grips with social change, are decisive in determining the role other classes will play in the future; and (6) it has shown itself capable of marshalling mass support. Wherever the salaried new middle class has become dominant in the Middle East, it has become the chief locus of political and economic power and of social prestige. There are few classes anywhere in the world of which this much can be said.[4]

✿   ✿   ✿   ✿   ✿

. . . An elite in power, whatever the social class from which it springs, faces problems and temptations in the very business of maintaining itself in power which will often distinguish it from those who have the same hopes and interests but not the same responsibilities. Membership in a particular social class is by no means the sole determinant of policy decisions. Differences in political choices among members of the new middle class, however, also reflect differences among the strata of that class and the variant character of its class consciousness.

Such differences are real enough, but they usually become polit-

---

[4] Hence we cannot accept the Marxist idea that the intelligentsia, since it does not start from an economic base of its own, is unable to act in its own interest but must ally itself with one class or another. In areas like the Middle East, Soviet analysts have talked about a "national bourgeoisie," composed of local industrialists, merchants, and bankers, a "lower middle class" which employs little or no outside labor, an "intelligentsia" of students and clerks, even a "military intelligentsia." (See Walter Z. Laqueur, "The 'National Bourgeoisie,' A Soviet Dilemma in the Middle East," *International Affairs*, July 1959, pp. 324–331.) They have failed to perceive, however, the central role of the class which contains such men as Ataturk, Nasser, Kassim, and Bourguiba and which not only leads the nationalist revolution, but is the harbinger and architect of a decisive change in the social structure of the Middle East.

There are fundamental reasons for this failure of recognition. Perceptively, the Marxist philosopher Georg Lukacs has noted: "In such periods of transition, society is not dominated by any system of production. . . . In these circumstances it is, of course, impossible to speak of the operation of any economic laws which would govern the entire society. . . . There is a condition of acute struggle for power or of a latent balance of power . . . : the old law is no longer valid and the new law is not yet generally valid." He adds, "As far as I know, the theory of historical materialism has not yet confronted this problem from an economic perspective." (*Geschichte und Klassenbewusstsein*, Berlin, 1923, pp. 243 and 249.) As far as the present author is aware, this vacuum remains.

ically important only after the new middle class has achieved power. Earlier, all its members normally concentrate on the battle for power, mobility, and status in order to open up the controlling positions in society and administration. Soon after the triumph of the new middle class, however, it becomes apparent that there is simply not room for all of them—that some will be "in" and most will be "out." It also becomes clear that, although they are agreed on the need for the transformation of their society, they are not of the same mind as to what to do with their historical opportunity.[5]

Such differences, however, are never merely political, or merely social, or merely economic. All three realms are entwined as, for example, in one of the most profound of all tensions within the new middle class—between those who are salaried and those who would be like them but are not. Only a minority of the Middle East's new middle class actually holds jobs and draws salaries. The rest either can find no jobs consonant with their skills and values, or else work for status quo regimes which deny this group status and power. It would be quite misleading to exclude the "would-be" new middle class from this middle class. Both components of the middle class possess modern rather than traditional knowledge, and both are eager for a forced march into the modern age. Both are striving for the status, power, order, and prosperity that ought to go with middle-class existence. They resemble each other in every respect except success. This would-be middle class will therefore enlist itself in any movement that promises the kind of education that creates modern skills, the kind of job that opens a career, and the kind of action that gives a mere career individual rewards and social importance.

The inclusion of this group among the new middle class may be unexpected to those who restrict themselves to the classical economic definition of classes. In areas like the Middle East, however, where a modern economy is still to be created, and where control over the state and the forces of social change is more potent than ownership of property, property relations alone cannot serve to define class relations. In the midst of a profound transformation of society, it would also be quite wrong to define a social class statically, in terms of occupation, or employment at a particular moment in time. Each class must be defined in terms of its political, social, and economic role in the process of social change. In the present instance, that means taking account of all who either already perform the role of a member of the salaried middle class or who are bent by revolutionary action, if necessary, to gain a chance to perform this role and no other.

o   o   o   o   o

[5] At such a point, the intelligentsia may well split again and speak for different competing factions within the new middle class—another reason why it is not possible to use "intelligentsia" and "new middle class" interchangeably.

Partially overlapping the distinction between the working and job-less sections of the new middle class is the difference between the younger and older members of this class. "Youth" is not a passing phase in this region where half of all the people are under 20 years old, and where population grows so quickly and opportunities so slowly. In this situation men in their forties may still have almost all the naïveté of youth—being untouched by careers, status, and power—yet have none of youth's innocence, for they know what they have missed.

The plight of youth is obvious when the elite is recruited only from traditional classes. This plight is not resolved when the new middle class comes into its own. Initially, it grows worse. Those who have arrived often come to the top in their thirties (Ataturk, Nasser) or their forties (Kassim, Ayub). What they do can have more far-reaching results in the lives of their people than the actions of any preceding government. Yet almost all of them become authoritarians who do not intend to relinquish the reins of power until they die. Nor do members of the leading echelon of administrators and directors in government, business, journalism, schools, etc. mean to depart before the particular head of state to whom they owe their position. The older group of nationalists often learned patience and perseverance in the long struggle for power when a foreign state could always be made to bear the blame for the postponement of success. The younger men now find no target for their frustration except their own ruling elite.

✺   ✺   ✺   ✺   ✺

The sharp and often bitter competition among members of the new middle class, however, does not inhibit the acquisition of a common historical awareness that each of them suffers from the same burden of the past and the same frustrations of the present. In the very fact of their separate individuality lies the essence of their common fate.[6] Coming into being by influx from all social classes—uniting the Western-educated son of a landlord with the army-trained son of a postmaster—the new middle class is the first in Middle Eastern history for whom family connections can no longer help automatically to establish class membership. Also, being itself composed of new men, it is the first which cannot hope to rest on inherited status or existing opportunities. It is the first class for whom communication depends on successful persuasion of

---

[6] Some may concentrate on preserving their status, some on enlarging it, others on attaining it. Such competition, however, does not touch their class membership. Separate individuals, to amend only slightly a formulation by Karl Marx (*The German Ideology*, New York, 1938, p. 49), form a class only in so far as they play a common role in relation to social change, and have to carry on a common battle against another class or seek collaboration with it. Otherwise, they may be on hostile terms with each other as competitors.

other individuals; it cannot base itself on the implicit consensus of the past. The new middle class is distinguishable from all other classes in the Middle East by being the first to be composed of separate individuals. It is therefore also the first class for which the choice between democracy, authoritarianism, and totalitarianism is a real and open choice.

⚬〰⚬

20. POLITICAL PARTIES IN LATIN AMERICA*

robert j. alexander

THE NATURE OF THE MODERN PARTIES

The kind of political party that has evolved in Latin America since World War I differs fundamentally from the parties of the first century of independence. It is an organization with reasonably well-defined programs and ideologies. The various parties represent the widest spectrum of political philosophy. Often they are organizations representing or seeking to represent the interests of particular groups within the evolving society. It is upon the basis of their ideologies, platforms, and programs, and their appeals to special interest groups, rather than on the grounds of allegiance to a particular political leader, that they recruit their membership.

The new political party in Latin America also has a much more intensive internal life than did the older kind. It has local organizations throughout the country conducting activities of their own most of the year and not merely on the eve of an election or in the morning after a *coup d'état.* They hold periodic membership meetings. They gather for regular local, regional, and national conventions, and they do so even when no election or other change in government is in the offing.

* From "The Emergence of Modern Political Parties in Latin America" by Robert J. Alexander in *The Politics of Change in Latin America* edited by Joseph Maier and Richard W. Weatherhead, Frederick A. Praeger, Inc., Publishers, New York, 1964. Selections from pp. 103–122. By permission.

These parties involve relatively large numbers of citizens drawn from various classes. They often carry on organized activities within the ranks of labor unions, professional associations, and other non-political groups. Many support a variety of periodicals and publish pamphlets and even books. Some have organized groups within them to carry on a continuous study of the economic and social problems of their countries— regardless of whether they are, at the moment, in the government or in the opposition. These studies may form the basis for policy and be published. Sometimes, though by no means always, the parties collect dues from their members and issue membership cards or other means of identifying those who belong.

Finally, the new parties are *civilista*. Although they have certainly not completely eschewed political cooperation with groups among the military (including participation in *coups d'état*), such contacts tend to be circumstantial and temporary, and their attention is centered on political action in the civilian field. Generally they seek, at least in principle, to keep the military out of politics.

TYPOLOGY OF PARTIES

There are many possible ways of analyzing the types of organizations that we have included under the heading of "new" or "modern" political parties in Latin America. We shall divide them here into three basic groups, each with its own subgroupings.

There are, first of all, the old traditional parties, which have been able to adapt themselves and their programs to the changing circumstances, the Conservatives and the Liberals.

Secondly, there are the parties of more recent origin following or seeking to follow European models. They include the Radicals, Socialists, Christian Democrats, Fascists, and the Communists and their splinters.

Finally, there are what may be called the indigenous parties of change, which have developed in recent decades. This type may be subdivided into what we shall call the national revolutionary parties and the personalist revolutionary parties.

✥   ✥   ✥   ✥   ✥

THE TRADITIONAL PARTIES

In most of Latin America, the traditional parties of the nineteenth century have ceased to be a major factor in political life or have disappeared altogether. . . .

Only in Honduras, Nicaragua, Colombia, and Uruguay are the traditional parties still the dominant competitors for power, and even in these nations, as we shall see, the Liberals and Conservatives have greatly changed in character. In Panama, Ecuador, Chile, Argentina, and Paraguay, they still have an important role in national politics, but they share the stage with more recent parties.

In countries where the traditional parties have maintained a foothold in the political arena, they have done so at the cost of a radical change in outlook. They have adapted themselves to changing circumstances by appealing to particular interest groups and by modifying their programs and methods of action.

The Conservatives

Where the Conservatives continue to be a factor of importance, they are, in most cases, the party of the large landowning class engaged in a rear-guard struggle to maintain its privileges, or, as the Partido Blanco in Uruguay, the spokesmen of the rural areas against the encroaching power of the cities. Their voting strength in Ecuador and Chile comes largely from the ability of landlords to march their tenants and agricultural workers off to the polls to vote for Conservative Party candidates.

However, even in the Conservative parties, the "winds of change" have not failed to leave things untouched. Generally, the Conservatives are no longer distinguished principally as supporters of the secular power of the Church. . . .

❖   ❖   ❖   ❖   ❖

The Liberals

With the exception of Chile and Nicaragua, the Liberal parties have become the spokesmen for important new segments of the population that have arisen in the wake of the economic and social revolution in Latin America. Thus the Liberal parties of Colombia, Honduras, and Ecuador are the principal political vehicle for the urban workers employed in factories and modern transportation, public utility, and agricultural enterprises. In Colombia and Honduras especially, the influence of the Liberal politicians is extensive within the organized labor movement itself.

❖   ❖   ❖   ❖   ❖

Many of the newer-style political parties which during the last two generations have challenged the Conservatives and Liberals were patterned after European models. These include at least one Radical Party roughly similar to the Parti Radical Socialiste of France, various Socialist parties, the Christian Democrats, the Fascists, and the Communists of various shades.

The emergence of European-patterned groups reflects the impact of Old World ideas on Latin America. In not a few cases, immigrants from Europe sought to establish in their new countries the kind of political organizations with which they had been familiar at home. As was perhaps inevitable, most parties took on their own characteristics. At times they moved far from the original European pattern.

The Radicals

The oldest of these European-oriented parties is undoubtedly the Partido Radical of Chile. It was established in the last decades of the nineteenth century as a left-wing offshoot of the Liberals. Like its counterpart in France, the Radical Party of Chile has been the typical expression of the middle class. At first a favorite among artisans and small shopkeepers, it subsequently became the party of the white-collar class, particularly the government bureaucracy.

Like the French Radicals, too, the Chilean party has oscillated violently in political philosophy and orientation. At times proclaiming themselves as socialists, they have at other times participated in Conservative government coalitions. Although they consider themselves to be of the left, they have more truly been the fulcrum of national politics, determining at any given instant whether the left or the right was to have the majority in Congress and even in public opinion.

☼   ☼   ☼   ☼   ☼

The Socialists

The Socialists were among the first political groups on the Latin American scene to advocate a fundamental transformation of their economies and societies. During the 1860's, 1870's, and 1880's, numerous immigrants who had been active in the First International and the first

European Socialist parties found their way to America. They established small groups, and some of them sought affiliation with the International. Although most of them remained relatively isolated from the political life of the Latin American countries, a few became nuclei around which Socialist parties were organized.

    ◦   ◦   ◦   ◦   ◦

Unfortunately, most of the Socialist parties of Latin America have abandoned the camp of Democratic Socialism. In some cases, they have been heavily infiltrated or influenced by the local Communist parties. In most instances, they have adopted xenophobic nationalist positions that have made them violently anti-United States and pro-Soviet. Only the Argentine Social Democratic Party and the Ecuadorean Socialist Party have remained more or less loyal to the ideas they originally espoused.

The Christian Democrats

The Christian Democrats are a relatively new type of party in Latin America. They reflect the emergence of a more socially conscious wing of the Roman Catholic Church, a phenomenon produced largely since World War II. Although the Uruguayan Unión Cívica and the Chilean Falange Nacional antedate the war, all of the others have emerged subsequently.

The Christian Democrats find their philosophical inspiration in the principal papal encyclicals on social problems: *Rerum Novarum*, *Quadregesimo Anno*, and *Mater et Magistra*. Although their main constituency is found among the middle class, they have in a number of instances successfully sought to gain influence in the organized labor and peasant movements. They are strong advocates of basic social and economic change. The quality of their leadership is generally high. They include among their ranks some of the outstanding intellectuals of the region, particularly those of the younger generation.

The three most important Christian Democratic parties are those of Uruguay, Chile, and Venezuela. . . .

    ◦   ◦   ◦   ◦   ◦

The Latin American Christian Democrats regard themselves as counterparts of the European parties of the same name. They all belong to the Christian Democratic International. In a congress of the International in Santiago de Chile in August, 1961, the Venezuelan and

Chilean parties sponsored a successful resolution urging a general alliance between Christian Democrats and other parties of the democratic left in Latin America.

The Fascists

The European totalitarians have had counterparts in Latin America as well. There were Fascist parties in a number of Latin American countries, particularly in the 1930's and 1940's, when fascism was at its apogee internationally. In Brazil and Chile, the Fascists, known respectively as Integralistas and Nacistas, were for some years parties of considerable consequence. They had all the trappings of their European brethren, including uniformed storm troopers and anti-Semitism. With the international defeat of fascism, the Chilean Partido Nacista disappeared, but the Brazilian Integralistas transformed themselves into the Partido de Representação Popular, which in its new form has tried to eschew its Fascist past.

❖   ❖   ❖   ❖   ❖

The Communists and Their Splinters

Among the European-patterned parties there are, finally, the Communists. There is now a Communist Party in every Latin American country. Some of them date from the early years of the Comintern, others arose in the 1940's and 1950's. Generally, the Latin American Communist parties follow the pattern of such organizations in other parts of the world. Over the years they have had two basic objectives: to serve the purposes of the Soviet Union and to establish the when and where of possible dictatorships of their own parties. They have followed faithfully the zigs and zags of the international Communist line.

The nature of the Communist appeal has varied from time to time. Generally, they have sought to picture themselves as the only real advocates of social change in Latin America and as the only true defenders of the working class. They have consistently pointed to the Soviet Union and other Communist countries as models that the Latin American nations should follow, first in terms of social revolution and more recently in terms of rapid economic development. In recent decades, they have sought to make the utmost use of nationalism and to turn it especially against the United States.

Until the advent of the Castro regime in Cuba, the Communists in most Latin American countries were little more than nuisance groups. Since 1959, however, they have achieved new importance. Their support of Castro has opened wider fields of contact with other political groups and has removed them from their almost complete isolation of the 1950's. The Castro phenomenon has also made the Communists more willing to use methods of violent insurrection and guerrilla war than they had been during most of their history. Moreover, the Cuban Revolution has sharpened the issue of social and economic revolution in Latin America. Thus, it has created a wider audience for the Communists' propaganda that only their particular totalitarian way would provide the kind of rapid change that the situation demanded.

¤   ¤   ¤   ¤   ¤

THE INDIGENOUS PARTIES OF CHANGE

In addition to the parties that derived their ideological and programmatic inspiration from Europe, there are two groups of parties that have grown out of the changing situation in Latin America itself: the national revolutionary parties and the personalist revolutionary parties.

The National Revolutionary Parties

The single most important group of democratic political parties in Latin America are the national revolutionaries. They have grown out of the particular circumstances of their countries. Because of the similarity of problems in various Latin American nations, however, they have tended to adopt broadly similar ideologies and programs. They include the Acción Democrática of Venezuela, the APRA Party of Peru, the Liberación Nacional of Costa Rica, the Movimiento Nacionalista Revolucionario of Bolivia, the Febrerista Party of Paraguay, the Partido Revolucionario Dominicano, and the Partido Popular Democrático of Puerto Rico. The Partido Revolucionario Institucional of Mexico might also be placed in this category.

These parties present in their platforms a program for the democratic transformation of their particular countries and of Latin America as a whole. They advocate an agrarian reform adapted to the specific needs of their respective nations. They favor extensive social and labor legislation and the development of strong trade union and peasant movements under democratic leadership. They are nationalist without being xenophobic. They seek to bring the key elements of their countries' national economies into the hands of local citizens or the national government. While not rejecting foreign investment, they seek to establish conditions for its entry that will not compromise their national sovereignty. They favor mixed economies, with the government performing the key function of stimulating and directing rapid economic development. Above all, they stand for the firm establishment of political democracy.

In recent years the national revolutionary parties have borne the responsibility of government in Mexico, Bolivia, Venezuela, Puerto Rico, the Dominican Republic, and Costa Rica. To be sure, conditions have varied considerably in each case. In general, however, these nations have been in the vanguard in Latin America because of their insistence on effecting basic social revolution through democratic means. . . .

☼   ☼   ☼   ☼   ☼

All the national revolutionary parties recognize a kinship among themselves. On several occasions they have held international conferences. They have joined with some of the more advanced liberal parties to establish an Institute of Political Education in Costa Rica for the training of second-rank leaders, and they have lent moral support to one another in moments of great crisis.

Personalist Revolutionary Parties

The second category of indigenous parties consists of two organizations, the Partido Peronista of Argentina and the Partido Trabalhista Brasileiro (PTB). These two parties are similar in origin and are likely to evolve in somewhat similar directions in the years immediately ahead.

Both were organized by socially minded dictators, Juan Perón and Getúlio Vargas. In both instances, they were designed as vehicles for organizing working-class support for the dictators and their tenure in power.

Since the disappearance of their founders—Perón is in exile and Vargas committed suicide—the parties have seemingly taken different directions. Yet, there is good reason to believe that they may both end up in the camp of the national revolutionary parties.

☼   ☼   ☼   ☼   ☼

THE DECLINE OF PERSONALISM

This review of the complex network of political parties in Latin America has indicated the key role they play in civic affairs. Among the many effects they have had on the traditional political structure and behavior, one of the most important has been that of diminishing the influence of "personalism" in Latin American politics.

Traditionally, Latin American politics have been viewed only in terms of the conflicting ambitions of rival leaders. During much of the nineteenth and early twentieth centuries, there was considerable justification for such a viewpoint. However, the emergence of political parties of the various types we have noted has been a principal factor in converting politics into something a good deal more complex than a game between personal rivals.

It would be foolish to maintain that leadership is a matter of no importance in the present parties. Particular individuals have played exceedingly important parts in determining the orientation of the older parties and bringing into existence the newer ones. . . . The fact remains, however, that the purpose of these parties is not to advance the fortunes of these men, nor will the parties disappear if they pass from the scene. The parties we have discussed were organized by groups of individuals, not by a single leader, and they were established to advocate and carry out a program.

21. THE POLITICAL BEHAVIOUR OF THE INDIAN PUBLIC*

s a m u e l j. e l d e r s v e l d

Scholars of "developing societies", such as India is, constantly emphasize the interrelationship between political, social and economic change. Theoretically, at least, what happens in the sphere of politics is intimately related to social and economic development. Political behaviour sets the limits and provides the political context for social change. It also

* From "The Political Behaviour of the Indian Public" by Samuel J. Eldersveld, Monthly Public Opinion Survey, Vol. IX, No. 4 (1964), pp. 3–9. By permission of The Indian Institute of Public Opinion Private Ltd.

helps explain why the social and economic development which takes place occurs in the form and at the time it does. A "development crisis" is presumably, therefore, as political as it is social or economic. This thesis may be argued at length. But certainly no one, not even the most extreme advocates of the irrelevance of politics, would deny that the political culture and behaviour patterns of a society have to be taken into account by the development planners, or that the political actions of the public in a changing society contribute much to the success or failure of the most beautifully conceived economic and social plans.

The surveys which the Indian Institute of Public Opinion has conducted in the past ten years provide a beginning empirical base for the type of analysis suggested above. Unfortunately, most of our research on developing societies is not "developmental". That is, if there is empirical research at all, it consists primarily of research at one point in time. What is needed is sound "historical" or "longitudinal" analysis which permits generalisation about the society at various stages at its development, and which is able to determine to what extent the society is moving towards political or social or economic goals. Such systematic data over time usually cannot be retrieved. In the Indian case, from the middle 1950's on at least, data are available on the political behaviour patterns of the Indian people. . . .

     ✿   ✿   ✿   ✿   ✿

THE PERVASIVENESS OF POLITICAL INTEREST

In a developing society, such as India, operating as it does on democratic premises, one may argue that political leadership needs an increasingly larger and broadly-based "attentive public" which is informed about public policy, concerned about it, and willing to be at least minimally active in the political arena. Such a public need not be very large at the outset; indeed, it would be unrealistic to expect it to be large. (Even in modernized societies this attentive public does not include even 50% of the public.) But though not large, it should be fairly representative of the social spectrum and its existence as an "interest section" should give the influential political elite both a motivation and opportunity for political communication, as well as provide a meaningful forum for criticism about governmental policy. . . .

There is a basic potential of political interest in the Indian public which appears to have been relatively prevalent already in 1955 and has shown signs of deepening and expanding. **The Institute's data from two of its studies, which approached this problem in an identical manner,**

POLITICAL SYSTEMS

suggest that up to a third of the Indian public is interested in public affairs (See Table 1). In 1961, over 40 per cent of the urban public manifested an interest in politics, compared to 34% of the rural public. And this percentage was a clear increase in both cases over the level of admitted political interest two years previously, in 1959. It is also a percentage which, if substantiated by adequate proportions of political knowledge and actual involvement, is not too dissimilar from political interest levels which studies in a country like the United States have documented. In fact, many scholars are willing to take the position that an attentive public of one-third or two-fifths is probably optimal for democratic support and social change in modern political systems.

TABLE 1

Levels of Political Interest

(Do you take an interest in political matters? % "Yes")

Particular Social Groups

	Urban	Rural	Illiterates Urban	Illiterates Rural	Age Group 21-35 Urban	Age Group 21-35 Rural	Income Groups Rs. 1—100 Urban	Income Groups Rs. 1—100 Rural	Income Groups 350+Rupees Urban	Income Groups 350+Rupees Rural
1959 Study	32.1	28.9	6.4	10.2	38.2	33.3	25.2	24.1	65.3	57.7
1961 Study	43.7	33.9	8.1	12.1	46.1	36.5	26.5	25.2	58.6	62.2

One may become somewhat more worried about the level of political interest in particular subsectors of Indian society. Thus, as Table 1 reveals, the lowest educational and income classes have a relatively low proportion of politically interested citizens. The illiterates are a particular cause for concern, since they represent over 50 per cent of the Indian public. The fact that less than 10 per cent of the illiterates in urban areas say they are interested in politics is indeed significant, and dysfunctional to the development of political self-consciousness among the Indian people. The rural illiterates are slightly more interested, surprisingly enough. The same observation is not true, however, for those at the lowest economic levels—fully one-fourth of those making less than 100 rupees a month (less than 22) are interested in politics; this is true also of those who are in the "blue collar" working class (the skilled and unskilled urban workers, the agricultural labourers, and the unemployed), 22% of whom were politically interested in 1959, compared to 43% of those in the higher "white collar" occupational brackets. Above all, it is interesting to note that political interest is increasing among almost all of these social groups. (The only exception is the urban wealthy who professed less interest in 1961.) It seems, then, that the body of potential politically interested citizens is sizable enough, partially inclusive of major social groups, and revealing an accentuation of potential attention rather than a decline in such attention.

TYPES AND CORRELATES OF POLITICAL ACTIVITY

Political activity beyond the mere assertion of interest in politics is, as one would expect, lower. But, if one takes into consideration the particular forms of political participation which are prevalent in the Indian environment, they cannot be considered low (Tables 2 and 3).

TABLE 2

The Channels and Evidences of Political Participation

	Attend public meetings		Join demonstrations		Listening to speeches of Political Leaders and Candidates		Read Newspaper reports about political matters	
	Urban	Rural	Urban	Rural	Urban	Rural	Urban	Rural
1959 Study	20.9%	—	5.5	—	23.6	—	28.9	—
1961 Study	28.8	27.2	10.3	12.3	31.8	28.5	39.7	25.6

TABLE 3

The Political Participation of Selected Social Groups (Urban only)

	Illiterates		Graduates		Lowest Income (Under Rs. 100)		Upper Income (350+Rupees)	
	Attend Meet-ings	Listen to speeches	Attend Meet-ings	Listen to speeches	Attend Meet-ings	Listen to speeches	Attend Meet-ings	Listen to speeches
1959 Study	3.7	4.5	38.9	44.9	18.8	19.7	34.7	46.9
1961 Study	4.7	5.4	40.8	46.0	20.1	21.7	34.4	42.7

The "occasional" pattern of newspaper reading is probably the most serious problem inhibiting political sophistication in India. . . . With the high degree of illiteracy, this is, of course, understandable. But only 8% were regular daily radio listeners in the total adult population. Despite this problem, Indian adults do engage in other types of political activity—up to 30% attend public meetings and hear political leaders or candidates speak, and close to 10% people took part in political demonstrations or rallies. . . .

It is the low level of participation by the illiterates which again is the disturbing finding. In 1961 these were the findings from the Institute's study of urban and rural illiterates:

% OF WHO HAVE AN INTEREST AND PARTICIPATE

	Urban	Rural
	%	%
Attending public meetings	3.7	8.5
Listen to political leaders and candidates	4.5	7.1
Join demonstrations or rallies	3.3	4.0
Read Newspaper Reports	2.7	1.9
Have an interest in politics	8.1	12.1

Only an extremely small minority of the adult illiterates (who number over 100 million) either have an interest or seem to have the time to take the trouble to implement this latent interest through political interaction with others. It is, perhaps, amazing that in rural areas, where illiterates seem most politically interested, as many as 8.5% do attend public meetings and try to inform themselves about politics. In this connection it is significant to note that in 1961, 59% of the urban illiterates and 68% of the rural illiterates intended to vote in the national elections. We will return to this problem subsequently.

LEVELS OF POLITICAL KNOWLEDGE AND OPINION CRYSTALLIZATION

When we move beyond mere assertions of political interest and types of political activity and ask how well informed the Indian public is on current political issues, there is a greater cause for concern (Table 4). There is a great wealth of information in the Institute's studies on attitudes towards economic issues. We have taken a few examples from these for illustrative purposes. The "don't know" category of respondents is large—a category which it must be recalled includes both those who are ignorant and those who are ambivalent and have not been able to make up their minds on the question. . . .

On the other hand, opinions of the political leadership elite seem somewhat better structured, although large proportions of the public apparently do not know who the leaders are. **Over 90 per cent of the urban public have opinions about Nehru (and in 1961 only 1% rated**

TABLE 4

Political Information and Knowledge—Urban and Rural

	Don't know which party can best provide cheaper food		Don't know which party can best provide more jobs		Have no opinion		Have no opinion whether there should be a "liberal but non-socialist opposi- tion" party	
					(Urban only)			
	Urban	Rural	Urban	Rural	Nehru	Desai	Urban	Rural
1959 study	42.6	46.1	44.5	—	15.6	61.5	61.7	73.8
1961 study	52.5	54.5	53.2	54.7	9.0	37.9	45.4	73.2

his performance as Prime Minister "bad"). The rural public was less well informed—21.9 per cent having "no opinion". But the other leaders are not as familiar to the public, particularly in rural areas. Lal Bahadur Shastri, now often mentioned as Nehru's successor, in the 1961 study was unknown to 75% of the rural public (41.5% of the urban), compared to 74% and (38%) for Morarji Desai, 70.5% (and 34%) for V. K. Krishna Menon. Yet, there is evidence that the public is becoming more familiar and opinionated about its top leadership, though if anything there is less opinion certainty on the issues of the day.

Some of the findings on critical aspects of governmental policy are indeed alarming in this respect. In the field of foreign policy, 55% of the urban public did not know whether they supported the directions of Indian policy in 1959; from 61% (urban) to 79% (rural) had no opinion about Eisenhower and the United States, virtually the same percentages which emerged when they were asked about Premier Khrushchev and the Soviet Union. When asked whether they thought a military dictatorship for India would be good or bad, 46% (urban) and 65% (rural) had no opinion. In the area of Community Development, on which India's leaders are pinning much of their hope for improving economic and social conditions in the countryside, including agricultural development, from 66% (urban) to 76% (rural) admitted they were not informed about Community Development. And on the critical issues of expanding "the public sector" and restricting "the private sector" of the economy a whole series of questions reveal a basic lack of political knowledge and an incapability to respond to even very general queries. From 50% (urban) to 74% (rural) of the public say they simply "don't know".

These general levels of political ignorance are high enough to raise serious questions as to whether the political capacity of the Indian public, based on adequate knowledge, is in fact "developing" and whether a government which in fact operates on the principle of democratic responsibility, and which also admits that it relies on public support for the implementation of its programmes and plans, can function effectively in its present "style" of political and administrative strategy. It is somewhat ironic that although political interest is present and increasing, and political participation activities are at least at credible levels, the public is not revealing a higher degree of clarity in understanding and responding to the issues of the day. In short, "the don't-know level" of the Indian public, particularly the rural public, is extremely high—*both* for issues and for the successors to Nehru. This level of withdrawal from or unfamiliarity with political reality should be a danger signal to the Indian government.

The degree to which this level of political opinion (ignorance or ambivalence) can be disturbing emerges sharply from an analysis of specific social sectors (Table 5). The "intellectuals" and university graduates are relatively capable of articulating an opinion, particularly on

TABLE 5

Political Ignorance or Ambivalence by Social Group (1961)

No opinion or undecided upon	Illiterates Urban %	Rural %	Graduates Urban %	Rural %	Low Income (Under Rs. 100) Urban %	Rural %	High Income (Over Rs. 350) Urban %	Rural %
Which party can best provide cheaper food?	85.2	72.6	51.8	44.7	60.7	58.7	44.6	43.3
Would the Congress Party be justified in curtailing the private sector?	95.3	93.9	28.7	44.6	83.6	84.1	35.0	50.0
Would you like to see a liberal but non-socialist party in opposition?	96.0	94.1	20.0	21.5	66.2	81.8	26.7	50.3
Who would you favour as a successor to Nehru?	91.2	91.4	25.7	4.6	66.0	77.2	29.9	55.6

the socialism question, the type of party system preferred, and who should succeed Nehru. They are not unanimous on these questions.

For example, 19.3% of the urban graduates preferred Desai, 21.1% wanted Jai Prakash Narayan, 9.1% preferred Menon and 4.5% Shastri (in 1961). But the great majority of the educated do have opinions. The same is generally true of those in the upper income brackets, with great diversity in opinion present in the findings. But the lowest income group (under Rs. 100 a month) and the illiterates have extremely high rates of political ignorance or indecision on these questions. And the rural illiterates are in some cases better able to express an opinion than is true in urban areas. But, with two-thirds or more of the low income groups having no opinion, and over 30% of the illiterates being uninformed, one wonders whether economic or social planning through India's democratic processes really is reaching and motivating the great mass of the adult public. **The suggestion in these revealing data is clear, and documented by all the studies of the Institute—only a small minority, the educated and well-to-do, are aware and informed of India's political issues and problems and are able to think intelligently about them. While the lower classes may be interested, so far the politics of their developing society has not penetrated to their political consciousness, nor enabled them to respond meaningfully to political controversies— whether these are controversies over what system shall prevail, or the solution of contemporary problems, or what leadership shall be entrusted with the country's future.**

⌒෴⌒

22. *ELECTIONS IN DEVELOPING COUNTRIES**

r. s. m i l n e

The number of Nuffield-type studies of elections in developing countries is rapidly growing.[1] But there has been a corresponding lack of discus-

* From "Elections in Developing Countries" by R. S. Milne, *Parliamentary Affairs*, Vol. XVIII, No. 1 (Winter, 1964–65), pp. 53–60. By permission.
[1] Notably, to list only some major publications in book form: W. J. M. Mackenzie and Kenneth E. Robinson (eds.), *Five Elections in Africa* (Oxford, 1960); M. Venkatarangaiya, *The General Election in the City of Bombay, 1952* (Bombay, 1953); Jorge R. Coquia, *The Philippine Presidential Election of 1953* (Manila, 1955); R. L. Park and S. V. Kogekar (eds.), *Reports on the Indian General Elections 1951–52* (Bombay, 1956); H. Feith, *The Indonesian Elections of 1955* (Ithaca, N. Y., 1957); I. D. S. Weerawardana, *Ceylon General Election, 1956* (Colombo, 1960); G. Bennet and C. G. Roseberg, *The Kenyatta Election: Kenya 1960–1961* (Oxford, 1961); K. W. J. Post, *The Nigerian Federal Election of 1959* (London, 1963).

sion of the assumptions underlying the use of elections in these countries.[2] The *forms* of western-type elections change when they are exported. Can it be assumed that the "functions" remain the same?

Experience of what happens to Western institutional and conceptual exports to developing countries suggests that changes may occur before elections are "domesticated" into the indigenous political system.[3] For instance, some aspects of election ritual may be 'nonfunctional' in the new environment, but may be practised from habit, just because they formerly served useful purposes in elections in developing countries. On the Northeast coast of Malaya the Pan-Malayan Islamic Party owes most of its support to its being identified with Islam and to the activities of religious leaders; yet the party maintains a quite elaborate, and probably partly unnecessary, organization to compete with its more secular rival party, the Alliance. Obviously the environment in developing countries is bound to be different. In some African elections the influence of tribalism is strong, and the support of the chiefs is important.[4] The parties may be relatively weak. In Northern Nigeria the Northern People's Congress is "at present little more than a 'front' for traditional institutions."[5] Party organization, on the other hand, is often 'elementary',[6] and branch membership, in the sense of paying membership, minute.[7] Electors may not be responsive to appeals couched in terms of national issues. They may have to be approached in terms of local issues[8] or of their trust in the personality of the candidates. Many of the differences may be attributed to the difficulty of 'communication' in such countries, whether resulting from physical obstacles, from illiteracy or from traditional limitations on dealings with members of other tribal, or ethnic, groups. On the highest level the obstacles to effective communication would include the absence of an adequate volume of informed *criticism* of a government's policies. A commentator on the Indian 1957 General Election has pointed to the generally passive, unquestioning and uninformed state of the public, the immunity from critical examination of the Prime Minister's declarations and the absence of political columnists of the calibre of Walter Lippman or James Reston.[9]

These are a few of the obvious general differences between elec-

[2] But see Mackenzie; Ch. VIII in Mackenzie and Robinson, *op. cit.; Free Elections* (London, 1958); "The Export of Electoral Systems", *Political Studies*, Vol. V, No. 3 (1957).
[3] Mackenzie and Robinson, p. 463.
[4] Dennis Austin, "Elections in an African Rural Area', *Africa*, Vol. XXXI, No. 1 (1961), p. 12.
[5] Mackenzie and Robinson, p. 478.
[6] Austin, p. 14.
[7] Post, pp. 134–5, 153. On Indonesia see Feith, *op. cit.*, p. 9.
[8] Austin, p. 3.
[9] J. R. Roach, "India's 1957 Elections", *Far Eastern Survey*, Vol. XXVI, No. 5 (1957), p. 76.

tions in developed and developing countries. Other detailed variations derive from them. For instance, in the 1955 Malayan election, the multi-racial Alliance Party ran some Chinese and Indian candidates, although at that time the overwhelming bulk of the electors were Malays. Their non-Malay candidates were therefore believed to be vulnerable to opposition by a strong Malay candidate. Partly for this reason the Alliance attempted to keep their nominations secret until the last possible moment. Such manoeuvres are in contrast to the practice in many Western countries, where it is believed to be an advantage to choose the candidate early so that he and his name may become familiar to the electors. Differences of this kind are roughly what might be expected when the sequence of operations that constitutes a general election is attempted in a developing country. . . .

        o   o   o   o   o

It is not easy to say exactly where "free" elections begin or end. In practice there are many degrees of "freedom" in elections. Even in Western countries there may be biases built into the system, such as the tendency in Britain for the Labour Party to need a higher proportion of the vote than the Conservatives in order to win a given number of seats, or the distortions inherent in the United States system because of the existence of Presidential electors. There may be *ad hoc* electoral laws introduced to favour particular parties such as the French system of *apparentement* of 1951. Varying degrees of government control of the Press may exist, and also, as in France, great disparities in the amount of radio and television time allowed to government and opposition parties. The financial resources available to various parties may differ widely.[10] Even once the objective conditions under which elections are held have been listed, there is still the *subjective* element in Mackenzie's definition to be considered; in brief, do the electors *consider* that they have a real choice? Perhaps, therefore, we should refrain from calling elections "unfree", unless there is wholesale interference with opposition parties, rampant "stuffing" of ballot boxes or unless an independent judiciary to interpret electoral law and an honest, competent, non-partisan administration to run elections [11] are obviously lacking. Otherwise, perhaps elections should be described merely as "less free" or "more free" than some other elections.[12]

The reasons usually put forward to justify the holding of free elections in Western societies may be summarized as:

[10]   *The Journal of Politics*, Vol. 25, No. 4 (1963), special issue, "Comparative Studies in Political Finance".
[11]   Mackenzie, *Free Elections*, p. 14.
[12]   Cf. C. G. Field, *Political Theory* (London, 1956), p. 43 on the definition of democracy.

1. To make possible peaceful changes of government;

2. To give the ruled a sense of commitment to the decisions made by the government and a sense of participation in their execution. In Western societies a high proportion of the electors will feel a sense of commitment (2) to a government, only if they are convinced that the elections which brought it into power were relatively "free". These generally recognised advantages of free elections in Western societies are similar to those put forward by Professor W. J. M. Mackenzie.[13] They may also be expressed in terms of legitimacy. Changes of government are accepted as legitimate, only if elections are widely regarded as free.

In some developing countries a fairly high and influential proportion of the electors share the western view that it is important that elections could produce a change of government. In the Philippines there has actually been a change of Administration three times since the Second World War, in 1946, 1953 and 1961. In 1949 the elections may not have been free, in the sense that there were claims "that the election results officially proclaimed did not reflect the will of the Filipino electorate as expressed in the ballots".[14] In other countries, such as India and Malaya, a change of government is possible, in principle, at a general election, although a single party has been dominant in each country since independence.

But in elections in some developing countries the emphasis may be on the "commitment" function of elections (2) rather than on the possibility of changes of government (1). Thailand is perhaps an extreme case. Thai elections seem to be one of the ways in which legitimacy is conferred on a government, although *changes* in government take place mainly through *coups*, which are not entirely peaceful. "In the old days the king was made legitimate by the splendid trappings and ceremonial of his court. Under the constitution the ceremonial of election is required for the group in power. The public, in fact, seems not so concerned about the political outcome of elections as that they be held in a seemly clean and orderly manner".[15] To say that in Thailand the nature of political parties and the conduct of elections "distort" the political

[13] *Political Studies*, pp. 255–6. In *Free Elections*, pp. 13–14 he puts forward two reasons which are substantially the same. See also a review of Bennet and Roseberg, *op. cit.*, by D. J. R. Scott, *Parliamentary Affairs*, Vol. XV, No. 3 (1962), pp. 399–400. Maurice Cowling in *The Nature and Limits of Political Science* (Cambridge, 1963) disagrees with Professor Mackenzie for being normative and for admiring Western-democratic political arrangements too much (pp. 35–7). In fact, in *Free Elections*, Mackenzie immediately makes qualifications about the circumstances under which it is prudent to introduce free elections (p. 14). He is also misquoted by Cowling. Mackenzie's statement that the doctrine of responsibility to an electorate ". . . is the best for ordinary use . . ." (p. 14) is reproduced in Cowling as ". . . is the best for electorate use . . ." (p. 36).

[14] Coquia, p. 3.

[15] David A. Wilson, "Thailand" in G. McT. Kahin (ed.), *Government and Politics of Southeast Asia* (Ithaca, N. Y., 1959), p. 56.

process is for the observer implicitly to set up norms of what Thai elections "are for".[16]

It has been argued that it is unnecessary for governments in developing countries to attempt to bolster up their legitimacy by going through an election ritual. Government can be equally legitimate, says Cowling,[17] where no election has occurred, or where elections are not part of the normal political process. Perhaps, but this is the argument of a dealer in logical categories rather than of an observer of the process of development. Elections are not a necessary condition of legitimacy in developing countries, but they have been widely used as *one* of a number of devices for acquiring legitimacy. The developing countries, almost without exception, have accepted the western export, "democracy". . . . But, although the developing countries have, by and large, accepted "democracy", they have reserved the right to define it in their own way.[18] Sometimes their definition does not include elections at all, or does not include elections which in form resemble western elections, as in Indonesia's "guided democracy" or Pakistan's "basic democracy".[19] Sometimes elections, ostensibly of the western type, are included. But even here the user country determines their exact form and the degree to which they should be "free".

Quite apart from considerations of democracy, in developing countries there may be other reasons for holding (or not holding) elections, whether relatively free or relatively unfree. One of these may be the wish to promote consensus or heightened national consciousness. This would not be an important reason in most western countries, although clearly it is relevant in even well-developed communist countries, such as the U.S.S.R. The view has been advanced that in some African countries orderly elections have in a sense become "the badge of national consciousness, maturity and independence". Election day "has become something of a solemn national occasion. . . ."[20] This link has also been noticed in Malaya. "Through a series of elections at local, state and federal government levels more people are being brought to deal, not only with the problems of democracy, but also at the same time with the issue of nationhood. At each election and in every political party more of the politically conscious are being made to affirm their loyalty to the nation and gradually to identify that nation with the political system which they are learning to manipulate".[21] Clearly, these consequences

[16] Saul Rose, *Politics in Southern Asia* (London, 1963), p. 319.
[17] *Op. cit.*, p. 37.
[18] See Hugh Tinker, *Ballot Box and Bayonet: People and Government in Emergent Asian Countries* (Oxford, 1964); Rupert Emerson, "The Erosion of Democracy", *The Journal of Asian Studies*, Vol. 20, No. 1 (1960).
[19] See especially Tinker, *op. cit.*; Marguerite J. Fisher, "New Concepts of Democracy in Southern Asia", *Western Political Quarterly*, Vol. XV, No. 4 (1962); Michael Brecher, *The New States of Asia* (London, 1963), Chs. 2 and 3.
[20] Mackenzie and Robinson, p. 467.
[21] Wang Gungwu, "Malaya Nationalism", *Royal Central Asian Journal*, July–Oct., 1962, parts 3 and 4 (July–October, 1962), pp. 324–5.

are regarded as advantageous, primarily because they tend to promote political development. The emphasis is on the educative effect of elections rather than on their actual results in determining who shall rule.

It is possible, however, that, in some countries, instead of *promoting* national consciousness, elections may actually have a *divisive* effect. An account of the 1955 general election in Indonesia claimed that it had the desirable result, *inter alia*, of strengthening all-Indonesian consciousness through the participation of a large number of electors.[22] The absence of any subsequent general election suggests that similar desirable consequences would no longer follow. It has been suggested that violence may occur because of the 'popular public festival' aspect of elections, reminiscent of British elections before the secret ballot was introduced in 1872.[23] Elections may convey too much of an "all-or-nothing" impression to Africans.[24] "A general election . . . is thus a civil war without bloodshed, and its result must be the same as that which would have been achieved by such a war." Consequently the question of minority rights becomes irrelevant.[25] If this diagnosis is correct, then elections may actually retard the spread of national consciousness.

Another authority disputes this view that African elections necessarily have such a divisive effect on society. The losing side does not feel it has "lost everything", and traditional society has a great ability to "return to laughter" after a period of conflict.[26] Generalisations on a subject as wide as "African elections" are perhaps risky, at least at this time. However, it would seem that, if little national consciousness already exists in a country, this will probably be reflected, in the way in which the campaign is conducted. . . . In short, unless there is a certain minimum degree of consensus to begin with, elections will not increase the degree of consensus.

The "functions" of elections in developed societies are not so obvious as they were once thought to be.[27] Their "functions" in developing societies are even less obvious. In such countries elections may bear an unexpected relation, or no relation at all, to "democracy". The decision whether or not to hold them may be determined by considerations which are important to the government—for instance, the effect on the promotion of national consciousness, but which have nothing whatever to do with democracy.

⟨≈⟩

---

22 Feith, pp. 89–90.
23 T. L. Hodgkin, *African Political Parties* (Penguin, 1961), p. 132.
24 D. J. R. Scott, "Problems of West African Elections", *What are the Problems of Parliamentary Government in West Africa?* (London, 1958), p. 73.
25 Roy Price, "Italy at the Poll", *Parliamentary Affairs*, Vol. IX, No. 3 (1956), p. 77.
26 Austin, p. 16.
27 Cf. Graeme Duncan and Steven Lukes, "The New Democracy", *Political Studies*, Vol. XI, No. 2 (1963).

C. Factors in Policy-Making

23. LATIN AMERICAN CONSTITUTIONS: NOMINAL AND REAL[*]

j. lloyd mecham

If the drafting of democratic constitutions serves as preparation for practice in the art of popular government then, indeed, Latin Americans are well prepared. Since gaining independence the twenty republics have essayed a grand total of 186[1] *magna cartae*, or an average of 9.3 each. A breakdown per country reveals the following: Argentina 4; Bolivia 14; Brazil 5; Chile 7; Colombia 6; Costa Rica 7; Cuba 2; Dominican Republic 22; Ecuador 16; El Salvador 10; Guatemala 5; Haiti 18; Honduras 10; Mexico 5; Nicaragua 8; Panama 3; Paraguay 4; Peru 12; Uruguay 4; and Venezuela 24. Today thirteen of the Latin American republics are governed by constitutions adopted since 1940, and only two antedate World War I.[2] There seems to be no end to constitution making.

This points up an anomaly: on the one hand apparent devotion to constitutionalism as a cure for national problems, and on the other, lack of respect for constitutional mandates. Nowhere are constitutions more elaborate and less observed. Politically, Latin Americans seem to be unqualified optimists, for the long succession of constitutional failures has never dampened hopes that the perfect constitution—a cure-all for national ills—will be discovered eventually.

THE NOMINAL CONSTITUTION

Since it is the objective of the present inquiry to show how widely government in operation departs from constitutional mandate, we first

[*] From "Latin American Constitutions: Nominal and Real" by J. Lloyd Mecham, *The Journal of Politics*, Vol. XXI, No. 2 (May, 1959), pp. 258–272. By permission of the publisher and the author.

[1] There is no agreement concerning the total number of Latin American constitutions. This is because many amended or revised constitutions were promulgated as new instruments. "It has been the habit of new political regimes to adopt new constitutions rather than to run the risk of loss of prestige by operating under the instrument identified with an opposing and defeated party." William W. Pierson and Federico G. Gil, *Governments of Latin America* (New York, 1957), p. 160.

[2] Argentina (1853) and Colombia (1886); both extensively revised.

note the constitutional norm, *i.e.*, a composite or average constitution of the Latin American republics.

The Composite Constitution

This constitution is a lengthy instrument of about 35 pages, in contrast to 13 pages for the Constitution of the United States. . . .[3]

The composite constitution contains no preamble. It sets about forthrightly to declare that the nation is sovereign, independent, and unitary or federal as the case may be; that the government is republican, democratic, and representative; that sovereignty is vested in the people who express their will by suffrage which is obligatory and secret for all citizens, male and female, over 20 years of age.[4] No literacy or property tests are required. This is universal suffrage in its most liberal sense.

The guarantees of individual liberty, the familiar rights of man, are spelled out in great detail. These include: the freedoms of speech, press, assembly, and petition; equality before the law; *habeas corpus;* no unreasonable searches or seizures; due process; no retroactive penalties; and no capital punishment. Religious freedom is guaranteed, and all cults receive the equal protection of the state.[5] The minute enumeration of the inalienable rights of the individual is inspired by a desire to erect a constitutional barrier to tyranny.

The effectiveness of this barrier is weakened, however, by provisions for the suspension of the individual guarantees in times of stress. This device is called "declaration of state of siege," a temporary annulment, by presidential decree, of all constitutional guarantees and privileges. This important presidential power is restricted only by the formality of securing congressional approval before the act if the Congress is in session, and after the act when that body is convened. The easy suspension of the constitutional guarantees is evidence of the fact that they are considerably less than absolute.[6]

One of the most detailed and lengthy sections of the constitution deals with "social rights and duties," a recent addition to Latin American constitutional law. Conforming to contemporary conceptions of

---

[3] Using Russell H. Fitzgibbon (ed.), *The Constitutions of the Americas* (Chicago, 1948), as a basis for comparison. Since issue of this collection new constitutions have been adopted in the following countries: Costa Rica (1949), El Salvador (1950), Nicaragua (1951), Uruguay (1952), and Venezuela (1953).

[4] In some of the states the minimum age is eighteen years, if married.

[5] For the status of religion in the respective states, see J. Lloyd Mecham, *Church and State in Latin America* (Chapel Hill, N. C., 1934).

[6] See Segundo V. Linares Quintana, *La denaturalización del estado de sitio como instrumento de subversión institucional* (Buenos Aires, 1946). See also Harold E. Davis (ed.), *Government and Politics in Latin America* (New York, 1958), pp. 280–282.

social justice, social rights and duties are enumerated *in extenso* under the subheads: labor, family, education, and the economic order.

✿ ✿ ✿ ✿ ✿

The supreme powers of government are divided for their exercise, by application of the principle of the separation of powers, into the legislative, the executive, and the judicial. Two or more of these powers shall never be united in one person or group of persons, for by counterbalancing and checking each other they will prevent the establishment of a tyranny.[7]

The legislative power is vested in a Congress composed of two houses, a Chamber of Deputies and a Senate. Both deputies and senators are chosen by direct popular vote, for terms of four and six years respectively. . . . In general both houses of the national legislature possess the same powers and perform the same functions. They are equal partners in the legislative process. Although each chamber possesses certain special powers these are of no particular consequence.

✿ ✿ ✿ ✿ ✿

The executive power is exercised by the president with a council of ministers. The president is chosen by direct vote of the people (even in the federal states), serves for a term of four years, and is not eligible for re-election until after one term intervenes. There is no provision for a vice-president because this heir apparent might become the magnet for conspiracies against the constituted government.[8]

The powers of the Latin American president are relatively greater than those of the president of the United States, for, in addition to the customary executive grants, he is authorized to directly initiate legislation in the national Congress, expel foreigners on his own authority, suspend the constitutional guarantees, and in federal states impose his will on state administrations by exercise of the power of intervention. His decree-making power is so broad as to be quasi-legislative in character; indeed, the constitution authorizes the Congress to delegate, in emergencies, extraordinary legislative powers to the president. Constitutional checks on dictatorship are thus cancelled out by contrary con-

---

[7] On the application of the classic separation of powers see Óscar Morales Elizando, *El principio de la división de poderes* (Mexico, 1945).

[8] Of the twenty republics only eight (Argentina, Bolivia, Brazil, Cuba, Ecuador, Honduras, Panama and El Salvador) have retained the vice-presidency.

stitutional delegations.[9] The end result is that dictatorships are possible within the terms, if not the spirit, of the Constitution.

The composite constitution provides that the president shall be assisted by ministers of state, the superior chiefs of their respective departments. . . .

The judicial system, independent and coordinate, is composed of a hierarchy of courts; [10] a supreme court, appellate courts, and inferior courts or courts of first instance. . . . The justices are appointed and serve for limited terms. The Latin American countries base their legal system on the Roman Law and so do not make use of trial by jury. United States influence is discovered however, in the constitutional provision conferring on the supreme court the power to declare laws unconstitutional.

In addition to the regular courts there are a number of special courts, notably the administrative tribunals and the electoral tribunals. . . .

In its organization of local government the composite constitution for the unitary state provides a highly centralized system as in France. The nation is divided, principally for administrative purposes, into departments, and each department has a governor appointed by the president, and directly responsible to the minister of interior. There is no departmental assembly. Insofar as self government exists on the local level it is found in the municipalities which have their own elected mayors and councils.[11] It should be recognized however, that neither mayor nor councilman actually has much to do. The various national ministries, particularly the *gobierno* or ministry of the interior which controls the police, absorb most of the local jurisdiction. Local self-government functions under highly restrictive limitations both in law and custom.[12] Within the respective states of the federal unions the organization of local government conforms rather closely to that of the unitary nations.

Reflective of the prominence which the military assumes in the political life of the Latin American nations, a separate constitutional chapter is devoted to "the armed forces." In addition to national defense the military are assigned the role of "guaranteeing the constitutional powers." This provides a basis for political intervention despite the injunction that the armed forces are "essentially obedient and not delib-

[9]   See Oswaldo E. Mirando Arenas, *El jefe de estado en las constituciones Americanas* (Santiago, Chile, 1944), and Karl Loewenstein, "The Presidency Outside the United States," *Journal of Politics*, XI (August, 1949), 447–496.
[10]   See Helen L. Clagett, *The Administration of Justice in Latin America* (New York, 1952), pp. 21–41.
[11]   For municipal democracy see Carlos Mouchet, "Municipal Government," Davis, *op. cit.*, pp. 389–390.
[12]   Austin F. Macdonald, *Government of the Argentine Republic* (New York, 1942), pp. 398–402.

erative." This is another of the numerous but ineffective constitutional word-barriers to the rule of force.

The constitution is easily amended. The proposed amendment must receive a two-thirds vote in two consecutive legislative sessions. The executive cannot object. This is meaningless, however, since the amendment would have little chance of adoption if the president opposed. There is no popular ratification of constitutional amendments; indeed, the original constitution itself was not popularly ratified.

THE OPERATIVE CONSTITUTION

The foregoing, in broad outline, is the composite "paper" constitution of the Latin American republics, together with certain distinctive variations. It is now in order to describe that constitution as actually operative. With the exception of Uruguay, and the doubtful addition of Costa Rica, Chile and Mexico, democratic government does not exist in Latin America.[13] A majority of the countries are either undisguised personalistic dictatorships or pseudo-democracies. In either case the proud constitutional assertions that these are popular, representative, democratic states, and that all governmental authority derives from the people in whom sovereignty resides, are mere verbiage, or at best declarations of ideal aspirations.

Divergences in Actual Practice

Universal suffrage, provided by more than half of the constitutions, is actually exercised by only a fraction of those qualified, even in countries where voting is supposed to be compulsory.[14] These few votes must then run the gamut of the "official count." It is a well-known fact that a requisite more important than honest voting is the honest poll of the votes. Since governments in power are usually in control of the voting and the tabulating of the vote, it is a commonplace that Latin American administrations never lose elections. On the rare occasions when this happens, as in Cuba in 1944 when Batista "allowed" the election of Dr. Grau San Martin, the shock of the unusual event reverberated throughout Latin America.[15]

[13] See Russell H. Fitzgibbon, "A Statistical Evaluation of Latin American Democracy," *The Western Political Quarterly*, IX (September, 1956), 607–619.
[14] For electoral practices see Frank R. Brandenburg, "Political Parties and Elections," in Davis, *op. cit.*, pp. 216–218.
[15] Since 1945 opposition parties have won presidential elections in Brazil, Chile, Ecuador and Peru. This may indicate a wholesome democratic trend. For description of electoral trickery see William S. Stokes, *Honduras: An Area Study in Government* (Madison, Wis., 1950), pp. 231–264.

POLITICAL SYSTEMS

What shall we say about the observance of those fundamental guarantees of individual liberty: the freedoms of speech, press, assembly and conscience? What of the guarantees of domicile and all of the components of what we know as due process of law? Since from the earliest days of their independence, Latin Americans have been so profoundly engrossed in the constitutionalizing of an ever expanding enumeration of civil liberties, it seems that they should, by this time, have attained a status of sanctity and respect. This however is not the case.[16] The guarantees are respected only at governmental convenience and by sufferance. The constitutions generously supply the executives with the means to be employed in emergencies, to suspend the guarantees. This device, known as "state of siege," is abused by overuse for it is the customary resort to overwhelm opposition and entrench dictatorship.[17] It is ironical that democratic constitutions bestow so lavishly on the executive the means to destroy the feeble manifestations of democracy. With respect to the status of the individual guarantees, therefore, much depends on the attitude of the president.

A principle of the "paper constitution" which is transformed beyond recognition in the operating constitution is the separation of the powers. Theoretically the three powers—executive, legislative and judicial—are separate, coordinate, and equal. Numerous safeguards, many of which are found in our own constitutions, are provided to prevent wanton exercise of authority by any one of these powers. Because of the well-founded belief that it is the executive which will be most prone to irresponsibility and be acquisitive of power, the most numerous constitutional limitations are those imposed on the presidents. Despite all this, and responsive to the strongman tradition in Latin governments, the executive overshadows the other two powers. Latin American governments are emphatically of the strong presidential type.

That the president is the dominant power in the government is never doubted. His supremacy derives from his dual position as constitutional chief-executive and as extra-constitutional *caudillo*, chief or boss. From the earliest days of their independence Latin Americans have shown a strong disposition for *caudillos*, preferably for those with a military background, for the magnetic attraction of the man on horseback can always be expected to reinforce the lure of demagogues.[18] The *caudillo* embodies the program of his political partisans; he is the platform of his pseudo-party. This is what is called *personalismo* in Latin

[16] "Rights are null, declarations are mere words, if means are not provided to make them effective; these means are the penal code, responsibility of authorities, inflexible punishment of all attack on the conceived rights. This and nothing else constitutes the guarantees." Justo Arosemena, *Estudios constitucionales sobre los gobiernos de la América Latina* (Paris, 1888), II, 303.

[17] Hector R. Baudón, *Estado de sitio* (Buenos Aires, 1939).

[18] Charles E. Chapman, "The Age of the Caudillos: A Chapter in Hispanic American History," *Hispanic American Historical Review*, XII (August, 1932), 281–300.

American politics, which means placing emphasis on individuals rather than on public policies. The *caudillo* because of his hold on the popular imagination, but more significantly because of his control of the army, meets with docile acceptance. Neither the disguised dictatorship, nor the pseudo-democracy is a government of laws, all are governments of men. One of the least effective of the constitutional checks on ambitious presidents is the no-reelection provision. *Caudillismo* and *personalismo* have transformed the constitutional office of the presidency beyond recognition.

In consequence of the dominance of the executive it is hardly necessary to indicate the position of the congress and the courts. Both are subordinate to the executive. . . .

Freedom and equality of the courts is also a fiction, for the judiciary, like the legislature, is subordinate to the executive, numerous constitutional provisions to bulwark the power and independence of the courts to the contrary notwithstanding. . . .

It is not necessarily because the presidents have ways of getting rid of objectionable judges which accounts for their surrender of independence; rather it is because of a long standing tradition of Spanish origin that there must be no interference by the judiciary with the policies of the chief executive. The old principle that the king can do no wrong is observed by the deference paid by the courts to the wishes of the president. . . .

         ✿   ✿   ✿   ✿   ✿

Equally as fictitious as Latin American federalism is the constitutional mandate that the army does not deliberate, *i.e.*, intervene in politics. Any practical discussion of Latin American politics which omits reference to the political role of the army would be sadly unrealistic, for the most significant feature of Latin American politics has always been the predominance of the military authority over the civil. It is an old story dating from the independence period when the possession of governmental authority became the prize of contesting arms. None of the countries has escaped the blight of military political intervention, and today the military are in control, openly or disguised, in most of the nations of Latin America.

The very nature and purpose of the army invites political activity, for it is designed more to preserve internal order and support the regime than to defend the frontiers against foreign invaders. Several of the constitutions impose on the army the responsibility of guaranteeing the fulfillment of the constitution and the laws. The militarists do not shirk this obligation for they regard themselves as the most competent, unselfish, and patriotic interpreters of the national interest. . . .

Violence Institutionalized

One of the most patent facts of Latin American government, and certainly the best-known to Anglo-Americans, is recurring *revolution*. The term is a misnomer, for it usually refers to nothing more than a *coup d'état* or a *cuartelazo* (barrack revolt), the classic "substitution of bullets for ballots," the ousting of the "ins" by the "outs," or perhaps the enforcement of the principle of "alternability of public office." These are not popular movements, for relatively few people participate, outside the military. The rabble, of course, assembles in the main plaza to acclaim impartially each succeeding *caudillo*.[19]

Since the great revolution for independence early in the nineteenth century there have been few authentic revolutions in Latin America, that is if we restrict the term to those deep-seated popular movements aimed at fundamental change in the political, social, and economic orders. Only a limited number of the demonstrations of force so common to the political scene are worthy of designation as revolutions; this, notwithstanding the crying need in most of the countries for a thorough revamping. What Latin America needs, paradoxically, is not less but more revolutions. Fundamental revolution may be the specific for the cure of chronic pseudo-revolution.

---

[19] William S. Stokes, "Violence as a Power Factor in Latin American Politics," *The Western Political Quarterly*, V (September, 1952), 445–468.

24. PUBLIC-POLICY-MAKING IN AVANT-GARDE DEVELOPMENT STATES*†

y e h e z k e l   d r o r

CHARACTERISTICS AND DOMAIN
OF VALIDITY OF THE PURE TYPE
"AVANT-GARDE DEVELOPMENT
STATE" CONSTRUCT

Development states vary considerably in their level of technology, man-power resources, history, ideology, financial means, social structure and political regimes; therefore every generalization on "development states" in general has many exceptions. In order partly to overcome this difficulty, we shall direct our remarks at a "pure" development-state-type to be called "avant-garde development state". The main character-istics of this composite construct of one type of development states include: a very low level of technological development; strong tribal or communal structure which is in the process of breaking up; a mass leader with a small political elite aspiring to achieve radical social-economic transformation within a short time and having a strong grip on the masses, both through charisma and force; nearly no middle class; a long history of colonial rule terminated recently after a period of mil-itant nationalism; and a large scope of public-policy-making, including economic activities. This composite picture fits well most of the Central and West African and some of the Southeast Asian new states. It also fits to a significant degree many North African and Middle Eastern states and applies in the main to Communist China. Most of the characteristics do not fit some development states which either do not yet engage in radical directed social change (such as Liberia and Ethiopia) or which are already well developed in some respects (such as India, Israel,

---

* From "Public-Policy-Making in Avant-Garde Development States" by Yehezkel Dror, *Civilisations*, Vol. XIII, No. 4 (1963), pp. 398–405. By permission.
† This article was written while the author was a Fellow at the Center for Ad-vanced Study in the Behavioral Sciences.

Puerto Rico and the United Arab Republic [Egypt]); but even in respect to these, some of the characteristics do apply. Therefore the characteristics of public-policy-making to be presented fit fully some of the development states—namely those approaching the avant-garde pure type—and fit in part most other development states.

MAIN CHARACTERISTICS OF PUBLIC-POLICY- MAKING IN AVANT-GARDE DEVELOPMENT STATES

Having completed the necessary preliminary steps, we can now take on our main task, namely presentation of the main characteristics of public-policy-making in avant-garde development states. Relying on the conceptual framework presented above, we shall proceed by discussing first some general findings, then findings on input, output, structure and process respectively.

1. General Findings

(1). Both the actual quality and the maximum feasible quality of public-policy-making in the development states are much lower than those in modern states. The maximum feasible level is lower because of the dearth of resources which—even if fully utilized—are insufficient for high quality public-policy-making. The real level of public-policy-making is even lower because of a variety of factors which prevent full utilization of available resources, to be detailed in the following findings. While, therefore, the actual level of public-policy-making could be increased with available resources, it is unavoidable that for a considerable time—and even assuming the best of conditions—the overall quality of public-policy-making in the development countries will be significantly lower than that in the modern countries. This remains true, though to a lesser degree, even if large public-policy-making resources are transferred from the latter to the first.

(2). Contemporary public-policy-making systems as a whole, and most of their aspects and components in particular, are in all countries the result of historic evolution tempered by conscious renovations. These renovations were in most cases either improvisations directed at imminent crises, or/and reforms following radical changes in the political and value environment. All in all, systematic efforts to direct human intelligence at improving public-policy-making systems have been limited in scope and effect, though growing in importance and of significant aggregative impact in the modern countries. In the avant-garde development states, historic evolution and personal accidents are relatively

even more important, conscious, systematic and rational reforms necessarily being as yet a very minor force in shaping the public-policy-
making system.

(3). The basic strategy of public-policy-making in the avant-garde
development states is one of maximax (that is, directed at achieving the
maximum of positive results with relative disregard of possible negative
consequences) with a low security-level. In other words, achievement of
the desired goals requiring a sharp break with the past. Very little
experience in accelerated and directed large-scale social change being
available, incremental change cannot be utilized and "muddling
through" (in the sense of cautious and marginal action through slow trial-
and-error) is of no avail.[1] The only possible strategy of public-policy-
making fitting the goals and conditions of avant-garde development
states is one of far-reaching change involving high risks.[2] The real
danger implied in such a strategy is much reduced because of the
assured survival (see finding 13 below) which makes a maximax strategy
in development countries much less dangerous than in modern and more
risk-sensitive states.

(4). Public-policy-making in the avant-garde development countries
penetrates both less and more into social activities than in the modern
countries. It penetrates more in respect to the selected issues with which
it deals, because of the radical change aimed at and the near monopoly
of public-policy-making as a method for dealing with social problems
(which results both from the absence of private policy-making and the
pro-central-public-policy-making basic ideology). It penetrates less, because public-policy-making concentrates on some clusters of problems—
mainly those involving economic development—mono-focal objectives and
scarcity of resources making necessary abandonment of many spheres of
social activity to non-directed change. This often leads to unbalanced
development which creates new acute social problems, which earlier or
later will become foci for public-policy-making.[3]

[1] On this problem, see Charles E. Lindblom, "The Science of 'Muddling Through'",
Public Administration Review, Vol. 19 (1959), pp. 79 ff. and Yehezkel Dror,
"Muddling Through—'Science' or Inertia?" (forthcoming).
[2] The fact that most of the relevant experience in extensive "social engineering" is
concentrated in the USSR and that their experts are more predisposed to radical
action, presents a serious challenge for Western Democracy in the struggle over the
future political orientation of the avant-garde development states. Much care must be
taken not to transfer philosophic approaches and solutions based on totally different
conditions to the development states. In this respect, experts coming from democratic
countries which did engage in large-scale directed social change—such as The Netherlands and Israel—may have a significant advantage.
[3] This may sometimes be an important advantage, decreasing the burden on public-
policy-making and encouraging strenuous efforts. See Albert O. Hirschman, *The
Strategy of Economic Development* (New Haven: Yale University Press), 1958, and
Albert O. Hirschman and Charles E. Lindblom, "Economic Development, Research
and Development, Policy Making: Some Convergent Views", *Behavioral Science*,
Vol. 7 (1962), pp. 211 ff.

(5). Value-priorities and, to some extent, operational goals, are relatively more developed because of the clear predominance given to technological and economic development. A number of inconsistent values remain—such as raising the educational level of the masses ("primary education for all") vs. education directed at preparing manpower for economic development.[4] Basically, many values accepted in modern states are regarded as expendable, thus enabling concentration of resources on fewer goals and facilitating public-policy-making.

(6). A basic paradox of public-policy-making in nearly all avant-garde development countries is the intense predisposition toward radical social change on one hand and strong conservatism in regard to the basic design of public-policy-making itself on the other hand. In some respects, it seems to be easier to uproot whole tribes and change patterns of social action going back many generations than to change personal patterns of work and reorganize small circles of collaborators so as to increase the quality of public-policy-making.

(7). The value-ecology within which the public-policy-making system operates and which conditions its basic characteristics is not conducive to optimality. Especially disturbing is the absence of a basic pro-rational orientation deeply rooted in culture, as found in Western societies. Also the after-effects of the traumatic experience of becoming an independent nation have a tendency to lead either to highly emotional patterns of activity and/or to apathy, both being barriers to the optimistic matter-of-fact approach required for optimum public-policy-making.

2. Findings on Input

(8). The total resources available in development societies are very limited. Especially scarce are qualified manpower and data, which are the most important resources for public-policy-making. Considerable resources are required for basic collections of data and surveys of the physical and social ecology which are taken for granted in modern countries. Even though there is a strong tendency for the better-qualified manpower to go into the public-policy-making occupations, the absolute scarcity of available qualified manpower results in lack of suitable personnel and reliance on under-qualified persons in many important policy-making positions.

(9). The resources-input into public-policy-making is determined in a rather haphazard manner. Increasing attention is paid to resources-allocation to substantive operations and various techniques, such as performance budgeting, are sometimes introduced for that purpose. But public-policy-making as such is often regarded as a sort of "overhead costs" or "administrative expenses", with the concomitant tendency to

4   I am indebted to Frederick Harbison and Charles Myers for this illustration.

try and save money by cutting these expenses. This tendency is reinforced by the absence of measurable or obvious output-changes, which make input items into public-policy-making a favorite target for so-called "efficiency drives". On the other hand, the forces of inertia often prevent any really penetrating reform in the established patterns of resources allocation.

(10). More specifically, public-policy-making lacks especially the following inputs: resources for research; resources for comprehensive information-collecting, storing and retrieval; resources for thinking-units; and resources for policy-training.

(11). In regard to manpower input, it is possible to distinguish between two main relevant occupations: politics and civil service. The degree of differentiation and turnover between these two policy-making occupations varies between different avant-garde development countries, the tendency being towards some fusing of the two. Recruitment to both occupations is characterized by the dearth of qualified manpower and the priority enjoyed by persons who were active in the independence-movement. Little conscious activity to train reserves of policy-making cadres takes place.[5]

(12). A unique resources-source is foreign aid, in the context of public-policy-making—mainly foreign experts. Foreign experts, supplied partly by the various international agencies under the auspices of the Technical Assistance Board of the United Nations and partly through bilateral and multi-lateral agreements, present an unprecedented effort at import of public-policy-making resources. Their overall contribution to the improvement of public-policy-making in the avant-garde development countries is impressive but limited. Foreign experts are more difficult to utilize in public-policy-making than in more technical activities because of the higher political sensitivity of many policy-issues and because many foreign experts are quite ignorant of the relevant socio-political background. Also, no amount of foreign experts can compensate for lack of data on one hand and lack of rational patterns of behavior on the other. Therefore, while foreign experts have very beneficial short- and long-range effects on public-policy-making, they cannot fully compensate for the lack of local qualified manpower resources and the absence of rational values and behavior patterns.

3. Findings on Output

(13). One of the most interesting features of public-policy-making in all development countries are the relationships between the maximum

[5] For a series of relevant papers, see INCIDI, *Staff Problems in Tropical and Subtropical Countries* (Bruxelles: International Institute of Differing Civilizations), 1961.

feasible and real output-results on one hand [and] the objective survival level and minimum aspiration level on the other. The basic findings to be noted are that however low the actual quality of public-policy-making, the objective survival level is nearly always achieved (the exception being problems of possible external aggression); and that even if the maximum feasible level of public-policy-making were achieved, it would fall far below the level of minimum aspiration, not to speak of the much higher aspiration level of "satisfactory achievement".

The explanation of these findings is quite simple: The basic social structure of the development countries is still autonomous from public-policy-making and would survive even if all (non-local) public-policy-making were to break down. A complex modern society would not survive any real breakdown in public-policy-making, in the simplest meaning of nearly all the population dying unless a very complex network of services, depending *inter alia* on quite high-quality public-policy-making, is maintained. The less complex development societies are not as sensitive and are well able to survive the worst public-policies or even a total breakdown of the public-policy-making system.[6] On the other side of the picture, in most modern societies the gap between actual policy-results and the medium aspiration level is not very high; in the avant-garde development states the aspiration level has been imported by the elite from modern countries and is quickly becoming diffused in the population. This aspiration level—while not defined in detail—includes a standard of living and levels of economic activity patterned on the highest developed Western societies, to be achieved in "the near future"—and this is simply impossible, even with optimal public-policy-making and tremendous assistance from the modern states. This large gap between what is wanted and often promised and what is possible, constitutes a most serious source of tension which may well lead to social explosions once the expectations are clearly frustrated. Substitution of more realistic levels of aspiration for the utopian ones is, therefore, a basic long-range requirement for preserving environmental conditions for high-quality public-policy-making and for the highest feasible rate of actual socio-economic progress.

(14). Despite the predisposition to plan, overall desired output determination for public-policy-making is non-existent because of the concentration of public-policy-making on limited issue-clusters (see finding 4 above). Even in regard to limited projects, realistic target-setting is found only in the relatively more developed development-countries,

---

[6]   Therefore, they are less sensitive to nuclear warfare. Assuming that radioactivity would not wipe out all life, but that all central directory and regulatory activities would be disrupted, most of the population in modern countries would die because of lack of food, water, energy and medical services. Nothing comparable would happen in the development countries, where most of the population still lives in self-sufficient local units.

such as India. In most of the avant-garde development states both the necessary knowledge and action-patterns are absent, realistic planning being more often imposed from abroad as a condition for financial assistance than being practiced on local initiative.

4. Findings in Regard to Structure

(15). The public-policy-making structure is much simpler than in the modern states. Individual and small-group decisions play a relatively greater role than organizational processes and the aggregation-functions are less complex and easier to observe. Private individuals and legislatures have much less influence on public-policy-making, being more passive material for manipulation and channels for recruitment of support respectively than active contributors to public-policy-making. Private intellectuals are nearly non-contributing to public-policy-making, being either non-existent or influence-less and politically apathetic. Interest-groups are active, but are smaller in number and more integrated; they operate more in the manner of cliques than as autonomous social units. Leaders have a predominant influence, being aided by small cadres of followers.

(16). Most of the occupants of the central public-policy-making roles have a predisposition to improvisation and extra-rational decision-making, which is a carry-over from the pre-independence period. During the pre-independence period, the politicians of the independence movement operated mainly through improvisation, one of the main required skills being an ability to improvise in the face of quickly changing circumstances in which every small opportunity had to be taken advantage of without delay. The main qualifications for success were highly developed political acumen and charisma, there being little scope for rational long-range policy-making. These patterns of behavior were tremendously reinforced through the successful achievement of independence; therefore, when the pre-independence leaders took over the new policy-making positions they brought with them strongly ingrained behavior-patterns which are not congruent with those required for optimal public-policy-making in a development state. Some outstanding politicians did change their patterns of behavior but most of them neither feel the need nor are able to do so.[7] It may therefore take some time until natural and non-natural turnover of leaders bring to the main policy-

---

[7] In some development countries the pre-independence type of leader is still essential for building up a unitary nation, a task for which extra-rational and even mystic modes of operation may be optimal. Under such conditions, the quality of public-policy-making as such cannot as yet serve as a relevant criterion, other tasks being more important. In these cases, the problems of incongruency between actual and needed patterns of behavior by the senior political stratum are delayed but not avoided.

making positions persons whose action-patterns fit the requirement of optimum public-policy-making.

(17). The consequences of the last observations are strongly reinforced by the weaknesses of the higher civil service. With a few exceptions, most of the senior positions had been occupied during the pre-independence period by foreigners. When independence was achieved, these positions were taken over in most countries by persons who were often highly intelligent and devoted, but never had the opportunity to acquire the knowledge and patterns-of-work needed for public-policy-making under development conditions. The insufficiency in the contribution of the government bureaucracy to public-policy-making is further aggravated by an overload with new problems and programmes. Also, in some of the development countries the new indigenous civil service absorbed the patterns of social behavior of the former senior class of expatriates, which do not fit the new conditions and which seriously impair contact between the civil servants and the new political leaders and/or the masses. The cumulative result is that in most development countries the senior civil service necessarily contributes much less to public-policy-making-optimality than their counterparts in the modern countries, thus compounding the non-optimal action-patterns of the politicians instead of compensating for them.

5. Findings in Regard to Process

(18). Extrarational processes play a tremendous role in public-policy-making. In some avant-garde development countries intuition is explicitly regarded as superior to knowledge, a phenomenon associated with some kind of *Führer* ideology. In most cases, rationalization (in the psychological sense) to justify public policy is extensively relied upon.

(19). As a result of the already mentioned facts, most of the elements needed for high-quality public-policy-making are little developed. Especially weak are the rational elements, most of which are in an embryonic stage. The extra-rational elements are relatively better developed, but also not very much so.

SOME IMPLICATIONS

The actual state of affairs in respect to public-policy-making in avant-garde development states must be compared with both their aspirations and their often expressed intention to base activities on the best available knowledge. The gap between actual public-policy-making and optimal, knowledge based, public-policy-making is very large indeed. In part this is unavoidable; in part this gap can be bridged, but only with the help of vigorous action, whole-hearted devotion and determination similar in intensity—but not in direction and method—to those which enabled these countries to achieve independence. At the same time, considering the critical role of public-policy-making for the achievement of their goals and the large gap between reality and minimum aspiration level, improvement of public-policy-making is one of the most urgent and promising challenges faced by the avant-garde development states.

25. PROBLEMS OF EMERGING BUREAUCRACIES IN DEVELOPING AREAS AND NEW STATES*

s. n. e i s e n s t a d t

I

In all developing countries, bureaucracies very rapidly tend to develop and extend their scope. As the post-colonial new states attained independence, and as some of the older states (e.g., Latin America or the Middle East) surged toward modernization and expanded the range of state activities, they took over many organs of public administration remaining from the former period; the scope of their activities greatly expanded, and new organs were created. Each became a very important part of the political framework in these countries. Since, in most of these countries, the government plays a great role in economic development, the bureaucracies also began to engage significantly in the activities of the economic sphere. The bureaucracy's activities could then have great

* From "Problems of Emerging Bureaucracies in Developing Areas and New States" by S. N. Eisenstadt. Reprinted from: *Industrialization and Society*, by F. Hoselitz and W. E. Moore, eds., (Mouton/Unesco, 1963), with the permission of Unesco. Selections from pp. 159–171.

influence on the direction and tempo of the country's economic development.

❊   ❊   ❊   ❊   ❊

I I

One of the striking facts about the bureaucracies of the developing
areas is that, in most of these areas there exist not one but usually two or
three, bureaucracies—or, at least, different layers of bureaucratic organization and structure. First, there is what may be called the "pre-
modern" or "pre-development" layer, which had developed before the
attainment of independence or the introduction of modernization. The
second stratum has, as a rule, developed since World War II. It was
engendered by the dual impacts of the attainment of independence and
of modernization and of establishing new social, political, and economic
goals.

In the post-colonial new states, the "old" colonial civil service still
survives in remaining personnel, organizational structure, and tradition.
The structure and organization of the old civil service provided the
basic framework for the extension and development of bureaucratic
administration after the attainment of independence.

Within these societies, the initial emergence of bureaucracies had
been rooted in the need of the colonial powers for various resources and
for the maintenance of law and order. The bureaucracy was based on
over-all political control by the metropolitan powers; the administration
participated minimally in the indigenous political and social life of the
community. This necessarily limited its activities, confining them to the
basic administrative services. It also dictated some of the bureaucracy's
structural characteristics, such as the high degree of centralization, the
great adherence to legal precepts and rules, and the relatively small
internal differentiation. Thus the pre-independence bureaucracies
helped establish the framework of modern, universalistic legal and
administrative practices and organizations. On the other hand, they
were highly apolitical. They did not meddle in politics, and they kept up
the ideal of a politically neutral civil service. They were also apolitical in
that they never really participated in the indigenous political life of the
countries in which they served. Their very limited goals were prescribed
by the colonial powers, who were not responsible to the political groups
and opinions of the countries which they ruled. . . . It is significant that
the scope and impact of the activities of the colonial civil service were
much greater in countries, such as India, in which "direct rule" was
applied, than in countries governed according to precepts of "indirect

rule," where the native population was left more or less alone to manage its own affairs, especially on the local level.

The second main layer of the bureaucracies in the new states consists of those departments and echelons which were developed after the attainment of independence. Here a new civil service—"new" in personnel, goals, departments, and activities—evolved. This stratum had to be staffed with new recruits—frequently with inadequately trained recruits whose chief claim to or qualification for office was their former participation in the nationalistic political movements. These new bureaucratic organs have had new types of goals, like economic development, social betterment, educational advancement, or community development.

Unlike members of the "colonial" civil service, most of the recruits to the new have usually had a clear and articulated political orientation and sense of political responsibility. They have very often perceived themselves as representatives of their respective movements, parties, or sectors. Moreover, they frequently have seen themselves as fulfilling chiefly political functions—either as implementing political goals, or as representing, articulating and regulating the political interests and activities of different groups and social strata.

The relations between the older bureaucracy and the new echelons have not always been easy. In the first period after independence, particularly, the nationalist leaders' prevailing attitude toward the remnants of the older colonial services was distrust. In some cases, this led to the almost complete destruction of the older structure. In most instances, however, some sort of *modus vivendi* has been evolved between the older and newer echelon. One or the other is usually predominant; but necessarily the implementation of new social, political, and economic goals has been strongly emphasized, and the involvement in the political process has been much greater than before.

An even more explicitly politically oriented type of bureaucracy has tended to emerge in most of the new states. This type consists of the different "party" bureaucracies which grew out of the leading nationalistic movements which became dominant parties—e.g., the Congress in India, the PCP in Ghana or the Neo-Destour in Tunisia. These party bureaucracies have been oriented more to the political manipulation of groups of population and to the provision of political support and loyalty to the new regime than to the upholding of universalistic legal norms, the development of public services, or the creation of new public administrative services. In personnel or over-all political supervision, the party bureaucracy has often been very similar to the new echelons of the governmental bureaucracy, and has sometimes also been closely related to it, especially through the activities of prime ministers and cabinet ministers. However, the basic patterns of activities and orientations of the members of the party bureaucracy have frequently differed to a very great extent from those of the governmental bureaucracy, and have sometimes clashed.[1]

III

The bureaucracies in developing countries which have not been under colonial rule exhibit a somewhat different, although not entirely dissimilar, pattern. Within each there existed, first, a traditional bureaucracy—whether "royal" (as in the Middle Eastern countries) or "oligarchical-republican" (as in most Latin American countries). These bureaucracies usually dominated the political scene until the end of World War II. Within them, some traditional elements were mixed with more modern ones. Frequently, the modern elements were copied from some European country—for example, the French pattern had strong influence in most Latin American countries.

These administrations were usually concerned with supporting the interests of the ruling oligarchies, and with implementing rather limited social and economic objectives. Whatever tendency to modernization they may have exhibited—e.g., in the fields of military affairs or education —their major political aim was to restrict modernization to those minimal spheres in which it was necessary to maintain the viability of the then existing system.

With increasing modernization, with the growing impact of internal democratization, and with the development of new social, political, and economic goals, these bureaucracies had to extend the scope of their activities and to recruit new personnel. However, the older pattern usually continued to leave its imprint on the new echelons and departments, in administrative training, organization, and to some extent also in social and political orientation.[2] . . .

In most of these older countries, the party bureaucracies were usually less important than in the new states. . . .

Both within the formerly colonial societies and in the states with longer traditions of independence, another distinct type of new bureaucratic organization has also emerged—the big economic or business corporation. Within the older countries, these corporations are usually more concentrated in the private sector; in the new states, more in the

---

[1] See D. Apter and R. A. Lystad, "Bureaucracy, Party and Constitutional Democracy," in G. M. Carter and W. O. Brown (eds.), *Transition in Africa* (Boston, 1958).
[2] See the papers by G. Blanksten and D. Rustow in G. A. Almond and J. S. Coleman (eds.), *The Politics of the Developing Areas* (Princeton, N. J., 1960). See also the papers by W. R. Sharp (on Egypt), A. Lepawsky (on Bolivia), F. Heady (on the Philippines), and J. N. More (on Thailand), in W. J. Siffin (ed.), *Toward the Comparative Study of Public Administration* (Bloomington, Ind., 1957).

public or mixed sectors. In all these societies, however, the corporations play an important role in the economic and political life of the country.

IV

We see thus that, in each emerging country, the pattern of development of bureaucracies has been very mixed and heterogeneous. Each part of the bureaucracy developed under somewhat different conditions and in response to different types of needs and pressures. It was only after the attainment of independence, and/or the development of goals and programs of modernization, that these parts were brought together into a common framework and confronted with the need to find some *modus vivendi* in order to deal with the new tasks which they faced.

Perhaps the most important general problem which faced all the bureaucracies was the necessity to adapt themselves to the goals, new spheres of activity, and new social needs that arose from the growing differentiation and diversification of the social structures, the extension of the scope of social and political participation of many groups in the society, and the development of new social and political goals. In trying to adapt themselves, the emerging bureaucracies developed several characteristics which were greatly influenced by their heterogeneous origins and by the conditions in which they found themselves.

※   ※   ※   ※   ※

The first and most important development in the social and political orientations of these bureaucracies is their high involvement in the political process in their respective countries. This is manifested in several ways.

In many of these countries, for example, the bureaucracy becomes not only the administrative arm of an executive, supervised by the legislature; it also constitutes itself as an effective executive or a component thereof, and plays a basic part in establishing, determining, and implementing political goals and major policy directives. In many nations, the bureaucracy may be the main or the only body which, apart from the head of the executive, is capable of formulating clear political and administrative goals and objectives.

The second major aspect of the bureaucracy's involvement in the political process is grounded in the fact that it tends to evolve as one of the principal instruments of political regulation—one of the main channels of political struggle in which and through which different interests are regulated and "aggregated"—and it tends to be very important, even predominant, in this facet of the political process. In some cases, e.g., in some Latin American countries, the bureaucracy also becomes a powerful pressure and interest group in its own right, strongly allied to other oligarchical groups.

Thus, in all these countries, the bureaucracy may tend to fulfill different types of political functions and—like parties, legislatures, and executives—become a center of various kinds of political activity. Although, through such activities, it may establish some of the basic frameworks of modern politics, it may also minimize the extent of differentiation of divers types of political roles and activities. In the latter case, it would greatly impede the development of autonomous and differentiated political activities, organizations, and orientations.

The second basic characteristic of the social orientations of emergent bureaucracies is that they are also major instruments of social change and of political socialization in their respective countries.

These bureaucratic organizations are (at least initially) based on universalistic and functionally specific definitions of the role of the official and the role of the client. The majority of the population of these countries, however, have a different orientation. In social life, their traditional orientations and structures, such as the extended family, are predominant. In these societies, most of a person's role relations are set within traditional groups; and rights and duties are defined in terms of personal relationships. Previous experience with bureaucratic organizations was restricted, and was rarely of any great significance.

Thus, the contacts of the public with governmental organizations provided a framework for a wider process of political socialization. The public's accommodation to the new political structure became, to a considerable extent, dependent upon its successful learning in these situations of contact. This has very often forced the bureaucracies to go beyond their proper specialized roles and to assume various roles of social and political leadership and tutelage—without which they could not have effected the necessary changes in the behavior of the population at large. This need to foster change often extended the scope of the activities of bureaucrats beyond their specific goals, and made them reach also into the realm of family, kinship, and community life of wide strata of the population.

✿   ✿   ✿   ✿   ✿

v

All these forces—the cultural orientations prevalent in these societies, the political and economic processes and pressures—necessarily have their repercussion on the structure of the bureaucracies and on their ability to implement major political and social goals and to provide continuous services to the population.

Among the most important of such structural problems, the following have often been noted:[3] (a) the low density of administrative structure, i.e., the relatively small ratio of officials to population and tasks; (b) the lack of fully qualified and adequate personnel; (c) the small extent of diversification of functions, and consequent overlapping between different organizations; (d) inadequate communication between different echelons and departments; and (e) overcentralization, poor co-ordination, and lack of autonomy and initiative of the linestaff.

Riggs has aptly summarized some of these problems, especially as they apply to older independent countries:

Obstacles to identification of personal with program goals are especially conspicuous in the way the work load and responsibilities of different officials are allocated, that is, in "organization and management." These often make it impossible for anyone to carry out a constructive project without waiting for the concurrence of many others, whereby many people have the power to block action. One result is often to elevate the level of settlement of even minor disputes to ministerial, cabinet, and chief executive levels. Top administrators become embroiled in continual interagency conflicts while subordinates piddle away their energies waiting for requisite approvals. Moreover, because many persons far from the scene of action become involved in decision making, questions are often referred to persons with only remote interest in them, it becomes difficult to assign responsibility for action, and final decisions hinge on the outcome of power struggles among individuals only indirectly concerned.[4]

In some countries, elaborate ministerial secretariats, staffed by generalists, who rotate frequently between headquarters and district assignments, have been placed in the line of communication and command between ministers and executive or administrative departments and divisions. Invariably, great delay ensues while secretariat officials review more and more of the work nominally assigned to and originating in the departments. We may quote the words of a distinguished former civil servant in India about the result:

The head of the department is deprived of all initiative and instead of being allowed to attend to and make progress with his own work, has to spend a great deal of time submitting unnecessary reports, explaining the position in individual matters to the Ministry and getting its orders on points which lie well within his own sphere of authority.

Because of overcentralization and lack of delegation, those close to the goals

[3] See, for instance, J. L. Quermonne, "La sous-administration et les politiques d'équipement administratif," *Revue française de science politique,* IX, No. 3 (Septembre, 1959), 629–67.

[4] F. W. Riggs, "Public Administration—A Neglected Factor in Economic Development," *Annals of the American Academy of Political and Social Science* (May, 1956), pp. 70–81.

of action cannot easily cooperate with their colleagues in other agencies whose work directly affects the success of their own efforts. Characteristically, to overcome this stagnation, new agencies are often set up in the hope that, outside the bog of established structures, action may be possible. But the new agencies simply add to the intra-bureaucratic conflict and competition, increasing the burden on the top of the hierarchy to impose coordination.[5]

The relative importance of these problems naturally varies in different countries. In the post-colonial countries, the most critical problems seem to be lack of adequate staff, overcentralization, and too little diversification. In the independent countries, the most vital problems are the excessive control, rigidity, and lack of initiative of the officials, and their regarding their offices as sinecures. However, there is much overlapping between these different structural aspects. And beyond all these, there always hovers the double specter of corruption and growing inefficiency of the bureaucracy.

26. CORRUPTION IN DEVELOPING COUNTRIES[*]

ronald wraith
and edgar simpkins

Throughout the fabric of public life in newly independent States runs the scarlet thread of bribery and corruption. This is admitted by everybody; very little can ever be proved about it.

The reaction of the educated citizens of these countries to this state of affairs is that of any other people; they are angry, ashamed, indifferent, cynical according to their different temperaments. What distinguishes them from people who live in a more fortunate atmosphere is that circumstances force even the angry and ashamed into a resigned apathy. Those who have tried to live as moral men in an amoral society

5   A. D. Gorwala, *Report on Public Administration* (New Delhi, 1951), p. 39. See also Paul H. Appleby, *Public Administration in India; Report of a Survey* (New Delhi, 1953), Sec. II, especially p. 21.
°   From Ronald Wraith and Edgar Simpkins, *Corruption in Developing Countries* (London: George Allen and Unwin Ltd., 1963), pp. 11–31. By permission.

have generally given way sooner or later under agonizing pressures; the pressure of legitimate ambition which can only be achieved by illegitimate means; the pressure from families, insatiable for help; the slow, insidious pressures of a society in which material success is adulated (even by the standards of the twentieth century), and where moreover material failure is ruthlessly mocked; the pressure of increasing defeatism, on realizing that public opinion stigmatizes the transgressor so lightly, and that so little seems to be gained from trying to swim against the tide. This is the general picture. Within it, some go on trying, a few with rare persistence; corporately they achieve little, since most of them are teachers or civil servants, firmly enmeshed in the system which they want to destroy, and silenced by the terms of their official employment.

✧   ✧   ✧   ✧   ✧

It is frustrating to try to write, one's phrases wrapped in a cocoon of ambiguity, about something which everybody knows, which no one dares openly to acknowledge, which can rarely be proved and which may lead to serious trouble if one is in the least incautious. Perhaps that is why studies of contemporary corruption are rare.

What can be said about corruption among the mandarins, and in the high places, can amount to no more than a few careful generalizations. Of corruption among the common or less gifted citizens one may write a little more freely. It is only of municipal corruption that one is able to write at large, free from the shadow of the law of libel; to write also with some precision, since the field especially in Nigeria has been admirably documented by successive Commissions of Inquiry, whose published works, now assuming a considerable bulk, are among the livelier contributions to contemporary Nigerian literature. It is a pity they are not better known.

Some years ago Dr Nkrumah shocked many Christians by permitting the base of his statue outside the Law Courts in Accra to be inscribed with the words—carved imperishably out of granite—'Seek ye first the Kingdom of Politics and all else shall be added unto you'. It is clear from subsequent events that this was hardly an over-estimate so far as some of his own supporters were concerned, and the Osageyfo himself was courageous enough in 1961 to compel his own Ministers to declare their business assets and commercial interests, and to do a full-time job for a full-time salary. This is no final solution, since people cannot be compelled to be honest, and a man of influence in public life has many opportunities to circumvent the letter of the law, through relatives, agents and foreign bank accounts. But the Osageyfo's gesture gave hope to many Africans.

✧   ✧   ✧   ✧   ✧

POLITICAL SYSTEMS

The writer has been told in more than one West African country, however, that corruption among top people must be seen with an understanding eye. It is not necessarily concerned with personal enrichment, or at least only in moderation. The root of the matter is that political parties need money, and the small subscription from the average man is not available. The large subscription from the man of influence must therefore take its place, and the accession of certain large sums to the party funds represents something not reprehensible, but notably self-sacrificial, on the part of those who are the channels of this communication. An unofficial percentage on a contract (and there are some big contracts), the compulsory purchase of land at an unorthodox price, a little wise direction in the development of real estate—these must not be too hastily condemned. It may well be.

It is unfortunate that Ministers, among whom are men of ability and integrity, should almost gratuitously have made themselves a butt, defined by the Oxford Dictionary as 'an object of teasing or ridicule', by possessing motor cars of embarrassing size and living in houses which are commonly said to have cost the taxpayer well over £30,000. Anyone who happens to travel in a car of extravagant aspect is now liable to have the word 'Meenister' shouted after him by the local urchins. . . . West Africa is sadly afflicted by the love of ostentation, and thousands of men on the middle and lower rungs are crippled financially because of it. Ministerial ostentation can perhaps be excused on the grounds of dignity of office, or more straightforwardly because Ministers can afford it; but it is an unfortunate example, and gives rise to cynicism.

How much is true and how much is false about corruption in high places nobody outside a small circle can ever know for certain. What *is* certain, and can be said without circumlocution, is that to wander through the corridors of power in these countries is to wander through a whispering-gallery of gossip, in which the fact of corruption at the highest levels is taken utterly for granted, and the only interest lies in capping the latest story with one that is even more startling.

There is of course an illicit glamour about alleged ministerial corruption which causes it to be talked about more perhaps than it deserves. It is certainly unfair to those Ministers who are free of it that they should be linked in the generic word 'ministerial' with those who are not.

It is indeed always unfair to speak of people in categories instead of as individuals. In the writer's experience the civil services in West Africa can, as a corporate whole and at the time of writing, be proud of their general integrity; on the other hand there is little doubt that the depredations of some civil servants are considerable. Those who deal direct with the public and are in a position to bestow benefits on individuals, or to influence their bestowal, are of course more vulnerable than the rest, and the known fact that some such men have avoided or declined promotion to higher salaried grades tells its own story.

✿ ✿ ✿ ✿ ✿

The problem has been openly and officially recognized in Ghana and Nigeria by the appointment of Advisory Commissions on the suppression of corruption in the public service, and more than one Government maintains an Anti-Corruption Officer on its normal strength.

✿

The economic effects of all this on a country may not be very considerable. The sum total of illicit gains is no doubt small in relation to the revenue, and there is no evidence from more developed countries where large-scale corruption is common that corruption and inefficiency are necessarily correlated. The taxpayer is of course being robbed, either directly in cash or indirectly by unsuitable appointments being made on his behalf. But by far the more serious loss is the loss of self-respect and the growth of frustration and cynicism. It is above all a moral problem, immeasurable and imponderable. And politicians and civil servants who are guilty are more guilty only in degree than the mass of people whom they represent and are supposed to serve.

✿

For while some of the corruption of which one hears in high places has at least a robust and buccaneering flavour, the corruption which one experiences oneself, or learns of at first hand through the tribulations of African dependants, is depressingly mean and squalid; and it is all-pervasive.

It is distressing that people who in the life of family, clan or tribe are generous with one another to the point of destitution should in the world of cash services, and among strangers, become so mean that the simplest service is extorted, quite illicitly, for a 'dash' or rake-off.

It is incongruous that in the merciful professions of nursing and medicine the out-patient must find his twopence for admission, at the head of the queue, to his rightful place; that in the most ignominious of human emergencies the bed-pan can only be secured for a penny; that the pound note is looked for under the pillow of the consulting room of the Government doctor.

To put a man in the way of a job at £5 a month ought, one would have supposed, to be a simple human kindness among people so underprivileged that to have a job at all is to be an aristocrat. To spoil it by the demand of a rake-off of several shillings a week for a year seems grasping and callous.

○   ○   ○   ○   ○

One turns to corruption in local government with a mixture of relief and dismay—relief because the actual facts have been more precisely investigated, and can be quoted; dismay because as matters stand at the time of writing local government in the southern Regions of Nigeria [1] has reached the point of being a conspiracy against the public, so riddled is it with bribery, nepotism, politics and corruption.

For many years the critics have been pointing to the folly of the colonial administration in forcing a veneer of British local government on West African territories, supposing in their blindness that a plant which has only been known to flourish in the temperate, misty and kindly atmosphere of England and Wales could be transplanted to the harsh, exotic climate of the African tropics. They happen to have been wrong in their facts, because the colonial administration, from the Colonial Office to the District Officer, has done its best to restrain West African governments from adopting *in toto* a system that they knew could never work; the pressure for its adoption came from within West Africa, and was based on the suspicion that differentiation meant discrimination, that modification meant the second best. . . .

The adoption of British local government, with ultimate power in the hands of elected councillors, but shorn of the restraints of British convention, compromise and mutual respect between elected representative and paid officials has amounted to an open invitation to corruption, an invitation eagerly if incredulously accepted.

The only supposition on which the English kind of local government can rest is that elected councillors are people who for one reason or another wish to serve the community. It may be due to the inherent goodness of their natures alone, or this may be fused in varying degrees with the love of power, the satisfaction of public regard, or an inability to mind their own business; but whatever the motive it could hardly be financial. In West Africa the position is otherwise. A government, presumably in its right senses, proposed to confer on councillors, with minimal constraints, the right to allocate market stalls, to control paid appointments and to award contracts. Even if the bribe required to get on the council in the first place were increased many times over, it would still become a sound investment. . . .

[1]   The North is less well documented.

It may seem strange to an English councillor that the allocation of market stalls should be of such importance to serious men, but among market-minded people in West Africa the possession of a stall in a big market means a comfortable income, of a strategically placed stall comparative wealth, and the control of a number of stalls for illicit subletting an enviable unearned competence. . . .

The tendency of councillors to allocate stalls to themselves, their wives, their relations, and then to the highest bidder can only be described as pronounced.

If a man has spent a month, as the author of the Aba Report did, in investigating such a highly specialized racket, he may presumably lose a little of the calm and detachment proper to an administrative officer. At any rate his language was more forthright than that of some of his colleagues working in the same general field, though with their wider opportunities and more varied interests. He was moved to say in his conclusions that he could

'only gasp at the entirely shameless conduct of the councillors and the executive staff. No moral principle and no prick of conscience appears to have entered their minds at any stage. . . . I find that all the councillors must be held jointly responsible for their decisions and actions. Not one has resigned in protest, and not one has asked that his name be recorded as voting against the scandalous allocations of . . . The Chairman of the Council is principally noteworthy for his sanctimonious announcements, deliberately calculated to deceive the public. This makes his deeds even more intolerable . . . My impression of Mr . . . , as a witness and as Chairman of the Markets Committee, is that he is without scruple.'

Although the language is slightly exceptional, the facts, regrettably, are not. There is even a silver lining to his Report, as he postulates the possibility of an honest council:

'Unfortunately, a policy that, in the hands of an honest council, operates satisfactorily and with justice may become an instrument of evil and oppression in the hands of a venal council. One needs two policies: one for the honest council and one for the corrupt council. Regrettably however it is not possible to devise any policy which can wholly defeat the depredations of a dishonest council. At some stage, when it comes to allocating market stalls, it is essential to separate the sheep from the goats if genuine traders only are to be allocated stalls. That means interviews and that in turn means opportunities for corruption.'

Others working in the sphere of local government find it difficult to grasp the concept of an honest council, since such a thing has never come their way; they have grown up with the racket and they assume— who can blame them?—that that is what local government means.

✧　✧　✧　✧　✧

A more sinister trend is the tendency of councillors not only to demand bribes for securing employment but for retaining it—what is known in more conventional gangster circles as protection money. The fact that influential councillors have been to council employees 'in the night' [2] and said that if they do not produce a given sum within a given time they will be sacked, has long been known to students of local government, who are grateful to Mr Nicholson in his Report on Ibadan for bringing it into the light of day. A considerable section of this Report (p. 20 onwards) is devoted to the almost incredible case of councillors who, to the Commissioner's satisfaction, blandly informed four 'revenue collectors' at the same car park that failure to pay £10 each would result in their dismissal. It is an interesting reflection that the councillors had no doubt that people who collected money on car parks, although presumably earning a bare living wage, would be in a position to pay this money. . . .

* * * * *

The word corruption, as usually employed, means the illicit gain of money or employment, and that is the principal sense in which it is discussed in these pages. A reference to corruption in local government would however be incomplete without some mention of political jobbery, which is corruption of another kind.

Local councils in Africa have tended to become extensions of national or regional political parties; they may be said to combine in one body what in Britain would be found in the local authority, concerned with the administration of services, and the local constituency organizations of the political parties, concerned with winning the next election. This has resulted in some painful situations; dismissal of council staff who were not politically acceptable; the appointment of party men with minimal qualifications for the job, or sometimes less; and the suppression of conscience.

In the higher reaches of the Lagos Town Council Mr Storey felt compelled to write as follows:

'Looked at from whatever angle you will, the incident (of the appointment of the Town Clerk) is calculated political jobbery without a single redeeming feature. It shows a callous disregard for the principles of honest local government, and is a matter of which the Democratic Party in the Lagos Town Council may even now feel ashamed. I condemn it without reserve.'

[2] A phrase widely used in Nigeria to cover a shady transaction; it does not necessarily mean that the deed was done after the hours of darkness, though these are favoured, but indicates rather a state of mind.

An election is traditionally the *locus classicus* of bribery and corruption, and it is impossible that Nigeria should escape the general infection. On the other hand one does not contemplate the conduct of an election in Nigeria with any great sense of outrage; it is the grotesque rather than the venal that weighs upon the spirit.

At the approach of an election considerable numbers of people lose their heads, and even leaders of ability and standing revert to a tender mental age. Wild and intemperate accusations fill the air. All sense of shame evaporates. The conduct of a campaign is, to put it mildly, uninhibited. This pandemonium, however, is caused by a few people and by the newspapers. Small stage armies of party agents, supporters and hangers-on, concerned more to draw attention, *fortissimo*, to the huge delinquencies of their opponents than to disseminate a creed, roam the streets and tear along the main roads, filling them with sound and fury. The newspapers, who must sell to an unsophisticated public (the lesser ones being themselves barely literate) treat all this as if it were an adult activity. It signifies, in fact, very little.

It has an occasional ugly side, since from time to time the police will find an electioneering van with weapons of a murderous kind. Their investigations generally reveal small parties of thugs on the loose, disowned by their parties, execrated by the mass of the people, and even they themselves whipped up not so much by a lust for blood as by an obsessional conviction that their opponents are doing the same thing; they are beastly, but in the total picture unimportant.

To see the picture in perspective, one has only to consider election day itself, when the melodramatic curtain-raiser is over and the general public takes the stage for the play itself. Almost invariably, election day is calm, level-headed, mature. The ordinary man and woman, unaffected by the vapourings that have gone before, behaves like a textbook citizen. It is a pity that the parties do not rise to the level of the people.

The serious thing from the point of view of national self-respect is the unquestioned assumption that opponents will cheat, and the inordinate effort that goes into the prevention of remote and improbable types of fraud. That fraud takes place, and that some of it is of a wildly improbable kind, is not to be denied; but that it has any significant effect on the results of an election is equally improbable.

In the fevered imaginations of party organizers their opponents plan to insert ink, glue or nitric acid into their ballot boxes,[3] to tear off their names and symbols from them, to forge ballot papers (in which they overestimate their technical proficiency), to bring in lorry loads of illicit voters, to bribe polling officers.

---

[3] Each candidate has his own, with his name and the symbol of his party pasted on it.

In cold fact, very few specific allocations are ever made, and most of these dissolve into a mist at the touch of the precise, searching question.

✿   ✿   ✿   ✿   ✿

But—and it cannot be too often repeated—all this activity, often degrading, sometimes farcical, is largely carried on by a few people whose professional business it is to do so, and in whom the electorate is not interested. It does not fairly represent the temper of the people, who are on the whole very sensible about elections.

It may be that the most venal aspect of elections, and the most harmful to the national interest, is that about which no vestige of proof can be offered—the purchase of candidatures and seats by bribery. It is rare that anyone who bribes or is bribed reaches the point of saying so, and the chances of ever discovering the facts about this matter are remote.

On the fringe of the problem, light relief is occasionally afforded by the hopeless independent candidate, who invests his deposit in the full intention of withdrawing at the last moment, as some regulations allow, and accepting a consideration from the rival who is in most fear of his vote being split. Occasionally also there are engaging arguments as to whether a 'feast' or any other form of the customary, almost obligatory, African hospitality constitutes 'treating', a cold and inappropriate word for an alien concept.

But the central and troubling question of what proportion of the candidates bribe, how they do it and how much they spend are unanswerable. There are not lacking those who claim to know; but when it comes to the point they will not say. It is clear that a high degree of corruption in government and administration makes candidature a sound and profitable investment, and it is assumed by all that the investment is widely made.

political and social problems

A broad array of complex social and political problems, many of which have already been identified, confront the developing states. Some of these problems involve the fundamental questions concerning the unit that is to constitute the state, the state's social and political institutions, and the system of law upon which political authority is to rest. Another group of problems concerns the basic policies to be pursued for the solution of major issues. Priorities must be set and decisions reached on the general allocation of scarce resources for purposes of modernization and development, for example. A third group consists of problems of a more specific nature. Decisions must be made on a variety of issues, such as the allocation of funds for specific projects, the location of roads, schools, and industry, the provisions for fire and police protection, public housing, health, and sanitation, and all the other routine problems confronting any state. Of course, no clear distinctions can be drawn between these several groups of problems; a problem that may deeply divide one society may be of quite secondary importance in another, and problems that at one time appear to be of major significance for a society may later seem to be of much less importance. Nevertheless, a broad distinction can be drawn between the problems that concern the very existence of a state and those that involve policy decisions on a wide range of social and economic questions.

In any society, most problems other than those involving the basic issues of human survival are "created" in the sense that existing conditions are regarded as unsatisfactory and alternatives are perceived to exist. In the developing states, many problems have been created by the gradual exposure of persons to different social, economic, and political values and institutions through various types of contact with the outside world. In many states, however, the masses (particularly in the rural areas) only dimly perceive the prospects for, or advantages of, change, though this condition is being altered, in some instances very rapidly. The limited physical and intellectual world in which the masses generally still live has conditioned them to accept life as inevitably harsh and often cruel. This attitude itself constitutes a major obstacle for the modernizing elite, who identify many more conditions in society as problems capable of resolution than do the masses. On the other hand, once the desire for change is stimulated, policies must be developed, taking into account the consequences of different alternative solutions to the problems that have been identified.

As the previous chapter has indicated, many of the transitional states have not as yet been able to develop stable political institutions and processes. Until a broader consensus is developed on the basic framework of the state and its principal institutions, efficient, effective decision-making is impeded. The development of such consensus is itself obstructed, however, by the ineffectiveness of the decision-making process in many states in resolving the increasing number of problems that have been identified as capable of political solution. Conversely, the demonstrated effectiveness of political institutions in achieving popular solutions usually tends to promote support for the institutions, processes, and individual leaders.

Among the most basic political problems confronting any state are those of defining the geographical limits of the state and the relationships of the constituent parts to the whole. In some of the developing states, great difficulty has been encountered in establishing the geographical basis for statehood. The Federation of Malaysia, for example, created in 1963, was fractured by the withdrawal of one of its constituent states, Singapore, in 1965. Similarly, in the Middle East, Egypt's unification with Syria in 1958, establishing the United Arab Republic, collapsed in 1961 when Syria reasserted its independence. In sub-Saharan Africa, several unsuccessful attempts have been made to create viable federations. The Mali Federation, initially agreed upon by Senegal, Soudan, and Upper Volta in 1959, was disrupted within one month by the withdrawal of Upper Volta and collapsed completely in 1960. The Central African Federation, established by the British in 1953 for its colonies of Northern and Southern Rhodesia and Nyasaland, disintegrated in 1963 when Nyasaland, renamed Malawi, became a fully independent state and withdrew from the Federation. Northern Rhodesia, taking the name Zambia, achieved its independence in 1964, while Southern Rhodesia proclaimed its independence as Rhodesia in 1965, despite the vigorous opposition of the British Government. Undoubtedly the greatest disappointment to most observers of the developing states was the disruption in 1967 of the Nigerian Federation, created at the time independence was granted by the British in 1960. A notable exception to this list of failures to organize new states was the creation in 1964 of Tanzania out of the formerly independent states of Zanzibar and Tanganyika.

In several other states, dissident minorities have sought, unsuccessfully so far, to establish their own independent states or autonomous regions. The Karens, along with several other groups in Burma, have demanded their own states, as have the Kurds in Iraq, who have occasionally resorted to armed conflict to support their claims to independence. A long period of conflict and the eventual dispatch of military forces under United Nations authority in 1960 resulted from the attempt of Katanga, one of the principal provinces of the newly established Republic of the Congo, to assert its independence. Ethnic and other regional groups have from time to time voiced their demands for independence in other states in Asia and Africa, as in Thailand and India, sometimes taking up arms against the central government in support of their demands.

The specific issues that have encouraged efforts to merge several independent states, and those that have contributed to the disintegration of states and the demands for independence, have varied from case to case. Economic advantages and ethnic or racial ties are usually the motivating forces for mergers, as in the case of the Mali Federation. The threat of possible discrimination, the right of self-determination, and the economic advantages of independence, on the other hand, are the principal justifications cited by those groups and their leaders who seek to create new, independent states. In the case of Pakistan, for example, independence from India was demanded on the grounds that the Muslim population would be discriminated against by the dominant Hindu population. Katanga sought its independence primarily because it did not wish its advanced economy to be burdened by the backward conditions existing in the other provinces of the Republic of the Congo.

In addition to the problem some states have had in establishing a legal identity, boundary disputes have also disrupted attempts to create stable, geographically defined nation-states. In Latin America, the boundaries of most states have remained fixed for some time, though Paraguay and Bolivia engaged in a bitter war from 1932 to 1935 over the Chaco territory, and Argentina and Chile have a long-standing controversy over parts of their long common border. In Asia and Africa, boundary disputes are more common, in part because of the imprecise boundaries drawn by the colonial powers, and in part because of traditional rivalries and the refusal to recognize boundaries agreed upon by earlier governments. Recent examples of boundary disputes, in some cases leading to hostilities, include China's controversy with India, Malaysia's disputes with Indonesia and the Philippines, Pakistan and India's long rivalry over Kashmir, and the controversies between the several Arab states, and between them and Israel. Most of the developing states have had difficulties, at some time in their history, in fixing firm boundaries, and border disputes remain an important source of contention between states in many areas.

For many of the developing states, a much more urgent problem than that of boundaries is the problem of establishing a stable political system. A number of these states, as noted earlier, have either discarded the constitutions adopted at the time independence was achieved, or they have modified in important details the institutional arrangements of their governments. In many cases, e.g. Burma, Pakistan, Indonesia, Nigeria, and a number of Latin American states, the overthrow of the civilian government by the military destroyed the previous constitutional framework of government and initiated the search for new institutional arrangements. The need for stronger, more efficient and effective political authority has been the usual justification for replacing one form of government with another. The urgent problems of nation-building and social and economic development require, many leaders assert, the vigorous leadership that only the armed forces can supply. Even where the military has not assumed direct control, it frequently is a principal agency through which the developmental programs are executed.

Aside from, but intimately related to, the problems of creating a stable, geographically defined state and its political system, none of the problems facing the governments of the developing states is more basic than that of the lack of national unity and identity on the part of many groups and individuals in society. This problem is particularly acute in many of the new states in Asia and Africa, but it is found in almost all of the other developing states as well. Traditional loyalties to ethnic, regional, linguistic, tribal, and religious groups frequently take precedence over national loyalties. In those states that attained their independence only after a protracted struggle, these groups often cooperated against the colonial power, but the primary identification of most individuals remained with their own groups. These traditional loyalties not only threaten the continued existence of some states, as evidenced above in the demands for separate states or autonomy within the state, but they also undermine the stability of governments and thwart the implementation of national policies. To encourage a sense of national identity and purpose, the governments of the developing states employ a variety of techniques and policies. In some cases, force has been necessary to prevent secessionist movements from succeeding. The resort to force to preserve national unity is, of course, by itself an unsatisfactory solution since it often increases the solidarity and isolation of the dissident group. Persuasion, rather than coercion, is more conducive to the development of national loyalties and the stability of the state and its government.

Many of the policies designed to encourage nationalism have, in addition, their own intrinsic or practical justification. The establishment of an educational system, for example, is supported as essential for the development of individual dignity and intellectual growth as well as for the development of those skills necessary for a modern economy. At the same time, however, these policies may also, at least in their more immediate consequences, result in increased tensions and strains within the society. An increasing educational level may, using our example, stimulate demands for more rapid changes than can be successfully executed, or it may lead to a greater awareness of the differences among the several groups in society, each seeking to protect its unique characteristics. Thus, in devising and coordinating policies that will promote national unity and development, account must be taken of the possible adverse effects of these policies in the transitional period before their full advantages can be realized.

Despite the possibility of adverse consequences, leaders of the modernizing states place great emphasis upon the development of a comprehensive educational system not only because an increasingly literate and skilled population is necessary for economic development, but also because national unity will be strengthened. The assumption is that as achievements are registered in raising the standard of living and in creating a more interdependent economy, national unity will increase. Yet, in planning and executing their educational policies (and this applies in other policy areas as well), the leaders are obstructed by a combination of psychological and material factors. The funds that can be allocated to educational programs are, of course, limited. The general shortage of qualified teachers is intensified in the rural areas, since many teachers are reluctant to accept the low pay and often poor working conditions in these areas, preferring the more favorable urban environments. In addition, the leaders' emphasis on technical training in higher education runs counter to the traditional preference of students for education in law and the humanities; technical training is commonly regarded as inferior education and socially unacceptable.

The attempt to establish an official language for the state, to be used as the medium for instruction in the schools as well as in business and governmental transactions, has sharply divided a number of states. While there is general recognition of the utility of a single language in promoting national unity and the economic and social development of the states, there is often little agreement on which language to choose. Some of the Westernized elite prefer to retain the language of the former colonial power. Some of them have used this language so long that they are far more competent in it than in any of the indigenous languages in their states. Further, they prefer the Western language on grounds that it facilitates trade and other relationships with Western states on whom they must rely for aid, both in financial matters and in the supply of technical skills. Other leaders and groups, however, demand the use of an indigenous language, asserting that the use of one of their languages will protect and promote their cultures and establish their identities apart from the former colonial powers. The choice of a single indigenous language, however, poses its own difficulties. The decision in favor of any language is often vigorously contested by those groups whose language and culture are to be accorded a secondary position. The conflict over an official language in India and several other states has, at times, become so intense that the basic structure of the state has been threatened. In India, lingual states have had to be recognized to preserve the national state. This solution is opposed, however, by many leaders in other states who regard a single language as essential to unity and progress.

Industrial expansion, with its corollary development of transportation and communication networks, is also regarded as a means to promote both the unity and the welfare of society. Although general support for programs of industrialization is common, the leaders must again overcome many obstacles in addition to those concerning the financing of new industries. The traditional values and habits relating to work, savings, and investment are frequently not conducive to rapid expansion of industrial production. Further, hostile reactions have often arisen from groups who believe that their welfare is being threatened by the industrial policies of their national leaders. The specific location of industries is frequently vigorously contested. While the location of government-sponsored industries and developmental projects, such as dams and irrigation works, is also a politically involved issue in more developed states, the economic and political implications of such decisions in the developing states are more acute because of the relatively greater role of the government in economic development programs, the relatively greater impact of individual industries on the economy of an area, and the existing higher level of social fragmentation.

In addition to the economic and social policies designed to promote the unification of the state, leaders also attempt to evoke an emotional response to the nation-state. They seek to develop a sense of pride in the accomplishments of the state, stressing that these were possible only as a result of the unified efforts of the people. Those common elements (such as religion) of the various groups in the state are emphasized, while the divisive factors are ignored as far as possible. Single mass political parties, as has been indicated, are another means used to promote unity, as are the ideologies articulated by the leaders. Thus, through ideas as well as material advances, attempts are being made to advance the level of consensus among the disparate groups in society.

Even in the relatively well-integrated states, a number of problems demand the attention of the governments. Rapidly growing populations, particularly in urban areas, create a number of social and economic problems. The fastest rate of population growth is, with a few exceptions such as the United Arab Republic, occurring in Latin America, with an average increase of 2.4 per cent, while in Asia and Africa the figure is about 2 per cent annually. (In the United Arab Republic the rate is 2.8 per cent.) At the present rates, therefore, the population of these areas may double in thirty-five years. India's large population, for example, is growing at the rate of about nine million a year, a figure that has alarmed Indian leaders and led them to consider drastic measures, such as raising the legal age for marriage and instituting programs of birth control, to reduce the growth rate. Jobs must be found for the ever-increasing work force, particularly in industry, since few workers can be absorbed by the agricultural segment of the economy. Indeed, as agricultural methods improve through increasing mechanization, fewer agricultural workers will be required in the future. Additional pressures for the expansion of industrial job opportunities result from the increasing life span of the workers, the disinclination of the educated youth to accept the standard of living provided by the traditional agrarian economy, and the increasing number of women who are seeking employment.

The attempts to reduce the growth rate in those states in which it has become a serious problem frequently encounter much opposition, even though in many cases of a largely passive nature. Religious principles, such as those of the Catholic Church, may inhibit the use of birth control devices. The use of such devices, even where not prohibited because of religious considerations, is often scorned by those persons who prize large families. In many cultures, large families not only give social prestige but are also a form of economic security for the non-productive years of the parents. Since few governments as yet have extensive old-age assistance or medical care programs, families must rely largely on their own resources for support in cases of illness and unemployment.

The provision of basic services in the expanding urban areas has been difficult in many states. One reason is that the tax base of the cities has usually grown far less rapidly than have the demands for services, since the movement of large numbers of persons into the cities has preceded the expansion of business and industry. In addition, the population turnover in the cities tends to be high as many persons move from city to city seeking jobs or else return to the rural areas. Appalling slums have developed in most cities. In many cities, supplies of water and electricity are inadequate, as is fire and police protection. Crime rates are often high. At present, little progress is evident in solving the complex problems of the urban areas.

The changing conditions—and the aspirations for even more extensive changes—in the social, economic, and political systems of the developing states have thus created innumerable problems for their political leaders. Heavy demands are placed upon them to devise policies that will enable their societies to progress in an orderly fashion to the goals to which they aspire. As yet, it is too early to estimate the chances for success for most states; what is certain is that a profound social, economic, and political revolution is reshaping the societies that until recently were of little concern to the major powers of the world.

SUGGESTED READINGS

Alexander, Robert J., *Organized Labor in Latin America*. New York, The Free Press, 1965.

Beling, Willard A., *Modernization and African Labor*. New York, Frederick A. Praeger, Inc., 1965.

Binder, Leonard, *Religion and Politics in Pakistan*. Berkeley, Calif., University of California Press, 1961.

Black, Cyril E., *The Dynamics of Modernization*. New York, Harper & Row, 1966.

Braibanti, Ralph, and Spengler, Joseph J., eds., *Tradition, Values, and Socio-Economic Development*. Durham, N. C., Duke University Press, 1961.

Coleman, James S., ed., *Education and Political Development*. Princeton, N. J., Princeton University Press, 1965.

Cowan, L. Gray, O'Connell, James, and Scanlon, David G., eds., *Education and Nation-Building in Africa*. New York, Frederick A. Praeger, Inc., 1965.

Crozier, Brian, *The Morning After: A Study of Independence*. New York, Oxford University Press, 1963.

Curle, Adam, *Educational Strategy for Developing Societies*. London, Tavistock Publications, 1963.

Deutsch, Karl W., and Foltz, William J., eds., *Nation-Building*. New York, Atherton Press, 1963.

Fisher, Sidney N., ed., *The Military in the Middle East: Problems in Society and Government*. Columbus, Ohio, Ohio State University Press, 1963.

Froehlich, Walter, ed., *Land Tenure, Industrialization and Social Stability*. Milwaukee, Wisc., The Marquette University Press, 1961.

Geertz, Clifford, ed., *Old Societies and New States*. New York, The Free Press of Glencoe, 1963.

Hoselitz, Bert F., and Moore, Wilbert E., eds., *Industrialization and Society*. Paris, UNESCO, 1963.

Janowitz, Morris, *The Military in the Political Development of New Nations*. Chicago, University of Chicago Press, 1964.

Montgomery, John D., and Siffin, William J., eds., *Approaches to Development: Politics, Administration and Change*. New York, McGraw-Hill Book Company, 1966.

Nayar, Baldev R., *Minority Politics in the Punjab*. Princeton, N. J., Princeton University Press, 1966.

Pike, Frederick B., *The Conflict Between Church and State in Latin America.* New York, Alfred A. Knopf, 1964.

Pye, Lucian W., *Aspects of Political Development.* Boston, Little, Brown and Company, 1966.

————, and Verba, Sidney, eds., *Political Culture and Political Development.* Princeton, N. J., Princeton University Press, 1965.

————, *Politics, Personality, and Nation Building: Burma's Search for Identity.* New Haven, Conn., Yale University Press, 1962.

Schramm, Wilbur, *Mass Media and National Development.* Stanford, Calif., Stanford University Press, 1964.

Sinai, I. R., *The Challenge of Modernization.* New York, W. W. Norton & Company, Inc., 1964.

van den Berghe, Pierre L., ed., *Africa: Social Problems of Change and Conflict.* San Francisco, Chandler Publishing Company, 1965.

Wolf, Eric R., *Peasants.* Englewood Cliffs, N. J., Prentice-Hall, Inc., 1966.

Yu, Frederick T. C., *Mass Persuasion in Communist China.* New York, Frederick A. Praeger, Inc., 1964.

⌒〰⌒

A . Nation-Building

27. POLITICAL INTEGRATION AND POLITICAL DEVELOPMENT[*][†]

m y r o n   w e i n e r

It is often said of the developing nations that they are "unintegrated" and that their central problem, often more pressing than that of economic development, is the achievement of "integration." The term "integra-

[*] From "Political Integration and Political Development" by Myron Weiner, *New Nations: The Problem of Political Development, The Annals,* Vol. 358 (March, 1965), pp. 53–62. By permission of the publisher and the author.

[†] This article is a preliminary version of a portion of a study I am preparing for the Social Science Research Council Committee on Comparative Politics. The final and full version will be published in a volume entitled *The Political System and Political Development.* I want to take this opportunity to express my appreciation to the Committee for granting me permission to publish this version at this time, and to express my intellectual appreciation to my four collaborators in this study—Lucian

tion" is now widely used to cover an extraordinarily large range of political phenomena. It is the purpose of this article to analyze the various uses of this term, to show how they are related, then to suggest some of the alternative strategies pursued by governments to cope with each of these "integration" problems.

DEFINITIONS

(1) Integration may refer to the process of bringing together culturally and socially discrete groups into a single territorial unit and the establishment of a national identity. When used in this sense "integration" generally presumes the existence of an ethnically plural society in which each group is characterized by its own language or other self-conscious cultural qualities, but the problem may also exist in a political system which is made up of once distinct independent political units with which people identified. . . .

(2) Integration is often used in the related sense to refer to the problem of establishing national central authority over subordinate political units or regions which may or may not coincide with distinct cultural or social groups. . . .

(3) The term "integration" is often used to refer to the problem of linking government with the governed. Implied in this usage is the familiar notion of a "gap" between the elite and the mass. . . .

(4) Integration is sometimes used to refer to the minimum value consensus necessary to maintain a social order. These may be end values concerning justice and equity, the desirability of economic development as a goal, the sharing of a common history, heroes, and symbols, and, in general, an agreement as to what constitutes desirable and undesirable social ends. Or the values may center on means, that is, on the instrumentalities and procedures for the achievement of goals and for resolving conflicts. . . .

(5) Finally, we may speak of "integrative behavior," referring to the capacity of people in a society to organize for some common purposes. At the most elementary level all societies have the capacity to create some kind of kinship organization—a device whereby societies propagate themselves and care for and socialize their young. As other needs and desires arise within a society we may ask whether the capacity grows to create new organizations to carry out new purposes. In some societies the capacity to organize is limited to a small elite and is only associated

Pye, Leonard Binder, Joseph LaPalombara and James S. Coleman, not only for their comments on this manuscript and for the many ideas of theirs which found their way into these pages, but for the intellectual excitement of the entire venture. Needless to say, I alone am responsible for any errors and follies which this essay contains.

with those who have authority.[1] Only the state, therefore, has a capacity to expand for the carrying out of new functions. In still other societies organizational capacities are more evenly spread throughout the population, and individuals without coercive authority have the readiness to organize with others. Societies differ, therefore, in the extent to which organizational proclivities are pervasive or not, and whether organizations are simply expressive in character—that is, confined to kinship and status—or purposive.

. . . As diverse as these definitions are, they are united by a common thread. These are all attempts to define what it is *which holds a society and a political system together.* Scholars of the developing areas have groped for some such notions of integration, for they recognize that in one or more of these senses the political systems they are studying do not appear to hold together *at a level commensurate with what their political leadership needs to carry out their goals.* If each scholar has in his mind a different notion of "integration," it is often because he is generalizing from one or more specific societies with which he is familiar and which is facing some kind of "integration" problem. Since there are many ways in which systems may fall apart, there are as many ways of defining "integration."

✧   ✧   ✧   ✧   ✧

FORMS AND STRATEGIES

Transitional or developing political systems are generally less integrated than either traditional or modern systems. This is because these systems cannot readily perform the functions which the national leadership—or in some instances, the populace too—expects them to perform. . . . When we speak of political development, therefore, we are concerned first with the expanding functions of the political system, secondly with the new level of integration thereby required to carry out these functions, and, finally, with the capacity of the political system to cope with these new problems of integration. . . .

National Integration

It is useful to ask why it is that new nations with pluralistic social orders require more national integration than did the colonial regimes

---

[1] For an analysis of the attitudes which inhibit organized activity see Edward Banfield, *The Moral Basis of a Backward Society* (Glencoe, Ill.: Free Press, 1958). Though Banfield's study is confined to a single village in Italy, he raises the general problem of analyzing the capacities of a people to organize for common purposes.

which preceded them. The obvious answer is that colonial governments were not concerned with national loyalties but with creating classes who would be loyal to them as a colonial power. Colonial governments, therefore, paid little or no attention to the teaching of a "national" language or culture, but stressed instead the teaching of the colonial language and culture. We are all familiar with the fact that educated Vietnamese, Indonesians, Nigerians, Indians, and Algerians were educated in French, English, and Dutch rather than in their own languages and traditions. Although the colonialist viewed the development of national loyalties as a threat to his political authority, the new leadership views it as essential to its own maintenance. Moreover, since the colonial rulers permitted only limited participation, the parochial sentiments of local people rarely entered into the making of any significant decisions of essential interest to policy makers. Once the new nations permit a greater measure of public participation, then the integration requirements of the system are higher. Moreover, the new elite in the new nations have higher standards of national integration than those of their former colonial rulers and this, too, creates new integration problems.

✧   ✧   ✧   ✧   ✧

How nations have handled the problems of national integration is a matter of historical record. Clifford Geertz [2] has pointed out that public policy in the first instance is effected by patterns of social organization in plural societies. These patterns include (1) countries in which a single group is dominant in numbers and authority and there are one or more minority groups; (2) countries in which a single group is dominant in authority but not numbers; (3) countries in which no single group by itself commands a majority nor is a single group politically dominant; and (4) countries of any combination in which one or more minorities cut across international boundaries. Examples of the first group are prewar Poland (68 per cent Polish), contemporary Ceylon (70 per cent Sinhalese), and Indonesia (53 per cent Javanese). The dominant minority case is best exemplified by South Africa (21 per cent "white"). The best examples of complete pluralism with no majorities are India, Nigeria, and Malaya and, in Europe, Yugoslavia and Czechoslovakia. And finally, among the minorities which cross international boundaries, the most troublesome politically have been the Kurds, the Macedonians, the Basques, the Armenians, and the Pathans. In contemporary Africa, there are dozens of tribes which are cut by international boundaries, and in Southeast Asia there are substantial Chinese and Indian minorities.

[2] See Clifford Geertz, "The Integrative Revolution: Primordial Sentiments and Civil Politics in the New States," *Old Societies and New Nations*, ed., Clifford Geertz (New York: Free Press of Glencoe, 1963).

In general there are two public policy strategies for the achievement of national integration: (1) the elimination of the distinctive cultural traits of minority communities into some kind of "national" culture, usually that of the dominant cultural group—a policy generally referred to as assimilationist: "Americanization," "Burmanization," "detribalization;" (2) the establishment of national loyalties without eliminating subordinate cultures—the policy of "unity in diversity," politically characterized by "ethnic arithmetic." In practice, of course, political systems rarely follow either policy in an unqualified manner but pursue policies on a spectrum somewhere in between, often simultaneously pursuing elements from both strategies.

The history of ethnic minorities in national states is full of tragedy. If today the future of the Watusi in East Africa, the Hindus in East Pakistan, the Turks in Cyprus and the Greeks in Turkey, and Indians in Burma and Ceylon is uncertain, let us recall the fate of minorities in the heterogeneous areas of East Europe. . . .

It is sad to recount an unpleasant historical fact—that few countries have successfully separated political loyalties from cultural loyalties. The dominant social groups have looked with suspicion upon the loyalty of those who are culturally different—generally, though not always (but here, too, we have self-fulfilling prophecies at work) with good reason. Where killings, population transfers or territorial changes have not occurred, the typical pattern has been to absorb the ethnic minority into the dominant culture or to create a new amalgam culture. . . . It remains to be seen whether the ideal of unity and diversity, that is, *political* unity and *cultural* diversity, can be the foundation for modern states. Perhaps the most promising prospects are those in which no single ethnic group dominates—Nigeria, India, and Malaysia. . . .

Territorial Integration

The associations of states with fixed territories is a relatively modern phenomenon. The fluctuating "boundaries" of historic empires, and the fuzziness at the peripheries where kinship ties and tributary arrangements marked the end of a state are no longer acceptable arrangements in a world where sovereignty is characterized by an exclusive control over territory. In time the control over territory may be accompanied by a feeling of common nationality—our "national integration," but there must first of all be territorial integration. For most new states—and historic ones as well—the establishment of a territory precedes the establishment of subjective loyalties. A Congo nation cannot be achieved, obviously, without there being a Congo state, and the first order of business in the Congo has been the establishment by the central government of its authority over constituent territorial units. Some scholars have distinguished between the state and the nation, the former referring to the existence of central authority with the capacity to control a given territory and the latter to the extent of subjective loyalty on the part of the population within that territory to the state. There are, of course, instances where the "nation" in this sense precedes the "state" —as in the case of Israel and, according to some, Pakistan—but more typically the "state" precedes the "nation." "Nation-building," to use the increasingly popular phrase, thus presumes the prior existence of a state in control of a specified—and, in most instances, internationally recognized—territory. Territorial integration is thus related to the problem of *state-building* as distinct from *nation-building*.

☆   ☆   ☆   ☆   ☆

Value Integration

The integration of values—whatever else it encompasses—at a minimum means that there are acceptable procedures for the resolution of conflict. All societies—including traditional societies—have conflicts, and all societies have procedures for their resolution. But as societies begin to modernize, conflicts multiply rapidly, and the procedures for the settlement of conflict are not always satisfactory. There are societies where the right of traditional authority to resolve conflict remained intact during the early phases of modernization—Japan comes readily to mind—and were thereby able to avoid large-scale violence. But these are the exceptions. Why does the system require a new level of value integration?

First of all, the scale and volume of conflict increases in societies experiencing modernization. The status of social groups is frequently changed, even reversed, as education opens new occupational opportunities, as the suffrage increases the political importance of numbers, and as industrial expansion provides new opportunities for employment and wealth. A caste or tribe, once low in status and wealth, may now rise or at least see the opportunity for mobility. And social groups once high in power, status, and wealth may now feel threatened. Traditional rivalries are aggravated, and new conflicts are created as social relationships change.

The modernization process also creates new occupational roles and these new roles often conflict with the old. The new local government officer may be opposed by the tribal and caste leader. The textile manufacturer may be opposed by producers of hand-loomed cloth. The doctor may be opposed by a traditional healer. To these, one could add an enormous list of conflicts associated with modernization: the conflicts between management and labor characteristic of the early stages of industrial development, the hostility of landlords to government land-reform legislation, the hostility of regions, tribes, and religious groups with one another as they find it necessary to compete—often for the first time—in a common political system where public policies have important consequences for their social and economic positions. Finally, we should note the importance of ideological conflicts so often found in developing societies as individuals try to find an intellectually and emotionally satisfying framework for re-creating order out of a world of change and conflict.

There are two modal strategies for integrating values in a developing society. One stresses the importance of consensus and is concerned with maximizing uniformity. This view of consensus, in its extreme, emphasizes as a goal the avoidance of both conflict and competition through either coercion or exhortation. A second view of the way integrative values may be maximized emphasizes the interplay of individual and group interests. Public policy is thus not the consequence of a "right" policy upon which all agree, but the best policy possible in a situation in which there are differences of interests and sentiments.

Since most developing societies lack integrative values, political leaders in new nations are often self-conscious of their strategies. . . .

. . . The problem has been one of finding acceptable procedures and institutions for the management of conflict. It is striking to note the growth of dispute-settling institutions in modern societies. When these bodies are successful, it is often possible to prevent conflicts from entering a country's political life. Here we have in mind the social work agencies, churches and other religious bodies, lawyers and the courts, labor-management conciliation bodies and employee councils, and inter-racial and interreligious bodies. The psychiatrist, the lawyer, the social worker, and the labor mediator all perform integrating roles in the modern society. In the absence of these or equivalent roles and institutions in rapidly changing societies in which conflict is growing, it is no wonder that conflicts move quickly from the factory, the university, and the village into political life.

A modern political system has no single mechanism, no single procedure, no single institution for the resolution of conflict; indeed, it is precisely the multiplicity of individuals, institutions, and procedures for dispute settlement that characterizes the modern political system—both democratic and totalitarian. In contrast, developing societies with an increasing range of internal conflict, typically lack such individuals, institutions, and procedures. It is as if mankind's capacity to generate conflict is greater than his capacity to find methods for resolving conflict; the lag is clearly greatest in societies in which fundamental economic and social relationships are rapidly changing.

Elite-Mass Integration

The mere existence of differences in goals and values between the governing elite and the governed mass hardly constitutes disintegration so long as those who are governed accept the right of the governors to govern. . . . The integration of elite and mass, between governors and the governed, occurs not when differences among the two disappear, but when a pattern of authority and consent is established. In no society is consent so great that authority can be dispensed with, and in no society is government so powerful and so internally cohesive that it can survive for long only through the exercise of cohesive authority. We need to stress here that both totalitarian and democratic regimes are capable of establishing elite-mass integration and that the establishment of a new pattern of relations between government and populace is particularly important during the early phase of development when political participation on a large scale is beginning to take place.

It is commonplace to speak of the "gap" between governors and the governed in the new nations, implying that some fundamental cultural and attitudinal gaps exist between the "elite" and the "mass," the former being secular-minded, English- or French-speaking, and Western-educated, if not Western-oriented, while the latter remain oriented toward traditional values, are fundamentally religious, and are vernacular-speaking.[3] In more concrete political terms, the government may be concerned with increasing savings and investment and, in general, the postponement of immediate economic gratification in order to maximize long-range growth, while the public may be more concerned with immediate gains in income and, more fundamentally, equitable distribution or social justice irrespective of its developmental consequences. . . .

Perhaps too much is made of the attitudinal "gap" between governors and governed; what is more important perhaps is the attitude of government toward its citizens. Nationalist leaders out of power are typically populist. They generally identify with the mass and see in the "simple peasant" and the "working class" qualities which will make a good society possible. But once the nationalist leadership takes power and satisfies its desire for social status it tends to view the mass as an impediment to its goals of establishing a "modern," "unified," and "powerful" state. From being the champion of the masses the elite often becomes their detractor.

[3] For a critique of "gap" theories of political development, see Ann Ruth Willner, "The Underdeveloped Study of Political Development," *World Politics* (April 1964), pp. 468–482.

In all political systems, those of developing as well as developed societies, there are differences in outlook between those who govern and those who are governed. In a developed system, however, those who govern are accessible to influence by those who are governed—even in a totalitarian system—and those who are governed are readily available for mobilization by the government. In modern societies governments are so engaged in effecting the economy, social welfare, and defense that there must be a closer interaction between government and the governed.[4]

. . .

But whatever their fear of the masses, governmental elites in new nations cannot do without them. While the elite may be unsympathetic to mass efforts to exercise influence, the elite does want to mobilize the masses for its goals. In some developing societies an organizational revolution is already under way as men join together for increasingly complex tasks to create political parties, newspapers, corporations, trade unions, and caste and tribal associations. Governmental elites are confronted with a choice during the early stages of this development. Should they seek to make these new organizations instruments of the authoritative structures or should these organizations be permitted to become autonomous bodies, either politically neutral or concerned with influencing government? When the state is strong and the organizational structures of society weak—a condition often found in the early phases of postcolonial societies with a strong bureaucratic legacy—then government leadership clearly has such an option.[5] It is at this point that the classic issue of the relationship of liberty and authority arises, and the elite may choose to move in one direction rather than the other.

The choices made are often shaped by dramatic domestic or international crises of the moment. But they are also affected by the society's tradition of elite-mass relations. . . . [T]he behavior of many African leaders can often be understood better by exploring the customary patterns of authority in traditional tribal society than by reference to any compulsions inherent in the development process.

In the analysis of elite-masses relations much attention is rightly given to the development of "infra-structures"—that is, political parties, newspapers, universities, and the like—which can provide a two-way communication channel between government and populace.[6] Much attention is also given to the development of a "middle strata" of individ-

---

[4] Karl Deutsch has pointed out that governments of industrial societies, whether totalitarian or democratic, spend a larger proportion of their GNP than do governments in underdeveloped economies, irrespective of their ideologies.

[5] This theme is amplified by Fred W. Riggs, "Bureaucrats and Political Development: A Paradoxical View," *Bureaucracy and Political Development*, ed., Joseph La-Palombara (Princeton, N. J.: Princeton University Press, 1963).

[6] For a discussion of the role of infra-structures in political development, see Edward Shils, *Political Development in the New States* (The Hague: Mouton, 1962).

uals who can serve as links—newspapermen, lobbyists, party bosses, and precinct workers. While in the long run these developments are of great importance, in the short run so much depends upon the attitude of the governmental elites, whether the elites fundamentally feel—and behave— as if they were alienated from and even antagonistic to the masses as they are, or whether the elites perceive the values of the masses as essentially being congruent to their own aims.

28. THE POLITICS OF NATION-BUILDING: PROBLEMS AND PRECONDITIONS*

a r n o l d   r i v k i n

The problems of nation-building are so formidable that, out of cynicism or realism, many political leaders in the new and emerging states have taken refuge in the unreality of the doctrine of supranationalism. Out of this flight into unreality has come the principal political problem confronting would-be nation-builders—definition of the physical proportions, the geographic configuration, the legal limits of the unit within which the nation is to be built. The supranationalist phenomenon has appeared in the aftermath of World War II as Pan-Africanism in Africa, Pan-Arabism in the Middle East, and the export variety of Chinese communism in Asia and Castroism in Latin America. All would override territorial boundaries and build regional or continental nations. Somehow, by some undefined mystique or magic their protagonists appear to believe, the problems of finding and building national identities for the newly independent peoples of the world would disappear in the new messianic-like movements searching for regional-wide or continental-wide personalities. This at any rate is the dynamic of supranationalism in the underdeveloped areas of the world today.

*   From "The Politics of Nation-Building: Problems and Preconditions" by Arnold Rivkin, *Journal of International Affairs*, Vol. XVI, No. 2 (1962), pp. 131–143. Reprinted by permission.

Related but separable is the second principal political problem of today's nation-builders—the structure of the state within which to build the nation once the geographic limits are defined. In the conflicts raging around the structure of the state in such widely-dispersed areas as the new state of the Congo in the heart of Africa and the somewhat less new state of Burma in Southeast Asia, this problem has frequently been oversimplified as one between strong centralized unitary states and weak decentralized federal states. Thus Prime Minister Lumumba risked his political role, and paid with his life, in his campaign to translate the ill-defined unitary structure of the state envisaged in the *Loi Fondamentale* of the Congo into a centralized reality; and Prime Minister U Nu found himself under arrest . . . for his seeming failure to resist ardently enough the pressures of various national groups in the Burmese union seeking to find expression in a federal structure.

Related to the problems of defining the national unit and building a state structure within which to develop the nation is the third principal political problem of the nation-builders—the approach and techniques to be employed in constituting the nation, in investing disparate groups within the state with a consciousness and sense of national identity, in making Nigerians out of Yorubas, Ibos and Hausas, in forging a national consensus.

Under the three headings—the concept of the national unit, state-structure and methodology—are subsumed, in our opinion, the problems of the politics of nation-building. . . .

THE CONCEPT OF THE NATIONAL UNIT

Mamadou Dia, Prime Minister of Senegal, in his book, *The African Nations and World Solidarity,* confronted the political problem of the concept of the national unit. He recognized the reality of the territorial limits which the new states have inherited from the colonial period, but in his anxiety to escape from the reality—the artificially contrived but nevertheless vested boundary lines of the new states—he propounded a theory of African national units ("nations") transcending the territorial limits of legal boundaries of the new states.[1] This led him to champion the founding of the Federation of Mali.

In an epilogue to his book, a sadder but wiser Mamadou Dia, writing about the abortive attempt to constitute the Federation of Mali, confessed that his "theories on the formation of the African nation and . . . theses on the process of setting up of large economic complexes" were in fact wrong. In his words:

[1] See Mamadou Dia, *The African Nations and World Solidarity* (New York: Praeger, 1961), p. 7 ff.

Taking our ideal for a reality, we thought we had only to condemn territorialism and its natural product, micronationalism, to overcome them and assure the success of our chimerical undertaking. . . . We are faced with micronationalisms that need be tamed, micronations that will have to be organized. Thus it is necessary for us to start with these micronationalisms and micronations, which are the realities of this strange twentieth-century African universe. Then we can build modestly, gradually, the bases of a great African nationalism and the foundations of a great African nation.[2]

⸰ ⸰ ⸰ ⸰ ⸰

What then are the elements of the Mali lesson? In essence the dissolution of the Federation of Mali within a little over a year of its birth, if one includes the longest period of its existence in the pre-independence period, poses the question of the necessary preconditions for establishing the geographic parameters within which a nation may successfully be built. First and foremost, the Mali experience raises the issue of timing. Does grouping together territorial units which have not yet (and this is true without exception in Africa) forged a national consciousness, found a national consensus and evolved a national identity aid or hinder the task of nation-building? The union of Senegalese and Soudanese at their respective stages of development in the Federation of Mali before either had developed cohesiveness as national units or widespread modern economies merely served to compound the difficulties of welding together disparate ethnic, tribal, cultural, linguistic, religious, political and economic groups into a national unit. The Mali experience suggests that, at a minimum, a certain degree of political development and economic growth is desirable and probably indispensable if territorial units are to be merged successfully and a nation built within enlarged national frameworks. Otherwise, as in the Mali case, the conflict for control of power at the center will divert energy from the basic tasks of nation-building; political consensus and building of the economy, the life blood of nation-building in the component parts, are likely to be neglected and retrogression probably will set in. Both Senegal and the Soudan (which has retained the name Mali) suffered, and will continue to, as a result of the bitterness engendered by the ill-fated attempt at political union. The rail link between the Senegalese capital of Dakar, Mali's only outlet to the sea, and Bamako, the capital of the new state of Mali has been cut, to the mutual disadvantage of both states.

Second, the Mali case also puts in issue the possibility of two essentially one-party states successfully uniting without, as a precondition, one or the other of the monolithic and exclusive parties agreeing to subordinate its identity to the other. Neither the Senegalese section of

[2] *Ibid.*, p. 138, 140 and 143.

the *Parti de la Fedération Africaine* nor the *Union Soudanaise* could tolerate the political incursions of the other in its theretofore exclusive domain. And yet an inevitable consequence of a union of territorial units would seem to be a free flow not only of manpower and capital across territorial lines and within the united area but also of political ideas and their proponents, *i.e.*, political party spokesmen. . . .

    ✿   ✿   ✿   ✿   ✿

THE STRUCTURE OF THE STATE

Behavioral scientists notwithstanding, next in importance to the political issue revolving around the size and shape of the basic nation-state is the political question of the structure of the state within which the multiple efforts are to be made to compose into national units disparate groups, including the so-called "detribalized" Africans who have given up or been deprived of the security deriving from the relatively static system of the subsistence sector. Even the charismatic leader needs a framework within which to operate, and his success in leading into nationhood his state and its transitional society, somewhere on the scale between traditionalism and modernity, depends to a significant degree on the suitability of the state structure circumscribing his efforts. For example, the late Prime Minister of the Congo, Patrice Lumumba, was foredoomed to failure as a nation-builder. Once the artificial constraint of the colonial power was removed, only a gradualist approach reflected in a federal structure was likely to lead to building a single Congolese nation. Lumumba's concept of a unitary state, which he read into the *Loi Fondamentale*, required building in one thrust a Congolese nationality in a huge area with no tradition of unity and justified the use of violence and terror to accomplish this purpose.

Even the Federation of Nigeria, with a background of at least ten years of careful preparation for independence and with much stronger ties binding together its three very different regions than the Congo had linking its six very different provinces, owes much of its performance to a state structure which affords the national leadership time to develop the concept of Nigerian nationality. Obviously, the appropriate structure does not insure adequate performance, but it does afford the opportunity for it. A unitary structure in Nigeria would probably have prevented the emergence of a single state, and if by some chance the state had emerged as a unitary one, it might well have ended in a series of secession bids by one or another of the groups not in power.

    ✿   ✿   ✿   ✿   ✿

THE POLITICAL SYSTEM

The questions of dispersion of political power and recognition of cultural differences lead naturally to the third major political issue confronting the nation-builders. In political terms, what system of government should be employed? Should it be, to oversimplify, a system which views national unity as identical with uniformity and hence accepts as inevitable, and even as desirable, the achievement of unity through exhortation, organization, coercion and compulsion? Or should it be a system which seeks unity amidst diversity and seeks to evolve plural loyalties which at various levels will be compatible—to the nation-state, to the region or tribal grouping, to religious institutions and so forth?

For many of the African leaders one-party authoritarian systems are the answer—the way to forge national unity, to build a nation-state, to create a nationality. Perhaps most eloquent on this score is President Sékou Touré of Guinea. First, he posed the issue of nation-building this way:

Is it necessary to repeat that the people of Guinea has not been mobilized to satisfy the needs of such and such an individual, but that each individual has been mobilized to satisfy the needs of the people of Guinea? [3]

Then he proceeded to answer it with these observations:

Each one must consider himself as a "part," an element indissociable from a "whole" and subject to the laws and exigencies of this "whole." [4]

And again:

Our fundamental principles are simple; we recognize valuable only that which serves the cause of the people, and which accelerates the pace of the history of the nation. This discipline to which we freely submit and this orientation which constitutes the main task of a vanguard democratic party, this is indeed dictatorship. . . . As far as we are concerned . . . in giving preeminence to the people, in letting it participate directly in all the important decisions that can bind the nation, we expressly want this dictatorship to be popular and democratic.[5]

For other African leaders—perhaps fewer in number than the authoritarian-minded but often cast in significant roles, such as the leadership of Nigeria—the task of nation-building and the political approach to it are seen in vastly different terms than those of Sékou Touré. Prime Minister Sir Abubakar Tafawa Balewa of Nigeria formulated the problem in these words:

[3] Sékou Touré, *Toward Full Re-Africanisation* (Paris: Présence Africaine, 1959), p. 53.
[4] *Ibid.*
[5] *Ibid.*, p. 55.

The . . . point concerns the problem of national unity. No problem is more urgent and none more difficult of solution. . . . It is true that Nigeria was the creation of the British, but it is no longer a mere geographical expression. The various peoples in the geographical area called Nigeria have lived together for almost a century and have developed common sentiments and a feeling of belonging together. It would be a great pity if nothing was done to forge a secure link which would, for all times, band all these peoples together as members of one nation.[6]

The Prime Minister then prescribed what must be and is in fact being tried in Nigeria:

The leaders of the various political parties and various other associations must place loyalty to Nigeria above other loyalties. If the leaders are willing to foster national unity, the common man will respond. . . . [After the 1959 General Elections] . . . the NPC [Northern People's Congress] and the NCNC [National Council of Nigeria and the Cameroons] agreed to form a coalition government because both parties believed that the only way to preserve the unity of the country was for the two parties to enter into coalition. . . . The present arrangement is the only one which in the circumstances can ensure the continued growth of parliamentary government in Nigeria. . . . The prospects for the survival of parliamentary democracy in Nigeria are favorable; however, this goal can only be attained if we address ourselves to the task of nation building with honesty, tolerance and devotion.[7]

These two dramatically opposed approaches to nation-building are at the ends of the African spectrum. The intermediate shadings are to be found in different countries. Interestingly enough, Guinea and Nigeria are also at opposite ends of the spectrum on Pan-Africanism and nationalism in one state, and on the issue of unitary and federal structures—a circumstance which suggests something more than coincidence. We can only suggest the hypothesis here [8] that there is at least a meaningful correlation, and perhaps even a causal interrelationship, between the views of African states on Pan-Africanism, the structure of the state and the political system chosen.

‡ ‡ ‡ ‡ ‡

BEYOND AFRICA

Nation-building is in process across the broad expanse of Asia and beyond it in most of Latin America. In vastly different circumstances, the underdeveloped states of these two continents are confronted by

[6] Sir Abubakar Tafawa Balewa in the Foreword to the book by Chief H. O. Davies, *Nigeria: The Prospects for Democracy* (London: Weidenfeld and Nicholson, 1961), p. xi.
[7] *Ibid.*, p. xii.
[8] To be examined in the author's forthcoming study, tentatively entitled *The African Presence in World Affairs.*

common political problems and by the common need to establish the necessary preconditions if their nation-building efforts are to be successful.

Because of the many significant differences between Africa and the other two continents—in population density, availability of food, social structure and class system, land ownership, traditional culture and religion, and many other factors—their responses to the political problems they all share are likely to vary considerably. And in any event, the psychology of nationalism in the many different states in the three continents will probably lead to different results in the individual states. Nevertheless, the underlying unities imposed by the similarity of problems to be faced and preconditions to be established by the new states and the re-awakening old states wherever they may be in pursuit of the goal of nation-building are likely to impart discernible lines of development which will allow for comparative study.

A quick look . . . would seem to confirm that the same trio of difficult political problems—determination of the concept of the nation, state structure and political system—confronts the nation-builders of all these continents.

☙❦❧

29. CAUSAL FACTORS IN LATIN AMERICAN POLITICAL INSTABILITY*

k e n n e t h f. j o h n s o n

THE INSTABILITY SYSTEM

Political instability occurs when the governing institutions of organized society are ineffective in gratifying popular wants and expectations. In that sense, governments are "maximizers," to use David Apter's term,

* From "Causal Factors in Latin American Political Instability" by Kenneth F. Johnson, *Western Political Quarterly*, Vol. XVII, No. 3 (September, 1964), pp. 435–441. By permission of the University of Utah, copyright owners.

sending out streams of satisfactions.[1] Failure of governments to gratify popular wants leads to political alienation in varying degrees of intensity. Alienation, in turn, is not a fixed quality but varies according to a number of causal factors. Political alienation may be defined as a deeply felt resentment toward social and governing institutions which is so intense as to be manifested in happenings which contribute to political instability. Political instability, accordingly, is defined as a state of conflict between governments and (competing) power groups which is characterized by overt acts of violence, by support for extreme political radicalism, or by apathy in the face of movements which are committed to extreme, radical, or violent dislocations of the status quo.[2] Thus, political alienation is seen as a widely shared attitude-potential and instability is viewed as those phenomena proceeding therefrom.

✿　✿　✿　✿　✿

Causal factors in Latin American political instability may be viewed as actors in a circular or self-reinforcing system. Their cumulative effect is a barrier to the drives of Latin American nations toward economic development and political stability. As a result of low socioeconomic development, maldistribution of wealth reaches critical levels; frustration of mobility expectations is widespread and produces popular and elite alienation, disaffection, and outright aggression toward the state.

Political instability in Latin America results from the circular interaction of three general categories of factors: (1) entrepreneurial deficiencies (includes passive and flight capital, social values and cultural influences, religious institutions, illiteracy); (2) high degrees of role substitutability among politically relevant performance entities; and (3) accelerated urbanization and overpopulation.

Entrepreneurial Deficiencies

As a human dynamic, entrepreneurship is defined as "the function of perceiving and effectuating new combinations of factors of production in order to take advantage of existing or anticipated market situations."[3] The commercial entrepreneur deals in ideas, supported by capital from

[1] David E. Apter, "A Comparative Method for the Study of Politics," *American Journal of Sociology*, 64 (1958), 225.

[2] Apathy on the part of politically relevant populations is considered a reinforcement factor in the sense of tacit endorsement through inaction.

[3] Charles Wolf and Sidney Sufrin, *Capital Formation and Foreign Investment in Underdeveloped Areas* (Syracuse: Syracuse University Press, 1958), p. 21—derived from Joseph Schumpeter, "Economic Theory and Entrepreneurial History," in *Change and the Entrepreneur* (Cambridge: Harvard University Press, 1949), pp. 23–24.

credit or familial sources, in such a way as to realize a marginal profit. Governmental entrepreneurship relates largely to leadership expertise at problem-solving through public policy and administration. Both entrepreneurial forms require available active capital for effective functioning. The relative absence of entrepreneurship accounts for much of Latin America's backwardness and contributes to political instability.

Chronic to all underdeveloped countries is illiteracy, a tremendous entrepreneurial deficiency. . . .

Social attitudes and values act to inhibit entrepreneurial growth in Latin America. Throughout the area, there is a general lack of individual preparedness to take big financial risks in order to capture lucrative gains. Although many Latin Americans are willing to invest in stocks, bonds, mutual funds, and securities, the majority of investors prefer something safer such as land or independently issued credit at high rates of interest. One frequently hears stories of private money caches both great and small. According to informal reports, one would expect fairly impressive sums to appear if all of these passive investors were to declare their resources.

Because a genuinely competitive and collaborative spirit is lacking, Latin Americans are suspicious of impersonal institutions which control and allocate capital. Investors prefer to keep their funds out of banks and government-sponsored lending institutions where they might otherwise be available for entrepreneurial use as development capital. Reluctance to mobilize capital for entrepreneurship accompanies failure to achieve volume marketing conditions through increased unit output. According to testimony and empirical observation in Colombia and Mexico, there seems to be an ingrained notion that it is better to sell a few items at a high price than to improve one's total income through promotion of volume sales at a reduced price.[4]

Another entrepreneurial deficiency lies in the problem of excessive centralization of decision-making where allocation of credit for commercial development is concerned. In Mexico, for instance, major credit decisions are regularly made at the "home office" level which normally means the capital city.[5] Moreover, thousands of decisions of relatively small consequence also require central validation. Interviews in both Mexico and Colombia revealed the belief among businessmen that provincial locations are definitely less favored than central ones where credit dispensation is concerned. . . .

[4] In Bogotá, for instance, the author learned that there are hundreds of dwellings remaining vacant much of the year because proprietors favor a high and prestigeful rental price even though a lower one might bring more tenants and an improved total income for the landlord.

[5] Paul Lamartine Yates, *El desarrollo regional de México* (México: Banco de México: segunda edición, 1962), p. 205.

Still a further barrier to effective entrepreneurship is found in Latin American religious institutions. Drawing on the works of Tawney and Weber, the general proposition may be made that the Roman Catholic ethic, being preoccupied with achieving and preserving grace in the sight of God, discourages the vigorous competitive spirit needed for accomplishment within an entrepreneurial value hierarchy.[6] Besides Roman Catholicism, anthropologists have noted in certain Indian societies value systems which discourage capital formation for other than ceremonial purposes. Eric Wolf found that the Maya Indians of Mexico and Guatemala accumulate capital for annual religious displays which wipe out family savings.[7] Specifically Wolf says of the Maya, "he is not a capitalist nor free of restrictions; his economic goal is not capital accumulation but subsistence and participation in the religio-political system of his community." [8]

Ultimately, in the deep recesses of Latin American culture, one comes to the inescapable conclusion that collusion rather than collaboration is the dominant characteristic of human enterprise. . . . The absence of a truly collaborative spirit is an enormous entrepreneurial deficiency which Latin America cannot easily overcome.

Entrepreneurial deficiencies constitute a market imperfection which allows capital to flow into passive rather than active forms. The process is circular and affects the public and private sectors of the economy jointly. Exploitive tributary taxation and corrupt fiscal allocation by governments discourage private investment and capital formation. Public fiscal dishonesty inspires nonpayment of taxes and wastes much of whatever funds are collected. Accumulated capital is hoarded or invested in ritual and prestige items or in usurious investments with proceeds concealed from taxation or exported abroad. Public treasuries are thus impoverished and public services remain at low levels. Controlling value systems sustain corrupt public officials and inhibit adoption of policies aimed at socioeconomic betterment. Low entrepreneurial growth means that Latin American economies cannot absorb rapid population increase without hardship. Frustration of mobility expectations is therefore widespread and dictates to political alienation and instability.

[6] R. H. Tawney, *Religion and the Rise of Capitalism* (New York: Harcourt Brace, 1926). Tawney speaks of barriers to entrepreneurship in the sense of ideology rather than specifically in terms of capital formation. In contrasting Roman Catholic and Calvinist-Puritan views toward commercial enterprise he says that Puritanism "insisted, in short, that money-making if not free from spiritual dangers . . . could be, and ought to be, carried on for the greater glory of God." P. 199.
[7] Eric R. Wolf, *Sons of the Shaking Earth* (Chicago: University of Chicago Press, 1959), p. 216.
[8] *Ibid.*, p. 224.

Role Substitutability Among Politically
Relevant Performance Entities

Gabriel Almond's definition of a pre-industrial political system emphasized the relative ease with which performance entities could usurp each other's natural role. This condition has been endemic to Latin America and is a major causal factor in political instability. George Blanksten notes that in some Latin American countries the army performs a number of unspecialized and undifferentiated functions ranging from administering public education to conducting elections.[9] With increasing functional differentiation in the private economy, Blanksten sees the possibility of a trend toward "more specialized functions of political institutions . . . and basic alterations in the commitments of governing elites." [10] Whereas in Colombia, Peru, and Ecuador the Church is landowner, public educator, and political practitioner as well as a religious institution, "with the march of the developmental process it is likely that the last of these functions will tend to become the exclusive, specialized and differentiated role of the Church." [11]

The prevailing lack of role specialization and interdependence among performance entities in Latin America is a continuing invitation to armies and government bureaucracies to usurp each other in a power grab. Likewise, the failure of Latin American universities to become specialized seats of learning has relegated student groups to extreme and radical political roles. The same may be said for trade unions which, in countries such as Bolivia, Venezuela, and Argentina, constitute veritable "parties" in themselves and are frequently embroiled in extreme acts which contribute to political instability.

The apparent ease with which performance entities have usurped each other in Latin America may be partly explained in terms of the relative absence of social pluralism within that political culture. Involving as it does a multiplicity of overlapping group memberships, social pluralism has a decidedly moderating effect upon political behavior. One's performance in a given membership context is certain to have implications for other memberships as well. Social pluralism is one of the hallmarks of Latin America's incipient middle class which has been viewed by Charles Wagley as moderately conservative.[12] According to John J. Johnson, the Latin American middle sectors are "harmonizers"

---

[9] George I. Blanksten, "The Aspiration for Economic Development," *Annals*, 334 (March 1961), 17.

[10] *Ibid.*, p. 19.

[11] *Ibid.*, p. 17.

[12] Charles Wagley, "The Brazilian Revolution: Social Changes Since 1930," in *Social Change in Latin America Today*, ed. Lymon Bryson (New York: Harper, 1960), pp. 221–22.

which avoid the dangers inherent in strictly negative and absolute postulates.[13]

Because of the relative lack of social pluralism in Latin America, performance entities become psychologically compartmentalized and politically semi-autonomous. Vocational roles tend to circumscribe social attitudes and political attachments. Armies, bureaucracies, legislatures, are found each with its own highly subjective *élan vital*, an aggressive expansionist force marked by the all-consuming lust for control and easily infused with a moral purpose to justify intrusion upon other roles. For many Latin Americans, a career in the army or government bureaucracy is life's only road to socioeconomic mobility. . . .

Urbanization and Overpopulation

During the past several decades, urbanization in Latin America has taken on proportions of acute social change.[14] Rural-to-urban migratory patterns complicate efforts to promote urban economic growth and to stimulate new agrarian entrepreneurship. Displaced peasants seek welfare and opportunity in great cities. Frustration of their expectations produces alienation and, thus, urbanization exacerbates existing symptoms of political instability.

The following causes of Latin America's accelerated urbanization may be listed at this point: (1) urban industrialization and the promise of a better life lures unemployed groups from the country; (2) exploitation of rural workers by *latifundistas* forces exodus as does material impoverishment of *minifundistas*; [15] (3) terror and violence perpetuated by bandit groups especially in Colombia, Venezuela, and Peru make rural life unbearable; [16] (4) certain legal structures promote social and economic development of a capital or central city at the expense of the rest of the country as in the case of Haiti; [17] (5) many peasants are motivated to leave their farms because of exploitation by the bureaucracy of an agrarian reform program as in the case of Mexico; [18] and (6) in at least one country, Colombia, there is specific evidence that service in the military brings many young peasants into the city who are unwilling to

[13] John J. Johnson, "The Political Role of the Latin American Middle Sectors," *Annals*, 334 (March 1961), 25.
[14] This contention is based on the author's "Urbanization and Political Change in Latin America" (Ph.D. dissertation, Ann Arbor, University Microfilms Inc., 1963).
[15] See Robert Carlyle Beyer, "Land Distribution and Tenure in Colombia," *Journal of Inter-American Studies*, 3 (April 1961), 281–91, *passim*.
[16] See Roberto Pineda Giraldo, *El impacto de la violencia en el Tolima: El caso de El Líbano* (Bogotá: Universidad Nacional de Colombia, 1960).
[17] Achille Aristide treats this problem in *Problemes Haitiens* (Port-au-Prince: Imprimerie de L'Etat, 1958).
[18] See Rodrigo García Treviño, *Precios Salarios Mordidas* (México: Editorial América, 1953).

return to an agrarian life upon completion of their duty.[19] These motivational factors for rural-to-urban migration have meaning for the majority of Latin American nations. Urbanization has brought increased demands upon governments and socioeconomic systems for accommodation of the expanding work force. Because of the entrepreneurial deficiencies discussed earlier, popular expectations for achievement and mobility are frustrated which leads to political alienation and instability.

A concomitant of urbanization has been overpopulation in both urban and rural areas. Though government programs of disease control have sharply reduced infant mortality throughout Latin America, urbanization has not produced a significant decline in over-all fertility rates.[20] While rural populations have continued to grow, rural food production has not always kept pace with urban needs. This keeps food prices high and militates against the already depressed and alienated social sectors. Migrants to the cities find that large families are no longer the asset they were in the country as family incomes are dissipated by nonproducing members who continue to consume. With children under fifteen years making up approximately 40 per cent of Latin America's total population, the need to provide for these dependents heavily burdens the head of a household. He is at a major disadvantage in seeking to improve his level of living through accumulation of capital for investment or for family emergency.[21]

As Latin American overpopulation continues, pressure mounts upon the already inadequate rural land forcing more and more persons into the great cities where entrepreneurial deficiencies make it doubtful that their wants will be gratified. Growing popular frustration and alienation are manifest in popular support for aggressive radical movements which voice mistrust of government and hatred for the dominant classes.[22] At this point, opportunities for usurpation of governing roles may be seized upon by armies, bureaucracies, or other power groupings and political instability moves across the continuum from latent to overt.

⟨∽∾⟩

[19] Kenneth F. Johnson and Fernando Gallo C., "Encuesta para un grupo de infantes de marina" (Cartagena: Facultad de Economia de la Universidad de Cartagena, 1962, unpublished sample survey).
[20] Pertinent here are a series of studies done by Harold L. Geisert and Carr B. Lavell which were published by George Washington University Press in 1959 and 1960: cf. Geisert, *Population Problems in Mexico and Central America*, and *The Caribbean: Population and Resources;* and Lavell, *Population Growth and Development of South America.* On the topic of birth control, see J. Stycos, Curt Back, Reuben Hill, "Contraception and Catholicism in Puerto Rico," *Milbank Memorial Fund Quarterly*, 34 (April 1956), 150–59.
[21] Geisert, "Population Problems . . . ," *loc. cit.*
[22] This theme is prominent in Oscar Lewis' study of the slums in Mexico City: *The Children of Sanchez: Autobiography of a Mexican Family* (New York: Random House, 1961), p. xxvii.

B. *Political Development*

30. *THE CONCEPT OF POLITICAL DEVELOPMENT**

l u c i a n   w.   p y e

Some members of the Committee on Comparative Politics of the Social Science Research Council have suggested that it may be useful to conceptualize the processes of political development as involving essentially six crises that may be met in different sequences but all of which must be successfully dealt with for a society to become a modern nation-state.[1]

The Identity Crisis. The first and most fundamental crisis is that of achieving a common sense of identity. The people in a new state must come to recognize their national territory as being their true homeland, and they must feel as individuals that their own personal identities are in part defined by their identification with their territorially delimited country. In most of the new states traditional forms of identity ranging from tribe or caste to ethnic and linguistic groups compete with the sense of larger national identity.

The identity crisis also involves the resolution of the problem of traditional heritage and modern practices, the dilemma of parochial sentiments and cosmopolitan practices. . . . As long as people feel pulled between two worlds and without roots in any society they cannot have the firm sense of identity necessary for building a stable, modern nation-state.

The Legitimacy Crisis. Closely related to the identity crisis is the problem of achieving agreement about the legitimate nature of authority and the proper responsibilities of government. In many new states the crisis of legitimacy is a straightforward constitutional problem: What

---

* From *Aspects of Political Development* by Lucian W. Pye. Copyright (c) 1966, Little, Brown and Company (Inc.). Reprinted by permission of the publisher, Little, Brown and Company (Inc.). Selections from pp. 63–67.

[1] The following analysis of the "crises of development" is based on the forthcoming study by Leonard Binder, James S. Coleman, Joseph LaPalombara, Myron Weiner, and Lucian W. Pye, which will be published by the Princeton University Press as the seventh volume of the Series in Political Development sponsored by the Committee on Comparative Politics of the Social Science Research Council.

should be the relationship between central and local authorities? What are the proper limits of the bureaucracy, or of the army, in the nation's political life? Or possibly the conflict is over how much of the colonial structure of government should be preserved in an independent state.

In other new states the question of legitimacy is more diffuse, and it involves sentiments about what should be the underlying spirit of government and the primary goals of national effort. For example, in some Moslem lands there is a deep desire that the state should in some fashion reflect the spirit of Islam. In other societies the issue of legitimacy involves questions about how far the governmental authorities should directly push economic development as compared with other possible goals. Above all, in transitional societies there can be a deep crisis of authority because all attempts at ruling are challenged by different people for different reasons, and no leaders are able to gain a full command of legitimate authority.

The Penetration Crisis. The critical problems of administration in the new states give rise to the penetration crisis, which involves the problems of government in reaching down into the society and effecting basic policies. . . . [I]n traditional societies government had limited demands to make on the society, and in most transitional systems the governments are far more ambitious. This is particularly true if the rulers seek to accelerate the pace of economic development and social change. To carry out significant developmental policies a government must be able to reach down to the village level and touch the daily lives of people.

Yet, . . . a dominant characteristic of transitional societies is the gap between the world of the ruling elite and that of the masses of the people who are still oriented toward their parochial ways. The penetration problem is that of building up the effectiveness of the formal institutions by government and of establishing confidence and rapport between rulers and subjects. Initially governments often find it difficult to motivate the population or to change its values and habits in order to bring support to programs of national development. On the other hand, at times the effectiveness of the government in breaking down old patterns of control can unleash widespread demands for a greater influence on governmental policies. When this occurs the result is another crisis, that of participation.

The Participation Crisis. . . . The participation crisis occurs when there is uncertainty over the appropriate rate of expansion [of popular participation] and when the influx of new participants creates serious strains on the existing institutions. As new segments of the population are brought into the political process, new interests and new issues begin to arise so that the continuity of the old polity is broken and there is the need to reestablish the entire structure of political relations.

In a sense the participation crisis arises out of the emergence of interest groups and the formation of a party system. The question in many new states is whether the expansion in participation is likely to be effectively organized into specific interest groups or whether the pressures will lead only to mass demands and widespread feelings of anomie. It should also be noted that the appearance of a participation crisis does not necessarily signal pressures for democratic processes. The participation crisis can be organized as in totalitarian states to provide the basis for manipulated mass organizations and demonstrational politics.

Integration Crisis. This crisis covers the problems of relating popular politics to governmental performance, and thus it represents the effective and compatible solution of both the penetration and the participation crises. The problem of integration therefore deals with the extent to which the entire polity is organized as a system of interacting relationships, first among the offices and agencies of government, and then among the various groups and interests seeking to make demands upon the system, and finally in the relationships between officials and articulating citizens.

In many of the transitional systems there may be many different groupings of interests, but they hardly interact with each other, and at best each seeks to make its separate demands upon the government. The government must seek to cope with all these demands simultaneously. Yet at the same time the government itself may not be well integrated. The result is a low level of general performance throughout the political system.

The Distribution Crisis. The final crisis in the development process involves questions about how governmental powers are to be used to influence the distribution of goods, services, and values throughout the society. Who is to benefit from government, and what should the government be doing to bring greater benefits to different segments of the society?

Much of the stress on economic development and the popularity of socialist slogans in the new states is a reflection of the basic crisis. In some cases governments seek to meet the problem by directly intervening in the distribution of wealth; in other cases the approach is to strengthen the opportunities and potentialities of the disadvantaged groups.

The Sequences of Development. The particular pattern of development in any country depends largely upon the sequence in which these crises arise and the ways in which they are resolved. It is noteworthy that in the history of England, the model of modern democracies, development tended to follow a path in which the crises arose somewhat separately and largely according to the order in which we have just outlined them. The English developed a sense of national identity early, the issue of the legitimacy of the monarchy and government was well established before the problem of expanding participation appeared and, finally, serious issues of distribution did not arise until after the political system was relatively well integrated.

In contrast, development of the continental European system followed more chaotic patterns. In Italy and Germany the prelude of nation-building did not involve a resolution of the issue of national identity. In France questions of legitimacy and the realities of inadequate integration have persistently frustrated national performance and intensified the crisis of distribution. It was, indeed, the cumulativeness and simultaneity of the crises on the continent that produced the striking differences between the European and the British systems.

The story in modern Asia and Africa seems to be closer to the continental experience than either the British or American. In most of the new states the crises are all appearing simultaneously, and governments are, for example, striving to use the distribution crisis to resolve the identity problem. The efforts to raise the standards of living in these cases are in large part related to creating feelings of basic loyalty to the nation, and this procedure raises the question of how stable such states can become if their citizens' sense of identity is tied too closely to the effectiveness of particular policies.

∽✕∾

31. POLITICAL DEVELOPMENT AND POLITICAL DECAY*†

s a m u e l   p.   h u n t i n g t o n

"Among the laws that rule human societies," de Tocqueville said, "there is one which seems to be more precise and clear than all others. If men

° Excerpts from "Political Development and Political Decay" by Samuel P. Huntington, World Politics, Vol. XVII, No. 3 (April, 1965), pp. 386–411. By permission.
† I am grateful to the Center for International Affairs, Harvard University, for the support which made this article possible and to Edward C. Banfield, Mather Eliot,

are to remain civilized or to become so, the art of associating together must grow and improve in the same ratio in which the equality of conditions is increased." [1] In much of the world today, equality of political participation is growing much more rapidly than is the "art of associating together." The rates of mobilization and participation are high; the rates of organization and institutionalization are low. De Tocqueville's precondition for civilized society is in danger, if it is not already undermined. In these societies, the conflict between mobilization and institutionalization is the crux of politics. Yet in the fast-growing literature on the politics of the developing areas, political institutionalization usually receives scant treatment. Writers on political development emphasize the processes of modernization and the closely related phenomena of social mobilization and increasing political participation. A balanced view of the politics of contemporary Asia, Africa, and Latin America requires more attention to the "art of associating together" and the growth of political institutions. For this purpose, it is useful to distinguish political development from modernization and to identify political development with the institutionalization of political organizations and procedures. Rapid increases in mobilization and participation, the principal political aspects of modernization, undermine political institutions. Rapid modernization, in brief, produces not political development, but political decay.

* * * * *

There is thus much to be gained (as well as something to be lost) by conceiving of political development as a process independent of, although obviously affected by, the process of modernization. In view of the crucial importance of the relationship between mobilization and participation, on the one hand, and the growth of political organizations, on the other, it is useful for many purposes to define political development as the institutionalization of political organizations and procedures. This concept liberates development from modernization. It can be applied to the analysis of political systems of any sort, not just modern ones. It can be defined in reasonably precise ways which are at least theoretically capable of measurement. As a concept, it does not suggest that movement is likely to be in only one direction: institutions, we know, decay and dissolve as well as grow and mature. Most significantly, it focuses attention on the reciprocal interaction between the ongoing social processes of modernization, on the one hand, and the

Milton J. Esman, H. Field Haviland, Jr., and John D. Montgomery, for their helpful written comments on an earlier draft.
[1] *Democracy in America* (Phillips Bradley edn., New York 1955), II, 118.

strength, stability, or weakness of political structures, traditional, transitional, or modern, on the other.[2]

The strength of political organizations and procedures varies with their *scope of support* and their *level of institutionalization.* Scope refers simply to the extent to which the political organizations and procedures encompass activity in the society. If only a small upper-class group belongs to political organizations and behaves in terms of a set of procedures, the scope is limited. If, on the other hand, a large segment of the population is politically organized and follows the political procedures, the scope is broad. Institutions are stable, valued, recurring patterns of behavior. Organizations and procedures vary in their degree of institutionalization. Harvard University and the newly opened suburban high school are both organizations, but Harvard is much more of an institution than is the high school. The seniority system in Congress and President Johnson's select press conferences are both procedures, but seniority is much more institutionalized than are Mr. Johnson's methods of dealing with the press. Institutionalization is the process by which organizations and procedures acquire value and stability. The level of institutionalization of any political system can be defined by the adaptability, complexity, autonomy, and coherence of its organizations and procedures. So also, the level of institutionalization of any particular organization or procedure can be measured by its adaptability, complexity, autonomy, and coherence. If these criteria can be identified and measured, political systems can be compared in terms of their levels of institutionalization. Furthermore, it will be possible to measure increases and decreases in the institutionalization of particular organizations and procedures within a political system.

☼   ☼   ☼   ☼   ☼

Social mobilization and political participation are rapidly increasing in Asia, Africa, and Latin America. These processes, in turn, are directly responsible for the deterioration of political institutions in these areas. As Kornhauser has conclusively demonstrated for the Western world, rapid industrialization and urbanization create discontinuities which give rise to mass society. "The *rapid* influx of large numbers of people

[2] The concept of institutionalization has, of course, been used by other writers concerned with political development—most notably, S. N. Eisenstadt. His definition, however, differs significantly from my approach here. See, in particular, his "Initial Institutional Patterns of Political Modernisation," *Civilisations,* XII (No. 4, 1962), 461–72, and XIII (No. 1, 1963), 15–26; "Institutionalization and Change," *American Sociological Review,* XXIX (April 1964), 235–47; "Social Change, Differentiation and Evolution," *ibid.,* XXIX (June 1964), 375–86.

into *newly* developing urban areas invites mass movements." [3] In areas and industries with very rapid industrial growth, the creation and institutionalization of unions lag, and mass movements are likely among the workers. As unions are organized, they are highly vulnerable to outside influences in their early stages. "The rapid influx of large numbers of people into a new organization (as well as a new area) provides opportunities for mass-oriented elites to penetrate the organization. This is particularly true during the formative periods of organizations, for at such times external constraints must carry the burden of social control until the new participants have come to internalize the values of the organization." [4]

So also in politics. Rapid economic growth breeds political instability.[5] Political mobilization, moreover, does not necessarily require the building of factories or even movement to the cities. It may result simply from increases in communications, which can stimulate major increases in aspirations that may be only partially, if at all, satisfied. The result is a "revolution of rising frustrations." [6] Increases in literacy and education may bring more political instability. By Asian standards, Burma, Ceylon, and the Republic of Korea are all highly literate, but no one of them is a model of political stability. Nor does literacy necessarily stimulate democracy: with roughly 75 per cent literacy, Cuba was the fifth most literate country in Latin America (ranking behind Argentina, Uruguay, Chile, and Costa Rica), but the first to go Communist; so also Kerala, with one of the highest literacy rates in India, was the first Indian state to elect a Communist government.[7] Literacy, as Daniel Lerner has suggested, "may be dysfunctional—indeed a serious impediment—to modernization in the societies now seeking (all too rapidly) to transform their institutions." [8]

Increased communication may thus generate demands for more "modernity" than can be delivered. It may also stimulate a reaction against modernity and activate traditional forces. Since the political arena is normally dominated by the more modern groups, it can bring into the arena new, anti-modern groups and break whatever consensus exists among the leading political participants. It may also mobilize

[3]   William Kornhauser, *The Politics of Mass Society* (Glencoe 1959), 145.
[4]   *Ibid.*, 146.
[5]   See Mancur Olson, Jr., "Rapid Growth as a Destabilizing Force," *Journal of Economic History*, XXVII (December 1963), 529–52; and Bert F. Hoselitz and Myron Weiner, "Economic Development and Political Stability in India," *Dissent*, VIII (Spring 1961), 172–79.
[6]   See Daniel Lerner, "Toward a Communication Theory of Modernization," in Lucian W. Pye, ed., *Communications and Political Development* (Princeton 1963), 330 ff.
[7]   Cf. Karl W. Deutsch, "Social Mobilization and Political Development," *American Political Science Review*, LV (September 1961), 496.
[8]   Daniel Lerner, "The Transformation of Institutions" (mimeo.), 19.

POLITICAL AND SOCIAL PROBLEMS

minority ethnic groups who had been indifferent to politics but who now acquire a self-consciousness and divide the political system along ethnic lines. Nationalism, it has often been assumed, makes for national integration. But in actuality, nationalism and other forms of ethnic consciousness often stimulate political disintegration, tearing apart the body politic.

Sharp increases in voting and other forms of political participation can also have deleterious effects on political institutions. In Latin America since the 1930's, increases in voting and increases in political instability have gone hand in hand. "Age requirements were lowered, property and literacy requirements were reduced or discarded, and the unscrubbed, unschooled millions on the farms were enfranchised in the name of democracy. They were swept into the political life of the republics so rapidly that existing parties could not absorb many of them, and they learned little about working within the existing political system." [9] The personal identity crises of the elites, caught between traditional and modern cultures, may create additional problems: "In transitional countries the political process often has to bear to an inordinate degree the stresses and strains of people responding to personal needs and seeking solutions to intensely personal problems." [10] Rapid social and economic change calls into question existing values and behavior patterns. It thus often breeds personal corruption. In some circumstances this corruption may play a positive role in the modernizing process, enabling dynamic new groups to get things done which would have been blocked by the existing value system and social structure. At the same time, however, corruption undermines the autonomy and coherence of political institutions. It is hardly accidental that in the 1870's and 1880's a high rate of American economic development coincided with a low point in American governmental integrity.[11]

Institutional decay has become a common phenomenon of the modernizing countries. *Coups d'état* and military interventions in politics are one index of low levels of political institutionalization: they occur where political institutions lack autonomy and coherence. According to one calculation, eleven of twelve modernizing states outside Latin America which were independent before World War II experienced *coups d'état* or attempted coups after World War II. Of twenty states which became independent between World War II and 1959, fourteen had coups or coup attempts by 1963. Of twenty-four states which became independent between 1960 and 1963, seven experienced coups or

[9] John J. Johnson, *The Military and Society in Latin America* (Stanford 1964), 98–99.
[10] Lucian W. Pye, *Politics, Personality and Nation Building* (New Haven 1962), 4–5.
[11] See, in general, Ronald E. Wraith and Edgar Simpkins, *Corruption in Developing Countries* (London 1963).

attempted coups before the end of 1963.[12] Instability in Latin America was less frequent early in the twentieth century than it was in the middle of the century. In the decade from 1917 to 1927, military men occupied the presidencies of the twenty Latin American republics 28.7 per cent of the time; in the decade from 1947 to 1957, military men were presidents 45.5 per cent of the time.[13] In the 1930's and 1940's in countries like Argentina and Colombia, military intervention in politics occurred for the first time in this century. Seventeen of the twenty Latin American states experienced coups or coup attempts between 1945 and 1964, only Chile, Mexico, and Uruguay having clean records of political stability.

In many states the decline of party organizations is reflected in the rise of charismatic leaders who personalize power and weaken institutions which might limit that power. The increasing despotism of Nkrumah, for instance, was accompanied by a marked decline in the institutional strength of the Convention People's Party. In Turkey, Pakistan, and Burma, the Republican People's Party, Muslim League, and AFPFL deteriorated and military intervention eventually ensued. In party organizations and bureaucracies, marked increases in corruption often accompanied significant declines in the effectiveness of governmental services. Particularistic groups—tribal, ethnic, religious—frequently reasserted themselves and further undermined the authority and coherence of political institutions. The legitimacy of post-colonial regimes among their own people was often less than that of the colonial regimes of the Europeans. Economists have argued that the gap between the level of economic well-being of the underdeveloped countries and that of highly developed countries is widening as the absolute increases and even percentage increases of the latter exceed those of the former. Something comparable and perhaps even more marked is occurring in the political field. The level of political institutionalization of the advanced countries has, with a few exceptions such as France, remained relatively stable. The level of political institutionalization of most other countries has declined. As a result, the political gap between them has broadened. In terms of institutional strength, many if not most of the new states reached their peak of political development at the moment of independence.

The differences which may exist in mobilization and institutionalization suggest four ideal-types of politics (see Table 1). Modern, developed, civic polities (the United States, the Soviet Union) have high

[12] These figures are calculated from the data in the Appendix of Fred R. von der Mehden, *Politics of the Developing Nations* (Englewood Cliffs, N. J., 1964).
[13] Computed from figures in R. W. Fitzgibbon, "Armies and Politics in Latin America," paper, 7th Round Table, International Political Science Association, Opatija, Yugoslavia, September 1959, 8–9.

levels of both mobilization and institutionalization. Primitive polities (such as Banfield's backward society) have low levels of both. Contained polities are highly institutionalized but have low levels of mobilization and participation. The dominant political institutions of contained polities may be either traditional (e.g., monarchies) or modern (e.g., political parties). If they are the former, such polities may well confront great

TABLE 1. TYPES OF POLITICAL SYSTEMS

Social Mobilization	Political Institutionalization	
	High	Low
High	Civic	Corrupt
Low	Contained	Primitive

difficulties in adjusting to rising levels of social mobilization. The traditional institutions may wither or collapse, and the result would be a corrupt polity with a high rate of participation but a low level of institutionalization. In the corrupt society, politics is, in Macaulay's phrase, "all sail and no anchor." [14] This type of polity characterizes much, if not most, of the modernizing world. Many of the more advanced Latin American countries, for instance, have achieved comparatively high indices of literacy, per capita national income, and urbanization. But their politics remains notably underdeveloped. Distrust and hatred have produced a continuing low level of political institutionalization. "There is no good faith in America, either among men or among nations," Bolivar once lamented. "Treaties are paper, constitutions books, elections battles, liberty anarchy, and life a torment. The only thing one can do in America is emigrate." [15] Over a century later, the same complaint was heard: "We are not, or do not represent a respectable nation . . . not because we are poor, but because we are disorganized," argued an Ecuadorian newspaper. "With a politics of ambush and of permanent mistrust, one for the other, we . . . cannot properly organize a republic . . . and without organization we cannot merit or attain respect from other nations." [16] So long as a country like Argentina retains a politics of coup and countercoup and a feeble state surrounded by massive social forces, it cannot be considered politically developed, no matter how urbane and prosperous and educated are its citizens.

In reverse fashion, a country may be politically highly developed,

[14] Thomas B. Macaulay, letter to Henry S. Randall, Courtlandt Village, New York, May 23, 1857, printed in "What Did Macaulay Say About America?" *Bulletin of the New York Public Library,* XXIX (July 1925), 477–79.
[15] Simon Bolivar, quoted in K. H. Silvert, ed., *Expectant Peoples: Nationalism and Development* (New York 1963), 347.
[16] *El Dia,* Quito, November 27, 1943, quoted in Bryce Wood, *The Making of the Good Neighbor Policy* (New York 1961), 318.

with modern political institutions, while still very backward in terms of modernization. India, for instance, is typically held to be the epitome of the underdeveloped society. Judged by the usual criteria of modernization, it was at the bottom of the ladder during the 1950's: per capita GNP of $72, 80 per cent illiterate, over 80 per cent of the population in rural areas, 70 per cent of the work force in agriculture, a dozen major languages, deep caste and religious differences. Yet in terms of political institutionalization, India was far from backward. Indeed, it ranked high not only in comparison with other modernizing countries in Asia, Africa, and Latin America, but also in comparison with many much more modern European countries. A well-developed political system has strong and distinct institutions to perform both the "input" and the "output" functions of politics. India entered independence with not only two organizations, but two highly developed—adaptable, complex, autonomous, and coherent—institutions ready to assume primary responsibility for these functions. The Congress Party, founded in 1885, was one of the oldest and best-organized political parties in the world; the Indian Civil Service, dating from the early nineteenth century, has been appropriately hailed as "one of the greatest administrative systems of all time." [17] The stable, effective, and democratic government of India during the first fifteen years of independence rested far more on this institutional inheritance than it did on the charisma of Nehru. In addition, the relatively slow pace of modernization and social mobilization in India did not create demands and strains which the Party and the bureaucracy were unable to handle. So long as these two organizations maintain their institutional strength, it is ridiculous to think of India as politically underdeveloped, no matter how low her per capita income or how high her illiteracy rate.

Almost no other country which became independent after World War II was institutionally as well prepared as India for self-government. In countries like Pakistan and the Sudan, institutional evolution was unbalanced; the civil and military bureaucracies were more highly developed than the political parties, and the military had strong incentives to move into the institutional vacuum on the input side of the political system and to attempt to perform interest aggregation functions. This pattern, of course, has also been common in Latin America. In countries like Guatemala, El Salvador, Peru, and Argentina, John J. Johnson has pointed out, the military is "the country's best organized institution and is thus in a better position to give objective expression to the national will" than are parties or interest groups.[18] In a very different category is a country like North Vietnam, which fought its way into independence

---

[17] Ralph Braibanti, "Public Bureaucracy and Judiciary in Pakistan," in Joseph LaPalombara, ed., *Bureaucracy and Political Development* (Princeton 1963), 373.
[18] Johnson, *Military and Society*, 143.

with a highly disciplined political organization but which was distinctly weak on the administrative side. The Latin American parallel here would be Mexico, where, as Johnson puts it, "not the armed forces but the PRI is the best organized institution, and the party rather than the armed forces has been the unifying force at the national level." In yet a fourth category are those unfortunate states, such as the Congo, which were born with neither political nor administrative institutions. Many of these new states deficient at independence in one or both types of institutions have also been confronted by high rates of social mobilization and rapidly increasing demands on the political system. . . .

C. Social Problems

32. SOME ASPECTS OF EDUCATIONAL PLANNING IN UNDERDEVELOPED AREAS*

adam curle

. . . In the last fifteen years an unprecedentedly large amount of aid has flowed from the rich to the poor countries; but viewed as a whole, the results have been disappointing: the "take off," as Rostow [1] calls it, has been achieved by very few of the underdeveloped nations. The character of this help has been largely based on the assumption that the chief lack of the underdeveloped countries was capital, and the technical personnel required to form capital. This assumption is now being vigorously challenged by many economists, who maintain that underdevelopment is not merely an economic but also a social phenomenon. Galbraith [2] in particular makes this point vigorously, stressing that a literate

---

* From "Some Aspects of Educational Planning in Underdeveloped Areas" by Adam Curle, *Harvard Educational Review*, Vol. XXXII, No. 3 (Summer 1962), pp. 293–300. By permission of the *Harvard Educational Review* and the author.
[1] W. W. Rostow, *The Stages of Economic Growth: a non-communist manifesto* (Cambridge, England: Cambridge University Press, 1960).
[2] J. K. Galbraith, "A Positive Approach to Foreign Aid," *Foreign Affairs*, Vol. XXXIX, No. 3 (April 1961).

population and a highly educated elite are just as important for development as the inflow of capital. He goes on to list three other items relating to the social system as being of equal importance. These are social justice, an efficient administration, and clear understanding of what development entails.

EDUCATION AND THE SOCIAL STRUCTURE

The significance of education in particular is now generally maintained, as was demonstrated by the recent conference of the OECD on *Economic Growth and Investment in Education* (Washington, October 1961). Some economists have attempted to quantify the contribution of education to economic expansion. Schultz,[3] for example, maintains that less than a third of the increase in the national income of countries can be explained by quantitative increases in factor inputs. The residual has not been accurately broken down, but the most important factors appear to be the improvement of the human material through better health and training, and through the development of science and technology.

Encouraging though such developments may be, it is perhaps limiting that many people who are concerned about speeding the educational growth of underdeveloped countries think in rather narrow terms of increasing the supply of skilled manpower. If we stop to consider the social context responsible for the previous failure to produce this manpower, we see that the problem is wider than this. Underdeveloped societies are underdeveloped because they are not geared to the types of activity which development entails, and one of these is education in the general sense of the word. Many of these societies espouse systems of belief which are antipathetic to the flexible, empirical spirit necessary to technical achievement. Their social systems are often of a sort which would impede the growth of large commercial or industrial undertakings, or of individual capital accumulation. Large proportions of their populations, being chronically malnourished or diseased, are physically incapable of taxing technological work or agricultural innovation even if they were emotionally oriented and intellectually prepared for it. The enormous poverty of the majority of people in the underdeveloped world forms an almost unbreakable vicious circle with sickness, disease—and underproduction. The perimeter of this circle is very often reinforced by either political considerations, or the non-egalitarian character of the society, or both.

[3] Theodore W. Schultz, "Capital Formation by Education," *Journal of Political Economy*, Vol. LXVIII, No. 6 (1960), pp. 571–583, and his other writings. H. M. Phillips gives even greater weight to education in "Education as a Basic Factor in Economic Development," *Final Report* of Conference of African States on the Development of Education in Africa (Addis Ababa, May 1961; Paris: UNESCO, 1961).

It is common knowledge that the ruling classes of many nations have been reluctant to spend much money on the education of those who might then compete with or supplant them. The differences between these classes and their poorer compatriots reflect and are similar in principle to the differences between nations.[4] Even without explicit government policy, the enormous gulf between rich and poor, powerful and impotent, well educated and illiterate is incredibly difficult to bridge. Underdeveloped societies tend to be highly stratified in terms of race, religion, tribe, region, class, or caste. In consequence the path of advancement for any one born in the lowest strata is hard and steep. He has to cross obstacles in the shape of indifferent schooling, of his own physical difficulties—malnourishment and chronic disease—and of social inertia. Eventually he has the final problem of establishing himself in a world in which there is no ready-made place for him.

For all these reasons, only a fraction of the potential talent of the underdeveloped countries is put to productive use, and it is very largely for this reason that they remain underdeveloped. The problem is one which education is qualified to tackle, at least in part, so long as it is borne in mind that we are not thinking simply of producing the people, but also of changing the society; or rather of producing the people who will change the social structure as they contribute to the economy. Naturally these things always go together, but the emphasis we lay on one or other aspect of the development continuum affects our priorities.

One of the main things lacking in the underdeveloped countries is a middle class. In the traditional land-based economy there is little to stimulate the entrepreneur, while the growth of the technical, professional, and administrative class has been so slow, because of the inadequate educational system, that its members have tended to align themselves with the existing power groups. Thus the small emergent middle class, instead of establishing its own standards of competence, of professional integrity, and of appointment in terms of ability and training, has often striven to become as exclusive as the old elite, emulating rather than rivaling it. This proclivity is reinforced and illustrated by the difficulty of filling the intermediate posts, which is almost as serious an impediment to development as the complete lack of trained persons. Compare, for example, the figures for doctors and less highly trained medical personnel in the United Kingdom and in India.

The reasons for the inversion of the British pattern are complex, but one implication is that hierarchy matters even to the "new class" and that it frequently sets up barriers as strong as those through which its members have themselves broken. The high prestige of the top grade occasioning the lack of intermediate personnel is one cause of slow

4 This is neatly illustrated in "Problems of Regional Development and Industrial Location in Europe," *Economic Survey of Europe in 1954* (Geneva, 1955).

professional growth; it also leads to inefficiency and waste, as when a doctor spends half of his time as his own laboratory technician.

This is not to say that education is doing a bad job, but that to have its full social effect, it must have a sufficient volume. If the middle class is to be influential enough to break through resistances against effective economic behavior, to establish high standards of efficiency in administration, industry, and business, and gradually to draw together the extremes of the population, then it must be sufficiently large.

TABLE 1 [5]

Type of personnel	Per number of persons	
	India	United Kingdom
1 doctor	6,300	1,000
1 nurse	43,000	300
1 health visitor	400,000	4,710
1 midwife	60,000	618

In the old days when the British Colonial Office was planning a slow socio-educational evolution for Africa, it was assumed that the middle class would grow gradually over a period of decades. But political pressures and the urgency of reaching what Sax calls the Demographic Transition [6] give us very much less time. The African countries, among others, feel the urgency most keenly, and ambitious plans of educational expansion are being everywhere developed. From the point of view of the arguments I am putting forward, this is excellent, but when we get down to the details there are vast difficulties.

ECONOMIC CONSIDERATIONS

First there is the problem of how much a country can spend on education, and I will not attempt to answer this, except to say that the answer will to some extent depend on the apportionment of resources between activities which have a more and a less rapid impact on the economy. . . .

. . . There can be little doubt that the most immediate short-term returns can be obtained from investment in adult education. On-the-job training in metal, engineering, and building trades, agricultural extension, apprenticeship schemes, and all the educational activities which go

[5] Government of India, Planning Commission, *The First Five Year Plan* (New Delhi, 1952), p. 490.
[6] Karl Sax, *Standing Room Only: The World's Exploding Population* (Boston: Beacon Press, 1955). This is "the transition from a high-birth-rate, high-death-rate culture (with low living standards) to a low-birth-rate, low-death-rate culture (with relatively high living standards)," p. 4.

with community development will obtain results in weeks or months, whereas schemes involving formal education may take ten years or more to mature.

There is another extremely important side to this. A poor country's capacity to absorb trained personnel is not great. For one thing, the jobs are few; for another, the wage expectation of the small number of educated persons is relatively much higher than in a richer country. In Ghana, for example, a primary school teacher is paid four times more relative to the national average income than one in the U.S.A. Therefore the poor countries can afford proportionally fewer trained people than the rich ones, although their need is so much greater. Here is one of the many vicious circles of underdevelopment. If primary education is expanded as rapidly as political pressure and national pride demand, the result—as in many West African countries—is the unemployed primary school graduate. In the Philippines and India [7] the academic level at which unemployment occurs is higher, but the principle is similar. There are no jobs at a level which young people consider proper for themselves, and so, having wasted their country's money on their education, they proceed to waste their family's resources on their maintenance. Given time, the number of available jobs will go up, or the aspiration of the school leaver go down, but again we have not got this kind of time and we cannot afford this kind of waste.

The speediest way in which an underdeveloped country's absorptive capacity can be increased is through its main industry of agriculture. This appallingly neglected field could absorb, as extension workers, community development workers, assistant agriculture officers, and the like, millions of young men and women who at present scorn it as a form of activity representing the backwardness they are attempting to escape from, and who see very slender rewards to be gained from it. (It takes 75 per cent of the working population of Asia to produce an inadequate 2,500 original calories per head per day for the inhabitants of the continent. In the U.S.A. 15 per cent of the working population produce 10,000 original calories per head per day. These figures illustrate the size and the urgency of the problem.) But if suitable training for different levels of scholastic attainment were devised and adequate possibilities of promotion established, the people might well be attracted to types of work which have an immediate impact on the economy, rather than to the normal favorite avocations of clerk or school teacher.

If agriculture can do most to absorb skilled and semi-skilled labor, industry comes second and can do more to increase a nation's wealth. However, the poorer a country is, the less it can sustain those factors which tend to strengthen the labor force and to increase production.

[7] It is calculated that there are 50,000 unemployed graduates in India. In the Philippines there are 250,000 college and university students, most of whom are working for qualifications which are both academically worthless and useless for obtaining employment.

Two of these factors, the amount of vocational training and the membership of labor unions, tend to vary proportionately with national wealth,
as is shown by the following figures for underdeveloped areas.

TABLE 2 [8]

Group of countries	Percentage of secondary school population (age 12–19) in vocational training, according to national per capita income			
	up to $100	$100–250	$250–500	$500–750
Africa	3.5	25.3	— [o]	—
Asia	2.4	14.6	20.9	48.8
Latin America	47.1	41.4	36.5	61.0

[o] Only the Republic of South Africa comes within this group.

An entirely untrained and unadapted labor force drifting between
agricultural under-employment and the alien life of the factory town is
cheap and easily obtained labor in which management is not inclined to
invest. Nor is it attractive to install new plant calling for skilled handling. So industry lacks efficiency and the labor force lacks the steady

TABLE 3 [9]

Per capita gross national product		Percentage of population in labor unions
Up to $100	(21 countries)	0.82
$100–$250	(20 countries)	2.59
Over $250	(15 countries)	6.42

Note: The average for the lowest income group has been almost doubled by the figure for Bolivia of which 7.7 per cent of the population belongs to labor unions.

employment which would make it efficient. But these workers, by the
very fact that they have shaken loose from the traditional life and sought
industrial employment, are part of the nucleus of the new class which
will transform society. Anything spent on their appropriate training or
on efforts to organize them will have both a short-term productive and a
long-term social effect.

A STRATEGY FOR EDUCATIONAL
EXPANSION

If I seem to have strayed away from the field of education proper, it
is because I wanted to stress that we have to use the term widely in

[8] Derived from Norton Ginsburg, *Atlas of Economic Development* (Chicago: Chicago University Press, 1961), and from UNESCO, *Basic Facts and Figures* (1960).
[9] Derived from Ginsburg, *op. cit.*, and Gabriel A. Almond and James S. Coleman,
eds., *The Politics of Developing Areas* (Princeton, New Jersey: Princeton University
Press, 1960).

relation to the underdeveloped countries. I also wish to show why educational planning and especially planning of the long-term investment in schools, universities, and technical colleges, has to be related in the widest sense to all other aspects of social and economic planning. A country's capacity to absorb persons of different educational levels and abilities; the factors which can be brought to affect this capacity; the relationship between the educational, social, and economic factors in productivity—all these and many other things have to be borne in mind when planning the rate of expansion of an educational system and the priorities to be assigned within that system to its several parts.

Nevertheless, despite the fact that every country presents its own problems, it is possible to suggest some of the broad lines of the strategy of educational expansion. Firstly, common sense would advocate an absolute maximum ratio of growth for primary education of 10 per cent per annum. But common sense is unlikely in this case, as in many others, to prevail against political expediency. We are forced to the next best thing, which is a series of measures designed to reduce the damage to standards caused by over-rapid expansion. This means emphasis on teacher training (including upgrading of existing teachers) and on such methods as will enable teachers both to deal with more children and help bad teachers to teach better. The growth of secondary education is far more significant to economic development, and it is on this that resources should be concentrated. Universities are, of course, also of great importance, but their expense is enormous and in any case the greatest shortage is of persons educated up to secondary level (particularly where there has been a considerable component of vocational or technical training).

The great problem is to determine the rate of growth. . . . This is an almost universal dilemma: a country needs a considerable number of trained and educated persons to build up and consolidate its development, but until it is developed it has not the resources to educate the people.

What can be done, however, is to place heavy emphasis initially upon such activities as will without great cost bring about rapid improvements in the economy. Such activities would be training rather than education in the broadest sense; vocational rather than general. They would be directed towards key sectors of the economy. Agriculture and industry have already been mentioned in this connection: training for management is also extremely important. A further principle would be to make full use of existing potentialities, of the people already employed. Both public and private employers would be encouraged to provide in-service training to upgrade their staff.

To concentrate heavily upon this form of technological training is, of course, only a short-term expedient designed to strengthen the economy and to increase the absorptive capacity so that, in the next phase, the weight can be gradually transferred to the formal system of education. From this will come men and women who not only possess the necessary skills, but an outlook sufficiently broad to contend with the extreme problems of a society undergoing rapid change.

33. DICHOTOMIES IN THE CHURCH *

j o h n j. k e n n e d y

Questions concerning the role of the Church in society and its relation to the state have persistently formed one of the central issues in the politics of Latin America. As the Latin-American nations move through a period of accelerated social change and transition, it is unlikely that these questions will disappear. In the process of a profound social transformation, however, it is probable that they will be restated and re-examined. . . .

❂   ❂   ❂   ❂   ❂

There is little doubt that the situation of the Church today is radically different. Contrasts between 1930 and 1960 establish the difference. At the earlier date, rightly or wrongly, the Church was widely regarded as exerting what pressure it could on behalf of the *status quo* in opposition to incipient social change. Now, when pressing social demands portend yet deeper and more far-reaching transformation, the Church appears to have given a vigorous endorsement to those demands. Most of the alliances with reaction have long since disappeared. Conservative and Catholic are no longer interchangeable symbols in the

* From "Dichotomies in the Church" by John J. Kennedy, *Latin America's Nationalistic Revolutions, The Annals,* Vol. 334 (March, 1961), pp. 55–62. By permission of the publisher and the author.

language of party politics. The Christian Democratic movements that have developed in Chile, Venezuela, Brazil, and Argentina have not inherited the function once attributed to conservatism. That is to say, they do not claim to be the political spokesmen of a political and religious combination. Moreover, Christian Democratic leadership has taken pains to emphasize the nonconfessional character of these parties.[1]

The contrast also emphasizes the vigor with which the Catholic episcopacy in several countries has, in recent years, been willing to speak out officially and collectively. A generation ago, the Mexican bishops were engaged in an unequal contest with Calles and Obregón. In the 1950's Perón, Rojas Pinilla, Pérez Jiménez, and Batista provoked statements of condemnation, criticism, or stern counsel from the Argentine, Colombian, Venezuelan, and Cuban hierarchies. In each case, these pronouncements had the effect of linking the Church with other groups which disapproved and opposed repressive regimes. When these regimes shortly came to an end, the Church, in the aftermath, seemed to stand conspicuously with the victors who had destroyed unappetizing dictatorships and to have won, thereby, sympathy and cordiality in quarters where such would not normally have been expected. According to the latter point of view, it might be claimed that in a certain sense the several episcopacies had redeemed the Church in their respective countries.

Needless to say, this is not a view which will be shared by churchmen, who see the justification of the Church not in terms of its response to progressive norms but rather in accordance with the measure of zeal with which it fulfills a divine mandate. To seek on this latter basis alone, however, an explanation of current ecclesiastical attitudes will hardly prove more helpful than that which sees the Church as a late convert to liberalism. For if the real goals of the Church are not of this world, the historical truth of Western civilization, including the Latin-American segment, is that the Church has been very much involved in the things of this world.

PERMANENT INVOLVEMENT

✧　✧　✧　✧　✧

Series of Crises

The permanent involvement of the Church in Latin America can, at least partially, be delineated by reference to the series of crises through which it has passed in its relation to the state. This series undoubtedly

---

[1] A definite statement on this point may be found in *Politica y Espiritu*, Año 6 (August 1955), No. 139, pp. 15–18.

begins in the period following liberation when two important and related problems were Church patronage and recognition by Rome of the new governments. In connection with the latter, papal hesitancy or reluctance to deal with the new and unstable authorities probably gave rise to a certain tension between a nascent nationalism and the Church, which was not entirely dissipated by the eventual extension of recognition. This problem was, however, less important and less enduring than that of the *patronato*. If the state could approach this question in terms of national interest and authority, the Church viewed the matter against the background of traditional Spanish regalism which represented a potential encroachment on its own authority.

The important consideration here, however, lies less in the conflict over the appointment of bishops and other ecclesiastical officials than in the fact that neither side could produce a solution without the other. It was not in the logic of the times for public authority, on the one side, to regard the authority which a bishop possesses as being beyond the scope of concern of the state. The implications of such authority for public order were too obvious to be ignored. It was equally impossible for the Church to forego or abandon an official recognition of its functions by the state. In what other way could it secure assurance that its functions would be tolerated?

In the course of a century and a half, the Church, in many countries, has, of necessity, learned that it can function without this recognition, but there is no denial of the fact that, in certain cases, the circumstances of withdrawal of this recognition confirmed the earlier fears of the Church. Within the same period, many Latin-American governments have modified or given up their regalistic positions. . . .

Regalism per se raises questions that are truly political in nature. Some of the crises through which the Latin-American Church has passed, however, have posed issues that have been less strictly political than they have been sociological or even—in the view of the Church—theological. Some general questions in these areas relate to the effort to laicize certain functions which the Church has claimed as primarily within its own sphere of authority. The most important have centered in legislation concerning marriage and education.

Marriage

In regard to marriage, modern formulation of Catholic doctrine does not deny the competence of the state to regulate the civil effects of matrimony. It does not, for example, oppose the issuance of a marriage license. Catholic teaching does, however, regard marriage as a sacrament, and the Church claims authority over the administration of sacraments—even though, in this case, the ministers of the sacrament are the parties to the marriage contract, not the clergyman officiating at the ceremony. Basic regulation of the conditions of marriage, then, is claimed by the Church. In many parts of Latin America, the Church has seen its claims threatened and opposed by the state in two respects. The more important one so far is the requirement of civil marriage to validate a union between man and wife. The other is the authorization of civil divorce. . . .

Education

Conflicts in the field of education have, on the whole, been less clear-cut but probably no less prevalent. Three areas of possible discord may be noted: the maintenance of schools under religious auspices, religious instruction in the public school system, and the existence of universities under Catholic auspices. Conflicts in any one of these areas may, of course, arise out of the directly opposing claims of Church and state. Generally, however, the problem is not so simple. Where the maintenance of Catholic schools has been in question, the question has often appeared in the context of a more intricate problem, such as the legal status of a religious order or a general breakdown of relations between Church and state, as happened in Mexico.

The introduction of religious doctrine classes into the public school system may appear as a drastic and, to many, an unpalatable settlement of the competition between Church and state in education. The Argentine experience, however, between 1944 and 1954, strongly suggests that this arrangement provides no real solution. . . .

✿　✿　✿　✿　✿

EXPECTATIONS

In evaluating the Church, there is always the danger of oversimplification of a most complex organization. Taking that risk for the moment, may one not discern a single element pervading the whole involvement of Church and state over human conduct? This element is the authority claimed by the Church. This is an authority which, by definition, cannot be determined by the state. Yet the state is asked to recognize it. The recognition originally demanded was an official endorsement of the necessity of the Church in society in accordance with its own credal concepts of the nature and destiny of man. Up to this date, the Church has not revised its creed; nor is such an eventuality at all likely. The Church has, however, undoubtedly learned from experience that, in practice, official recognition is not quite the *sine qua non* that it is in theory. The important consequences of this lie in the greater possibility of flexibility in the Church's adjustment to society as managed by the state. It would be a serious error, however, to interpret flexibility as relinquishment or abdication of authority.

An emphasis on this element should not be understood as excluding other considerations from the concern of the Church. For the latter, as for any other interested party, the paramount fact today is that Latin America is in a process of rapid and profound social transformation. Within the Church, there may be many views and evaluations of this process as it unfolds in various countries. Collectively, however, the forces of Catholicism cannot be unaware of the opportunities to exert moral and ethical influences on this process. Such opportunities are open not only to the hierarchies as the official spokesmen of the Church, but also to the citizen as he participates in the social life of his country.

Undoubtedly, one of the stimuli to action in both the preceding respects is an ultimate awareness that social stagnation and repression may pave the way to a Marxist revolution which, acting in concert with international communism, could produce the least of all desirable situations from a Catholic point of view. Evaluation of current Catholic attitudes on this negative basis alone, however, is probably inadequate. The affirmative drive of Catholic forces, especially in the laity, is shown, if nowhere else, in the large area of identity between their professed aspirations and those of contemporary nationalism in general.

34. THE SOCIAL, ECONOMIC, AND TECHNOLOGICAL PROBLEMS OF RAPID URBANIZATION*

p h i l i p   m.   h a u s e r

Urban problems and the problems of rapid urbanization are quite different in the economically advanced and the economically underdeveloped

* From "The Social, Economic, and Technological Problems of Rapid Urbanization" by Philip M. Hauser. Reprinted from: *Industrialization and Society*, by F. Hoselitz and W. E. Moore, eds., (Mouton/Unesco, 1963), with the permission of Unesco. Selections from pp. 201–211.

areas of the world respectively. In the economically advanced nations, urbanization is both an antecedent and a consequence of high levels of living. It both makes possible and is a manifestation of great increases in division of labor and specialization, in technology, in skill, and in productivity. In the economically underdeveloped areas, it does not usually have these properties. There, large concentrations of urban population are only to a minor degree symbols of man's mastery over nature—they represent more the transfer of underemployment and poverty from an overpopulated rural countryside to an urban setting. In consequence, the social, economic, and technological problems of rapid urbanization must be considered separately for the underdeveloped and the developed areas of the globe respectively.

ECONOMIC PROBLEMS

The economic antecedents of urbanization in the economically more advanced areas differ greatly from those of the less advanced areas. Although much remains to be learned, the emergence of the urban agglomeration has been reasonably well traced for Western civilization. . . . In the West, urbanization is both an antecedent and consequence of rapid industrialization. There are no highly developed economies in the world in which large cities and a high degree of industrialization are not present.

Urbanization in the economically underdeveloped areas of the world is the product of very different forces. The "primate" cities in South and South-East Asia are less the result of indigenous economic development than they are the product of economic development oriented essentially to one or more foreign countries. They developed as links between the colonial and mother country. Today, they usually still have an external orientation, serving as a link between the local elite and the outside world, rather than as an economic outpost of the national economy.[1] Urbanization in Latin America is characterized by the hypertrophy of capital cities. These, reflecting unique aspects of Latin American history, are concentrated on the seaboard, or in the mountain districts in the tropics.[2] In Latin America—as in Asia and Africa—prior to World War II, economic and urban development was largely directed

[1] Philip M. Hauser (ed.), *Urbanization in Asia and the Far East* (Calcutta, 1957), pp. 86 ff; Mark Jefferson, "The Law of the Primate City," *Geographical Review* (April, 1939); Norton S. Ginsburg, "The Great City in Southeast Asia," *American Journal of Sociology* (special issue on "World Urbanism"), LX, No. 5 (March, 1955), 455–62.
[2] UNESCO, *Report by the Director-General on The Joint UN/UNESCO Seminar on Urbanization in Latin America* (Paris, 1960), p. 6.

toward external markets in the framework of patterns established under colonial administration. Moreover, the process of urbanization in the underdeveloped areas has been accelerated by the low land-population ratio arising from excessive population growth in relation to agriculture resources; by the disruption and disorganization produced by the last war, which forced refugee populations to choke already swelled populations in cities; by the lure of urban existence, to which large parts of the peasant population were exposed as the result of military service and other wartime dislocations; and by various other forces which pushed population to the city instead of attracting it by economic opportunity of the type experienced in the West.[3]

Thus, the underdeveloped areas of the world are "over-urbanized," in that larger proportions of their population live in urban places than their degree of economic development justifies. In the underdeveloped nations, a much smaller proportion of the labor force is engaged in non-agricultural occupations than was the case in the West at comparable levels of urbanization.[4] Furthermore, during the postwar period, the rate of urbanization in the underdeveloped areas has continued proceeding more rapidly than the rate of economic development.

To say that the underdeveloped areas of the world are over-urbanized is to pose the major economic problem with which they are confronted, namely, that they do not at the present time have an adequate economic base to support present urban populations by the standards of the Western world. They must find a way of achieving higher levels of economic development to support their present, let alone their prospective, urban population. Continued rapid rates of urbanization are, therefore, likely to aggravate, rather than alleviate, present urban poverty and distress. In general, the outlook for the remainder of this century is a dismal one indeed. It is very doubtful that, over this span of time, the underdeveloped nations can attain economic development of adequate dimensions to meet Western standards of living for their present and future city dwellers.[5] The fundamental economic objective of the underdeveloped areas is that of increasing productivity; and the many difficulties they meet in their efforts to attain this objective are likely to be exacerbated rather than ameliorated by present and prospective rapid rates of urban growth.[6]

---

[3] Hauser, *Urbanization*, pp. 33 ff; UNESCO, *Report by the Director-General*, p. 15.
[4] Kingsley Davis, "Urbanization and the Development of Pre-Industrial Areas," *Economic Development and Cultural Change*, III, No. 1 (October, 1954).
[5] Philip M. Hauser, "Demographic Dimensions of World Politics," *Science*, CXXXI, No. 3414, 16–43.
[6] United Nations, *Determinants*, chap. xv; United Nations, *Report on the World Social Situation* (New York, 1957), chaps. ii, vii, viii, ix; Joseph J. Spengler, "Population and World Economic Development," *Science*, CXXXI, No. 3412, 20.

This general problem may be analyzed into a number of components.[7] Virtually all of the underdeveloped nations have ambitious programs for economic development. The cores of these programs generally
consist of plans to increase industrialization. At the present levels of
productivity and limited savings, a central problem is that of allocating
resources for development between the agricultural and industrial sectors of the economy. If the criterion of maximizing product per head be
accepted as the objective of economic development programs, then it is
possible, at least in the short run, that the advancement of the agricultural sectors of the economy may be more productive than efforts to
induce industrialization. The achievement of adequate balance between
agricultural and industrial development is a major difficulty which confronts almost all of the economically underdeveloped nations.

Another issue involves the allocation of scarce investment resources
between "social investment" and "productive investment." This problem, although it exists both in the urban and rural sectors, assumes its
most acute form in the cities. Cities in the underdeveloped areas are
characterized by inadequate infrastructure development, precluding the
usual amenities of urban existence found in Western cities. The tempta-
tion to devote scarce savings to social purposes—e.g., piped water, sewerage, better housing, etc.—is great, particularly in view of the expectations
which have accompanied political independence and the opportunity for
self-determination. Yet social investment of this type, badly needed as it
may be, is possible only at the expense of decreased productive investment—investment in power plants and factories, or in tractors and fertilizers, designed to increase productivity.

Another difficult problem posed by the continued accelerated rates
of urbanization in the underdeveloped areas is that of the location of
industry. At the present time, numerous small commercial towns serving
agricultural areas are widely dispersed, largely in accordance with the
location of agricultural activity and the density of agricultural population. Larger towns are superimposed on the widespread distributional
pattern of the smaller commercial centers. They are usually near transport nodal points—river and road junctions and, more recently, railroad
junctions. These centers, and the seaports, are the "break-of-bulk"
points; their essential function is the transshipment and distribution of
goods between land and water and within the interior. Such cities have
increasingly become convenient points of location for processing and
light manufacturing industry. In most underdeveloped areas, the growth

[7] Discussion of economic problems is drawn largely from Hauser, *Urbanization*,
chaps. i, ii, vi, vii, UNESCO, *Report by the Director-General;* and *United Nations
Seminar on Regional Planning* (New York, 1958). These publications summarize the
UN/UNESCO Seminar considerations of economic problems associated with urbanization.

of towns and cities and industrialization, apart from primate and capital cities, has gone little beyond this point.

Efforts to increase industrialization, and to deal with the many pressing problems of swelling urban populations, are forcing decisions about the location of economic development projects. In the economically more advanced nations, the locations, as well as the size and function of urban places, were largely the products of the play of market forces. In the economically underdeveloped areas, these decisions are usually centrally administered. They involve considerations of raw materials, power sources, availability of labor, the location of consumer markets, national policy concerning centralization or decentralization of industry, regional development, and general national economic development. In centralized decision-making about the location of new industry, there are dangers of serious dis-economies.

Decentralization is necessary because the "great city" tends to be "parasitic," in that it usually retards the development of other cities in the nation, and may contribute relatively little to the development of its own hinterland because it is oriented primarily to the contribution of services abroad or to the indigenous or remaining Western elite inhabiting it. On the other hand, the decision to decentralize industry may produce dis-economies by ignoring the productive factors already available in the larger urban agglomerations. The larger cities in the underdeveloped areas represent already available labor supply, markets, and a wide variety of public services which may be utilized for industrial and business development. To duplicate such agglomerations of population in efforts to decentralize may well be redundant and wasteful.

Underdeveloped areas with rapidly growing urban populations face another difficulty in making policy with respect to employment opportunities. To provide work for hordes of unemployed and underemployed immigrants to urban centers, there is a tendency to emphasize labor-intensive techniques. If carried too far, this tendency may adversely affect the growth of the nation's net aggregate product by retarding labor-saving technological developments. In general, policy determination presumably must aim toward obtaining balance in industrial development between employment opportunities, in the short run, and technological advance to insure maximum product per head, in the longer run.

Low productivity and poverty are distinguishing traits in both rural and urban areas in underdeveloped nations. Because internal migratory flow from agricultural to urban centers is a major factor in the present and prospective increase in urban populations, programs designed to keep rural people in agricultural areas may be important in any effort to deal with urban, as well as national, economic development problems. Programs that raised the level of living of rural populations would undoubtedly moderate the excessive flow of migrants from rural to urban areas. In a number of underdeveloped nations, outmoded land tenure systems contribute to rural proverty. Agrarian reform resulting in higher productivity, giving the agricultural population a stake in the land and an opportunity to raise its level of living, may well be an important means of alleviating urban problems by helping to reduce the flow of city-bound migrants. Similarly, the establishment of cottage industries and small industries in rural areas may keep their population from emigrating.

Western cities have undergone development and transformation with changing industrial technology. Economically underdeveloped areas today have the choice of adopting twentieth- or nineteenth-century types of industrial equipment. The extent of actual choice depends, of course, on the availability of electric, as contrasted with steam, power; on cost factors for older, as against more modern, equipment; and on the emphasis placed on labor-intensive rather than automated equipment. The adoption of twentieth-century industrial technology would undoubtedly create patterns of urban development quite different from those which characterized the West during the nineteenth. Moreover, the problem of maintaining balance in economic development is also at stake in the decisions made with respect to the types of technology adopted in different sectors of the industrial economy.

Urbanization has an impact on income, levels of living, savings, and capital formation that requires brief mention, even though most of what can be said is necessarily speculative. Urban residents in the underdeveloped areas, in spite of underemployment and low productivity, are generally engaged in nonagricultural activities which provide them with a relatively higher money level of income and expenditure than is achieved in rural areas. While it is a moot point whether urban real income is higher than rural real income in such areas, the higher urban money income is undoubtedly one of the factors attracting populations to cities.

The transition from the rural to the urban economy involves a shift, of course, from a subsistence to a monetary economy in which mobilization of savings can be facilitated. Urbanization produces alteration in consumption patterns, in which the proportion of consumer expenditures for food tends to decrease below the rural level; while expenditures on amusement, education, transport, services, footwear, rent, and taxes tend to rise. . . .

Finally, in the underdeveloped nations another crucial decision is necessary: the interventions of government and of market forces respectively, in dealing with the economic problems of the nation as a whole, as well as with the specific industrial and urban developments, must be determined. For a number of reasons, historical and contemporary, central decision-making and management of economic affairs inevitably must play a more important role in the economically underdeveloped nations than they did in the history of the economically advanced nations. If the mix of central planning and government interventionism is increased, it may be expected that patterns of economic, as well as urban, development are likely to follow different routes than they did in the West. Some types of problems engendered by Western industrialization and urbanization may be avoided or ameliorated; but it is also possible that new and critical kinds of problems will be encountered, and that the dangers of serious dis-economies will be increased. The interplay of forces most conducive to efficient and balanced economic development and orderly urbanization is far from being fully understood. . . .

✧ ✧ ✧ ✧ ✧

PHYSICAL PROBLEMS

The most visible consequence of overurbanization and rapid rates of urban growth is the decadence of the urban environment in underdeveloped areas.[8] The physical city is characterized by a large proportion of shanty towns and tenement slums; inadequate urban services, including housing, water supply, sewerage, utilities, and transport; uncontrolled land use; excessive population densities; deficient educational and recreational facilities; and inefficient commercial and marketing services. Rapid urbanization in the underdeveloped areas is accompanied by not only a defective but, also, by a deteriorating urban environment. It is estimated that, in Latin America alone, some four or five million families live in urban shanty towns and slums. The miserable physical conditions of cities create great pressure for "social" instead of "productive" investments. However, many of the public housing and physical improvement programs which have been undertaken in such areas have necessarily tended to benefit families with moderate incomes rather than to meet the needs of the lowest-income families—the residents of the shanty towns and slums.

Of course, the underdeveloped nations are very aware of the need for city and regional, as well as national, planning. But the city planner in the underdeveloped country is confronted with insuperable difficulties. These stem largely from low income levels; from rapid population growth, including hordes of immigrants from rural areas who are ill-

[8] The materials on "physical problems" are drawn largely from Hauser, *Urbanization*, chaps. i, ii, xi; UNESCO, *Report by the Director-General;* and Philip M. Hauser (ed.), *Urbanization in Latin America* (UNESCO, 1961).

adapted to urban living; from inadequate urban infrastructure development—all in all, from a bewildering array of needs, each of which seems
to have first priority.

Although urban agglomerations of the size of Western cities are to
be found, the physical amenities associated with such in the West have
not yet developed—at least, not for the mass population. The amenities of
urban existence are available only to very small fractions of the total
urban population. It is in the impact on the already inadequate urban
physical plant that the rapid rate of urbanization produces some of its
more serious consequences.

☼　☼　☼　☼　☼

SOCIAL PROBLEMS

The city represents not only a new form of economic organization
and a changed physical environment. It also is a profoundly modified
social order affecting man's conduct and thought. Urbanization produces the city as a physical and economic artifact, and also produces
"urbanism as a way of life." [9] The size, density, and heterogeneity of
population—aspects of "social morphology"—affect the nature, intensity,
and frequency of contact, and, therefore, influence the nature of the
process of socialization and human nature itself. The city is a type of
mutation in culture that has far-reaching effects on social structure and
process and on social institutions, including the structure and function
of government. The transition from pre-urban to urban living necessarily
involves frictions, which are manifested in social and personal problems.
Rapid urbanization exacerbates these frictions.

. . . The chief effects of urban living on the personal level are,
probably, discernible in the changed nature of interpersonal relations
and in the relative flexibility of personal patterns of behavior. On the
cultural and social level, they are to be found in the changed nature of
the forces making for cohesion, in the changed genesis and function of
social institutions, and in the changed structure and role of government.

On the personal level, contacts in the urban setting become secondary, segmental, and utilitarian, rather than primary, integral, and senti-
mental as in the traditional social order. Personality tends to change
from a relatively rigid structure molded by the traditional social heritage to more fluid flexible patterns, arising from the necessity to exercise

[9] Louis Wirth, "Urbanism as a Way of Life." The framework materials in the
introductory part of "social problems" are drawn from the general sociological literature, and particularly from the works of the men to whom reference is made in the
text.

choice and from rationalism in behavior, as the hold of tradition loosens and new urban problems emerge. On the social level, cohesion in the urban social order becomes a function of interdependence engendered by increased specialization and division of labor; it is no longer the product of the constraint of convention in a relatively homogeneous and closed traditional order. Social institutions in the urban setting become "enacted" rather than "crescive" as older functions become attenuated or disappear and new instrumentalities arise to cope with unprecedented situations and problems. Even the basic social institutions—the family and the church—are subjected to forces which modify their structure, their role, and their hold on the behavior of the person.

In the urban setting, the role of government is one of increasing interventionism as organizational complexity and interdependence increase. In the West, the transition from a feudal to an industrialized and urbanized order has been characterized by the emergence of complex formal organization—bureaucracy—not only in government, but also in business, labor, voluntary associations, and virtually all organized aspects of the mass society.

      ✵   ✵   ✵   ✵   ✵

. . . The acute as well as chronic aspects of social problems that result from rapid urbanization are, perhaps, most discernible in the adjustment of in-migrants to urban living. The rural in-migrant to the city is typically from a relatively homogeneous origin. In the city, he is confronted with a bewildering and almost incomprehensible vastness and heterogeneity. He usually lives for some time with his fellow villagers or relatives and only gradually becomes accommodated to city life. He must adapt to new and unfamiliar ways of making a living; a money economy; regular working hours; the absence of warm family living; large numbers of impersonal contacts with other human beings; new forms of recreation; and a quite different physical setting, often involving new kinds of housing, sanitation, traffic congestion, and noise. One of the greatest adjustment problems centers around the transition from a subsistence to a monetary economy, and dependence on a job for subsistence.

Furthermore, the in-migrant often finds his area of first settlement is the shanty town, in which the decadence of the underdeveloped urban environment is manifest in its most extreme form. Consequently, superimposed on problems of adjustment there may be severe problems of health and nutrition, and of extreme poverty and squalor in living conditions. In such a setting, the in-migrant frequently displays personal disorganization as the subjective aspect of social disorganization. It is in the in-migrant family that the greatest incidences of personal and social pathology are found—delinquency, crime, prostitution, mental illness, alcoholism, drug addiction, etc.

Another element contributes to the social problems and is source of severe problems for the economy as well. This is the fact that rural in-migrant workers often lack rudimentary skills for industrial work, possess high rates of illiteracy, and are otherwise ill-prepared for city living. Throughout the underdeveloped countries, the need to increase literacy and to provide minimum vocational training for urban employment is acute. In fact, the provision of adequate educational and vocational training, both to the in-migrant and to the more permanent inhabitant of urban places, is among the most critical social problems which confront the underdeveloped areas.

Rapid urbanization is accompanied by increasing tempos of cultural, social, and personal change. A number of scholars have maintained that underdeveloped areas with non-Western cultures possess ideologies and value systems that tend to resist change in general and, therefore, changes of the type induced by urbanization. A rapid rate of urbanization, as contrasted with a slow one, conceivably increases the frictions of transition from non-Western to urban (and presumably Western) value systems. It is, of course, disputable whether Western values identified with urbanism as a way of life are an antecedent or a consequence of industrialization and urbanization; and whether they are the only values consonant with urban living. Conceivably, the difference between non-Western outlooks produces different kinds of "urban mentality" and interpersonal and social relations in the urban setting. Whatever the answer to this question may be, it *is* true that rapid urbanization increases the tensions and frictions of adjustment in value systems from pre-urban ways of life.

35. SOME SOCIAL CONCOMITANTS OF INDUSTRIALIZATION AND URBANIZATION *

j o s e p h a. k a h l

The transformation of society by industrialization and urbanization is currently of great concern to men of affairs and to men of science.[1] Since the second World War the rate of industrialization has increased as people in previously isolated or tradition-bound societies have entered the main stream of world history to demand the material benefits of modern technology. They often seek those material benefits while hoping to retain their traditional cultures, yet, since England pointed the way in the eighteenth century, experience indicates that their hopes are utopian, for a radical change in the mode of production has profound repercussions on the rest of culture. This generalization is as sure as any in all of social science, but it is so abstract as to offer little guide to one who wants to know what the specific consequences of industrialization are likely to be. . . .

The process of "development" involves a series of intertwined economic changes: 1) the integration of previously isolated, self-sufficient rural economies into a single national economy with strong ties to the international economy; 2) the dominance of production for sale over production for barter or for use, thus the increasing emphasis upon money; 3) the introduction of new technological devices in farming and in manufacture which are based on worldwide science and involve large capital expenditures; 4) a tremendous growth of the means of communication and transport; 5) a steady growth of towns and cities (through internal migration from the farms) as bases of manufacturing, trade, and political control which become consumers of surplus food produced on

* From "Some Social Concomitants of Industrialization and Urbanization" by Joseph A. Kahl, *Human Organization*, Vol. XVIII, No. 2 (Summer, 1959), pp. 53–69. By permission of The Society for Applied Anthropology.
[1] The author takes pleasure in recording his indebtedness to students in two seminars who have given bibliographic assistance, and to several of his colleagues from Washington University and beyond it who read the first draft of this paper and offered useful critical comments.

the modernized farms; 6) a steady development of specialization in the division of labor between occupations, between farm and city, and between regions.[2]

Although economic development, industrialization and urbanization can be conceived of as separate variables, in most real instances the three unfold as an over-all complex. The changes listed in the preceding paragraph occur together, and no country can go far along the road to development unless they occur in a fairly harmonious pattern. . . .

✿ ✿ ✿ ✿ ✿

I am going to stress the general, the universal—those social effects of the development process which tend to occur regardless of the traditions of the particular culture under consideration. Obviously, local traditions make a difference, and the final outcome will show a compromise between the ecumenical social forms of modern, industrial society and the local forms of a given culture. We do not yet know how much "leeway" exists, how much variation around the central theme of industrial society is possible. It is one of the prime tasks of current comparative research to find out.

POPULATION GROWTH

A traditional society composed of isolated, self-sufficient villages has a very slow rate of population growth: it takes at least a century for the population to double, and ordinarily the counteracting forces of plague and famine decimate the growth almost as fast as it occurs. Economic development changes that picture: better means of transport make it possible to move food from areas of plenty to areas of scarcity; economic resources become available which permit the basic devices of sanitation, namely, fresh water and adequate sewage disposal; and contact with the outside world permits the rapid importation of cheap devices, such as DDT and penicillin, for the control of contagious disease. When economic development goes a bit further, and the general standard of living rises and provides better nutrition and medical care, the reduction in the death rate is dramatic.

Population growth is obviously the result of an excess of births over deaths. Economic development affects both the birth rate and the death

---

[2] For background in economics the author relied principally upon Norman S. Buchanan and Howard S. Ellis, *Approaches to Economic Development* (New York: Twentieth Century Fund, 1955).

rate, but at different periods in the development process. During the early industrialization of Europe, improvements in transport, urban sanitation, and general nutrition reduced the death rate slowly over a long period of time; when the great discoveries of modern medicine appeared in the 19th century and further cut the death rate, the birth rate had *already* begun to decline as a result of those gradual changes in family life which generally lead urban people to prefer fewer children than do rural people. But nowadays the rate of change is faster and the sequence of steps is different: during the earliest stages of modernization, a country simultaneously improves its transport and communication, increases its food supply, cleans up its cities, and introduces scientific medicine by importing it from advanced countries. All of these changes can occur *before* any important alteration in the average size of family takes place as a result of urbanization. The consequence is a rapid reduction of the death rate, the maintenance of a high birth rate, and a population explosion.[3]

Recent data from Mexico . . . illustrate this process of sudden growth.[4] The pre-conquest population of Mexico is estimated at around nine million. The conquest in the early 16th century and its immediate aftermaths reduced the population by about one-half; thereafter, a stable though stagnant social system emerged and a very slow growth in population resulted. There were some six million by 1800, and twelve and a half million by 1895. Industrialization began under the Diaz dictatorship; just before the overthrow of his regime in 1910, the population reached 15 million. The severity of the civil war during the decade of the 1910's reduced it by almost one million people. Thus, 400 years after the conquest the population had only grown by about 60 percent.

In the 1920's peace was restored and a new surge of economic and social development began. The result was an unprecedented spurt in population: 16,553,000 in 1930; 19,654,000 in 1940; 25,791,000 in 1950; 33,000,000 in 1958.

The birth rate has probably been between 40 and 46 per thousand per year since the end of the revolution, but the death rate has steadily declined: it was over 30 before the revolution, about 25 during the 1920's and 1930's, about 20 in the 1940's, and is about 12 now.[5]

[3] Kingsley Davis, "The Unpredicted Pattern of Population Change," *Annals of American Academy of Political and Social Science*, vol. 305 (May, 1956).
[4] For statistical details, see Jose E. Iturriaga, *La Estructura Social y Cultural de México* (México: Fondo de Cultura Económica, 1951); Manuel Germán Parra, *La Industrialización de México* (México: Imprenta Universitaria, 1954); and Julio Duran Ochoa, *Población, México* (México: Fondo de Cultura Económica, 1955).
[5] Much of the decline in the death rate is due, of course, to diminishing infant mortality. The latter rate (deaths in the first year of life per thousand live births) has fallen from 317 in 1895 to 95 in 1953.

The disparity between the birth and death rates produces the annual rate of natural increase, and note its trend: from about 14 per thousand before the revolution, to about 19 in the 1930's, about 25 in the 1940's, and between 31 and 34 now (that is, a compounded growth of between 3.1 and 3.4 per cent per year).[6] The current rate of natural increase is sufficient to double the population *in less than 24 years* instead of in 400 years as was previously the case. But Mexico, although close to the top of the list of the countries of the world in current rate of increase, is by no means a special case. Other countries in Latin America, the Near East, and Asia are experiencing roughly the same phenomenon.

If a country is to progress in the economic sense—to raise the standard of living of its people and to have a surplus available for capital investment—it must increase its agricultural and industrial production faster than it increases its population. . . .

✿   ✿   ✿   ✿   ✿

Time is a crucial factor. For the development process to occur, a surplus must be available for capital investment. Factories must be built, mines sunk, farm machinery and fertilizers bought. Cities must be created as centers of industry and as sources of jobs to absorb the excess population from rural areas. Also, highways, railroads, schools, and hospitals have to be constructed. And to make matters more tense, the people, once aroused from a traditional way of life which assumes a fixed standard of living, start demanding new consumption goods; they institute a "revolution of expectations." Consequently, a country that once initiates the changes that lead it toward modernization must, to maintain self-sustained growth, increase its production considerably faster than its population; merely keeping even is impossible without chaos and revolution. There exists a critical period of rapid population growth which must be met by rapid industrialization before the gradual effects of urbanization can produce a decline in the birth rate and thus initiate a later period of slower growth.

FROM RURAL TO URBAN

The traditional world is a rural world; seventy percent or more of the people live on farms, and the surplus of food which they grow with their

6   All statistics in Mexico are suspect, and that is particularly true of vital statistics until recent years. Consequently, the estimates of natural increase given in the text have been adjusted somewhat to reflect growth as measured by the census, which is more accurate than growth measured by vital statistics. See Germán Parra, 1954, Table 23. Immigration has been negligible since the 17th century.

crude techniques of production can support but a few urbanites. Each village is self-sufficient in most of its needs, and engages in only a small amount of trade with the outside world.

But the modern world is an urban world. Less than ten percent of the population (given good farmland and scientific techniques of production) can feed ninety percent living in towns and cities. Even if the urban proportion is smaller than ninety percent, urban control in science, commerce, manufacturing, mass media, and politics comes to dominate. Modern culture originates in cities and spreads outward to farms.

During the period of rapid development, there is an enormous flow of young people from farm to city. If a farmer has eight children who reach maturity, only two may remain on the farm, if a stable rural population is to be maintained. Actually, in the early stages of development, there is usually a slow growth in the rural population as new lands are opened for exploitation and as old ones become more crowded (in the later stages of development, the absolute size of the rural population is likely to shrink, for farms become larger and are worked by machinery instead of by hand). But a slow growth in the rural population is not enough to absorb all of the farmers' children; many of them must move cityward when they are young adults to seek urban jobs.

❊   ❊   ❊   ❊   ❊

Cities are large and heterogeneous.[7] The contacts between men tend to be contacts in specialized roles rather than as total personalities. Work-place is different from home and both are different from worship-place. At each, a man has different associates. Salesman and customer, teacher and student, fellow members of the Society for the Preservation of Ancient Choral Music, even "neighbors," interact for particular purposes and do not allow themselves to become totally involved with one another: there is not enough time, and it would interfere with the efficiency of the specialized interaction (for example, a teacher is not supposed to consider "family background" in awarding grades to students—or, to use an overworked phrase, "business is business"). The immediate family and very few "close friends" are the limits of social relationships based on long contact, personal rather than business attitudes, emotional rather than rational purpose, total rather than specialized and thus superficial involvement.

The link between men in the city is mediated by money: urbanites buy and sell goods and services, and they play in ways which cost

---

[7] Louis Wirth, "Urbanism as a Way of Life," *American Journal of Sociology*, XLIV (July, 1938); reprinted in Hatt and Reiss, eds., *Cities and Society* (Glencoe, Illinois: The Free Press, 1957).

money so that only those with similar incomes can play the same games and join the same clubs. Even one's neighbors are determined by money, for the economic competition for space sorts out neighborhoods according to "quality" or cost. The cash nexus tends to replace kinship and local community as the main determinant of social position and consequently of social relationships.

. . . The key to city life is the multiplicity of group ties: each may have strong influence on the individual, but each is limited to a specific area of behavior and is balanced by others. In the folk society, the family group generally controls property, marriage, work, and much of religion. The individual is a member of a *single* small group whose activities cover all the important aspects of his life. In the city, the individual interacts with many groups: he has his own personal career and he meets on the job a team of workmates; at home, he sorts the claims of parents, extended kin, wife, and children into different compartments; he may belong to a church which tells him that the goals of business are not the only important ends of life, etc. He has a great range of choice, and can use one group to offset the other. He must manipulate their various claims by means of rational decision, and thus may at times seem like an extreme individualist organizing his life to suit himself. But the fact is that his own goals are taken over from various of these groups; he follows group codes, gets emotional satisfaction from group member-ships, thinks in terms of maximizing group performance. Work groups, recreational cliques, nuclear families—these are "tight" groups which bind the individual to them, shape him in their image. The typical urbanite is not an isolate; he is a group member whose total involvement in collective life is very great but whose involvement in any one group is limited.[8]

As long as the rapidly growing cities contain so many citizens who are migrants from rural areas, we must distinguish between their transitional way of life—combining rural and urban traits—and the more adapted pattern which eventually develops among those born and reared in city environments. Persons in transition may cling to many rural characteristics, such as devotion to the extended-family system, which give them security in their new situation. Indeed, many new city workers are temporary workers, leaving families behind in the villages. On the other hand, some transitional individuals throw over the rural patterns before they have time to learn functionally adapted urban ways, and their lives show the "disorganization" noticed in many urban stud-

[8] Perhaps some of the overemphasis upon individualism, even on isolation, in urban society stems from the attempts of Park's students in Chicago to find and portray "extreme" types of urbanites, like taxi dance hall girls and rooming house inhabitants. But such extremes cannot be used to construct an "ideal-type" of life in the city. Durkheim, in discussing his model of modern society, emphasized *both* the loosening of the old social controls of rigid tradition in small communities *and* the emergence of new social controls in terms of segmental groups functionally adapted to the urban milieu.

ies. But neither rural survivals nor temporary disorganization last through time; if we are to predict the future, we must concentrate on the city-bred persons who have turned their back on the farms and are committed to an urban style of life.

◦ ◦ ◦ ◦ ◦

NEW DIVISION OF LABOR

An urban population supported by industrial and commercial activity develops a division of labor markedly different from that of a rural population. The latter contains farmers plus a very few specialists (artisans, merchants, priests, soldiers, governors). The former contains thousands of different specialists (the United States Government catalogues over 20,000 in the Dictionary of Occupational Titles) whose existence is dependent upon an intricate system of exchange which integrates the labor of bricklayer, machine-tool maker, automobile assembly worker, and clerk, so that all end up with complete houses and automobiles. The occupational division of labor is the economically determined skeleton on which the flesh of modern social organization develops; it is somewhat analogous in function to the kinship system which is the base of much of primitive society. Therefore we can use the division of labor as a convenient index of the degree of industrialization-urbanization reached by any given society—it is probably the most meaningful index for sociological purposes.

The division of labor is conventionally portrayed by two distributions: that among branches of activity (industry, agriculture, and services, including commerce), and that among socioeconomic levels (professionals, clerks, laborers, etc.). Let us examine both measures. If we use the historical experience of the United States as a model (and it appears that other countries tend to follow the same general trends), we find that economic development involves a steady shift from an early period in which agricultural labor predominates, with a secondary emphasis upon industry and services, to an intermediate period in which there is a shift from agriculture into both industry and services in equal proportions, to a later period of maturity when industry stops growing and the remaining shift is from agriculture into services. In other words, there appears to be a limit upon the need for industrial labor, for as the system matures the machines get more efficient and increases in production can be obtained without increases in manpower.[9] However, services cannot so easily be mechanized, and they continue to absorb excess agricultural workers. . . .

[9] Colin Clark, *The Conditions of Economic Progress* (3rd ed.; London: Macmillan, 1957).

If we turn our attention to the distribution by socioeconomic levels, we get a complementary picture. . . . Here we notice that as the industrial system matures, there is a greater need for professional and technical people (they almost tripled in proportion from 1870 to 1950), and for clerks and salesmen (they increased fivefold). There is a smaller need for more workers at the semi-skilled level (they doubled). The skilled workers increased by a still smaller amount (about fifty percent), and the unskilled workers not at all. Thus there is a constant up-grading of the labor force as the system matures: from blue-collar to white-collar work, from lower levels to higher levels of technical competence.

The implications of these shifts in the labor force are far-reaching. For instance, it becomes less likely that a boy will become a farmer like his father and learn his occupation within the family context; instead, he follows a personal career and prepares for it by going to school, and that takes him out of the home (and often away from the community) and thus weakens the family while it strengthens the system of formal education. Furthermore, since many urban occupations are open to women, they are no longer thought of solely as daughters, wives and mothers, but become individuals who can pursue careers.

Finally, the interactions of city life become, as was suggested above, contacts between specialists acting in their occupational roles rather than human beings as total personalities. If the trading of the marketplace is the framework for the interaction, cold-blooded rationality and pursuit of personal gain will come to the fore. If entrepreneurship in long-range enterprises based on substantial capital is the focus, then attitudes of planning, of husbanding of resources, of efficiency in the use of expensive time and equipment will predominate. If bureaucratic organization is emphasized, the relationships between people will take on the coloration of attention to the rules, limitation of authority to the specifics of the job, a conservative and cautious approach toward life.[10] If the interaction is between professional and client, then the traditions of intellectual mastery, of pride, of devotion to the traditions of the professional group and its ethics will largely govern behavior.[11] If assembly-line workers are observed, a routinization of behavior and a psychological alienation from work will be noted. In general, the more specialized the job is, the more bureaucratized the organizational context in which it occurs, and the bigger the price tag on the product or service, the more narrowly is the interaction likely to be confined to the business at hand.

      ✧   ✧   ✧   ✧   ✧

[10] Robert K. Merton, "Bureaucratic Structure and Personality" in his *Social Theory and Social Structure* (Glencoe, Illinois: The Free Press, 1949).

[11] Talcott Parsons, "The Professions and Social Structure," *Social Forces*, XVII, No. 4 (May, 1939); reprinted in his *Essays in Sociological Theory* (Glencoe, Illinois: The Free Press, 1949).

EDUCATION

A complex division of labor demands a system of formal education to prepare men for their jobs—apprenticeship is too conservative, too slow, too clumsy. Consequently, instead of walking beside his father at the plow, a young man prepares for life by going to school.

A modern school system, like modern industry, tends to emphasize norms of impersonal efficiency: promotion is based upon demonstrated performance. As industrialization proceeds and men begin to recognize the extent to which formal education is the key to their careers, the demand for schooling grows, as well as the feeling that it ought to be available to everybody regardless of his position in society. Thus the state is led to establish free public schools, and progressively to adapt their curricula from the old-fashioned subjects which were designed to perpetuate the traditional lore of the local culture among the upper classes (i.e., to prepare the elite for a life of leisure, or of governance or theology) to the new-fashioned subjects designed to prepare men for industrial and commercial careers.

Modern schools tend to separate young men from their fathers (in ideas and skills, if not in space); they lead the minds of the young outward from the locality to the nation; they teach a *personal* skill which can be sold anywhere. Such schools unfreeze the social class order by permitting, even encouraging, geographical and social mobility. They make inherited capital and inherited family status less important as the determinants of a man's career, and make intelligence, personality, and will-power more important.

Each level of education is designed to prepare students for an appropriate level in the occupational hierarchy. Thus, university education leads toward professional, technical and executive positions, secondary education toward skilled and clerical jobs, primary education toward semi- and unskilled jobs.

*   *   *   *   *

SOCIAL CLASSES

A truly "primitive" society has no class system: all families live at about the same socioeconomic level. As agricultural production grows, and the society transforms itself into a settled, peasant-type of structure, a surplus of food is produced which is used to support landlords, priests, and rulers. Ordinarily, there exist only two classes: those who work with their hands, and those who engage in administrative or ritual activities and enjoy leisure. There may exist the germs of an in-between group of clerks and merchants who are aids to the leisure class, but they are relatively insignificant.

The development of a commercial civilization enormously expands the role of trade and thus the in-between group grows into an independent middle class. Industrialization speeds this process for it increases the flow of goods which are traded, it up-grades many hand-workers into skilled machine-tenders who have middle-class educations and incomes, and it produces enough surplus wealth to support many people in service activities which enrich the leisure hours of the majority of the people rather than just the upper class.

The new industrial class order is divided into a series of groupings which overlap with one another; there are no sharp divisions, and the terms we use such as "upper class," "middle class," and "working class" are but convenient rubrics, rather than precisely denotative classifications. There are gradations of occupation, education, and life-style within each broad class, and there is considerable mobility from one level to another. Instead of the great gap between landlord and peasant, we get the series of small gaps between factory worker, skilled laborer, foreman, engineer, plant manager, and company president, with young workers aspiring to be foremen and young engineers dreaming of the presidency. This series of small gradations means that communication from one level to another is easier and class-consciousness is weaker. Marx was wrong: industrial capitalism does not simplify the class order into two antagonistic groups, but rather makes it much more complex.

Stable city life is dependent upon a social class system. Public opinion in cities—that substitute for firm tradition maintained by the social controls of an homogeneous village—is never a single entity, but rather a series of opinions, each adapted to the needs of a given class level, and supported by networks of overlapping cliques which articulate basic values and teach them to new members. Ideals of family life (including the size of family desired), patterns of expected education for children, attitudes toward work and career, modes of consumption in matters of dress, food, house furnishings, and to some extent religious and political beliefs, all these emerge within the framework of relatively homogeneous strata of society which share a given level of education and a given type of job and income. The conversations of men on the job, and women and children in the area of residence (which is segregated by ecological competition according to income), create an appropriate style of life or class sub-culture.

○   ○   ○   ○   ○

THE FAMILY [12]

In general, urban-industrial society is conducive to the nuclear rather than the extended-family system; it tends to equalize the power of the sexes and the generations; it reduces the economic functions performed by the nuclear family to a minimum, and instead centers it upon sex, companionship, and the socialization of the very young. Let us examine these trends and their causes in some detail, and also note certain exceptions and countertrends.

In African rural life, the domestic unit frequently consists of more than one nuclear family. The members of the extended family cooperate in herding or agriculture, in the raising and distribution of the dowry or bride-wealth that permits young people to marry (thereby uniting not just individuals but family lines), in religious ceremonies (including ancestor worship), in the education of adolescents and its symbolization in *rites-de-passage*, in social control which keeps individuals from straying from the path of customary virtue, in political organization. All of these activities are based on the assumption that the crucial family members (the lineage, howsoever it be defined, and the spouses of its members) live and work in the same area; through the structure of kinship is organized the life of a homogeneous community. There results a strong sense of kin obligation and dependence: one shares with his relatives, one grows strong and safe through having many family ties that are actively functioning. One submits to family discipline because it pays off (and because there is no alternative).

At first, the urban migrant clings to the old family values. Indeed, he often goes to the city as a young man to raise money for his parents and expects to send cash home at regular intervals. But he quickly finds that the cost of housing and food absorbs most of his income, leaving little for remittance home. If he stays in the town and learns a skill which brings a higher income, he may be able to get a wife and settle down as an urbanite. Then he finds that rural relatives expect him to house them without pay when they come to town for a visit or a job; sometimes they send their children to him for schooling, or he sends his young children to the village to keep them from being "spoiled" by the undisciplined ways of city youth.

As long as it manages to stay alive during the period of transition from rural to urban life, this system of kinship obligations has several effects: it slows down the emergence of class differences, for wealthier men are called upon to give more to their relatives than are poorer ones;

[12] This section has greatly benefited from my conversations with my colleague Irving Kaplan.

it blurs the distinctions between town life and village life, for it stimulates interchange between them; it serves as a system of social security providing benefits during times of illness or unemployment. *Particularly during the period of transition,* while individuals brought up in the villages are trying to adjust to the demands of the city, are they likely to lean upon the family for help. . . .

As time passes, kinship obligations are put under more and more strain. They grew out of a village way of life which integrated all the institutions into a functioning equilibrium. That integration weakens in the city *because the wage job is an individualistic affair, and because the members of the kin-group no longer live close together.* A man eventually comes to feel that his wage income belongs to him and his wife and children, and he resists the claims of relatives. . . .

❁ ❁ ❁ ❁ ❁

The urban family tends to be smaller than the rural family. On the farm, children cost less to rear, for space is cheap, food is home-grown, and formal education unnecessary. From a young age, farm children contribute labor which is worth more than their upkeep. But, in the city, children are more expensive to rear and they do not start earning until a much later age. Especially in the middle classes, where economic wants (including the symbols of consumption necessary for upward mobility) tend to outrun income, children become a burden and parents gladly turn to methods of birth control.

I have stressed that individualistic jobs and geographic separation are the keys to the breakdown of close kinship solidarity beyond the nuclear family. But these two forces do not operate equally throughout city life. The urban proletariat (once stabilized) tends to be less geographically mobile than the middle class; working-class siblings may grow up in the same area and, when married, may exchange services such as baby-care or aid in housebuilding which tend to keep solidarity alive. These mutual exchanges can function well so long as social mobility is not present: if one of a pair of siblings climbs into the middle class, opportunity for equal reciprocity is lost, the less successful sibling feels awkward in the presence of the more successful one, and interaction declines. Thus, social mobility has effects similar to geographical mobility.

economic development

Few problems in the transitional states are regarded as more urgent than the problem of economic development. A widespread belief persists among most leaders of these states—as well as among those in the West who support foreign aid programs—that if substantial, long-term progress can be achieved in economic growth, many other problems confronting their societies will be far more readily resolved. But the problem of achieving substantial economic development is extremely complex, and despite a few significant exceptions, most of the developing states have not yet succeeded in generating and maintaining a high, continuous growth rate. The reasons are not solely economic, however; they also involve some of the social, political, and psychological characteristics of these societies.

There are many reasons that account for the high priority accorded economic development. One basic reason is, of course, that of eliminating the extreme forms of poverty found in many of these states. Large numbers of persons still suffer from inadequate food, clothing, and shelter, with premature death often the result. The extensive famines in India and China during the past decade were only a more acute form of a common problem. Humanitarian considerations require that the bare essentials of life be provided, either through increasing domestic production or through expanding exports that will earn the foreign exchange necessary for the importation of food supplies and other essential commodities. To meet the basic needs of their rapidly growing populations, particularly in the urban areas, states must increase the level of agricultural and industrial production.

There is also another form of poverty with which the leaders must contend. This form of poverty is more psychological and subjective than absolute. It springs from a recognition of the gap that separates the poor

329

from the rich, whether internally within a society, or externally among the states in the international community. In a world in which egalitarian political and economic ideas are becoming increasingly accepted, the continuation of gross disparities in standards of living leads to bitterness and frustration. Leaders in many new states held out the hope to their followers that once political independence was achieved and the oppressive economic conditions of colonialism were removed, a rapid development of the economy would ensue, bringing material benefits to all. Demands that these promises be fulfilled have led to intense pressures on these leaders to raise the standard of living. The prospect of a better life is increasingly stirring the masses to political action in their desire for a standard of living more commensurate with that of a privileged few.

A further reason for seeking economic development is to relieve the present heavy dependence on the export of one product, a situation found in many developing states. Since the export of this product, usually a raw material or food product, is often subject to extreme and sudden price fluctuations on the world market, the income from its sale is highly unstable. This instability of income, in turn, makes sound planning and financing of domestic programs difficult to achieve. By developing their other resources, these states hope to diversify their exports and attain a higher and more stable income. Simultaneously, the development of their other resources will also provide a more adequate base for the development of domestic industries. Such industries will enable these states to supply many of their domestic needs that must at present be imported.

Economic development is also sought for reasons that are more specifically social and political than economic. For example, many leaders view economic development as a means of promoting social and political unity among the diverse groups within their states. By creating a more complex, interdependent economy, regional, cultural, and economic groups are brought together in the common cause of economic progress. The transportation and communication networks that are created as part of the developmental schemes help to link regions and groups together not only physically but also psychologically. National pride is stimulated by the accomplishment of economic growth, particularly in the industrialized sector. Such growth, in turn, permits an expansion of educational facilities and other welfare programs, all of which, it is hoped, will further serve to unify the society.

Another objective served by economic development is the promotion of greater economic and social equality by narrowing the division between rich and poor within society. Industrialization results in the creation of a middle class of technicians, engineers, and managers, and a working class of skilled and unskilled laborers, all of whose incomes are higher than those of the rural masses. Programs of land reform are also usually included in the plans for economic development. These reforms are expected to result in increased income for the peasants and farmers. Together, agrarian reform and industrial development are viewed as a means to reduce the sharp differences in income that characterize the traditional agrarian economy.

Further, the self-interest of the political elite in promoting economic development cannot be overlooked. The modernizing elite may undertake industrialization as a means of restricting and diminishing the power of the recalcitrant, traditional, landed aristocracy and other traditional elites. Neither the industrialists nor the workers can be controlled economically or politically by the traditional elites as can the rural masses. Gradually, economic and political power is being transferred to the more forward looking middle and working classes whose geographical base is in the urban areas, not the countryside. Thus, industrialization develops increasingly powerful allies for the modernizing political elite in their struggle to reshape society. Through industrialization the economic and political power of the usually highly conservative, traditional elites can be diminished.

Even the more conservative political elites may feel constrained to promote economic development to maintain their positions. Failure to alleviate the poverty and suffering of the masses or refusal to acknowledge the demands for more rapid economic growth may result in an increase of the appeal and power of more radical groups such as the communists, military leaders, and professional and intellectual elites.

In addition to domestic considerations, leaders may promote economic development to enable them to play a more prominent role in international politics. A strong economy with a substantial industrial capacity is regarded as essential if power and influence are to be exerted in the international community. This assumption leads to a strong emphasis on the development of heavy rather than light industry or agricultural development. With heavy industry, modern, well-equipped military forces can be maintained and an independent foreign policy pursued, as in the case of Communist China.

A mixture of these motives is usually advanced by those leaders who are attempting to advance the level of economic development in their states. The goal of economic development is more easily stated, however, than realized. In plotting the strategy for economic development, these leaders must resolve a number of complex problems.

First, the decision to seek economic growth has to be balanced with other national objectives. While a high rate of growth is commonly desired, it is not the only goal that the leaders of the developing states are pursuing. The maximum theoretical growth rate is often sacrificed, for example, to maintain a large military force. Resources that might otherwise be allocated for agricultural or industrial development are often diverted for support of the military establishment. Frequently the military budget accounts for as much as fifty per cent of the total governmental expenditures. Similarly, resources are often diverted for expenditures designed to promote national unity. Transportation systems that must be heavily subsidized are nevertheless justified as a means of increasing interregional cooperation. Other appropriations have been made, as in Indonesia, for example, to construct huge stadiums in which national and international games and other events can be staged. Such expenditures on national showplaces, while often not economically profitable, are believed to contribute to feelings of national pride and unity. Again, the maximum growth rate is sometimes restricted by the determination of the modernizing elite to achieve greater income equality. Tax structures have been designed to favor low income groups at the expense of the wealthy even though the latter's ability and incentive to invest in economically productive enterprises are thereby reduced. Policies of this type have been employed in Cuba, the United Arab Republic, and Indonesia, among many others.

In designing their programs for economic development, the leaders of the developing states have had to determine the appropriate roles for the public and private sectors of the economy. As has already been indicated, many leaders are prejudiced against capitalism as the dominant economic philosophy because of its alleged economic inefficiency and the promotion of social injustices. The pattern of public and private ownership varies greatly from state to state, however, and even some of those who most vigorously espouse socialist principles have been forced to rely fairly heavily on private enterprise for increasing production. While the private sector is severely limited in states such as Communist China, much greater emphasis is placed on it in the Latin American states. In between these extremes are a number of socialist economies, such as that in India, in which the state owns many of the principal industries, but in which private enterprise plays a significant role as well. In almost all developing states, great emphasis is placed on central planning, both for the public sector and for controlling and guiding private investment.

The complex problems of financing the programs of industrial expansion and agricultural development continually confront the planners. Domestic investment capital is, of course, extremely limited in most of these states, and even the amount that is nominally available may be difficult to direct into investment. In many of the more conservative states, as in Latin America, the wealthy segment of the population is almost untaxed. Even in states where income and inheritance taxes are sharply progressive, inefficient collection systems and corruption frequently combine to reduce to a very low level the taxes actually collected. While many modernizing leaders regard high taxes on the poor masses as socially and politically undesirable, the masses in most states nevertheless bear the major share of the tax burden, paid largely through a variety of consumer taxes.

Private investment is often difficult to stimulate. Those persons who possess great wealth generally prefer either to invest in land (usually with little intention of reforming the traditional, semifeudal agrarian system) or to invest abroad, either in industry or banking. Merchants have traditionally sought high profits on a small turnover of goods and are often suspicious of mass production techniques and merchandizing methods that assume small profits on a high turnover. The instability of governments and the uncertainties surrounding future economic conditions are further obstacles to private investment.

In addition to taxes as a source for investment capital, some states have established monopolies in certain sectors of the economy, such as utilities and some exports. The excess income over operating costs can then be reinvested either in the same segment of the economy or in other areas. In other states, royalties on the resources extracted by foreign companies provide substantial capital, as in the case of oil royalties paid to several Middle East governments by American and European oil companies. Loans from international lending agencies such as the Export-Import Bank, the International Bank for Reconstruction and Development, and the Inter-American Development Bank of the Organization of American States, as well as loans and grants provided by the United States and other countries, have injected billions of dollars into the economies of the developing states for developmental purposes. Although this aid is often criticized as being too little, many of the developing states have not as yet been able to use efficiently and effectively the aid already extended. The internal problems of these states, such as the shortage of trained personnel, unstable governments, and a reluctance on the part of some leaders to undertake internal reforms of tax systems or agrarian reform programs, have all impeded the expansion of capital from external sources.

The financing of expansion programs is complicated by the great pressures on the economic planners to permit an immediate increase in the standard of living. In view of the low standard of living, the decision to restrict current consumption in favor of investment—and thus to achieve a higher rate of growth in the future—is difficult to make and maintain. In most states, an uneasy compromise has been achieved that attempts to increase the standard of living rapidly while at the same time expand investments.

As a result of these factors, inflation has been a serious problem for most of these states. Many governments have undertaken massive programs of expansion, the cost of which cannot be covered by the taxes collected. Large deficits have been incurred which have been covered by loans from central banks and foreign lending institutions. Since large amounts of money are poured into the economy as the development programs (such as industrialization) are executed, competition for the limited supply of goods has rapidly driven prices upward. Although wages have also been increased, they usually tend to lag seriously behind the increase in prices of all commodities. Thus the industrial workers, who depend upon their wages for subsistence, are in effect subsidizing the economic developmental programs in their societies. In some cases, inflation has exceeded 100 per cent a year, and price rises of 25 to 50 per cent are not unusual in many developing states. Although limited inflation may enable governments to expand their development programs, excessive inflation has disrupted sound planning and has forced some states to reduce drastically the scale of some schemes.

The planning for economic development is usually highly centralized in an official government planning board or commission. Even in states that do not subscribe to socialist principles, conditions have forced the governments to assume active leadership if systematic economic development is to be achieved. The planning boards usually have great responsibility and authority; they, along with the political leaders, make all major decisions relating to the type of development program to be pursued, its financing, and its general execution. Since the planning boards wield considerable power, they become deeply involved in the political bargaining process. A variety of interests attempt to influence their decisions both on major issues, such as land reform and foreign investments, and on the more specific issues, such as the precise location of industrial plants. The breadth and complexity of the problems they have to consider frequently impose severe strains on their limited manpower resources with the result that the plans developed are sometimes quite unrealistic in terms of the societies' actual capacities for development.

The severe shortage of skilled personnel and the lack of stable, efficient political and administrative institutions enormously complicate the task of economic development. In some cases, the acute shortage of skilled native personnel has been intensified as a result of nationalistic policies that have forced out many or all of the bureaucrats of the former colonial state. In Indonesia, for example, the intense hostility toward the Dutch eventuated in the withdrawal of almost all Europeans soon after independence was achieved. While the forced withdrawal was justified by the Indonesian leaders on grounds of national pride and the fear of further economic exploitation, the impact of their removal was immediately noticeable in the sharp decline in agricultural and industrial production. To replace the departed colonial bureaucrats, some states have eagerly sought the aid of other outside experts and advisers. Although technically competent, such advisers are sometimes inadequately attuned to the subtleties of the social and political structures of the states whose economies they are attempting to aid. Through programs such as the Peace Corps and scholarship programs to train students in the United States and other countries, efforts are being made to supply the developing states with a core of skilled technicians and administrators.

For programs of economic development to succeed, deeply rooted traditional values, attitudes, habits, and political and economic institutions often have to be modified or replaced. In rural areas, the patterns of life based upon subsistence farming are often quite resistant to change. Many agrarian development plans have floundered because of the failure accurately to assess the response of the rural inhabitants to changes that, to the urban bureaucrat, represent such obvious improvements. New types of grains have been rejected, for example, because they did not provide the desired taste even though they were more nutritious and produced higher yields. Programs for agrarian reform are usually vigorously opposed by the large landowners whose standard of living and traditional authority are threatened by these programs. Traditional business attitudes too, as indicated above, have not been conducive to economic development, nor have the attitudes of many workers toward their jobs. Only gradually, for example, is the long afternoon break in the Latin American's workday being eliminated. In many societies, the industrial work force is unstable, given the propensity of workers to return to their native villages as soon as possible. Under these circumstances, the development of a skilled labor force is difficult to achieve.

While a few states such as Mexico, Turkey, and the Philippines are making substantial progress in economic development, for many others the outlook is highly uncertain. Indeed, for some states the prospects of orderly development are simply bleak. As two advisers to the Iranian government have written concerning that state's program of land reform, it may be that "the situation can be so miserable and reforms so overdue that planned development is impossible." [1] If progress is often slow internally, the prospect of closing the gap between the poor and rich states in the world seems even more difficult to attain. A simple illustration indicates why this is so. If two economies, one of which provides a gross national product per capita income of $2,000 and the other of $200, each grow at an annual rate of 2 per cent, at the end of a year the former will have increased to $2,040 while the latter to only $204. Thus the initial difference in per capita income of $1,800 will have grown to

[1] P. Bjorn Olsen and P. Norregaard Rasmussen, "An Attempt at Planning in a Traditional State: Iran," *Planning Economic Development*, ed. Everett E. Hagen (Homewood, Illinois: Richard D. Irwin, Inc., 1963).

$1,836 at the end of one year. To maintain the initial difference of $1,800, the less developed state would have to grow at an annual rate of 20 per cent, or 10 times as fast, a figure that is unlikely to be maintained by many states over a period of years.[2] Yet since we are dealing with a problem that is in large part psychological, the inability to narrow the gap in absolute terms is undoubtedly of less importance to persons in the underdeveloped states than is the realization of immediate benefits resulting from substantial and sustained internal economic growth. However, even a modest increase in the per capita income is difficult to attain in many of these states in the face of their increasing populations. In our example, a population increase of 2 per cent would eliminate any increase in the per capita income. To attain an increase of 2 per cent in the per capita income simultaneously with an increase of 2 per cent in the population would, of course, require an annual economic growth rate of 4 per cent. Such a growth rate, while not necessarily unrealistic, would nevertheless provide only a very gradual increase in the standard of living and would not begin to close the gap between the rich and the poor nations.

The economic progress the developing states are able to make will continue to be a principal factor affecting the stability of their political institutions as well as the stability of the international community. Failure to meet the rising expectations for a higher standard of living is likely to produce frustrations and tensions that can have only a most disruptive effect upon the development of a more peaceful world.

SUGGESTED READINGS

Agarwala, Amar N., and Singh, Sampat P., eds., *The Economics of Underdevelopment.* New York, Oxford University Press, 1958.

Basch, Antonín, *Financing Economic Development.* New York, The Macmillan Company, 1964.

Galenson, Walter, ed., *Labor in Developing Economies.* Berkeley, Calif., University of California Press, 1962.

Gordon, Wendell C., *The Political Economy of Latin America.* New York, Columbia University Press, 1965.

Hagen, Everett E., ed., *Planning Economic Development.* Homewood, Ill., Richard D. Irwin, Inc., 1963.

Hambidge, Gove, *Dynamics of Development.* New York, Frederick A. Praeger, Inc., 1964.

Harbison, Frederick, and Myers, Charles A., *Education, Manpower and Economic Growth.* New York, The McGraw-Hill Book Co., 1963.

Heilbroner, Robert L., *The Great Ascent.* New York, Harper & Row, 1963.

[2] Hla Myint, *The Economics of the Developing Countries* (New York: Frederick A. Praeger, Inc., Publishers, 1965), p. 18.

Hirschman, Albert O., *Journeys toward Progress: Studies of Economic Policy-Making in Latin America.* New York, The Twentieth Century Fund, 1963.

Holt, Robert T., and Turner, John E., *The Political Basis of Economic Development.* Princeton, N. J., D. Van Nostrand Company, Inc., 1966.

Mellor, John W., *The Economics of Agricultural Development.* Ithaca, N. Y., Cornell University Press, 1966.

Myint, Hla, *The Economics of the Developing Countries.* New York, Frederick A. Praeger, Inc., 1965.

Onslow, Cranley, ed., *Asian Economic Development.* New York, Frederick A. Praeger, Inc., 1965.

Rostow, Walt W., *The Stages of Economic Growth: A Non-Communist Manifesto.* Cambridge, England, Cambridge University Press, 1960.

Smith, T. Lynn, ed., *Agrarian Reform in Latin America.* New York, Alfred A. Knopf, 1965.

Sufrin, Sidney C., *Unions in Emerging Societies.* Syracuse, N. Y., Syracuse University Press, 1964.

Walinsky, Louis J., *The Planning and Execution of Economic Development.* New York, The McGraw-Hill Book Co., 1963.

Wietz, Raanan, ed., *Rural Planning in Developing Countries.* Cleveland, The Press of Western Reserve University, 1966.

◦◦◦

36. AGRARIAN REFORM IN ASIA *

w o l f   l a d e j i n s k y

It is no longer news that land reform is a critical issue throughout Asia, the Near East and Latin America. We are not surprised to see the Shah of Iran going about the country sponsoring a drastic redistribution of private holdings. . . . President Macapagal in the Philippines, President Betancourt in Venezuela and Prime Minister Nehru in India have

* From "Agrarian Reform in Asia" by Wolf Ladejinsky, *Foreign Affairs*, Vol. XLII, No. 3 (April, 1964), pp. 445–459. Excerpted by special permission from *Foreign Affairs*, April 1964. Copyright by the Council on Foreign Relations, Inc., New York.

similarly been using "agrarian reform" in their search for answers to some of their countries' instabilities.

. . . [T]he problems . . . are fundamentally the same: How relieve the plight of cultivators working mostly for a pittance? How revive stagnating agricultural economies? How root the peasant securely and beneficially on the land he cultivates? The one important departure from the conditions of a bygone age is that the stated problems have the closest bearing on the overall economic development of Asia, as indeed elsewhere.

II

The answer to these questions constitutes what is broadly known as "agrarian reform." The term can mean various things to various people within the free world, let alone as between the Communist and non-Communist worlds. As exemplified by Soviet Russia and Communist China, agrarian reform is simple enough: it is a means to political power, based on a promise to the peasant of the one thing he wants most—ownership of the landlord's land—in exchange for his political support. Once the Communists are in power, all the land is confiscated, peasants become farm hands on collectives, communes and state farms, and harsh production and delivery quotas complete the rude awakening from an exhilarating but all-too-brief experience of freeholding.

In non-Communist Asia, agrarian reform is not without political motivation. The emphasis, however, is not on consolidating the power of the state *over* the peasantry but on increasing the state's well-being. The need for drastic changes stems from such questions as who owns or doesn't own the land, how it is used, who gets what out of the land, the productivity of the land, the rate of economic development, and, of course, social status and political power. These are not unique in any one part of Asia; all cut across cultural and national boundaries and together they represent the Achilles' heel of the Asian socioeconomic structure.

The mere enumeration of the issues points to the fact that no single panacea can deal with them effectively; even redistribution of the land will not do it unless it is accompanied by the necessary means to work and improve the land. The economic opportunity and psychological incentives which come with the possession of land or security of tenure must go hand in hand with a host of other developmental measures. For this reason, agrarian reform in the sense considered here encompasses all or most of the following elements: distribution of land among the landless and favorable financial arrangements for tenant land-purchases; security of tenure and fair rents; better methods of cultivation through technical assistance, adequate credit, co-operative marketing facilities, etc. Agrarian reform is a combination of a great many things, and not all of them are of equal importance. Important though the other ingredients are, unless those who work the land own it, or are at least secure on the land as tenants, all the rest is likely to be writ in water. And this is the most difficult step to achieve. It is relatively easy to use science to increase production, but only if the cultivator's relationship to the land and the state's treatment of him and of agriculture create incentives to invest, to improve the land and to raise productivity. Too many of Asia's cultivators are still waiting to find that incentive.

☼　　☼　　☼　　☼　　☼

Directly related to this problem is the fact that four-fifths of Asia's vast population are peasants; millions of them are on too little land, and hordes of others are crowding onto the same land. Inadequate tools, archaic methods of cultivation and institutional arrangements over which the peasant has no control underscore his plight and explain his resentment.

Newspaper headlines in Asia are snatched by the glittering economic development plans with their emphasis on industrialization as the cure-all. Yet agriculture, not industry, is the pivot of economic life there. The ambitious postwar schemes for industrialization throughout Asia no longer are mere blueprints, but so far they have made only a small dent in the continent's traditional character. The factory is bringing material advancement to some groups, but surely not to a degree, even in the foreseeable future, to obscure the fact that the heart of the problem of Asia still lies in the countryside. It is on the farm that solutions must be sought and found, if the empty rice bowls are to be filled, if something is to be added to the half-empty ones and if the economic development of the various countries is to proceed by their own efforts.

III

When looking at rural Asia today, nearly two decades after the start of the reform movement, we see that the old order in the countryside has been under attack—vigorously in some countries, much less so, and with results to match, in many more. The reforms have certain things in common, and not only with regard to the condition of the peasantry. Their purpose is the same whatever the wording of an official pronouncement. President Macapagal of the Philippines spoke for all of them when, in signing the recent Agrarian Land Reform Code, he observed: "Let this signing be recorded in our annals as an Act of Emancipation of the toiling farmer from his slavery to debt, poverty and misery and of his dignification as a human being and as a citizen. By this Act of Emancipation a new revolution is on." After a series of land reform failures in the Philippines over a quarter of a century, whether this is so remains to be seen, but it does mirror the ultimate hope often voiced by all Asian countries when this thorny subject is approached. To bring it about, the Philippine Code relies on two general features common to all attempted reforms in Asia: security of tenure and the creation of peasant proprietorships.

On issues of substance, however, the reforms speak in a variety of voices, which more often than not are a far cry from the exalted pronouncements made on the supposedly historic occasions. They reflect inevitably the political climate in the country concerned. This determines the will or lack of will to proceed with the task; the kind of specifics with which the general measures are or are not endowed; the care or lack of care with which the enabling legislation is formulated; the preparation or lack of preparation of the pertinent technical and administrative services; the presence or absence of technical agricultural services with their bearing upon success or failure; and, finally and most importantly, the drive or lack of drive behind the enforcement of the provisions of the law. For these reasons, the results of the reform movement in Asia are anything but uniform. They run the full gamut, from Japan and Taiwan where fulfillment in the widest sense has been achieved; to Korea where much land has actually been redistributed but with results far from satisfactory; to South Viet Nam where land reform has been carried out in its essentials, but engulfed by a civil war before it came to fruition. Then there are the Philippines, Nepal, Pakistan and Indonesia—all knowledgeable in writing reform laws, some of them at variance with their fervent preambles—where the record to date ranges between poor performance and non-performance. Finally, there is India, significant and encouraging for what it has attained in unprecedentedly difficult and bewildering conditions, and just as significant and discouraging for what it has failed to attain, and for the reasons why.

The picture, clearly, is mixed, and in order to assess it a number of questions must be raised. The primary one is: Why have some reforms succeeded, others fallen short of their goals, and still others failed to get off the ground?

Just as Soviet Russia was the progenitor of the Communist type of reform, Japan and Taiwan are the progenitors of non-Communist reforms in Asia. Japan, the leader, and Taiwan, the follower and innovator, provided between them all the pertinent elements of leadership, content and implementation which made for a successful reform.

In Taiwan as in Japan, reforms were not designed to satisfy the claims of both contending parties: the tenant was to gain at the expense of the landlord. Without going into details, we may cite a few main provisions to demonstrate the emphasis on the ideological underpinnings and the lack of vacillation about the real intent of the measures. Security of tenure is one of the cases in point. The sharp reduction of rents in Taiwan was an important move; but more important were the provisions that, for all practical purposes, the tenants could remain on the leased land undisturbed even after the expiration of a contract. This virtually insured the enforcement of rental provisions. Less carefully worded stipulations might have undermined this part of the reform program, as has been the case in India, not to mention others.

Provisions for security of tenure in overcrowded Asian villages, where tenants compete fiercely for the privilege of cultivating somebody else's land, are notoriously difficult to enforce; yet in Taiwan a land redistribution program for the benefit of tenants who cultivated 40 percent of the land became much more feasible as a result of such provisions. . . .

The idea that the reforms were meant to benefit the tenants is also apparent in the principal provisions about land redistribution and the creation of peasant proprietorships among tenants. Absentee landlords had to sell all of their land at fixed government prices; resident landlords were compelled to sell their land in excess of the permissible ceiling. Neither Japan nor Taiwan aimed to do away with tenancy as an institution; but with determination to enlarge the area of individual, private ownership, the low ceiling made it possible to extract a great deal of surplus land for redistribution. The result is that whereas before the reform 54 percent of Japan's land was owner-operated, after the reform the figure had risen to 92 percent; the respective figures for Taiwan are 60 and 85 percent.

What matters is not only at what level the ceiling is set, but also that it not be evaded. The problem of West Pakistan, to cite but one case, is not merely that the ceiling of 500 irrigated acres and 1,000 unirrigated acres is altogether too high where two-thirds of the owners average five acres each; it is also the exceptions and subdivisions of large holdings among members of a family which were made on the eve of the reform and which have combined to divest the ceiling and, by the same token, the entire land distribution program of any meaning. It is not surprising, therefore, that even if West Pakistan had implemented this part of the reform, only an estimated 7.5 percent of the country's 2,000,000 tenants might have obtained land. And Pakistan is no exception. In Japan and Taiwan, on the other hand, the acreage that could be retained by a landlord was fixed retroactively, both on the basis of the household as a unit and on the basis of land owned by that household.

With a low ceiling, no evasions and effective implementation, the majority of the tenants become peasant-proprietors.

A crucial feature of any reform not intended to result in out-and-out confiscation is price and method of payment. Whatever the differences displayed in Asia in formulating and implementing a program, there is a consensus on one point: the price fixed must be considerably below the market price. Land-purchase under a reform is not an ordinary real estate transaction where seller, broker and buyer meet in a free market. If it were, and if tenants were able to pay the "going price," there would be no need for a reform. The price fixed by a government is an arbitrary one, the degree of its arbitrariness depending upon how a reformer answers this question: "For whose benefit is the reform designed?"

The question of how to pay for the land is of paramount importance for government, landlord and tenant. No matter what the price, experience in Asia has shown that a government cannot pay in cash, in one lump sum. Here Taiwan provides a lesson worth pondering. In content, Taiwan's reform is in many respects similar to that of Japan, but in method of paying it is not. In Japan, what appeared to be a reasonable price when first fixed was later on swallowed up by a galloping inflation, virtually confiscating the landlord's land. To avoid this possibility, Taiwan tied the price of land to payments in two principal products of the land and to shares of stock in government-owned industrial undertakings. In practice this meant that 70 percent of the value of the land was in the form of commodity bonds, payable in 20 semi-annual installments over a period of ten years, and 30 percent was paid outright in stocks.

This novel method has worked well for all parties involved. . . .

○   ○   ○   ○   ○

. . . [W]ith the exception of important bright spots here and there in India, only very few . . . gains can be found in other Asian countries which have gone to the trouble of writing reform laws, but largely limited and vague in content and with just as limited intent to translate them into action. The writing of reform laws—and some nations have done it more than once—may be good practice in preparation for the day when the execution of such laws becomes unavoidable. But as of the moment, it may be said in general that the high hopes reposed in agrarian reform during the immediate postwar years have not materialized in action. Before suggesting why this is so, we will find instructive a brief review of India's vast experience in the course of 15 years of reform activities.

I V

It is safe to say that all the disabilities which peasant and land can suffer are to be found in many of the 600,000 villages of India. An observer will find many striking and promising manifestations of a resurgent agriculture; but these are still only tiny islands in the vastness of the debilitating conditions noted elsewhere. The result is that the yields of basic food crops are too low in relation to the potential of the land and existing food needs, and particularly in view of the grim fact that between 1961 and 1976 the Indian agriculture will have to provide food for nearly 190,000,000 additional people. To remedy the situation, the Indian Government after independence set itself to ease the lot of the peasantry by a drastic overhaul of the land system, the complexity of which almost defies description. This would-be agrarian revolution was to have been attained through the familiar pattern already described, and through the elimination of the "zamindari" system, a peculiarly Indian problem.

The zamindari system was a by-product of the early British rule under which a zamindar or intermediary was given the right to collect land taxes and undertook to pay the British administration a fixed revenue. In return, he was not only permitted to keep a portion of the revenue but was also recognized as the proprietor of the revenue-bearing land. In time the system covered more than 40 percent of the cultivated land of India, and it created, too, some of the worst abuses that can be perpetrated upon a peasantry, including a long chain of non-cultivating sublessees all getting a share of the highly inflated rent from the same piece of land and the same cultivator. As one student of the problem put it, "His landlords form a Jacob's ladder in which each rung is occupied not by an angel but a tenure holder, and the topmost by the proprietor." This ladder the Indian Government set out to do away with as almost the first order of agrarian reform.

Despite opposition and administrative problems, the zamindari tenures have been virtually abolished. . . . Why this measure succeeded is not difficult to answer. The zamindari system, with its absurdities and injustices, was the weakest enemy to attack, because it was imposed by a foreign power which handed out property rights to which neither the British nor most of the recipients had any claim. Thus abolition of the system became one of the symbols of freedom from the British rule, and it is not surprising that the abolitionists largely succeeded in eliminating it.

Getting rid of this system did not put an end to tenancy in India.

Even in the ex-zamindari areas the "home-farms" of the former middle-man continued to be operated by tenants, and not all the subtenants were eliminated. But above all there was the multitude of tenants—not to mention the millions of agricultural wage laborers—cultivating at least a fourth of the country's arable land in "ryotwari" areas (as distinguished from the former zamindari areas) where owner-proprietorship predominated. The Government of India decided to provide tenants with security of tenure and reduction of rents, and to confer landownership upon the tenants through the familiar ceiling device and officially fixed land prices. Under the guidance and continuous prodding of the Planning Commission, the States have enacted a voluminous body of legislation presumably designed to meet these goals.

Both from the point of view of the content of the legislation and the enforcement of it these reforms are in serious difficulties. . . .

Administrative problems are a formidable obstacle to implementation of the reforms. On the other hand, judging by the experience of the largest and most populated state of India, Uttar Pradesh, this is not an insurmountable difficulty—if there is the will to overcome it. More to the point is the faulty content in many legislative enactments. In India, the most glaring manifestation of this is the seemingly reasonable but ill-defined right of the landlord to resume tenanted land for what is euphemistically called "personal cultivation." As the writer saw in widely separated parts of the country, this has led to mass evictions of tenants; to "voluntary surrenders" of land by tenants in order to salvage some relationship to the land, even if it be as a hired hand; to augmentation of the ranks of agricultural workers; and, inevitably, to the failure of the new rent regulations.

The ceiling provisions did not fare well at all. While the tenancy reforms can claim achievements in a few states, the same cannot be said about ceilings as a means of acquiring ownership. . . . For the moment, the question of how much land might have been available for redistribution is academic; of India's 80,000,000 acres or more of tenanted land very little is available for redistribution. In anticipation of ceiling provisions, the landlords divided up the land among members of their families so as to make certain that holdings were *under* the ceiling; for the legislative provisions, unlike those in Japan and Taiwan, did not contain the teeth to preclude such transfers. More recent amendments designed to annul such transfers have had, so far, little effect on the evasions committed.

Needless to say, such developments do not produce the incentives which lead to better living conditions, investments in land, improvement of land and a rise in agricultural productivity. Yet these were the goals of the tenancy reforms—the goals that Mr. Nehru so aptly summed up in the phrase, "placing the peasant in the center of the piece."

V

From the experience of Japan and Taiwan and from that of India one may learn why so few reforms in Asia have succeeded and so many have not. Neither success nor failure can be attributed primarily to the presence or absence of experts or to a special reform mystique. The usefulness of facts, figures and preparatory work no one can deny; but reforms cannot be "researched" or "studied" into existence. Of far greater importance is the acceptance of the reform idea, to begin with, in such a manner that technical problems are not an excuse for inaction but something to be resolved. There is no country in Asia, however underdeveloped, which does not know how to write a reform law, or what its implications might be. They have written them, and many have not been carried out—precisely because the political decision-makers understood their implications and their inevitable repercussions.

The politicians make or unmake agrarian reforms. It is they who provide the impetus or lack of impetus, who decide between reform and "reform." They alone can create a condition "when the economic sails are filled with political wind." [1] There is no gainsaying the fact that the economic environment, population pressure on the land, and customary relationships sanctioned by a long history of social and religious traditions exert great influence on what happens to legislation designed to break old institutional molds. But this does not invalidate the main premise—that the content and implementation of agrarian reform are a reflection of a particular political balance of forces in a country. This premise assumes even greater significance in Asia because the peasants themselves, while discontented, have not developed a movement, whether in the form of tenant-unions like those of Japan before the reforms, or peasant political parties like those of East Europe after the First World War. For a time, the Communists in Hyderabad, Tanjore and Kerala exploited the peasant grievances for their own ends; the Communist Huks in Central Luzon played a similar role. For the most part, however, the peasants behaved as if any change in their condition depended upon somebody else. By their apathy they have disproved the reasonable assumption that in an agricultural country a government must have peasant support. The fact is that national and state legislatures in Asia do not represent the interests of the peasantry; if they did, reform might have taken on a different character altogether. The reality is that even where voting is free, the peasantry in Asia is not yet voting its own interests. Except in Japan, the peasants do not yet know that

[1] Doreen Warriner, "Land Reform and Development in the Middle East." London: Royal Institute of International Affairs, 1957, p. 9.

they can be bearers *and* recipients of political gifts; the idea that "we support those who support us" has yet to take root. More important, then, is the role of the articulate and politically powerful pro-reform groups.

VI

In Japan and in Taiwan both the forces which were indigenous and those which were created as a result of the war favored a drastic agrarian reform and a redistribution of income and social and political power. In the case of Japan, the defeat by the United States and the American influence as an occupying power were crucial in the timing of the reform but were of only limited importance in giving it a radical character. Other factors were also the memories of peasant rebellions; the numerous, if unsuccessful, prewar reform measures; the strong tenant-unions; the windfall of the Communist opposition to the "MacArthur reform"; the emergence of large groups of Japanese who were disillusioned with the old oligarchy; and an eager and active pro-reform leadership in the Ministry of Agriculture which drafted the enabling legislation. This "political wind" found expression in the firm proposition that "those who cultivate the soil of Japan shall enjoy the fruits of their labor." This meant clearly defined provisions, a minimum of half-measures and a minimum of loopholes. Similarly on the enforcement side, the reformers recognized not only that the cultivators had to be made aware of the essence of the main provisions, but that they—and only they—had to be the true implementors of the reform if it were to succeed. This attitude led to the creation of a practical enforcement agency, the local land commissions—so far shunned by all other countries engaged in reform save Taiwan.

The situation in Taiwan on the eve of the reforms was not the same as in Japan, but here, too, special circumstances—primarily non-economic or sociological—created the setting for action. The final decision rested with the politicians or, more specifically, with a political and military leader. The Communist victory on the mainland and the subsequent prevalent belief among the Nationalist politicians that the Communists won because of the promise of land to the tillers played a crucial role in creating the favorable climate. Certain elements in the Nationalist ideology worked to the same end, especially when the beleaguered government realized it needed greater social stability as a means to military security. But none of these factors might have sufficed were it not for the fact that General Chen-Cheng, then Governor of Taiwan and an influential member of the Nationalist Party, had resolved that rural Taiwan was to undergo a thorough change. . . .

To return to India: while the need for reform there is surely as great as in any country in Asia, the difficulties in the way are incomparably greater. Among them are the sheer size of the subcontinent; the administrative decentralization, with each state a law unto itself; the paucity of good land records; the fact that a third of the tenanted land belongs to owners with five acres or less; the fierce competition for any tillable plot of land on almost any terms; the lack of peasant initiative and his inability to comprehend the complex laws; the poor prospects for alternative occupations despite the country's progress of industrialization; and the millions more people added annually to the already overcrowded land.

All these are sufficient to give one pause before rendering any hasty judgment about the tortuous and far from successful path of Indian reforms (other, that is, than the elimination of the zamindari). And yet the handicaps, especially the technical handicaps, do not quite explain why so much of the intent of the reforms is still unrealized. There are States in India which have demonstrated that, given strong leadership, many of the problems can be overcome. What is significant is that most of the handicaps, including the principal one—poor enforcement or non-enforcement—are not always causes but in a large measure consequences of attitudes displayed by state politicians and legislatures. This anti-reform sentiment has proved to be a crucial element in thwarting India's expectations.

By extension, and with variations, the same is true of most Asian countries. . . .

Clearly, the key to successful reform in Asia is the degree to which the controlling political forces of a country are willing to support reform and their readiness to use *all* instruments of government to attain their goals. Those against whom the reforms are directed will not divest themselves of their property and of political and economic power simply because a government wrote out a decree. Besides, despite the threat of Communism, the great fears generated by the French Revolution or by the Bolshevik Revolution in 1917 are not immediately in evidence in Asia. The conclusion is inescapable: if the peasantry is to get what is promised, peaceful and democratically managed reforms are not going to fill the bill. Government coercion, whether practiced or clearly threatened, is virtually unavoidable.

37. ECONOMIC DEVELOPMENT: POLITICAL
PRECONDITIONS AND POLITICAL CONSEQUENCES*†

j. j. s p e n g l e r

Contemporary underdeveloped countries, especially those which are densely populated and poverty-ridden, face more difficult conditions than those which confronted Western European nations or America around 1800. Rostow distinguishes three periods in the history of presently developed countries. (1) Before economic development can really get under way, certain institutional preconditions—most of which are non-economic or partly non-economic—must be established. Legal, educational, familial and other arrangements must become sufficiently favorable to the formation of capital, the supply of skilled personnel, the activation of entrepreneurs and the animation of other agencies. Barriers to economic development must be sufficiently reduced.[1] Completion of this initial preparatory period, Rostow suggests, may have required as much as a century or more in some presently advanced countries. (2) The subsequent or take-off period usually lasted two or three decades. It was marked by a significant increase in the rate of capital formation (say from 5 to 10 per cent of national income), together with a sharp stimulus of some sort (e.g., economic innovation, opening of new markets); by the development of one or more important manufacturing or processing activities; and by the emergence or activation of institutions which served to propagate to other sectors of the economy stimuli originating in the initially expanding sectors. (3) The over-all growth accompanying the take-off became self-sustaining when enough growth had been generated in sectors other than those which initially underwent expansion; these latter tended, after a time, to experience a decline in rate of

* From "Economic Development: Political Preconditions and Political Consequences" by J. J. Spengler, The Journal of Politics, Vol. XXII, No. 3 (August, 1960), pp. 391–416. By permission of the publisher and the author.
† This is a revised version of a paper prepared for the Social Science Research Council Committee on Comparative Politics.
1 See W. W. Rostow, "The Take-off into Self-sustained Growth," Economic Journal, LXVI (March, 1956), 25–48, esp. pp. 27 ff.; also "The Stages of Economic Growth," Economic History Review, XII (August, 1959), 1–16; also B. F. Hoselitz, Sociological Aspects of Economic Growth (Glencoe, 1960).

growth, at least temporarily, and this decline had to be counter-balanced by increased growth in other sectors. Continuation of growth thus required maintenance of the initially heightened rate of capital formation, together with a continuing expansion of the supply of entre-preneurs, skilled personnel and other factors.

While some underdeveloped countries may be moving into the second stage, and several may even be approaching the third stage, many are in a traditional or pre-take-off stage. Many are handicapped in ways Western countries were not.[2] (1) It is unlikely, for example, that there are to be found in many so favorable a conjuncture of economic factors as was present in the Western world at the time its self-sustaining economic growth got under way. For today, although techno-logical progress might set such a growth process in motion, population growth is excessive, there often is not an abundance of natural resources, incomes and (hence) capital formation are low and venturesome entre-preneurship tends to be scarce. (2) Political and legal conditions fre-quently are unfavorable. Because of uncertainties associated with polit-ical instability, many underdeveloped countries cannot attract foreign capital as readily as did developing countries in the nineteenth century. Furthermore, the supply of both domestic and foreign capital sometimes is kept down by the progressive character of tax systems, by forces making for wage inflation, by the fear of loss of property through expro-priation and by the capital-consuming power of the emerging welfare state. (3) Sociological factors often are relatively unfavorable. A desire for conveniences and luxuries is widespread, though not necessarily ubiquitous, in the underdeveloped world; and it is not balanced by a correspondingly widespread disposition to work harder and to produce. (4) The introduction of technological improvements is retarded by the fact that the rate of gross capital formation is low, that displacement of workers tends to augment unemployment and that economies of scale and of full use of capacity often are not realizable. There is, of course, great scope for technological progress in the underdeveloped world, but it cannot be effectively mobilized unless enough capital is forthcoming. This capital will not be forthcoming, however, unless political and social and fiscal conditions become sufficiently favorable.

DETERMINANTS OF ECONOMIC DEVELOPMENT

The determinants of economic development have been variously classified. . . . There is merit . . . in lists of determinants such as the

[2] See Benjamin Higgins, *Economic Development* (New York, 1959), esp. Part 3; Simon Kuznets, "Under-developed Countries and the Pre-industrial Phase in the Advanced Countries: An Attempt at Comparison," World Population Conference (Rome, 1954), *Papers* (New York, 1955), V, pp. 947–968.

one Rostow has proposed. He suggests that growth depends upon certain propensities which reflect a society's underlying value system and summarize its response to its environment: (1) the propensity to develop fundamental physical and social science; (2) "the propensity to apply science to economic ends"; (3) "the propensity to accept innovations"; (4) "the propensity to seek material advance"; (5) the propensity to consume, by which saving also is conditioned; (6) "the propensity to have children." The propensities are related, on the one hand, to the more immediate economic causes of economic growth, and, on the other, to determinants or circumstances underlying the propensities in question.[3]

Typological studies suggest that growth-favoring factors, being intercorrelated, tend to cluster even as do growth-retarding factors. Facilitation of a society's economic development therefore initially entails the introduction and the strengthening of enough favorable factors. In proportion as these variables are loosely instead of tightly interconnected, initial growth-favoring changes must be large if they are to be propagated through the system of interrelated variables and bring about new, intervariable equilibria that remain sufficiently unstable to make for continuing growth.[4]

⚬   ⚬   ⚬   ⚬   ⚬

SPECIFIC ROLES OR FUNCTIONS
OF GOVERNMENT

The state, of course, may contribute, positively or negatively, to economic development by pursuing courses which indirectly or directly affect economic growth. It may contribute indirectly through actions suited to strengthen the private sector, and directly by carrying on appropriate activities in the public sector. An economy is not always reducible, of course, to terms of a private sector and a public sector. The two sectors may overlap and become intermixed, inasmuch as many of

[3] See Rostow, *The Process of Economic Growth* (New York, 1952), Chaps. 1–3. For yet another list of factors which directly or indirectly affect economic development, see J. J. Spengler, "Economic Factors in the Development of Densely Populated Areas," *Proceedings of the American Philosophical Society*, XCV (1951), pp. 21–24.

[4] See Talcott Parsons, *Structure and Process in Modern Societies* (Glencoe, 1960), Chaps. 3–4, and *The Social System* (Glencoe, 1951), Chap. 5; Harvey Leibenstein, *Economic Backwardness and Economic Growth* (New York, 1957), Chaps. 9, 12; W. E. Moore, "Problems of Timing, Balance and Priorities in Development Measures," *Economic Development and Cultural Change*, II (January, 1954), 239–248; G. A. Theodorson, "Acceptance of Industrialization and Its Attendant Consequences for the Social Patterns of Non-western Societies," *American Sociological Review*, XVIII (October, 1953), 477–484.

the choices available lie on a continuum running from one extreme to the other.[5]

The negative actions of government include failure to maintain law and order; corruption in public administration, together with plundering of commercial and other enterprising classes; exploitation of submerged classes, together with denial to them of access to superior occupations; abuse or exclusion of foreigners possessing requisite skills, enterprise, capital, new tastes, *etc.;* non-maintenance of essential public services; failure to provide critical assistance and stimuli to economic sectors in which development may be triggered off; unduly restrictive regulation of economic activities; diversion of an excessive fraction of the community's surplus above consumption into unproductive forms of public capital; imposition of taxes which are arbitrary, uncertain and of a sort to blunt incentive; waste of resources in war; premature development of effective trade unions, together with "welfare-state" legislation; denial of adequate returns on private investments in public utilities, *etc.;* and diversion of resources from economic to uneconomic activities.

Economic activity can be carried on in the private sector, with some prospect of eventuating in continuing economic development only if certain functions are satisfactorily performed by the government. These include: (1) the maintenance of law and order and security against aggression; (2) sufficient support of education and public health; (3) adequate support of basic research, of the introduction of scientific findings from abroad and of the diffusion of applied scientific knowledge through agricultural extension and similar services; (4) provision, insofar as economically indicated and possible, of certain basic forms of overhead capital. Just as, through (2) and (3), the state may foster the development of a more effective labor force, so through (1) it may augment the capacity of the society to withstand the tensions that accompany economic development.

Satisfying the money requirements of economic development presupposes performance of at least two sets of functions: (5) control of the issue and supply of paper money and bank credit, through an effective central banking system and in a manner capable of preventing marked inflation; (6) making provision, insofar as practicable and necessary, for action on the part of the central banking system and cognate agencies to prevent undue deflation. It does not seem advisable for an underdeveloped country to pursue monetary policies designed to maintain full

---

[5] In this section, I draw heavily upon William Arthur Lewis, *The Theory of Economic Growth* (London, 1955), Chap. 7. See also Parsons, *Structure and Process . . .* , Chaps. 3–4; R. A. Dahl and C. E. Lindblom, *Politics, Economics, and Welfare* (New York, 1953), pp. 6–8; and, on the limitations to which governmental development efforts are subject, P. T. Bauer and B. S. Yamey, *The Economics of Underdeveloped Countries* (London, 1957), and N. S. Buchanan and H. S. Ellis, *Approaches to Economic Development* (New York, 1955).

employment. Its situation, together with the nature of its unemployment (much of it in agriculture and of long standing), differs from that encountered in developed countries; moreover, factor immobility is too great and bottlenecks are too many to permit such policies to work. (7) Provision needs to be made for the establishment, under public or public-private auspices, of financial institutions suited to assemble small savings (e.g., savings banks), to supply short-term and intermediate credit, to channel long-term capital from its sources to securities markets and to facilitate the inflow of foreign capital. (8) The government may contribute notably to the formation of attitudes favorable to economic development. (9) It may influence the uses to which resources are put (e.g., through conservation policies, zoning regulations, etc.), the manner in which industry is dispersed in space (so as to prevent excessive concentration, depressed areas, etc.), the degree of specialization (e.g., to prevent monoculture, etc.). (10) Should the government undertake to influence income distribution, it must proceed warily lest capital formation, the acquisition of skill, the suitable distribution of the labor force, etc., be checked. (11) The system of taxes employed should be so constituted as to diminish private capital formation and economic incentive very little. (12) To meet the many needs of a developing economy, a well-tested, stable, appropriately-oriented, and explicit legal and administrative structure is required, together with effective administrative and judicial personnel. Among the needs that must be met are: provision for the establishment and operation of required types of business organization (e.g., partnership, private corporation, co-operative, public and quasi-public corporations, trade union) and for the associated forms of decision-making power; rules facilitating the holding and the conveyance of property; guarantees of mobility and of freedom of entry on the part of labor and other factors of production into employments for which they are technically qualified; suitable definitions and regulations relating to contractual content, sanctions, limitations, etc.; rules insofar as required to avert retardation of growth by quasi-monopolistic and related arrangements; and so on. (13) A government may facilitate economic development by institutionalizing public as well as private initiative, since both are likely to be required, and by drawing on the relevant experience of countries which have achieved high levels of development.

More positive action may be undertaken by a government. It may undertake reform of the system of land tenure. It may attempt to step up capital formation and investment through facilitation of foreign loans, higher taxation and limited inflation, or through the use of unemployed and under-employed manpower to construct economic overhead capital (e.g., highways, railways). The success of such measures turns largely on whether resources are diverted from consumption or from the formation of private capital (which, frequently, is put to more productive use than public capital), and on whether increases in money-income restore to non-savers (*e.g.*, wage-earners) what inflation and increased taxes have taken away from them. The state may draw up a plan to put resources to particular uses and attempt to implement it by giving to entrepreneurs acting in conformity therewith greater access to resources in short supply (*e.g.*, capital, foreign exchange, skilled labor). It may attempt to affect the course of development directly, by setting up a development corporation to which it channels public revenue, by utilizing public revenue to finance the construction of economic and social overhead capital, by establishing specific agencies to perform entrepreneurial functions, and so on.

✧   ✧   ✧   ✧   ✧

ECONOMIC DEVELOPMENT AND CHANGING POLITICAL CONDITIONS

As economic development proceeds, growth-affecting political conditions and requirements change. Per capita expenditure for education and health tends to increase significantly. Institutional provisions respecting "money" become more complex. There is greater emphasis upon preventing deflation; monetary policy is increasingly directed to narrowing economic fluctuations and fostering fuller employment; less attention is given to cushioning fluctuations in the prices of primary goods. Moreover, as an economy progresses, its banking system becomes more differentiated, and its ratio of paper to physical assets rises. The legal structure also becomes more complex and differentiated as does the public and the private organizational structure for which legal institutions must design appropriate rules.[6] Foreign economic relations tend to become subject to greater regulation, much of it restrictive, especially after external trade has begun to lag behind national income.

As an economy advances, it may tolerate larger amounts of growth-checking taxation and public expenditure, since the economic system itself becomes more autonomous and more able and willing to supply growth-capital. While emphasis upon governmental intervention and centralized economic planning may for a time increase as an economy progresses, it eventually tends to decline insofar as the need for economic and social overhead capital and for state aid to newly developing industries falls off. This outcome is quite likely. Such increase in emphasis upon the public sector may, for a time, make conditions worse in

[6] *E.g.*, see E. V. Rostow's account of the newly acquired rules of public law, in *Planning for Freedom* (New Haven, 1959).

the private sector, though this is not a necessary outcome. Development corporations are not likely to be continued after an economy has become autonomous and characterized by self-sustaining growth. Budgetary policy becomes of greater importance as the economy progresses, particularly if, as some believe, the advent of "affluence" makes greater freedom increasingly necessary, together with the supply of "cultural" and "collective" goods and services, the production and/or distribution of which are not considered well suited to private enterprise. Economic progress is attended also by a great increase in the competence of private criticism of governmental economic policies, though not necessarily in its effectiveness.

While highly skilled personnel are always in short supply, governmental personnel tend to improve in quantity and quality as an economy improves, thereby permitting the government to undertake more of those economic tasks of which it is empirically capable, given adequacy of personnel. Rising income is associated with the increase of skilled personnel, income and personnel interacting through time to augment each other.

In general, as has been implied, economic development tends eventually to be accompanied by both political and economic decentralization. It is accompanied by decentralization of both legal norm-making power and use-determining, economic decision-making power, with both forms becoming more widely distributed in space and among households and/or corporate groups. The disposition of economic power in space and among groups and individuals tends to be rather closely associated with that of political power. Political decentralization entails the distribution of norm-making power among a plurality of groups or organs, together with the subjection of centralized norm-making to restraints imposed by dispersed, norm-affecting groups whose initially heterogeneous aspirations enter into such consensus as comes to underlie norms held valid for all members of a society.[7] Economic decentralization requires that the mechanisms employed to discover what final goods and services should be produced reflect an ever widening range of consumer preferences, be these mechanisms "free markets" in which price and effective economic demand rule, or political devices designed to register such non-economic indicators as votes. Such decentralization results because, as an economy becomes more consumer-oriented, centralized determination of what is to be produced becomes increasingly difficult.

Among the concomitants of decentralization are the decline of one-party rule and the rise of the welfare state. An effective one-party

[7]   See Hans Kelsen, "Centralization and Decentralization," in Harvard Tercentenary Conference, *Authority and the Individual* (Cambridge, 1937), pp. 210–239, esp. 212–213, 216–217, 223, 227–229; also 231–232 on struggles for local autonomy, and 233–234 on federalism as a form of decentralization.

system, though often favorable to economic growth, appears to be incompatible with a complex economy in which consumer goods, together with a high level of education, have come to play a paramount role. Similarly, the welfare state, though initially incompatible with the effective development of economically retarded lands, eventually becomes a part of the set of arrangements whereby, in high-income economies, collective goods and services are supplied and expenditure is kept abreast of "full-employment" output in pacific times.

38. PRIORITIES IN ECONOMIC DEVELOPMENT *

bilsel alisbah
and albert berry

Economic development is a shorthand expression for certain goals which represent the hope for a better way of life. The active pursuit of these goals by underdeveloped nations reflects a decision to influence the allocation of scarce resources and a willingness to alter existing institutions. The determination of the goals, of the institutional framework and of the allocation of resources all call for priority decisions. The goals are ideally an expression of society's preferences, though in practice they are what leaders correctly or incorrectly perceive them to be. . . .

Most underdeveloped countries would cite as their major goals a rapid growth of per capita income, a low level of unemployment and some degree of income equalization. But there is often a lack of awareness, both inside and outside these countries, of the possible degree of incompatibility among the objectives. Such countries are usually faced by high rates of unemployment caused by the shortage of the complementary factors, capital and entrepreneurship. This leads to a conflict between growth and full employment in situations where a choice must

° From "Priorities in Economic Development" by Bilsel Alisbah and Albert Berry, *Journal of International Affairs*, Vol. XVI, No. 2 (1962), pp. 172–181. Reprinted by permission.

be made between a mechanized method of production and a less efficient labor-intensive one. . . . Income equalization, by reducing high incomes, also conflicts with growth in countries where such incomes provide a large portion of total investment. In these cases, if all incomes are at about the same level—necessarily low—savings may be very small. A dilemma thus arises: a country can have inequality of incomes now, with the resultant investment leading to higher future incomes, or it can have more equality of incomes now, low investment and less hope of higher incomes in the future. . . .

The second group of decisions, those concerned with possible institutional changes, are the subject of an important current debate. Some hold that land reform [1] and tax reform [2] are in many cases such crucial preconditions of growth that other efforts are wasted until these problems are solved. (This view has recently been widely publicized in connection with Alliance for Progress aid to South American countries; certain officials hold that the aid should be withheld until there is more evidence of serious intent to undertake the desired reforms.) Certainly some form of a reasonably stable government, a banking system and a revenue system will be essential. But the real question is one of degree. It can be persuasively argued that none of the now developed countries had achieved anything approaching an ideal taxation or banking system until the process of development was far along in its course.

. . . Today this function [of allocating resources] is performed largely through the rapidly mushrooming planning boards. Economic planning is, of course, far from homogeneous. It varies with respect to the importance assigned to it, its sophistication, the detail in which it is carried out and the relative size of the public sector. But the basic problem facing all the planners is the same: to assign priorities in such a way that resources will be allocated in the best possible manner.

This would be a conceptually easy task if the economist could measure the total contribution to national income of every possible investment. He would then select the ones which yielded the highest returns per dollar, and would allocate his resources among these in such a way that the last dollar's worth of resources in each use yielded equal returns. The best allocation of resources among different sectors would follow automatically without the need for any additional considerations.

[1] Land reform is often defined more in social than in economic terms; it usually refers to the breaking up of large estates so that the peasants will own the land which they cultivate. Sometimes this increases agricultural output by increasing the incentive to produce, but if the estates were well managed before the breakup, output may decrease. Even if this is true, however, there may be a net economic gain if ex-landholders invest their funds in industry.
[2] A major problem of taxation in underdeveloped countries is the political difficulty of imposing high taxes on the rich; this group usually has an influence far out of proportion to its size. Many other weaknesses are common as well, such as inefficiency and corruption in the gathering of taxes, the use of poor kinds of taxes, *etc.*

In underdeveloped countries, unfortunately, the estimation of a project's contribution to national income is especially difficult. Economists commonly divide this contribution into the direct effects and the indirect effects. The former refer to the value of goods and services produced less the value of raw materials used in production; this is equal to the sum of incomes generated by the project (*i.e.* wages, rent, profits, *etc.*). The latter simply include any other effects on national income. If, for example, an innovating entrepreneur sets up the country's first modern textile plant, the total effect on national income may surpass the direct effect since others may copy its technology and thereby increase their own productivity. Again, the establishment of a canning plant may lead to an increase in the incomes of local fruit growers (indirect effect) by cutting the wastage which is common in underdeveloped areas with their poor storage facilities; thus the increase in national income will be greater than the total rewards to the employees and owners of the canning plant.

Direct effects, while not particularly difficult to determine when the enterprise is operating, may be hard to predict beforehand, especially in a rapidly changing economy where in many cases a project may be the first of its kind. Indirect effects are always hard to estimate. . . .

☼   ☼   ☼   ☼   ☼

Along with . . . broad ideas concerning the appropriate balance (or imbalance) of growth, the planner will think in terms of "sectoral principles and generalizations." These revolve around two questions: what should be done and who should do it? The first deals with the most desirable allocation of resources among sectors, the most important of which are agriculture, industry, education and mining.[3] The second is basically concerned with determining the proper extent of the government's role.[4]

In the latter connection the balanced growth doctrine has important implications. Its requirements of sizable and more or less simultaneous

---

[3]   An alternative to this sectoral approach runs in terms of "bottleneck factors." In recent years writers have successively stressed a lack of natural resources, a lack of capital and a lack of high level manpower as being, in some sense, the "crucial missing link." At one point it was often implied that a country could be developed merely by pumping in enough capital. Currently this view is not popular and surprisingly low estimates of a country's ability to absorb capital are common. In any case, this general approach to the matter leads one to think of the priority problem less in terms of "which sector should a country develop fastest" and more in terms of "which factor should it try to get more of."

[4]   By the "government's role" we mean, as well as the operation of industries, any other methods used to influence the pattern of outputs and prices in the economy. We are primarily concerned with those economic reasons for this role which are especially characteristic of underdeveloped countries.

investments in all industries call for a "big push." This, in turn, requires the government to play a major role to insure the proper timing of investments and to see that the necessary funds are forthcoming. The government will have to indulge in heavy taxation or in forced saving by inflation (*i.e.* printing money and spending it), since the private sector cannot be expected to provide an adequate volume of savings voluntarily.

Certain other situations, peculiar to underdeveloped countries, also imply the need for government operation or intervention. Most underdeveloped countries still lack the infrastructure needed for development (roads, railroads, bridges, public facilities, *etc.*), and the fulfillment of this need is primarily a function of the government. Furthermore, the lack of entrepreneurial talent and experience, coupled with the desire to avoid risk-taking, means that many projects with a good chance of success will not be undertaken by the private sector. The public entrepreneur, who unlike his private counterpart is not risking his own capital, will be more likely to attempt such projects. Even where private entrepreneurial talent is not particularly scarce, investment is often channeled in directions which are not socially productive, *e.g.* the purchase of real estate or land, speculation on rising prices or the purchase of foreign bonds.[5] These investments, unfortunately, are usually less risky than truly productive ones, and hence highly attractive to the investor. An additional problem is the danger of monopoly power when a few new plants are set up to satisfy a fairly small market for some industrial product. Competition from imports will often be ruled out on "balance of payments" or "infant industry" grounds, enabling the lucky firms to relax and even stagnate to some degree while maintaining their profits by high prices. A final element in enlarging the government's sphere of activity is that international capital now largely takes the form of public loans and grants rather than private investment.

Although the above arguments imply the need for government operation, such operation on too large a scale has its own disadvantages. Some private entrepreneurial skills may be wasted because the government cannot attract them. Furthermore, some voluntary saving, which would have been induced by opportunities for private investment, will not occur. Saving will largely have to take the form of taxation, which is difficult and inefficient in most underdeveloped countries, and inflationary finance, which causes well-known disturbances and problems.[6]

[5] These investments are socially undesirable as compared, for example, with investment in factories, which increase the country's productive capacity. The purchase of land or real estate is merely a transfer of existing wealth, not a creation of new wealth.

[6] These considerations do not necessarily suggest that the government's role as a whole should be curtailed; they may alternatively imply wider use of other types of intervention besides government operation, *e.g.* subsidies, controls of various sorts, *etc.*

Viewing the public-private question as a whole, however, it seems clear that for some time to come governments should play an increasing role in developing economies. This statement remains valid to a considerable extent even if we cannot assume that administrators are as honest or efficient as their counterparts in developed countries, since much of what the government does would not be touched otherwise.

We turn now from broad considerations of growth as a whole to questions of inter-sectoral resource allocation. Probably the most widely discussed priority issue of this sort is "agriculture *vs.* industry." Many economists charge that underdeveloped countries consistently underestimate the importance of agriculture and consequently trip over this sector while chasing the dream of industrialization. Although the two sectors are often assumed to be in serious competition for scarce resources, we will argue that they can be, in fact, quite complementary. The only satisfactory course for most developing countries is the twofold one of industrializing *and* increasing agricultural output.

In dealing with the proper relationship of agriculture to industry it is very important to distinguish between the long and the short run. In the long run the relative contribution of industry to national income will definitely grow, since as incomes rise a greater percentage is always spent on industrial products. In all developed countries the ratios of industrial to agricultural output and of industrial to agricultural workers are higher than in underdeveloped countries. This holds true even for Denmark and New Zealand—the two most agriculturally oriented of the wealthy nations—both of which have less than 20% of their populations in agriculture. The real issue, therefore, is the priorities to be assigned in the next few years, *i.e.* the path to be pursued in moving toward a fairly definite long run position.

In some cases, where rural overpopulation is very serious and there are few unexplored avenues for increasing agricultural output, heavy emphasis on industrialization is a sheer necessity. In less extreme cases a relative increase in the industrial sector may remain desirable on other grounds.[7] It usually leads to greater total savings and investment by increasing the incomes of entrepreneurs, the major savers in underdeveloped countries. And the industrial sector, which is often coterminous

---

[7]   A number of unsound arguments for industrialization coexist with the valid ones. One of the most interesting and completely fallacious is the contention that, since the value of an industrial worker's daily output is greater than that of the farmer, national income could be raised by transferring workers to industry. This argument fails to consider the costs of the expensive machinery with which the typical industrial laborer works and to which his high productivity must be largely attributed. It may be that one more worker adds very little to the total output. In an extreme case other factors such as capital and entrepreneurship may be fixed in quantity with the maximum amount of labor already employed. In this case there would be nothing for the newcomers to do except to cheer on those already employed—at best a somewhat doubtful method of increasing production.

with the "money economy," is easier to tax than the agricultural sector, where the limited use of money makes attempts to determine incomes and transactions very difficult. Finally, industrialization makes people more receptive to change and progress by tearing them away from their traditions and instilling in them the "monetary incentive."

. . . [E]mphasis on agriculture, where marked increases in production are possible, has very important advantages of its own. Until industrial ventures become able international competitors, agricultural exports will, despite the disadvantages of severe price fluctuations, be a major means of payment for the various imports needed in development. An agricultural expansion will also ease the inflationary pressures caused, in a developing economy, by people's tendency to spend most of the increases in their incomes on food. Finally, since the agricultural sector is such a large portion of the economy, its general prosperity and buying power are very important to all the other sectors.

More arguments can be presented on either side, and it may appear that little can be said by way of generalization. The crucial point, however, is that in many cases agricultural output can be spurred by methods requiring relatively little capital or high level manpower, the factors especially necessary in industry. . . .

✧   ✧   ✧   ✧   ✧

We pointed out earlier that the importance of the industrial sector as a whole is virtually certain to grow over the long run as development proceeds. The optimal long run relation among specific industries is much harder to estimate because of the difficulty of predicting changing tastes, new inventions (nylon, for example, ruined the silk industry in Japan) and the discovery of new resources. One does not even know the latent industrial talents of the population itself. Unpredictable behavior by other countries further complicates the situation; a country which has a comparative advantage in steel production may not wish to specialize too much along this line if it feels power and prestige motives will lead other countries to build their own steel plants. Because of these difficulties, errors in the direction of specialization are a constant threat. Although the cost of such errors is somewhat mitigated in a growing economy, where excess capacity tends to come into use over time, the extreme scarcity of resources clearly calls for great care in their allocation.

One facet of the inter-industry allocation problem is the "heavy vs. light" issue. Despite economists' advice that developing countries, due to the scarcity of their capital, should specialize in light industry and acquire the products of heavy industry through trade, these countries continue to be lured by such symbols of industrialization as the steel plant. There seems, however, little cause to worry that they will quickly become exporters of heavy industrial products; advances in this direction have been rather modest so far. And such modest advances may be of considerable value, since in setting up heavy industry a country must import foreign technology and use rationalized procedures, some elements of which, hopefully, will spread to other parts of the economy.

Underdeveloped countries which are large and well endowed with iron ore and mineral fuels, or which feel that imports of industrial products are too uncertain to be relied on, may be quite justified in stressing heavy industry. Countries less well endowed must weigh carefully certain disadvantages of doing so. The most serious of these, probably, is that since heavy industry has a low labor-capital ratio, the greater the relative emphasis on it, the higher unemployment is likely to be. Light industry has the further advantage that it can more often be established in towns or villages. This means not only that the costs of transferring people to the cities can be avoided but also that the seasonal underemployment in agriculture—so typical of underdeveloped countries—can be reduced by having villagers work in industry for part of the year. Furthermore, since the typical firm in light industry is relatively small, the entrepreneurial function will be spread wider and valuable experience obtained. In view of the usual shortage of entrepreneurial ability,[8] this idea may appear implausible; the point, however, is that people not presently engaged in enterprise are more likely to make the jump if production is done on a small scale. Taking the "heavy vs. light" issue as a whole, it must be conceded that conditions vary too much from country to country for any valid generalizations to be made.

Finally, education, that sector of the economy which produces knowledge, has come increasingly to the forefront of allocation discussions. Decisions concerning the emphasis to be placed on education as a whole, and on the various levels and types of it, are perhaps the most difficult in the field of development. The problems of measurement here are gigantic. Even for the direct effects of different levels of education on an individual's income, it is extremely difficult to arrive at an accurate estimate. Analyses of these matters are just now beginning in developed countries; in underdeveloped areas most of the current discussion consists of educated guesses.

One view, which we tend to share, is that, in the short run it will be best to stress technical as opposed to general literary education. Considerable evidence shows that the latter is quickly forgotten when the student returns to the farm. In many cases it will be economically wise

---

[8] The unproductive bargaining skills of the middleman, which are so abundant in many underdeveloped countries, should not be mistaken for entrepreneurship. The time spent haggling in bazaars, while it may enrich the individual concerned, certainly makes no contribution to national income.

to postpone mass elementary education as well, since it may conflict sharply with the training of the technicians and engineers who are so important in development. We emphasize, however, that we are viewing this issue only from an economic point of view, and that in this case, perhaps more than in any other, one can expect the noneconomic considerations to be paramount.

39. INDEPENDENCE AND DEVELOPMENT: SOME COMPARISONS BETWEEN TROPICAL AFRICA AND SOUTH-EAST ASIA°

g u y   h u n t e r

. . . Almost all the societies under review, in Africa and in Asia, have from 60 per cent. to 80 per cent. of population engaged in agricultural and animal husbandry. Their low levels of income (running from about £20 to £100 per head per annum)[1] reflect their massive rural populations, and the higher figures among them reflect rich cash crops, such as Malaya's rubber, Ghana's cocoa, Philippine sugar, or minerals (Northern Rhodesian copper, Malayan tin). The agricultural problem is at once the social, the economic, and, one day, the political problem which dwarfs all others. . . .

Peasant agriculture is the crux; and here it may be that some parts of Africa have slipped quietly ahead. I could see no large-scale evidence that the critical break-through in peasant agriculture, involving land tenure, technical methods and marketing, which has been achieved notably in East African cotton and coffee, was yet in sight in South-East

°   From "Independence and Development: Some Comparisons between Tropical Africa and South-East Asia" by Guy Hunter, International Affairs, Vol. XL, No. 1 (January, 1964), pp. 52–58. By permission of the publisher and the author.
[1]   The low-level (£20–£30) group includes Burma, Indonesia and most Tropical African countries, including Nigeria. The middle level, Thailand (£35–£40), Philippines (£45–£50), Ghana (£75), Northern Rhodesia (£80). The highest, Malaya/Singapore (£100+).

Asia. The reasons may be various. In East Africa the colonial administration devoted three-quarters of its effort to rural affairs. A large, well-trained (and practically trained) extension service, working closely with District administration, was thrown into the battle. Good, residential secondary schools sited in rural areas produced African staff born to farming and trained in farming areas. Price policies for cash crops gave a good return to the grower—good enough to tempt him to accept better methods and harder work. Co-operatives were patiently fostered from below.

In much of South-East Asia these factors do not apply. The extension service appears in some cases to be four or five times smaller, per head of population, than its East African counterpart. In many areas the staff are urban trained in urban universities on chalk and talk; in some areas (rural Malaya was until recently one) non-residential secondary schools, or schools of poorer quality, have meant that qualifications could only be easily obtained in the towns. In some areas (Burma, Indonesia) prices to producers have been so low that land has been going out of cultivation or reverting to subsistence crops. In some areas (Philippines) 50 per cent. of holdings are tenancies to a landlord under conditions which give little incentive to improve techniques and yields.

But above all the difference seems to lie in the attitude of government and of the ruling group; and this may be of sinister import for the African future, since the main advances in Africa were achieved under colonial administration. It is not, I think, unfair to say that the developing countries of South-East Asia (with the exception of Malaya) are not wholeheartedly devoted to rural advance. All the excitements of the new era are concentrated in the capital city. Government, new industry, foreign embassies, the airport, the luxury hotel, new boulevards and motorways, the university, the nuclear research unit, United Nations agencies, with their growing staffs and expenditure, air-conditioning, smart restaurants, private medical practice, a world of prestige and importance and of money to be made (honestly or not), a world running on the standards of countries with a *per capita* income of £500 or more—this is what Rangoon, Bangkok, Djakarta, Manila offer—and perhaps Lagos and Leopoldville? There is one doctor to 1,000 in Bangkok; 1 to 30,000 in Thailand; 1 to 700 in Manila and 1 to 20,000 in the Philippines as a whole.

Certainly, there are multi-million schemes for rural development as part of every five-year plan. But these, planned in headquarters offices with all the panoply of foreign experts and international aid, are plans for great engineering works, sometimes for great state co-operatives, sometimes for extensive rural credit banks. They seemed, to me at least, to bear no relationship to the growth of an agrarian revolution as I saw it in Africa—the slow, patient teaching and persuasion, at the level of five-acre holdings, carried on year after year by Africans with mud on their boots, with applied research and authority behind them, and a good price, and a locally formed Co-operative to work with. There are indeed signs of real village work—in the Philippines through the PACD [2] and PRRM [3]—in Malaya at least in vigorous provision of physical facilities and new land clearance; but elsewhere the impression of vast schemes and little change remains.

The trouble goes deep. On the one hand, it is almost impossible to get the young graduate to go to the rural areas. Doctor or lawyer, engineer or biologist, teacher or administrator, he will opt for the town and modernity; if the town is full he will often go abroad. America and France have hundreds of Filipino or Vietnamese professional men who cannot find work in Manila or Saigon and would not look for it in the rural areas. It is not that manpower is short in South-East Asia; it is badly distributed.

Deeper still, one must ask if the efforts which are made to increase agricultural production are made in service to the people of the villages, or are made to provide exports—foreign exchange—spending money for the rulers, to be spent on the steel-works, the additional embassies abroad, and all the steel and concrete and glass which adorn the capital city. Certainly, the modern sector in developing countries must ultimately be financed from agricultural surpluses. But there is a sequence and a balance to be kept. The real revolution in peasant agriculture should be coming first, so that a good portion of a far larger surplus can go back to raising rural standards—health and education, transport and power, tools and equipment, small industry, educated men. The transfer of democracy, in the form of suffrage, to developing countries has often been neatly transposed into mass voting for the one-party system and its charismatic leader, or snapped up by a military dictatorship disgusted by the corruption which democrats elected by illiterates so easily find to hand. It will not be real until the 70 per cent. of population who are villagers are given the economic and educational power to take an intelligent part in it. At present, the funds, which developed nations and the United Nations are pouring into much of South-East Asia (and much of Africa may become the same) are going to widen the gap between Asian Metropolitan Man and the vast and poor populations whom he rules. The centralisation of wealth and power, the feebleness of provincial administration, luxury alongside extreme poverty and unemployment in the mushrooming cities, the many perversions of democracy—all in no small degree reflect a failure to see development primarily in terms of the people as a whole—the rural people. It is an uncomfortable foretaste of what could come in African states when 15 years of indepen-

[2] President's Assistant for Community Development.
[3] Philippines Rural Reconstruction Movement.

dence have passed. The tradition of service to the rural population (and it is a tradition of which Britain in particular may be proud) survives in some degree in Malaya, aided by Malay nationalism; will it survive in Africa? Can it be developed in Asia?

✿   ✿   ✿

Perhaps the strongest contrast between the African and South-East Asian societies lies in their present volume of secondary and higher education and their stocks of 'higher manpower'. In Tropical Africa it was true to say that, even as late as this year, there were shortages of graduates and technicians and above all secondary school teachers. Most 'manpower surveys', including the Ashby-Harbison report on Nigeria, were concerned to increase, as rapidly as possible, the output both from university level and from post-secondary training institutions— while noting with anxiety the growing unemployed, mainly primary school-leavers, at the lower end of the scale. It seemed as if there could never be enough graduates. But a shock was in store for me in South-East Asia. On the day of arrival I discovered that 35 per cent. of the engineers who graduated from Rangoon University in 1961 were found to be unemployed 18 months later, never having worked as engineers. In Thailand graduates were applying for jobs as junior clerks; in the Philippines they were driving taxis.

The sequence of events, much simplified, runs as follows. A shortage of higher manpower; a multiplication of secondary schools, with some reduction in standards; a lowering of university entrance requirements and the building of new universities; sudden surplus of graduates in relation to jobs; violent competition, making a degree even more vital; popular pressure for yet more secondary schools and universities, supported by vote-catching politicians; and so the cycle of expansion and surplus starts again.

There is little doubt that slogans which were current (and still are) in what might be called 'Manpower Planning Circles', mainly British and American, contributed to this situation by emphasising 'Investment in Human Capital' and implying that a country could hardly have too much of it. Two major confusions have led to this idea. First, once a country has passed the 'take-off' point, it is true that it is almost impossible to produce too many, or even enough graduates of higher education. But this is far from true with agricultural economies far, far short of take-off. Experience seems to show that once the main administrative, teaching, and skeleton medical services are filled, demand for qualified graduates rises only slowly, because the 'modern sector' expands slowly at first, and because graduates will not serve the subsistence economy, until it is modernised—this is the urban-rural problem again. Comparisons of graduates 'per head of population' conceal the fact that 60 per cent. to 80 per cent. of the population are villagers among whom there are few jobs for graduates and even fewer which they are willing to take. The calculation should be, for many purposes, 'per size of modern sector'.

The second confusion is between education as a tool of economic development or as a consumer good—a personal enrichment. You cannot have too much of a consumer good *if the economy can afford it,* and *if the consumer so regards it.* But both conditions may not be fulfilled; and in particular the consumer mainly looks at higher education as a qualification for a job, and is much frustrated if no job is available above the labourer or clerical level.

The situation in South-East Asia (again excepting Malaya which has not gone through the cycle) is hard to handle—unemployed and discontented graduates are not an economic or a political blessing.

The possible lines of action may be

(1) To distinguish clearly between 'tool' and 'consumer-good' education, so that at least the surplus over 'tool' requirements have a good *general* education rather than becoming unemployed specialists.

(2) To upgrade university entrance standards and provide alternative technician training which is badly needed.

(3) To upgrade training and qualifications for secondary school teachers.

(4) Above all, to tackle rural development, so that the 'surplus' of graduates (which is unreal, since the villages are short of doctors, nurses, teachers, agriculturalists, power, sanitation, etc.) is used for vital social purposes instead of vegetating in the capital city or endeavouring to get a doctorate in the most easy-going of American colleges.

There are, to my mind, some vital warnings for Africa here—not to downgrade university entrance out of impatience; to build up post-secondary training in quality and prestige; to be ready to switch the present correct emphasis on secondary education back to the primary level as soon as the 'tool' requirements begin to be met; to co-ordinate the agricultural with the educational programme, so that the huge needs of rural areas for men with better education begin to be met; to give real incentives for men to work in rural areas—house, car, salary, electric power, promotion prospects; to site institutions and small factories of every kind outside the main towns; to improve rural transport and communications. All these policies have the most direct bearing upon education and manpower. If they are not followed, the urban unemployed will not only be primary school-leavers; they will be university graduates.

✿   ✿   ✿

Both Africa and South-East Asia face largely identical problems in establishing a new industrial sector. They are problems of capital and of management. The management problem is far the more difficult. Those countries which welcome foreign capital investment and which have opportunities for its use (as there usually are) naturally stand in the safer position, since the foreign firm takes the risk. Most African and most South-East Asian countries accept this; Burma at present does not; Indonesia, partly through currency and administrative chaos and partly through nationalist pride, has made things extremely discouraging for the private investor. But government capital may be forthcoming, accumulated from marketing board surpluses or from foreign loans. It is the management problem which is so hard to solve.

Part of the trouble . . . is that the type of industry which is being introduced is the most modern product of the developed countries—steel works, oil refineries, electron microscopes (two in Burma, both out of action), maintenance of jet aircraft. As such, it is the product of countries where labour is scarce, capital is relatively less scarce, training and education is high, and consumption so large that it justifies mass production with refined electronic controls, and requires highly sophisticated accounting, extreme regularity and precision of the production schedule. These are not conditions likely to be found in Mandalay or Sumatra, Uganda or Kano. The technical skills can, indeed, be produced in time; the managerial skills, and the integrity (financial and technical), the devotion to the task, will take longer. Yet all these countries have already elements of enterprise and skill comparable to those elements which founded the industrial revolution in the West 100 years ago, capable of application to smaller units and more modest managerial tasks. If the developing countries are determined to have nothing but the largest, most modern and prestige-full industrial equipment, they will have to pay the price of reliance on foreign skills for many long years ahead; they may also find such enterprises economically unprofitable and politically indigestible—for they do not of themselves (by the very nature of their origin) provide much employment, nor (again, naturally) do they fit readily into the whole economic complex, from which they did not and could not have grown.

Indeed, it would have been more natural to expect industrial enterprise to be growing from the expansion of commerce and commercial skills; and these are far more readily available in Asia than in Africa—but with one defect: they are predominatly found among the overseas Chinese. Just as in Africa developing countries have sought to overtrump the Indian or Levantine trader by introducing far more sophisticated and capital-intensive Western industry (later to be Africanised in personnel and possibly nationalised in control); so in South-East Asia, American, British, Australian, Japanese or Russian investment, on terms leading ultimately to Malay or Thai or Indonesian control, may well be preferred to policies which stimulate skills and enterprise within the existing society, because those skills are Chinese.

$$\backsim\!\!\backsim\!\!\curlyvee\!\!\frown$$

40. OBSTACLES TO DEVELOPMENT: A CLASSIFICATION AND A QUASI-VANISHING ACT [*][†]

a l b e r t o. h i r s c h m a n

One could think of several ways of classifying obstacles: natural (lack of resources) and man-made (lack of law and order, lack of capital), objective (lack of resources or of capital) and subjective (lack of entrepreneurship and risk-taking, lack of a desire for change, contempt for material success), internal (all the factors so far named) and external (exploitation by a foreign power), etc.

I find it useful, however, to adopt a classification which is grounded in the concept of "obstacle" itself and which, in the process, questions its solidity from the outset. It is a principal contention of this note that the

[*] Reprinted from "Obstacles to Development: A Classification and a Quasi-Vanishing Act" by Albert O. Hirschman, Economic Development and Cultural Change, Vol. XIII, No. 4 (July, 1965), by permission of The University of Chicago Press. Copyright 1965 by The University of Chicago. Selections from pp. 385–393.

[†] This article was written as a contribution to a symposium on obstacles to economic development organized by Professor François Perroux. It will be published in French by the Institut d'Etude du Développement Economique et Social in a forthcoming volume of the series Etudes Tiers-Monde. The author is indebted to Terence K. Hopkins and Immanuel Wallerstein for helpful comments.

concept is far from solid, that it is not possible to identify either a finite number of "reliable" obstacles to development or a hierarchy among these obstacles which would permit us to arrange them neatly into boxes marked "basic," "important," "secondary," etc.

The traditional method of identifying an obstacle to development points immediately to the conceptual weakness we have in mind. The method consists in looking up the history of one or several economically advanced countries, noting certain situations that were present at about the time when development was brought actively under way in one or several of these countries (a temperate climate, a population belonging to the white race, "primitive" accumulation of capital, coal deposits, law and order, widespread literacy, a group of Schumpeterian entrepreneurs, a fairly efficient and honest civil service, agrarian reform, the Protestant Ethic, etc., etc.), and then construing the *absence* of any of these situations as an obstacle to development. This procedure could lead one to conclude that the more countries develop, the more difficult does it appear for the remainder to do the same, for each successfully developing country does so under a set of special conditions, thus lengthening the list of obstacles (i.e., the absence of these conditions) which have to be "overcome."

Fortunately, this conclusion is as implausible as it is dismal. The usual way of escaping from it is by the successive substitution of a newly discovered *fundamental* obstacle for those that held sway before the latest theoretical or historical insight. In this paper we shall proceed in a more empirical vein and attempt to classify obstacles in the order of their greater or smaller *reliability* as obstacles, on the basis of what evidence we have been able to collect.

Suppose some specific situation or condition can be shown to have been essential for the development of country X at time t; in other words, the absence of this condition performed as an insuperable barrier to the development of X. Now it is possible that the development experience of other countries confirms that of X; on the other hand, one can think of the following ways in which the barrier or obstacle would fail to perform as such in other countries:

(1) The obstacle does not constitute an *absolute* barrier in the case of country Y; certain forward moves are available to this country, and the obstacle, while still exerting a negative influence on development, can be dealt with, perhaps more easily, at a later time.

(2) The alleged obstacle, in view of another set of circumstances, turns out not to be an obstacle at all and therefore does not need to be removed, either now or later.

(3) The alleged obstacle, in view of yet other circumstances, turns into a positive advantage and asset for development.

ECONOMIC DEVELOPMENT

In justifying each of these possibilities—and, in the process, discovering several other variants—we shall invert the order in which they have been cited and thus start with the most extreme case.

I. AMBIVALENCE: ALLEGED OBSTACLES THAT TURN INTO ASSETS

How difficult it is to classify certain concrete situations as unequivocally hostile or favorable to economic development is well illustrated by the institution of the *extended* or *joint family*. Several Western economists belonging to quite different schools of thought have taken the position that the extended family dilutes individual incentives and that its demise and replacement by the nuclear family is required for dynamic development to occur.[1] This is, of course, a highly ethnocentric argument. Westerners who hold this view find it difficult to imagine that any one would want to exert himself if the fruits of his labors accrue largely to what they consider as distant relatives; implicit in the idea that the extended family is a bar to economic progress is therefore the judgment that no one in his right mind can really care for the welfare of his third cousin.

But suppose "they" do? In that case the argument against the extended family not only falls to the ground, but one can immediately perceive of several advantages in an arrangement in which the basic economic decision-making unit is not the nuclear family, but a wider grouping. For one, the special relationship existing among the members permits them to undertake new tasks requiring cooperation without prior mastery of such complications as hiring labor and keeping accounts.[2] Furthermore, the members may pool their resources not only for consumption, but equally for investment purposes; and thus it may be possible for them to finance business ventures as well as advanced education for the more gifted among them.[3]

Can we save the proposition for the rather special situation where the extended family still exists as a formal behavior code but can no longer command the full loyalty of the individual member of the society and is perhaps actively resented by him? In that case the strictures of

[1] P. T. Bauer and B. S. Yamey, *The Economics of Under-Developed Countries* (Chicago, 1957), p. 66; and Benjamin Higgins, *Economic Development* (New York, 1959), p. 256.
[2] C. S. Belshaw, *In Search of Wealth: A Study of the Emergence of Commercial Operations in the Melanesian Society of South-Eastern Papua* (Vancouver, 1955), Chs. 5 and 7.
[3] Peter Marris, *Family and Social Change in an African City* (London, 1961), p. 138. The importance of kinship ties in the early spread of banking and mercantile enterprise in the West is of course well established.

our economists would seem to apply fully. Yet, such is the variety of possible situations that even here we must tread with care. For example, the very desire to withhold extra earnings from one's family may deflect the more enterprising members of the family from a bureaucratic career (where earnings are fixed and a matter of public knowledge) into a business career (where earnings are uncertain and can be concealed).[4] Moreover, if there is any time lag between the newly won affluence of the individual and the famous moving-in of all the relatives to share in his newly won riches, then the institution of the extended family combined with the desire to escape from it provides a stimulus to ever new spurts of temporarily relative-exempt entrepreneurial activity.[5] Hence, even if the sharing implicit in the extended family system is resented, the obligation to share may act like those taxes that stimulate individuals to greater effort at securing non-taxable gains (and at tax evasion).

Our point is strengthened by the observation that, just as the extended family cannot be held to stunt growth under all circumstances, so the nuclear family will not always promote development. If the economic operator perceives no possibility of common interest, action, or gain with anyone outside his immediate blood relatives, then economic advance is likely to be severely hamstrung, as I have explained elsewhere and as has been documented by several empirical studies.[6]

A more general remark is in order at this point. We have said that an obstacle to development may usually be defined as the absence of a condition that was found to be present in a country which subsequently developed. But in many cases the question that ought to have been asked is *how much* of this condition was present. Too much may be just as deleterious as too little. It is too much rather than too little individualism and entrepreneurship and too little willingness to work with discipline in a hierarchical organization that plagues much of Southeast Asia and also other underdeveloped lands.[7] Too much law and order may be as stifling as too little is disruptive. . . .

     ❖   ❖   ❖   ❖   ❖

[4] *Ibid.*, p. 139.

[5] "The fact that, under the customary rules of inheritance, individual property was always in process of conversion to family property provided individuals with a great incentive to acquire additional lands, over which they had, for some time at least, unlimited control." Polly Hill, *The Migrant Cocoa-Farmers of Southern Ghana* (Cambridge, 1963), p. 16.

[6] A. O. Hirschman, *The Strategy of Economic Development* (New Haven, 1958), pp. 14–20; Edward C. Banfield, *The Moral Basis of a Backward Society* (Glencoe, Ill., 1958); Clifford Geertz, *Peddlers and Princes* (Chicago, 1963), pp. 42–47, 73 ff., 122 ff.

[7] "Malaya probably suffers from an excess of enterprise, since this is a factor which tends to disintegrate existing business." T. H. Silcock, *The Economy of Malaya* (Singapore, 1956), p. 44.

II. ALLEGED OBSTACLES WHOSE ELIMINATION TURNS OUT TO BE UNNECESSARY

We turn now to a somewhat less paradoxical type of situation: the presumed obstacle no longer changes colors and becomes a blessing in disguise; its existence simply leads to the charting of a hitherto unfamiliar path to economic progress, and the resulting, economically more advanced society exhibits a profile that is "different" because of the survival of certain institutions, attitudes, etc., which were originally thought to be incompatible with development. These situations can be difficult to distinguish clearly from the preceding ones, for if the presumed obstacle has at all survived, then one can frequently show that it is not only tolerated, but actually lends strength to the new state of affairs. Nevertheless, there is a difference, at least initially, between an obstacle that is being turned or neutralized and one that turns out not to be an obstacle at all, but a factor that promotes and propels development.

The confusion on this score is due to the somewhat shapeless notion of "challenge." Any difficulty or obstacle can be transmuted by a sort of semantic hocus pocus into a challenge which evokes a response. But these Toynbeean terms are not helpful, for they dissolve the concepts of difficulty and obstacle altogether, instead of permitting the differentiated analysis we are aiming at here. To recall an example from our preceding section, it is incorrect to say that the existence of the extended family is a "challenge" to developers; it is rather a real troublemaker in some respects and some situations and a valuable asset in others, as we have shown. The notion of challenge is similarly ineffectual in the case, now under consideration, of obstacles which have no positive dimension, but which do not preclude development via some "alternate route" (alternate to the removal of the obstacle). Let us take a country which lacks an important natural resource such as coal or whose history has not permitted any sizeable "primitive accumulation of capital"; when such countries substitute hydroelectric energy for coal, or bank credit and state finance for private equity capital,[8] they are not "responding" to a "challenge." They are merely encountering a different way of achieving growth which, of course, they might never have discovered had they been more "normally" endowed. "Believe me," says the Marquise de Merteuil in Laclos' *Les Liaisons Dangereuses*, "one rarely acquires the qualities he can do without." Yet, to acquire these very qualities is less a matter of responding to a challenge than of

---

[8] Alexander Gerschenkron, *Economic Backwardness in Historical Perspective* (Cambridge, Mass., 1962), Chs. 1 and 2.

discovering one's comparative advantage. In doing so a country may not even have been aware of the fact that the lack of a certain natural resource, institution, or attitudinal endowment constituted a special difficulty, an obstacle, or much less, a "challenge."

If a country lacks one of the conventional "prerequisites," it can overcome this lack in two distinct ways. One consists in inventing its own substitute for the prerequisite; as just mentioned, Gerschenkron has given us an exceptionally rich and convincing account of such substitution processes for the Marxian prerequisite of primitive accumulation of capital. The other possibility is that the purported "prerequisite" turns out to be not only substitutable, but outright dispensable; nothing in particular needs to take its place, and we are simply proven wrong in our belief that a certain resource, institution, or attitude needed to be created or eradicated for development to be possible. In other words, the requirements of development turn out to be more tolerant of cultural and institutional variety than we thought on the basis of our limited prior experience. . . .

❂ ❂ ❂ ❂ ❂

III. OBSTACLES WHOSE ELIMINATION IS POSTPONABLE

We are now ready for those obstacles which we come closest to recognizing as such, those that refuse to turn mysteriously into assets or to be accommodated in an unexpected fashion within an economically progressive society. They stubbornly remain factors detrimental to development which ought to be eliminated. In many cases, however—and this is the point to the present section—the priority which this task commands can be shown to be less rigidly defined than had been thought.

I am returning here to a theme which I have set forth at length in my previous writings. I have drawn attention to "inverted" or "disorderly" or "cart-before-the-horse" sequences that are apt to occur in the process of economic and social development; and I have argued that, under certain circumstances, these sequences could be "efficient" in the sense of making possible the achievement of stated goals of economic expansion within a briefer time period or at a smaller social cost than would be possible if the more orderly sequence were adhered to.[9]

The implication of this approach for the notion of barrier and

---

[9] See, e.g., *The Strategy of Economic Development, op. cit.,* pp. 80–81, 93–94, 154–55; *Journeys Toward Progress: Studies of Economic Policy-Making in Latin America* (New York, 1963), p. 260.

obstacle is evident. While it grants that insufficient electric power, inadequate education, or the absence of agrarian reform are serious defects, it is suspicious of theories that erect the elimination of such defects into *prerequisites* for *any* forward movement; in addition to the head-on assault on these defects, it will evaluate, look for, and scrutinize ways in which the economy can be moved forward elsewhere and how thereby additional pressure can be brought to bear on the acknowledged obstacles. If they are truly hindrances, then any forward move that can be instigated in spite of them is going to make it even more imperative than before to get rid of them; if, on the other hand, this additional pressure is not generated, then perhaps these obstacles are not to be taken quite so seriously, and they belong, at least in part, in our second category (assumed obstacles that, as it turns out, can be accommodated into an economically progressive society).

✿   ✿   ✿   ✿   ✿

As the search for the conditions of economic development has been unremittingly pursued by social scientists over the past years, increasing attention has been given to the role of attitudes, beliefs, and basic personality characteristics favorable to the emergence of innovation, entrepreneurship, and the like. While these theories, with their expeditions into psychology and psychiatry, are frequently fascinating, the message they leave behind is almost as dismal as that of the very first theories of development which attributed a decisive role to such unalterable factors as race, climate, and natural resources. Rooted, as they are purported to be, in childhood experiences and transmitted unfailingly from one generation to the next, the deplored attitudes or personality structure appear to be similarly refractory to any but the most radical treatment.

✿   ✿   ✿   ✿   ✿

Fortunately, while the behavioral scientists have become depth psychologists, the psychologists have come up with the discovery that attitudinal change can be a *consequence* of behavioral change, rather than its precondition! From a variety of approaches exploring this nexus, I shall single out the *Theory of Cognitive Dissonance*, which was originated in 1957 by Leon Festinger in a book bearing that title. Since then the theory has been widely investigated, tested, and discussed; much of the empirical evidence which has been gathered, together with a chapter on the applicability of the theory to problems of social change, can be found in a volume by Jack W. Brehm and the late Arthur R. Cohen, *Explorations in Cognitive Dissonance* (New York, 1962).[10]

Briefly and in non-technical language, the theory states that a person who, for some reason, commits himself to act in a manner contrary to his beliefs, or to what he believes to be his beliefs, is in a state of dissonance. Such a state is unpleasant, and the person will attempt to reduce dissonance. Since the "discrepant behavior" has already taken place and cannot be undone, while the belief can be changed, reduction of dissonance can be achieved principally by changing one's beliefs in the direction of greater harmony with the action.

The theory thus predicts significant shifts in attitude consequent upon commitment to discrepant behavior, and its predictions have been verified empirically. . . .

. . . A . . . fruitful field of application of the theory may be the process of attitude change which is required in the course of economic development. The following quotations from the Brehm-Cohen volume are suggestive:

> The theory is different in its essential nature than most other theoretical models in psychology. Where the major concern in other theories has been largely with the guidance of behavior—that is, with what leads to a given behavior or commitment—dissonance theory deals, at least in part, with the *consequences* of a given behavior or commitment (p. 299).
>
> Dissonance theory attempts to understand the conditions under which behavioral commitments produce cognitive and attitudinal realignments in persons (p. 271).

In other words, dissonance theory deals with the possibility of replacing the "orderly" sequence, where attitude change is conceived as the prerequisite to behavioral change, by a "disorderly" one, where modern attitudes are acquired *ex-post*, as a consequence of the dissonance aroused by "modern" type of behavior which happens to be engaged in by people with non-modern attitudes. One question will, of course, be asked, namely: how can a commitment to "modern" behavior be obtained from people whose values and attitudes preclude in principle such behavior? Actually, however, this is not much of a problem among *late coming* societies surrounded by modernity and by opportunities to transgress into or try out modern behavior; at one time or another, it is likely that the latecomer will stumble more or less absent-mindedly into such behavior as pursuit of individual profit, entrepreneurial risk-taking, promotion according to merit, long-term planning, holding of demo-

---

[10] It should be pointed out that the theory is by no means universally accepted. For a highly critical appraisal, see N. P. Chapanis and A. Chapanis, "Cognitive Dissonance: Five Years Later," *Psychological Bulletin* (January 1964), 1–22.

cratic elections, etc.; dissonance will thus arise and will then gradually lead to those changes in attitude and basic beliefs which were thought to be prerequisites to the just-mentioned modes of behavior. The art of promoting development may therefore consist primarily in multiplying the opportunities to engage in these dissonance-arousing actions and in inducing an initial commitment to them.[11]

One observation will conclude this section. A country which achieves economic advance and modernization through the process just described, i.e., where behavioral change paces attitudinal change, is likely to exhibit a personality rather different from the country whose elite right at the outset of the development journey is imbued with the Protestant Ethic and saturated with achievement motivation. Because, in the case of the former country these motivations are being laboriously acquired *ex-post* and en route, its path will be more halting and circuitous and its typical personality may well be subject to particularly strong tension between traditional and modern values.[12] While a country can well develop without being endowed at the outset with all the "right" values and attitudes, its development profile and experience cannot but bear the marks of the order and manner in which it accomplishes its various tasks.

◦〰◦

[11] If one were to extend the above-mentioned "refinement" of the theory to the development context, one would conclude that the conditioning of foreign aid on internal reform can do positive harm at the stage when an underdeveloped country is about to commit itself to new types of "modern" or reform actions; to reward such perhaps partly dissonant behavior would lead to less cumulative change than if the behavior could not be dismissed by the actors as something they did just to get hold of the aid funds. In this way, the theory throws some light on the difficulties of using aid as a means of promoting internal reform which have beset the Alliance for Progress since its inception. Besides many other constructive uses, foreign aid may be helpful in promoting reform and will serve as a reinforcing agent when it is conceived and presented as a means of reducing the cost of a reform to which the policy-makers in the recipient country are already firmly committed; but it is cast in a self-defeating role if it is proffered as a *quid pro quo* for the reform commitment itself.

[12] In *Journeys Toward Progress, op. cit.*, pp. 235 ff., I have drawn a related difference by distinguishing between societies which, in the process of tackling their problems, let motivation to solve problems outrun their understanding, and those that do not usually tackle problems unless the means to solve them are close at hand. Here also the two styles of problem-solving are shown to result in sharply differing development experiences.

international relations

Despite their limited industrial and military capacities, the developing states have had a profound impact on international affairs since the end of World War II. Not only have there been the organizational consequences for the world community resulting from the emergence of new states that have more than doubled the number of actors; much more basic have been the new directions in international politics stemming from the demands and aspirations of the developing states. No longer is the course of world history determined solely by the decisions of a few European and American powers, with the nations of Asia and Africa the pawns in the struggle for supremacy. Instead, the new states in these areas, as well as the older ones in Latin America, are vigorously participating in the decisions of the international community.

The principal goals that shape the foreign policies of the developing states are also those of the more advanced states: (1) the maintenance of political independence, (2) protection against aggression, (3) advantageous political, economic, and cultural relations with other states, (4) the respect of other states, and (5) the ability to influence the foreign policies of other states. The differing perceptions of these goals by the developing states and the more advanced ones arise from their different histories, internal conditions, and relative capacity to exert power and influence in the world community.

For many developing states, the effects of—and reaction to—the recently concluded period of colonialism are fundamental factors influencing their relations with other states. During the period of colonialism, trade patterns developed that are not easily modified. Ambiguous political relationships reflect the often bitter controversy leading to independence, the search for new allies, and the consequences of two major divisions in the world: the one economic, separating the rich from the poor states, and the other political, dividing the world along ideological lines. In addition, the foreign policies of the developing states are, of course, affected by their internal economic and political characteristics: an underdeveloped economy, a fragmented social structure, limited intellectual resources, and, in many cases, unstable political institutions and processes.

Since the developing states were dominated politically and economically by the major powers for so long, it is not surprising to find great emphasis on the development of policies that properly reflect the newly secured freedom to decide their own destinies. Leaders often appear obsessed with the need to demonstrate their independence. Many feel compelled constantly to remind the major powers that they no longer rule the world but must now treat the developing states as equals. The fear of new forms of political and economic imperialism is often reflected in the statements of these leaders. Warnings are issued to the major powers not to interfere in the internal affairs of the developing states, and in speeches to their followers, exhortations to watchfulness against this interference are frequently voiced. At the same time, there is usually a recognition of the benefits to be derived from the maintenance of close relations with both the former colonial powers and the other major nations. The result of these mixed feelings is, frequently, a rather schizophrenic attitude toward the major powers. On the one hand, there is widespread admiration for the economic and technological accomplishments of the advanced states. On the other hand, however, there is a feeling that these accomplishments were in large part the result of colonial policies that exploited the underdeveloped world, and that the major powers are not above future attempts to dominate the developing societies.

To protect their independence individually and collectively and at the same time profit from their participation in the international community, the developing states have sought to play active roles in the United Nations. In addition, a number of regional political and economic organizations have been created, and a wide variety of bilateral defense and economic agreements have been negotiated, both between the developing states themselves, and between a developing state and one of the major powers. Finally, unilateral pronouncements of policy also attempt to define the position of individual states on major issues.

A strong feeling of regional solidarity is evident in several of the developing areas. It is most noticeable, and has taken the most concrete forms, in Latin America and sub-Saharan Africa; it is somewhat less apparent in the Middle East (except in the spirit of opposition to Israel), and is least evident in Asia. Despite the many ethnic, cultural, and economic divisions within each of these areas, and despite the nationalism of the individual states, the bond provided by a common race, religion, or history has supported a number of attempts to promote regional cooperation within these areas.

The idea of eventual political unification of the Latin American states has existed ever since independence was achieved early in the nineteenth century. Although the realization of this objective seems remote, the Latin American states have established—in some cases with the participation of the United States—several regional institutions that enable joint action to be undertaken. The Pan-American Union, created late in the nineteenth century, and the Organization of American States, established in 1948, are the most inclusive organizations, designed to promote understanding and action on common problems. However, many Latin Americans regard these organizations as of limited utility today for purposes of regional cooperation. The feeling is widespread that the United States dominates these organizations to its own advantage, with little regard for the revolutionary changes occurring in Latin America. A mutual defense pact, the Treaty of Rio, was signed in 1947, providing for joint consideration of military threats to the hemisphere.

More significant efforts in regional cooperation have occurred in the economic field. Although many of the Latin Americans believe that the United States has until recently neglected their economic needs, the Alliance for Progress program, initiated in 1961, proposes to provide twenty billion dollars to the Latin American states over a ten-year period, with the United States supplying the larger share of the total. In addition, the Inter-American Development Bank was created in 1959 with a capital of one billion dollars to provide loans to the Latin American states. Not involving direct United States participation is the Latin American Free Trade Area, established in 1960 with the signing of the Treaty of Montevideo. Patterned after the European Common Market, the Latin American Free Trade Association now includes Argentina, Brazil, Chile, Uruguay, Paraguay, Peru, Mexico, Colombia, Ecuador, Bolivia, and Venezuela. The Treaty provides a twelve-year time span within which to complete the establishment of a duty-free trade zone among the signatory states, though no provision is made for a common protective barrier against the outside world. However, substantial difficulties have been encountered in reaching agreements on tariff reductions, and the Association has been only partially successful in attaining its goals. The five Central American states established their own Central American Common Market in 1962, which provides for both a reduction of trade barriers among themselves and a common tariff wall to the outside world. Within this Common Market, trade has quadrupled in five years. At the same time the Market was established, a Central American Development Bank, partly financed by the United States, was created.

What promises to be the most far-reaching agreement among the

Latin American states, however, is the "Declaration of the Presidents of America," agreed upon, except for Ecuador, at the Punte del Este Conference early in 1967. The Presidents pledged, with assistance from the United States, to create a comprehensive Latin American common market, beginning in 1970, to develop multinational road, railroad, and communications systems, to increase Latin America's share of international trade, and to limit military expenditures to essential defense requirements. Whether this bold declaration will in fact initiate a new phase in the history of Latin American economic development cannot as yet be determined.

At present, trade among the Latin American states is relatively limited, mainly because they are still principally producers of raw materials, with only a limited industrial capacity to provide the manufactured goods they need. The attempts to create common markets in Latin America reflect not only the advantages believed to exist in expanding the markets for the new industries in this area, however, but also the growing threat to the exports of the Latin American states to the European Common Market countries. Since the former colonies of France in Africa (and if Britain joins the Common Market, presumably for their former colonies) enjoy preferential treatment in the European Common Market, the Latin American states will have increasing difficulty in competing with the African exports of the same products. The Latin American common markets are also designed to decrease dependence on American manufactured goods by protecting and encouraging the growth of domestic industries. At the same time, however, the United States remains a major trading partner of most Latin American states. Fears continue to be expressed by many Latin Americans concerning the economic power of the United States over their economies. They fear the significant ability of the United States to determine the export prices of their commodities, and the economic and political consequences of the high level of United States investment in Latin American industries.

The Pan-African and Pan-Arab movements differ from each other as well as from the Pan-American movement. There are, in addition, several variations of the Pan-African movement itself. In one form, of little importance today, the term is used to denote the attempt to unite Negroes throughout the world in a struggle to destroy the derogatory image of Africans and Negroes. In another, more important version, the term is used to indicate those attempts to organize the states and peoples in sub-Saharan Africa. In still another form, one which has been given concrete expression in the Organization of African Unity, the term designates the movement to organize the African continent, including the northern, Mediterranean states.

The promotion of unification movements among the African people, whether on the basis of the Negro groups alone or on a continental basis.

has a long history. Even before independence was achieved, a number of conferences had been held in which ideas concerning unification were discussed, despite the fact that in the precolonial period there had never been widespread unity among the people on the continent. Initially, the objectives of the Negro leaders, many of whom lived in Europe and the United States, were the termination of racial discrimination by the European colonial powers, economic advancement for the Negro populations, and eventually political independence for the African societies. Once independence was achieved after World War II, the problem of unifying a large number of diverse states arose. Although the racial appeal of Pan-Africanism has had a strong emotional attraction, a number of factors have inhibited the emergence of a United States of Africa, the goal of some leaders (in particular Kwame Nkrumah, the former president of Ghana). The checkerboard division of Africa by the European powers, especially in West Africa, and the development of complex networks of economic, social, and political relationships between the colonial powers and their possessions have left the African states with relatively few substantive links with each other except for those of race. The individual economies are not particularly interdependent; they are more often competitive for world markets and are still quite closely linked with the former colonial powers. Competition for scarce development capital, urgently needed throughout all of Africa, also divides the states. Further, as noted earlier, the states that are relatively well developed have been reluctant to unite with less developed ones. In addition, strong leaders of individual states, capable of cooperation as equals, are not readily induced to yield their power and assume subordinate roles in a larger community. Finally, the nationalism within each state has inhibited unifying movements. Despite the emotional identification of Africans of all states with each other on the basis of race, the emotional attachment of politically conscious Africans to their individual states is strong and, it seems, often growing stronger. The longer unifying movements are delayed and individual governments successfully meet the minimum requirements of their people, the less likely political unity of a continental, or subcontinental, scope will occur.

Nevertheless, cooperative movements providing for less than full political unification have been initiated. The outstanding achievement has been the creation of the Organization of African Unity, established in 1963. This Organization brought together within one body several more limited organizations that had previously existed. The OAU has been instrumental in channeling the vigorous opposition of the African states to the Union of South Africa and to Portugal, which has no intention of granting independence to its African colonies. In addition, a wide variety of common problems have been considered by the Organization's several organs and commissions. In the economic field, limited economic cooperation has been achieved among fourteen signatories to the Charter establishing the Afro-Malagasy Organization of Economic Cooperation, first established in 1961 and reorganized in 1964. Although proposals for an African common market have been advanced, no agreement has been achieved on its establishment. Several limited customs unions have been created, though without notable success.

Less successful than the recent attempts to organize the African states have been the longer efforts to institutionalize the Pan-Arab or Pan-Islamic movements. Although the memory of Arab unity before the era of European domination exerts a strong appeal, deep divisions among the Arab leaders have prevented the Arab League, founded in 1945, from being an effective organization for promoting either common policies (even in opposition to Israel) or the creation of a united Arab state. The Pan-Islamic movement is even less organized, though the Islamic religion supplies a loose unifying element throughout much of the Middle East and Asia.

Although broad Asian cooperation has been supported by a number of leaders, the relatively greater national self-identity of the individual Asian states and several bitter disputes among them have not encouraged Pan-Asian unity movements. Before World War II, several conferences of Asian leaders were held, as among African leaders, to demand independence for the Asian states and to promote regional cooperation. Anticolonialism has been the principal issue on which agreement can be attained, however. Further cooperation is inhibited by a number of factors. A deep ideological division separates the communist states, led by Communist China, from the noncommunist nations. Religious and other issues, such as control of Kashmir, divide India and Pakistan, and boundary disputes continue between India and China. Sukarno's opposition to Malaysia led to military clashes, although relations between Indonesia and Malaysia improved after Sukarno lost his control of policy. Asian leaders are also divided over the United States involvement in Vietnam. In addition, while many leaders regard the economic strength of Japan as a threat to the economic development of their states, they have not been able to establish common policies to meet the Japanese challenge. These factors, among others, effectively override the emotional identification of Asians as a unified group.

The most significant effort to develop cooperation among the Asian states occurred at the Bandung Conference in 1955, attended by representatives of twenty-nine Asian and African states. However, the deep divisions among the delegates were clearly evident. Little agreement could be reached among the three groups of states—the pro-Western, the communist, and the neutralist—except on issues of independence for the European colonies and the desirability of peace. A "second Bandung" conference was scheduled to be held in Algeria in 1965, but it failed to materialize because of the bitter controversies among the Asian and

African leaders. No permanent organizational structures were created at the Bandung Conference to provide a medium for continual consultation or the development of common political policy, nor has any other organization been established. Economic cooperation has, however, been achieved on a limited basis, primarily through the Colombo Plan, first negotiated in 1950 and extended in 1964 through 1971. Twenty-two states have agreed to aid each other, largely through the exchange of experts and the training of students in order to increase the supply and efficient utilization of skilled personnel.

To aid the development of their economies, almost all developing countries have vigorously sought the financial and technological aid (provided either directly or through international organizations) of the more advanced states. Many billions of dollars have been made available to the developing states through grants and loans by the United States, Great Britain, France, and the Soviet Union, with smaller amounts from other European and non-European states such as Communist China and Australia. Further, private investments by American and European firms have added vast amounts to the funds extended through official government aid programs. Nevertheless, the developing states face a chronic shortage of capital, and severe competition exists for that aid which is available.

In addition to seeking financial support, most developing states have eagerly participated in technical aid programs. Many of these programs are conducted by the United Nations, while others are sponsored by individual states, such as the United States Peace Corps. Large numbers of students from the developing states have been sent to schools in the United States, Europe, and the Soviet Union for advanced training.

Not surprisingly, the states that extend aid have developed their assistance programs largely on the basis of political considerations. Both the competition for aid and the development of foreign aid programs have inevitably become involved in the ideological struggle between the communist and noncommunist states. The struggle for power and influence between the two major blocs has led many of the developing states to seek a third course that will enable them to play an active role in world affairs and yet avoid permanent alignments with either of the major blocs. Nonalignment has become the guiding principle of the foreign policies of most Asian and African states. At meetings in Belgrade in 1961 and in Cairo in 1964, the nonaligned states attempted to define their position and bring their collective persuasive power to bear on the major issues confronting the world. However, the nonaligned states have been divided on the interpretation of nonalignment. Some believe that the nonaligned states should create an organized third force; for others, any organization destroys the concept and utility of nonalignment. A few leaders have eagerly sought to play the role of mediator in major power disputes, while others have not been so inclined. In general, the nonaligned states have sought to reduce the tensions of the Cold War while remaining outside the orbit of either bloc.

The United Nations provides a major forum in which the developing states have sought to influence the decisions of the international community. The admission of the many new states in Asia and Africa has had a profound effect on that organization. In 1945, when the United Nations was established, the Western powers still governed the world, and the decisions of the United Nations reflected their dominant position. Now, however, the developing states control about three quarters of the votes in the General Assembly, and the decisions of that organ, as well as other agencies of the United Nations, reflect the interests and concerns of the developing nations as well as of the major powers. In particular, the issues of colonialism, racial discrimination, funds for economic development, and nuclear weapons have been emphasized by the developing nations. They have sought to develop common positions on these and other issues considered in the United Nations; caucusing groups have been established by the African and Asian states to provide the organizational framework for this purpose. A high level of agreement has often been achieved by these groups, along with the Latin American states, on problems of development. On major Cold War issues, however, they have not been able to attain such a degree of consensus.

For the developing states, the United Nations offers many advantages. As relatively weak states, they have frequently turned to the United Nations for protection. Further, the United Nations provides an arena in which through common policies these states may enhance their individually weak influence on world problems. The economic and social projects undertaken under United Nations auspices provide them with considerable aid in developing their societies. Finally, through their membership, they achieve the psychologically satisfying opportunity to participate directly with the major powers in the consideration of important issues. For these and other reasons, such as the relatively limited cost of maintaining relations with many states without the need for individual diplomatic posts, almost all of the developing states are firmly committed to the support of the United Nations.

SUGGESTED READINGS

Black, Joseph E., and Thompson, Kenneth W., eds., *Foreign Policies in a World of Change.* New York, Harper & Row, 1963.

Brzezinski, Zbigniew, ed., *Africa and the Communist World.* Stanford, Calif., Published for the Hoover Institution on War, Revolution, and Peace by Stanford University Press, 1963.

Goldschmidt, Walter, *The United States and Africa*, rev. ed. New York, Frederick A. Praeger, Inc., 1963.

Gordon, Bernard K., *The Dimensions of Conflict in Southeast Asia.* Englewood Cliffs, N. J., Prentice-Hall, Inc., 1966.

Hinton, Harold C., *Communist China in World Politics.* Boston, Houghton Mifflin Company, 1966.

Hovet, Thomas, *Africa in the United Nations.* Evanston, Ill., Northwestern University Press, 1963.

———, *Bloc Politics in the United Nations.* Cambridge, Mass., Harvard University Press, 1960.

Kahin, George McT., *The Asian-African Conference, Bandung, Indonesia, April 1955.* Ithaca, N. Y., Cornell University Press, 1956.

Kerr, Malcolm, *The Arab Cold War 1958–1964.* New York, Oxford University Press, 1965.

Legum, Colin, *Pan-Africanism*, rev. ed. New York, Frederick A. Praeger, Inc., 1965.

London, Kurt, ed., *New Nations in a Divided World.* New York, Frederick A. Praeger, Inc., 1963.

Macdonald, Robert W., *The League of Arab States: A Study in the Dynamics of Regional Organization.* Princeton, N. J., Princeton University Press, 1965.

Martin, Laurence W., ed., *Neutralism and Nonalignment.* New York, Frederick A. Praeger, Inc., 1962.

McKay, Vernon, ed., *African Diplomacy.* New York, Frederick A. Praeger, Inc., 1966.

Mecham, J. Lloyd, *A Survey of United States–Latin American Relations.* Boston, Houghton Mifflin Company, 1965.

41. *ASIAN NONALIGNMENT*[*]

s i s i r k. g u p t a

The concept of nonalignment originated in Asia. It was in Asia that it struggled against heavy odds to survive, and it is in Asia, again, that

[*] From "Asian Nonalignment" by Sisir K. Gupta, *Nonalignment in Foreign Affairs, The Annals*, Vol. 362 (November, 1965), pp. 45–51. By permission of the publisher and the author.

new challenges to nonalignment are becoming sharply manifest. The adherence of a large number of Arab and African countries to a policy of nonalignment has strengthened the concept and lent new meaning to it. The respectability which nonalignment has gradually achieved is largely a result of African and Arab support of it. Asian nonaligned countries alone would not have been able to make the doctrine acceptable. But none can deny the special contribution made by Asian countries in the evolution of the concept, in practicing nonaligned policies, and in withstanding pressures to align themselves with one power bloc or the other.

IRRELEVANCE OF EUROPEAN CONFLICTS

Asia is vitally linked with Europe, and there has always existed a valid geopolitical concept of the Eurasian land mass. Inter-European power conflicts had often tended to engulf Asia. Many of Europe's battles were fought on Asian soil. While West Asia has tended to be directly involved in nearly all European conflicts in modern history, southern and eastern Asia have also been considered vital in the outcome of power struggles within Europe. This involvement of Asia in European struggles might have been inevitable, even if the Asian continent had been free from Western dominance, but because of Western dominance in Asia, its involvement in European conflicts was passive, and the terms of its involvement were dictated by the colonial powers. This unequal relationship, entailing a subsidiary role for Asia in European quarrels, induced Asian nationalist movements to assert that inter-European controversies were largely irrelevant for them. If Asia were free, it would escape such involvement, at least in the way its participation was forced by European powers. Desire for noninvolvement in irrelevant political contests paved the way for subsequent emergence of the doctrine of nonalignment.

All sections of the Asian nationalist elites did not regard every European political conflict as irrelevant for their future. Western-educated and Western-oriented elites took great interest in European affairs and were emotionally involved in them, particularly during the 1930's, when great political issues were being debated in Europe. In the case of fascism, for example, one section of the nationalist leadership of India, led by Jawaharlal Nehru, felt the need for fighting this new menace as strongly as anyone in Europe. . . . [T]he new nations of Asia had two immediate foreign-policy objectives to achieve after independence: (1) focusing attention on non-European, particularly Asian, problems and (2) readjusting relations between Asia and Europe. It was evident to Asian nationalists that, with their enormous problems of underdevelopment and overpopulation, of social tensions and political instability, of upheavals and uncertainties arising out of the process of ending centuries-old stagnation, Asia was bound to attract the attention of the world. The old tendency to regard European problems as world problems was now out-of-date. Asia needed attention, and Asian countries were bound to become more influential factors in world politics, but only if they could prevent Asian embroilment in the Cold War and the conversion of their regional problems into issues of inter-European relations. Nehru told the United Nations General Assembly on November 3, 1958:

> May I say that we are equally interested in the solution of European problems; but may I also say that the world is something bigger than Europe, and you will not solve your problems by thinking that the problems of the world are mainly European problems. There are vast tracts of the world which may not in the past, for a few generations, have taken much part in world affairs. But they are awake; their people are moving and they have no intention whatever of being ignored or of being passed by.[1]

The other important foreign-policy task before the new nations of Asia was to readjust their relations with Europe, particularly with the erstwhile ruling powers. It was not easy to determine the best possible manner of this readjustment. On the one hand, there were the declared Asian political goal of "complete independence" and the accumulated distrust and resentment of the former European rulers. On the other hand, there were also vital economic and cultural links with Europe which it was not easy to sever. . . .

The concept of nonalignment was the answer to this complex problem of redetermining Asian relations with the West. Complete political independence, and a refusal to maintain any political or military link with the West, became necessary if only because in many other fields links had inevitably to be maintained and, in fact, promoted. The simple truth, as it appears in retrospect, is that nonalignment initially was a method of determining free Asia's relations with the West.

HIDDEN DIFFERENCES

This posture toward the West constituted the fundamental element of commonness in the attitudes of Asian nonaligned countries. On other problems of foreign relations, the new nonaligned Asian nations did not have a common outlook. At least, divergent nuances and emphases in foreign policy were evident among these states. In cases such as India, there was, perhaps, an unorthodox attitude toward power and power politics, accompanied by an emphasis on peace achieved by friendly

[1] Jawaharlal Nehru, *India's Foreign Policy: Selected Speeches, Sept. 1946–April 1961* (New Delhi: Publications Division, Government of India, 1961), p. 163.

relations, as distinct from peace founded upon balance of power. This unusual Indian attitude sprang partly from the traditional values of the Indian society and partly from the experiences of the national struggle. In other cases, like Indonesia, the attitude to power was less unorthodox; there was an obvious desire by the leaders to play a power role in the Asian context.

On the issue of communism in Asia, some nonaligned countries, like Burma, were more distrustful of the Communist bloc than were countries like India and Indonesia. In 1954–1955, Burma and Ceylon were openly critical of Communist powers and wanted nonalignment to develop a negative orientation toward the Communist bloc. At this stage, India and Indonesia regarded such a development as unnecessary. Nonalignment, it must be remembered, was only one aspect of the foreign policies pursued by its adherents; each nonaligned state in Asia had other distinct foreign-policy objectives in the context of the particular region to which it belonged. For many nonaligned countries, the doctrine facilitated pursuit of certain positive foreign-policy goals. In West Asia, for the United Arab Republic, for example, Arab nonalignment paved the ground for Pan-Arab unity. For Indonesia, nonalignment was relevant only if it helped restructure Southeast Asia, with a new and distinctive position for the Indonesian nation. As in other areas of the world, in Asia also a broad division existed between nonaligned nations favoring the *status quo* and those opposing the *status quo*, those content with their borders and those committed to border readjustments.

In the early postwar period, these fundamental differences among nonaligned Asian nations tended to be submerged, because the challenge to their common doctrine came from the West, toward which they had an identical posture. Even as some of the Asian countries were attracted to an emergent form of nonalignment, the Cold War entered Asia. The rise of a Communist regime in China, the war in Korea, and the crisis in Indo-China together made Asia a focal point of conflict between the two power blocs. To the leaders of the United States particularly, it seemed natural that countries recently attaining their freedom should contribute their share in what Americans regarded as the global struggle for the "freedom" of all peoples and nations. To Western strategists, it became vitally important to build a defense barrier around the Communist bloc in Asia. Perhaps because the United States was not itself a major colonial power, it underestimated the strength of anticolonial and anti-Western sentiment in Asia. And when Asian nonaligned nations refused to participate in Western pacts, they were branded as immoral. This American onslaught on nonalignment deferred Asian debates on the meaning of the concept and postponed exposure of the inherent contradictions and differences within the camp of the Asian nonaligned.

The Communist response sought to exploit the clash that developed between Western and Asian diplomatic strategies. In the beginning, Communist countries were surprisingly unaware of the strength of nationalism in Asia; Marxists persisted in applying their oversimplified class structures and formulations to the Asian situation. Communists discovered certain potentialities in nonalignment only after a crisis erupted in nonaligned Asia's relations with the West. Interestingly enough, it was the Chinese who first saw this new opening for successful Communist foreign-policy moves. But shortly afterward, the Soviet Union not only adopted a policy of more harmonious relations with nonaligned Asian countries; in time, it developed a more stable and friendly attitude toward them than Communist China.

CONFLICTING ATTITUDES

With the gradual acceptance of nonalignment by the leading Western countries on the one hand and the Soviet Union on the other, latent differences among the nonaligned countries of Asia began to be manifest. The process of acceptance of nonalignment as a valid foreign policy was accompanied, and indeed generated, by gradual realization of the dangers of Soviet-American confrontation and the resulting need for at least limited Soviet-American *rapprochement*. Paradoxically, this development—signifying achievement of a major objective of nonaligned policies—also marked the emergence of new problems and difficulties among the nonaligned nations themselves. Some Asian countries, like India, not only welcomed the Soviet-American *rapprochement* and urged acceleration of the process; in a way, they became the symbol and beneficiary of this process. Gradually, India became an area of substantial agreement between the United States and the Soviet Union; because of this fact, it attained an enhanced international status, without any obvious addition to its strength or power. From the point of view of both countries, India appeared to be accorded a special position in the Asian scheme of things. But inherent in India's new status was the problem of relationships between India and other nonaligned nations. Gradually, this found reflection in two sharply differing attitudes among the nonaligned states toward the questions of peaceful coexistence, of war and peace, and of the roles of the United States and the Soviet Union.

President Sukarno of Indonesia views the world as currently divided between the old established forces and the new emergent forces. The Soviet-American contest or ideological conflicts among the great powers possess no particular relevance for this larger and deeper conflict. Speaking at the Belgrade Conference of the Nonaligned Countries in 1961, President Sukarno said:

Prevailing world opinion today would have us believe that the real source of international tension and strife is ideological conflict between the great powers. I think that is not true. There is a conflict which cuts deeper into the flesh of man, and that is the conflict between the new emergent forces for freedom and justice and the old forces of domination, the one pushing its head relentlessly through the crust of the earth which has given it its lifeblood, the other striving desperately to retain all it can trying to hold back the course of history. We in Indonesia firmly believe that the ideological conflict is not, I repeat, is not a problem which affects the majority of mankind, such as poverty, disease, illiteracy and colonial bondage.[2]

✧ ✧ ✧ ✧ ✧

THE CHINA PROBLEM

Ideological differences among the nonaligned countries of Asia, particularly between the two largest—India and Indonesia—would, perhaps, be of little significance if they also did not reflect a radically altered pattern of Asian politics. The unstated, but crucial, element in this controversy is the attitude of each nation toward China and the Chinese global outlook. China has successfully struggled for the disintegration of the existing cold-war blocs and the emergence of a multipolar world; in Asia today, China is capable of making power thrusts without concerning itself with Communist-bloc discipline, and China's sympathy or antipathy toward other nations has vital consequences for Asia. What is more, China aspires for a restructuring of world politics which will accord her the status of one of the three superpowers. As a prerequisite for this, it is necessary for China to mobilize the support of Asia (and, if possible, Africa and Latin America) behind the concept of the division of the world between the rich and the poor, the colored and the white—a division putting the United States and the Soviet Union on one side and automatically making China the leader of the other side of the world. China's determination to alter the *status quo* makes her impatient with those nonaligned nations which do not endorse Chinese conceptions of the task before Asian and African countries. China's policy endears her to those countries which also want modifications of the *status quo* on a limited scale in their regions. In China's scheme of things, nonalignment as such is not of any relevance; what is relevant is the equidistance of the nonaligned nations as a whole from the two great powers. India's policy of nonalignment—with its emphasis on close and cordial relations with the two superpowers, on "equi-adjacence" to them—appears to

[2] *The Conference of Heads of State or Government of Nonaligned Countries* (Belgrade: Publicistics-Izdavacki Zavod, 1961), pp. 27–28.

China as, in fact, a policy of double alignment, amounting to betrayal of the Afro-Asian task of an intensified struggle against the developed and prosperous half of the world.

The major problem confronting Asian nonaligned states in regard to China, therefore, arises out of the fact that, in contrast to the Soviet Union and the United States, this new great power makes more demands upon Asian countries. Unlike the Soviet Union and the United States, it is prepared to use its power to express its displeasure with the policies of fellow Asian nations. Its antipathy for nonalignment is less benign, and its sympathy for nonalignment is more directly meaningful, as it seeks to achieve goals at the expense of other Asian countries. If the controversy between India and China, for example, regarding the importance of peaceful international co-operation for the solution of the problems facing the less developed societies, were confined to ideological polemics alone, India's nonalignment would confront a different kind of challenge. Unfortunately, this controversy has taken the form of a physical confrontation—military, political, and even economic. India's unorthodox attitude toward power and power politics has been shaken, leading her to pay greater attention to power controversies and to search for a new balance of power in Asia.

THE CHANGED CONTEXT

So long as inter-Asian problems were attributable to inter-European conflicts, nonalignment remained a relevant and viable policy. For, even as many conflicts in Asia originated in the West, their solution in power terms would also be achieved there. Asian nonalignment not only facilitated solution of such conflicts; it enabled adherents of the doctrine to play the role of the mediator in clashes between the two blocs. Yet the emergence of China as an independent power factor in Asia makes it incumbent on other Asian countries to think of a new Asian power balance. While nonalignment in regard to Soviet-American controversies is still variable, nonalignment in relation to China is becoming increasingly difficult to practice.

As in Europe, a distinction must be made between the smaller Asian countries which may well decide to remain outside the power contests and larger Asian countries which do not propose to do so. It is not yet clear which among the smaller countries of Asia will be able, like Switzerland, to gain acceptance for its neutrality, although several may attempt to do so. As emphasized earlier, China's demands upon fellow Asian countries are high, and, like China, other new centers of power in Asia may also become less tolerant toward the claim of neutrality by small states in Asia. In fact, the hope of the smaller Asian countries to remain neutral in inter-Asian conflicts will depend on the viability of the Asian balance of power.

Even now, a smaller Asian country, which directly or indirectly faces China's power threat, may make improvisations in its policy of nonalignment. These moves, without being unsuited to Chinese convenience, may retain for the country concerned a degree of freedom of action. . . .

For other Asian countries which, because of their size and power potential or because of their policy inclinations, aspire to play a power role in Asia, it is becoming imperative to develop a new Asian power balance. Thus, a country like Indonesia (while remaining nonaligned in regard to the Soviet Union and the United States) may envisage a power alliance with China to achieve its objective of restructuring the map of the Malayan region of Southeast Asia. Similarly, India, without altering its policy of nonalignment toward the major power confrontation of the world—the contest between the United States and the Soviet Union—may draw closer to like-minded countries in Asia, interested in guarding their present frontiers and preventing a forcible disturbance of the *status quo* in Asia. In the new situation, the possible role of Japan has recently been emphasized in India. It will be surprising if India's approach to nonalignment in the global conflict is not supplemented in the coming years by a policy of seeking a partnership with Japan to insure a stable peace and progress through international co-operation.

For the powers outside Asia, the relevance of Asian nonalignment in this new context is that it aspires to build a stable power balance in the Far East. While the great powers may play some role in sustaining a new Asian power balance, their role will be marginal. The task of building an effective Asian security system must be undertaken primarily by the Asian countries themselves. It is in this task that nonalignment remains a meaningful policy, even for the large and medium countries of Asia. . . .

42. THE "LATIN-AMERICAN BLOC" IN THE UNITED NATIONS*

w i l l i a m   g.   c o r n e l i u s

Much has been heard in the postwar years about "Hemispheric Solidarity." In popular belief, this concept not only has concerned matters of security for the Western Hemisphere but frequently has been extended to cover practically all of the international relations of the American states. Particularly, there has been the widespread assumption that the Latin-American states form a bloc in the United Nations—and, incidentally, a bloc of twenty votes in the pocket of the United States.

It is unlikely that the scholar or even the thoughtful layman would accept this assumption without first looking at the record. There he probably would seek the answers to such questions as: Is there a Latin-American bloc of twenty Members which invariably or usually votes with the United States? If not, to what extent does a Latin-American bloc or distinguishable smaller groups of these states exist?

In an effort to find answers to these questions and to others suggested by these, the present writer examined the complete record of proceedings for the first ten years in all United Nations bodies. . . .[1]

*   *   *   *   *

An examination of the record has readily revealed two facts. First, there was no bloc of twenty Latin-American members always or even usually to be found in the camp of the United States, notwithstanding the pressures of "Hemispheric Solidarity." Second, there was no solid

*   From "The 'Latin-American Bloc' in the United Nations" by William G. Cornelius, *Journal of Inter-American Studies*, III, No. 3 (July, 1961), 419–435. Reprinted by permission of the *Journal of Inter-American Studies*.
[1]   A check of the voting in recent years indicated that Latin-American voting patterns became sufficiently crystallized during the first ten years to justify basing an analysis on that period. For a general account of the role of the Latin-American states in the United Nations see John A. Houston, *Latin America in the United Nations*, (N. Y.: Carnegie Endowment for International Peace, 1956).

bloc of Latin-American states that loomed up in any of the three recognized positions—"for," "against," or "abstaining"—whenever a decision was made in the United Nations. In fact, not often did all twenty of these members participate, and rarely did all of the participating ones vote together.

It should be acknowledged, though, that some situations and some subjects produced a high degree of solidarity among the Latin-American states and, occasionally, of cohesion with the United States. Elections in the General Assembly provide illustration of Latin-American solidarity. Since elections are conducted by secret ballot, no conclusion regarding them can be established through the record. However, according to the general concession of delegates interviewed, these twenty states usually voted together whenever one of their number or a Latin-American individual was considered for election to a body or an office. As one delegate expressed it, they allocated among themselves the elective spots available to Latin America and then voted together in order to make sure of getting them.[2] Another delegate called attention to exceptions to this practice. He pointed out that there had been less solidarity in the election of individuals than of states. . . .

On matters that involved "security" considerations in the cold war, nearly all, if not all, of the Latin-American Members voted together and with the United States. This cohesion was tightest when the issue between the United States and the Soviet Union was sharpest and clearest; it was looser when such an issue was less clearly defined; and it became increasingly unsure as the apparent or alleged danger to the national security of the Latin-American states became more remote. . . .

. . . Latin America was divided in early phases of the consideration of international aspects of the Chinese Communist revolution; but when the issue became acute, especially after the outbreak of the Korean War in 1950, Latin America stood firmly with the United States in the Security Council and somewhat less firmly in the General Assembly. Nevertheless, a few Latin-American states did not support censure of the Soviet Union for allegedly prodding or abetting China in the Korean struggle. Moreover, there was no Latin-American consensus whatever on the closely-related question of the admission of Red China to the United Nations—specifically, of establishing general criteria for accrediting one delegation in preference to another to sit in the United Nations as a Member.[3]

✧   ✧   ✧   ✧   ✧

[2] Personal interview with the permanent representative of a Latin-American state to the United Nations, United Nations Headquarters, New York, Nov. 23, 1954. For obvious reasons, it is necessary that the delegates interviewed in the course of this investigation remain anonymous.

[3] U.N. General Assembly, Fifth Session, *Ad Hoc* Political Committee, *Official Records*, 60th Meeting (Nov. 28, 1950), pp. 388–89.

When an issue in the category of threats to international peace and security involved a dependent people, Latin America and the United States usually stood together in support of these peoples; but particular Latin-American states expressed stronger sympathy for the struggles of dependent peoples than other Latin-American Members or the United States. For example, Colombia and Cuba supported more positive action by the Security Council in behalf of the Indonesians than did Brazil, Argentina or the United States.[4]

At times, Latin-American Members had to choose between "security" considerations and principles historically professed by them. For instance, while a Latin-American state (Chile) initiated the challenge before the Security Council against the Communist *coup* in Czechoslovakia, the two Latin-American members of the Council (Argentina and Colombia) opposed conceding to the United States and the other Big Powers the prerogative of determining what was procedural and what was substantive among the questions on the issue. Their position was that such a concession would violate the principle of equality of states— the equality of Members in the United Nations.[5] Moreover, even in the handling of the Korean War, Latin-American groups of varying size expressed preference for pacific settlement of disputes, economic aid through international organizations and universality of membership in the United Nations. They indicated their position by abstaining from voting rather than opposing these principles as offered in Soviet bloc proposals.[6] These preferences were expressed more frequently by Argentina, Guatemala, and Mexico than by others. On the other hand, in the Guatemalan complaint of aggression against Honduras and Nicaragua in 1954, the Latin-American members of the Security Council, Brazil and Colombia, joined the United States in insisting that the disturbance be left entirely to the Organization of American States; that is, they supported the handling of a Western Hemispheric dispute by the Western Hemisphere rather than by the general international organization, even though the complainant had asked for the latter.[7]

Beyond the category of "security" questions, Latin-American cohesion with the United States was rarely manifested; but greater Latin-American unity frequently appeared. The record in a few subject areas will serve to illustrate.

Economic Questions. Throughout the ten-year period under study there was a pronounced Latin-American consensus on economic ques-

[4] U.N. Security Council, Second Year, *Official Records*, No. 68, 173rd Meeting (Aug. 1, 1947), pp. 1700–1703; U.N. Security Council, Fourth Year, *Official Records*, No. 9, 406th Meeting (Jan. 28, 1949), pp. 21–23.

[5] U.N. Security Council, Third Year, *Official Records*, No. 73, 303rd Meeting (May 24, 1948), p. 26.

[6] For a reflection of this outlook, see U.N. General Assembly, Fifth Session, First Committee, *Official Records*, 353rd Meeting (Oct. 4, 1950), pp. 58–60.

[7] U.N. Security Council, Ninth Year, *Official Records*, 675th Meeting (June 20, 1954), p. 37; *ibid.*, 676th Meeting (June 25, 1954), p. 34.

tions. For instance, these states consistently favored more direct United Nations concern with the problems of international trade—an attitude distinctly at variance with the position of the United States. Specifically, the Latin-American states stood fairly solidly for lower barriers against trade, stable prices for primary commodities, and multilateral as well as bilateral agreements dealing therewith. The prevailing Latin-American view was that these policies were necessary for the formation of capital in under-developed countries. On one occasion, at the Seventh Assembly, the United States joined in an appeal to industrialized states to reduce their restrictions on imports of primary commodities.[8]

A strong and broad Latin-American sentiment emerged for United Nations financing of economic development and especially of exploitation of natural resources in under-developed countries. For example, at the Sixth Assembly the Second (Economic) Committee considered a draft resolution to recognize that private capital was insufficient for the economic development of under-developed countries and to request the Economic and Social Council (ECOSOC) to submit plans for a special fund for grants-in-aid and low-interest, long-term loans. In the action by which this draft resolution was approved, fourteen Latin-American states voted in the affirmative; only Brazil from that area voted with the United States against the proposal; and three others abstained.[9]

Social Questions. This Latin-American consensus was not maintained with regard to every social question. The hammering out of the Universal Declaration of Human Rights produced glaring inconsistencies in position, instability of groups, and unpredictability in voting. The largest group of Latin-American states, however, usually supported efforts to widen or render more secure particular concepts of human rights; while a smaller group lined up with the United States in invariable resistance to such efforts. . . .[10]

☼　☼　☼　☼　☼

Dependent Areas. In questions concerning trust territories and other dependent areas, such as colonies, there was a more complete split

[8] U.N. General Assembly, Seventh Session, Second Committee, *Official Records*, 222nd Meeting (Nov. 29, 1952), p. 195.

[9] U.N. General Assembly, Sixth Session, Second Committee, *Official Records*, 166th Meeting (Dec. 13, 1951), p. 139. In the plenary meeting of the General Assembly, Mexico and Peru joined the supporters of the draft resolution; and lone Brazil, forsaking the opposition, abstained. The same session, Plenary, *Official Records*, 360th Meeting (Jan. 12, 1952), p. 338.

[10] As was frequently true in other subject areas, when a proposal was sponsored by a member of the Soviet bloc, the largest group of Latin-American Members customarily joined the United States in opposition to it. The construction of the Universal Declaration of Human Rights absorbed much of the attention of the Third Committee and the Plenary Meetings of the Third Session of the General Assembly.

between Latin America and the United States than in any other matter (except perhaps in matters of international trade and the economic development of under-developed countries.) The Latin-American Members strongly favored: 1) participation by indigenous peoples in the work of the United Nations relative to trust territories; 2) maximum accountability of states to the United Nations for their dependent areas (except for United States accountability for Puerto Rico); and 3) full independence in preference to mere self-government as the objective for non-self-governing territories of all types.

Crucial decisions found the participating Latin-American Members standing almost solidly in positions sympathetic to the desires of the peoples of the trust territories. A clear majority of Latin-American states insisted on retention by the trust territories of their separate identities. Especially did they object to political union or absorption of these territories with or by the administering authorities or other possessions of the administering authorities. . . .

☆ ☆ ☆ ☆ ☆

A re-examination of Latin-American voting as a whole reveals readily that Latin America supported the United States in questions of national security in the cold war; that, when Latin-American Members felt that the United States was stretching the invocation of "security" too far, some dropped away from the leadership of the United States; and that, when devotion to a principle such as universality of membership in the United Nations exerted a counter-attraction, some were drawn away from the United States, even though the applicants for membership might be within the Soviet sphere of influence.

Such an analysis reveals, further, that the Latin-American states frequently formed a solid or nearly solid bloc on questions dealing with dependent areas and such economic matters as the economic development of under-developed countries. When harmony between the United States and Latin America with reference to dependent areas appeared, usually it was a case of the delayed arrival of the United States at a position already taken by Latin America. In other words, Latin America led and the United States followed. On questions regarding the economic development of under-developed countries, it can hardly be said that *any* harmony between the United States and Latin America was achieved. In seeking to understand this portion of the record, one should take into account the condition of the Latin-American states as "under-developed countries" in contrast to the condition of the United States as a "developed" country.

Beyond these categories, rarely did the Latin-American Members stand staunchly either with the United States or with each other.[11] Indeed, rarely could a majority of them be found in the same position on a question ("for," "against" or "abstaining"). But if absolute solidarity and consistency are discounted, smaller groups that *tended* to vote together can be pointed out. These groups can be found even in those categories in which most of the Latin-American voting was with or against the United States.

☼　☼　☼　☼　☼

. . . [I]n an effort to determine whether voting patterns revealed any motivations, several hypotheses were put to the test of the record. The first was that security considerations moved the Latin-American Members to stick closely to the United States on "political" questions, especially on those issues that produced sharp conflict between the two poles of power, the United States and the Soviet Union. This hypothesis, based upon the nature of power politics in the world, was overwhelmingly substantiated by the record of voting. However, a logical corollary, that the Latin-American Members closest geographically to the United States adhered most closely to the United States in the handling of security questions, fared badly. For example, Mexico, although adjacent to the big power, followed a most dissimilar course in its voting; while Brazil and Peru, quite remote from the big power, frequently voted with it.

The second hypothesis, suggested by the historic cultural and philosophical orientation of Latin America toward France, was that the cultural leadership of France rivaled the political leadership of the United States for influence over the voting of Latin-American Members. The record revealed occasional similarity between the voting of France and that of large numbers of Latin-American Members in nearly every aspect of United Nations action. There was especially great similarity in their voting with reference to matters of human rights. However, the evidence fell far short of justifying a conclusion that France positively influenced the voting of the Latin-American Members. The situation appears to have been as explained by an experienced authority on United Nations affairs from a Latin-American country: that, even though France had exerted great influence on former generations of Latin Americans, the present generation was too remote from these contacts to be guided by France, especially in current political decisions.[12]

[11] Except, of course, when the entire membership of the United Nations voted together in a unanimous decision, or when all of the Members except a very few (for example, the Soviet bloc) voted together.
[12] Interview at United Nations Headquarters, New York, Nov. 27, 1954.

A third hypothesis suggested that the voting policies of the Latin-American states were strongly influenced by the nature of the internal regimes. This hypothesis held specifically that, partly because of "Yankeephobia" in Latin America and partly because of the peoples' incomplete understanding of the necessities of power politics, governments based on comparatively-broad popular foundations were forced by popular pressure to follow more independent courses; and that, conversely, rulers of dictatorships found it politically possible and strategically advantageous to support more consistently the nearest center of threatening or overwhelming power—the United States. Certainly Mexico, with comparatively broad participation in government, was highly independent of the United States; and Nicaragua, the Dominican Republic and Paraguay, with their strong-man regimes, often stood with the United States. But on the other hand, the record showed that Uruguay, perhaps the most advanced and stable democracy in Latin America, frequently voted with the United States on issues that produced sharp splits in Latin-American ranks; while Peronist Argentina was highly independent in its voting. More reliable evidence, although negative, was provided by Venezuela and Bolivia, which underwent revolution during the period studied. The former changed from popular to dictatorial military control, and the latter reversed this change. But the record with reference to neither of these two Members substantiated the hypothesis. The voting of each of them with and against the United States after revolution was not significantly different from their voting before revolution.[13]

Consequently, to judge from these tests, it would be hazardous to base upon the voting record any definite conclusions about motivations. Perhaps all that can be ascertained reliably is the influence of the security motive in a world of power politics. Beyond this point, the situation seems to be, as several Latin-American delegates pointed out to the writer, that to identify motives, one would have to consider separately each state and each issue. . . .

---

[13] The same must be said of Guatemala. . . . [T]he overthrow of the "pro-Soviet" Guatemalan government during the summer of 1954 did not produce significant changes in Guatemalan voting in the United Nations.

43. THE ROLE OF AFRICA IN THE UNITED NATIONS*

t h o m a s   h o v e t,   j r.

No one at San Francisco in 1945 could have conceived that in nineteen years Africa would be playing a major role in the United Nations. No one at San Francisco could have conceived that under the impact of an awakening Africa the Trusteeship Council would have about gone out of business, that a major concern of the United Nations would be the elimination of colonialism, and that the Economic and Social Council and the entire United Nations system would have a major involvement in the economic and social progress of the developing countries. In 1945 it would have been inconceivable that a Secretary-General of the United Nations might say in respect to the African states that "the United Nations is now, or will be, their Organization." Yet, Secretary-General Dag Hammarskjold did make that statement at a press conference on February 4, 1960. And who at San Francisco could have imagined that the head of a then non-existent African state would claim in a major address to the General Assembly that: "One cardinal fact of our time is the momentous impact of Africa's awakening upon the modern world." Yet, Kwame Nkrumah, the president of Ghana, made that statement on September 23, 1960, and it seemed at that time a self-evident fact. And, lastly, no one at San Francisco in 1945 could in their wildest dreams have imagined that Africa would have a major role in the United Nations, let alone imagine that its meetings would be filled with representatives from thirty-four independent African states, the largest continental representation in the organization.

✸   ✸   ✸   ✸   ✸

EMERGENCE OF AFRICA
IN THE UNITED NATIONS

Apart from South Africa, which is not an indigenous African state, there were only three original African members in the United Nations:

*   From "The Role of Africa in the United Nations" by Thomas Hovet, Jr., *Africa in Motion, The Annals*, Vol. 354 (July, 1964), pp. 123–131. By permission of the publisher and the author.

Ethiopia, Liberia, and Egypt. While Libya was admitted in 1955 and Morocco, Tunisia, and Sudan in 1956, it was not until the admission of Ghana in 1957 and Guinea in 1958 that it was apparent that there would be an African voice in the United Nations. The North African states—Egypt, Tunisia, Morocco, and Sudan—were not looking in the direction of Africa but toward the Arab world. The image of Africa in the United Nations in the first twelve years was an image of Trust Territories—British and French Togo, British and French Cameroons, British Tanganyika, Belgium's Ruanda-Urundi, and Italian-controlled Somaliland—and a vast number of colonial-dominated non-self-governing territories. But with the break in nationalism that brought independence to the French Trust Territory of the Cameroun on January 1, 1960, the wave of independence in Africa brought twenty-five new African states as members of the United Nations in the forty month period between September 20, 1960 and December 16, 1963. Suddenly, thirty-four of the 113 members of the United Nations were from Africa, and, with the pending independence of Nyasaland in June 1964, only the territories of Northern and Southern Rhodesia, Angola, and Mozambique remain as major areas in Africa that have not achieved independence and a seat in the United Nations.

CO-ORDINATION OF AFRICA IN THE UNITED NATIONS

The emergence of Africa into the United Nations has been accompanied by a number of developments that have sought to co-ordinate the voice of these African states. The first Conference of Independent African States met in Accra in mid-April 1958, and, for the first time, the voice of Africa spoke on the issues of self-determination, the plea for independence of colonial areas, the elimination of racial discrimination policies, and, more importantly, the necessity of seeking some means for co-ordinating their efforts in the achievement of these policies within the United Nations. Not only is the United Nations a center for public diplomacy which focuses the spotlight of world public opinion on crucial issues, but it is also a center of quiet diplomacy. Since the beginning of the United Nations, there have evolved a number of political groups of states that meet as a number of caucus groups behind the scenes of the public diplomacy—such as the Soviet bloc, Latin-American group, Arab group, Commonwealth group, Afro-Asian group, and so on. While the African states prior to the Accra Conference in 1958 had been members of the Afro-Asian group, it was not until after the Accra meeting that a separate African group was organized. In May 1958 the African ambassadors to the United Nations drafted an agreement on the creation of the African caucusing group—the so-called Informal Permanent Machinery.

This African group serves as an area of contact in the United Nations, it attempts to co-ordinate policies that may have been agreed upon in conferences between the heads of state and to see that their recommendations are implemented in the United Nations. Its secretariat performs a role not only in the exchange of views on issues of concern in the United Nations, but it also serves as a planning body for the organization of inter-African conferences outside the United Nations. Many of the African states operate on national budgets too small to enable them to establish embassies in all the other African states, and, therefore, the United Nations serves as the only place in which representatives from all the African states are in constant and immediate contact with each other. Thus, it is only natural that the African group should serve a role in facilitating and planning inter-African conferences. From its beginning, the African group has confined its concern with United Nations issues to African issues. As all the members of the group are also members of the Afro-Asian caucusing group, the African group has felt it should not become a pressure group on other than African questions in the Afro-Asian group or they would tend to split the Afro-Asian group more than its size—fifty-eight members in 1964—already does. Since the original creation of the African group in May 1958, all African states as they have become members of the United Nations have also become members of the group. In addition, representatives of nationalist movements in the African countries who have still to achieve their independence also participate in the meetings of the African groups. . . .

The theory of the existence of the African group is that, if the African states can agree on questions before the United Nations, they can be more effective as a united voice in achieving their policy goals. The group meets with considerable regularity, and every effort is made to have disagreements between African states be confined to the caucus rather than appear in the public sessions of the formal meetings of the United Nations. For a period, there existed two other African caucusing groups within the African group. With the wave of independence of African states in the summer of 1960, the former French Africa territories in October 1960 met informally to support the French position on Algeria and, by a meeting of their heads of state in Brazzaville in December 1960, these twelve—and eventually fourteen—states constituted themselves as the so-called Brazzaville or African and Malagasy Union (AMU) group. In essence, it represented the more conservative—more friendly to the former colonial powers—African states. The creation of the Brazzaville group was a factor in the establishment of the so-called Casablanca group, which came into existence after the Casablanca Conference in January 1961 between Morocco, United Arab Republic, Ghana, Guinea, Mali, and the provisional government of Algeria. This was the more radical wing of the African group. Efforts were made in conferences of heads of state in Monrovia in 1961 and in Lagos in January and June 1962 to attempt to heal this breach, but it was not until the Addis Ababa Conference in May 1963 that agreement was reached. As a result of this conference, which created the Organization of African Unity as a regional international organization, the Brazzaville and Casablanca caucusing groups were dissolved in the summer of 1963. Since that time, every effort has been made to have Africa speak in the United Nations as one voice, at least on African questions.

In the meetings of the group, every effort is made to arrive at a consensus, but the group is not what in the United Nations is called a bloc, because a majority of the members of the group cannot bind the group all to take similar positions and to cast similar votes. . . .

Since the demise of the AMU, or Brazzaville group, there has been some discussion as to whether the African group should become a bloc, in which a majority of the members could determine the position of all the members, but an analysis of the votes of the African states in the Eighteenth Session of the General Assembly in the Fall of 1963 seems to demonstrate that it is still just a caucusing group.

COHESION OF AFRICA
IN THE UNITED NATIONS

While there are many elements in the consideration of the degree of cohesion that has been developed among the African states as a result of their efforts through the group, because I have dealt with this in detail in my study on *Africa in the United Nations* I will consider only the main points here. As the African group has become more organized and unified, the degree of cohesion has increased. In many respects, the African states have generally been in complete agreement on African questions before the United Nations. Their differences on African questions have been more in slight degree of difference in details rather than any fundamental differences on principle. Certainly, when the Brazzaville group was a subgroup of the African caucus, these states differed with the majority of the group on such questions as the Congo and Algeria. On the Congo, they were in sharp disagreement with the Casablanca states on the role of the United Nations vis-à-vis Lumumba; on Algeria, they tended toward the French position. These basic disagreements seem to have been minimized as these states have had a longer period of independence and have become more involved with the other African states and less involved with France. Still, in many respects, their economic ties remain closely related to France. In the Eighteenth Session, the African states were completely united on African questions before the United Nations. This is understandable, because, if the African states are to have a major role in United Nations decisions on African questions, they have to be of one voice.

On non-African questions, there is less agreement among the African states. The degree of division might be illustrated by their attitudes on the question of Chinese representation. Fifteen of the African states —Sudan, United Arab Republic, Algeria, Tunisia, Morocco, Mali, Guinea, Somalia, Ghana, Tanganyika, Uganda, Zanzibar, Kenya, Burundi, and Senegal—recognize the People's Republic of China (Peking regime). All the other African states, except Ethiopia and Nigeria, recognize the Kuomingtang government on Formosa as the government of China. Ethiopia and Nigeria recognize neither Chinese government. While the Charter of the Organization of African Unity (Article III-7) affirms "a policy of non-alignment with regard to all blocs," it might not be stretching the facts to say that those states that recognize Peking tend to a more neutralist position while those that recognize Formosa tend toward the Western position in the East-West issues in the United Nations. However, even in the case of non-African issues in the United Nations, one can see a trend since 1960 toward greater unity. . . .

CONCERNS OF AFRICA
IN THE UNITED NATIONS

While it is apparent that the African states are concerned with such major issues as the elimination of colonialism in Africa and around the world and the elimination of policies of racial discrimination, it is useful to look into the very specific issues that currently concern them in the United Nations.

In many senses, the initial concern of the African states in the United Nations is to achieve adequate representation in the various organs of the United Nations. The African states came into the United Nations after many of the informal procedures of the organization had already been established, and this has meant that their first task, at least in point of tactics, has had to be a concern with obtaining "seats" on such bodies as the Security Council, the Economic and Social Council, the General Committee, and other less-than-full-membership committees of the General Assembly and the Economic and Social Council. For example, in the Security Council, in addition to the five permanent members, there are six elected seats. Since the beginning of the United Nations in 1946, these six seats have been allocated by the so-called "Gentleman's Agreements of 1946" whereby two of these seats were allocated to Latin America, one each to Western Europe, Eastern Europe, the Commonwealth, and a Middle Eastern or Arab country. In the earlier period of growth of the United Nations when a number of Asian states gained membership, their desire for election to the Security Council resulted in a number of bitter election fights. Initially, the African states have similarly challenged this "Gentleman's Agreement formula," but it generally ended in a bitter fight between African states, particularly the Arab versus non-Arab African states. As a result, the African states have led a fight to enlarge the Security Council and the Economic and Social Council, where the same situation exists, by an amendment to the Charter. Short of a Charter amendment, they have sought to reduce the number of European seats, arguing that they do not want to reduce the Latin-American seats because they, too, are underdeveloped countries and the developing countries should be united.[1] . . .

❖   ❖   ❖   ❖   ❖

To turn from procedure to substance, the primary concerns of Africa at the moment are efforts to achieve independence for the Portuguese territories, especially Angola and Mozambique, in Africa and for South West Africa, which was a South African Mandate under the League of Nations that was never established as a Trust Territory under the United Nations, and, lastly, to eliminate the discriminatory policies of apartheid in South Africa. They are also very concerned with the establishment of African representation in the Southern Rhodesian government before it moves to independence as well as with supporting efforts to eliminate colonialism in all the smaller territories in Africa.

While the African states are pushing all of these issues simultaneously, they appear to have established a priority in regard to the major African issues. First priority appears to be the drive against Portuguese domination of Angola and Mozambique, second the efforts to achieve independence for South West Africa, and third the drive against the apartheid policies of South Africa, which they generally refer to as the policies of the "so-called government of South Africa." . . .

While it is very conceivable that the African states with their thirty-four votes in the General Assembly might be able to parlay a majority, and possibly a two-thirds majority, in support of strong and potential sanctions resolutions against Portugal and South Africa, they recognize that the success of such sanctions resolutions will depend upon the active support of the United States and the United Kingdom. They appear to recognize that they have to move gradually in their efforts to get the support of these two major powers. As a result, they have evolved a sort of circular policy to achieve this end. In the Fifteenth

[1] An amendment to enlarge the Security Council from 11 to 15 and the Economic and Social Council from 18 to 27, adopted in 1963, came into effect on August 31, 1965. The term of office of the new members began on January 1, 1966. [Ed. note.]

Session of the General Assembly, the African states supported the now famous Declaration on the Elimination of Colonialism. In the Sixteenth Session, with their support, the Assembly established a committee to speed the implementation of this declaration—what is now called the Committee of Twenty-four on Colonialism. This circular policy involves taking the question of the Portuguese questions to the Committee of Twenty-four—where the Afro-Asians have sixteen of the twenty-four members—to seek a resolution, then to have the Committee of Twenty-four refer the question to the Security Council for action, and then to the General Assembly. The same sort of cyclic pattern has been true in the case of Southern Rhodesia and in the cases of South West Africa and South Africa, although other committees than the Committee of Twenty-four have been involved. Thus the process goes to the committees, the Security Council, the General Assembly, the committees, the Security Council, the General Assembly, and around again and again. In the process, at each stage, the Africans seek the adoption of a resolution stronger than the United States and the United Kingdom are willing to support, but the African states seem willing to compromise to get their support. At each stage, however, the resolutions gradually move closer and closer to the type of resolutions the African group would like to see adopted. The theory would seem to be that, step by step, the United States and the United Kingdom will get committed.

Parenthetically, this process illustrates that the African states recognize that they are small, and, even though they are united and can muster thirty-four votes, they recognize that votes of major powers are needed if any resolution is to be politically realistic.

IMPACT OF AFRICA
ON THE UNITED NATIONS

As Africa has emerged in the United Nations, it is apparent that impact of this wave of African nationalism has had an effect on the United Nations itself.

First, the emergence of Africa in the United Nations—as the emergence of Asian states—has given the United Nations a new and different focus. Prior to 1955, the United Nations was immersed in the East-West conflict. Now, as is easily observable, the so-called North-South axis on issues has developed over the differences between the needs and views of the developed and the developing states. The United Nations Conference on Trade and Development in Geneva, for example, is seen in different lights by the Asian-African-Latin-American states and the developed countries. This North-South axis of issues probably is more evident in the case of their economic and social problems. But the net effect has been an ever-widening concern of the United Nations with basic economic and social problems.

In another sense, the issues that concern Africa—and Asia—are what might be termed moral-political issues. Moral issues such as the elimination of racial discrimination, the elimination of colonialism, the needs of the developing countries have an impact on the major powers. One often hears that these African states are dominated by the Soviet Union, but any detailed analysis of the voting in the United Nations will show that it is not a question of the African states voting with the Soviet Union but of the Soviet Union voting with the African states. Because these issues that concern Africa have a moral overtone, or at least a moral argument, it is difficult for major powers to oppose the African position without appearing to be driving the African states to the other side of the East-West conflict. The United States, in particular, has been placed on the defensive, because, in order to support its allies in the East-West dispute, it often opposes—or at least does not support—the African positions on such questions as South Africa and the Portuguese territories. Thus, in gradual manner, the United States, which for almost all the history of the United Nations has dominated the organization, has been gradually losing its control. The United States is still able to muster the necessary one-third-plus-one vote to defeat "extremist" resolutions and force compromise resolutions. However, because these issues have a moral connotation, it seems inevitable that, unless the United States shifts its attitudes, there may come the day when the United States instead of the Soviet Union will favor the use of the Security Council instead of the General Assembly. As more African states become independent, the United States will be more pressed to control the Assembly and will have to rely on the protection of the veto in the Security Council. Of course, as the major contributor to the budget, the United States does, to some degree, have a financial "veto" in the General Assembly and will to that extent retain some degree of control. Still, there can be no question that the advent of Africa into the United Nations has had an impact on the traditional political balance in the United Nations.

The African drive for the elimination of colonialism has also resulted in what some observers might call a major informal amendment to the Charter. The Committee on Colonialism, that was created in the Sixteenth Session and has continued ever since has, to all intents and purposes, become a major organ of the United Nations. It meets in continuous session, and its resolutions continually activate the Security Council and the General Assembly. Even the Trusteeship Council is required to report to it. . . .

Another impact, and not as major an impact, of the African states has been influence felt in the United Nations from the African delegations. The African delegates have brought a blunt candor into the

United Nations debates. Their frankness has been more in the spirit of the debates by Her Majesty's Loyal Opposition rather than the bitter invective that has characterized the speeches of the Soviet Union. Some of the older delegates in the United Nations are appalled by the African bluntness and candor, but, to other observers, it has breathed life into otherwise dull formal debates. . . .

44. SOUTHEAST ASIAN RELATIONS WITH AFRICA *†

f r e d r. v o n d e r m e h d e n

The "normal" view of international relations envisions some sort of contact between and among states, including diplomatic relations involving an exchange of ambassadors, formal agreements, trade and other forms of international interaction. In the case of Southeast Asian relations with Africa, such contacts have been both sporadic and meager, and this in spite of constant references to Afro-Asian friendship, exchanges of students and missions, efforts by Africans and Asians to establish closer contacts and even the existence of periodicals solely interested in Afro-Asian problems. To be more precise about the current level of contact between Africa and the nine states of Southeast Asia it is necessary to analyze four factors, (1) regular diplomatic exchanges, (2) relations in formal international organizations, (3) Afro-Asian conferences, and (4) trade relations.

African-Southeast Asian Diplomatic Relations: Formal diplomatic exchanges between states in the two areas have been sparse and seemingly haphazard. There are comparatively few Southeast Asian embassies in Africa and even fewer African embassies in Southeast Asia, the

* From "Southeast Asian Relations with Africa" by Fred R. von der Mehden, *Asian Survey*, Vol. V, No. 7 (July, 1965), pp. 341–349. By permission.

† This is a revision of a paper originally prepared for presentation before the Asian-African Relations panel at the 17th Annual Meeting of the Association for Asian Studies, San Francisco, April 2–4, 1965.

tendency being for states south of the Sahara not to exchange embassies with smaller non-African powers. Only the United Arab Republic has exchanged embassies with a majority of the Southeast Asian states—Burma, Cambodia, Indonesia, Thailand, the Philippines and recently North Vietnam. Relations between Egypt and several Southeast Asian states have been of comparatively long duration. For example, in 1951 Indonesia was prepared to recognize King Farouk as king of both Egypt and the Sudan, and the Philippines opened an embassy in Cairo as early as 1957. However, outside of the North African region, there are only eight embassies from Southeast Asia and no obvious pattern has emerged among them. Indonesia has an embassy in Guinea, North Vietnam in Mali and Guinea, South Vietnam in Niger and Senegal, Thailand and the Philippines have diplomatic relations with Nigeria, Thailand with Ethiopia, and consulates have been established in the Union of South Africa by both Thailand and the Philippines. Burma, Cambodia, Laos and Malaysia have no embassies in Africa south of the Sahara.

To the extent that there is any pattern among these, Thailand and the Philippines have relations with more pro-Western powers and North Vietnam and Indonesia with the more "neutralist" states of Africa south of the Sahara. Nor have formal treaties of defense or friendship normally been formed between countries in the two regions, an exception being an Indonesian treaty of friendship with Egypt, established in the early '50's. There are no regional collective defense agreements involving both areas. This lack of formal exchanges is probably due to a combination of insufficient funds for embassies and the small amount of commercial and other business carried out between the two areas.

DIPLOMATIC RELATIONS BETWEEN AFRICA AND SOUTHEAST ASIA—1964

Embassies of Southeast Asian States in Africa

African state	Burma	Cambodia	Indonesia	NVN	Phil	Malaysia	SVN	Thai
UAR	X	X	X		X	X	X	X
Guinea			X	X				
Nigeria					X			X
Niger							X	
Senegal								
Sudan			X					
Mali				X				X
Ethiopia								
Union S. Africa					Con			Con

Africa and Southeast Asia in the U.N.: The one arena where constant contact does take place is within the United Nations, where there has been diplomatic interplay between countries of Southeast Asia and

Africa from the first years of the organization. However, except for a short period in the mid '50's the numbers and influence of the delegations from the two regions have not been equal. Up to 1955 the African states played only a small role in the Afro-Asian caucus, with the dominant members actually being Arab and South Asian. As of 1950, there were but four African states in the U.N. (Ethiopia, Liberia, Egypt and South Africa) and four Southeast Asian (Burma, Indonesia, Philippines and Thailand) out of a total of fifteen members from Afro-Asia. At this time the Afro-Asian caucus as a caucus had only recently been organized (in fact, the Afro-Asian group really took form as late as the Korean War crisis). The height of Southeast Asian membership in this period was in 1955 when it totaled six to the five delegations from Africa (Libya was by then a member, and two years later Malaya was voted in). During this first decade the Afro-Asian members did meet on common problems from time to time and voted in a generally cohesive pattern on questions such as Algeria, Tunisia and efforts at independence by various other colonial peoples (South African treatment of its non-white population, Indonesian independence, the West Iranian question and problems of self-determination in general). However, during the first years of Afro-Asian caucusing there was not a high degree of agreement within the caucus on other issues, and the caucus did not find itself with the majority of the General Assembly on a good many measures (next to the Soviet Bloc, the Afro-Asian Caucus voted least with the majority of the United Nations in the General Assembly).[1]

The second decade of the United Nations has seen a similar pattern of voting on colonial issues but in an entirely different atmosphere. With the withdrawal of Indonesia from the U.N., the Southeast Asian delegations have been reduced to six and have been swallowed by the over thirty-five African delegations in the Afro-Asian caucus. The present caucus thus has approximately 60% African members and about 10% Southeast Asian. Lest these figures provide an inaccurate perception of the role of Southeast Asia in the caucus, it should be pointed out that experience and merit have provided Southeast Asian delegations with a louder voice than the size of its membership alone would normally allow. Although it is difficult to assess the relative effectiveness of specific delegations within the U.N., it is interesting to note the number of

[1] For materials on U.N. voting, Thomas Hovet, Jr., *Africa in the U.N.* (Northwestern Univ. Press, 1963). In reviewing this material, ten General Assembly votes on questions relating to Africa and Asian problems (Indians in South Africa, Indonesia-Dutch relations, West Irian, Suez, Congo, etc.) were checked. These votes showed that Thailand and the Philippines did not always vote with the African states and other Southeast Asian states on African issues and that in the early years of their U.N. membership, Laos and Cambodia had a tendency to vote with France against the Africans. On such questions as the Congo, both areas were split. For a good analysis of such questions, see Somaan Farajallah, *Le Groupe Afro-Asiatique Dans Le Cadre Des Nations Unies* (Geneva: Librairie Droz, 1963).

high positions to which Southeast Asians have been elected and the recent election of countries from that region to the Security Council. However, the over-all impact of increased African representation in the General Assembly has been a decrease in the voice of the Southeast Asian states. As well, the expansion of the Afro-Asian caucus to some 58 members has made it almost unmanageable and with the resignation of Indonesia there is no strong spokesman from the Southeast Asian region within the caucus.

Within the U.N. there has been a mutual interest expressed in the regional problems of the respective areas. African delegates spoke, but did not always vote unanimously, on Southeast Asian issues such as the West Irian and Malaysian issues. At the same time Southeast Asian states have spoken in support of the independence of the former French North African colonies and have entered the debate on the Congo. Southeast Asian governments have also sent troops to Africa on U.N. peace-keeping missions in the Congo and Gaza strip.[2] However, no special relationship appears to have emerged between Southeast Asia and the new African states other than one based on the fact that they are all "underdeveloped states" with certain common problems.

Afro-Asian Meetings: A somewhat similar pattern has emerged with regard to Afro-Asian conferences held over the past two decades. Initial meetings were composed almost entirely of representatives of Asian states and the African delegations were often ill-prepared, at times only observers and generally outside of the mainstream of political influence. The first Asian Relations Conference, an "unofficial" meeting of 28 Asian states, was held in New Delhi in 1947 and had but one African delegate, Egypt. The meeting dealt almost entirely with Asian questions although many of these had a wider significance. The New Delhi conference on Indonesia held in 1949 was again dominated by the South-Southeast Asian representatives and had but two African delegations, Egypt and Ethiopia. At the first Asian Socialist Conference held in Rangoon in 1953, only Egypt sent an official delegation (there were eight Asian delegations including three Southeast Asian) although observers were sent from organizations in Algeria, Tunisia, Kenya and Uganda. The small degree of interaction in this early period is best shown by the first truly Afro-Asian conference in Bandung in 1955. Attending the conference were 29 countries, only five African (Ethiopia, Sudan, Egypt, Libya and what was then called the Gold Coast). Only two countries represented "black Africa" and they remained relatively silent. Although Nasser of Egypt did play a role (not as large as he

---

[2]   In the Gaza affair, Burma, Indonesia and the Philippines offered aid to the UNEF and Indonesian forces served until September 1957. In the Congo operation Malaya sent 1,518 officers and men, Burma a contingent of 9 and Indonesia 1,152. D. W. Bowett, *U.N. Forces* (New York: Praeger, 1964).

hoped or has since) the African delegation was so ineffective that not one of its members was on the sub-committee on colonialism (which led the Ethiopian delegation to raise objections, but unsuccessfully). Even the Egyptian resolution on French North Africa was attacked as too mild. The final communique of the conference, while taking up South Africa and French North Africa, was largely silent on other questions relating to that continent.

At Bandung several Southeast Asian states were very active, Indonesia being the host country and along with Burma one of the five proposers of the conference. Indonesia, Burma, Cambodia, Thailand and the Philippines all actively participated in discussions and special meetings at Bandung, although there was disagreement among the Southeast Asian representatives on major issues before the conference. Spokesmen from Thailand, the Philippines, Laos and, to a lesser extent, Cambodia were more suspicious of the intentions of the Communists in general and China in particular than were Burma and Indonesia. The Philippines, Thailand and Cambodia were among the early leaders attacking Communist as well as Western colonialism. To the extent that splits developed at Bandung, these states plus Laos generally lined up with the "pro-Western" camp while Burma and Indonesia were to be found among the "neutralists."

The years since the Afro-Asian conference at Bandung have not seen the hoped-for development of Afro-Asian relations as such. Instead, conferences have tended to go in two directions, a concentration on their own problems among African members resulting in the formation of organizations composed of only African states and, secondly, the calling of conferences of a wider geographic significance and narrower ideological content. Thus the Africans have become involved in discussions within the organization for African unity and splinter groups such as the Brazzaville, Monrovia and Casablanca groupings. With regard to Afro-Asian meetings, the past several years have seen the inauguration of neutralist and other conferences of Afro-Asians and Latin Americans or of countries from respective regions whose policy was oriented along specific ideological lines. The Cairo Afro-Asian economic conference did have primarily Afro-Asian states and the Southeast Asians at that time, 1958, did have a strong voice. However, the conference of Chiefs of State of Non-Aligned Governments held in Belgrade in 1961 was composed of states somewhat ideologically oriented in terms of neutralism and included Latin American states. It should also be noted that at this time the Africans began to show their strength and there were 13 African states and only 3 Southeast Asian among the 25 delegations. The only Southeast Asians to take active roles in the conference were President Sukarno of Indonesia and, to a lesser extent, U Nu of Burma. The Conference of Economic Development held in Cairo in 1962 was composed of 31 delegations, including 13 African and but 4 Southeast Asians, and also included Latin American members. The initiative for this conference, unlike some earlier ones, did not come from Asia but from Presidents Nasser and Tito. Other ideologically oriented conferences took place at Conakry and Moshi, Tanganyika, where the Afro-Asian Peoples Solidarity Conferences were held. These meetings were composed of official or non-official delegations from "leftist" organizations and states; only Indonesia and North Vietnam of the Southeast Asian states attended as active participants. Even the tenth anniversary of the first Asian-African Conference at Bandung this year displayed this continuing tendency for meetings along ideological lines as a number of the more "pro-Western" states sent their regrets or sent lesser officials as delegates. The decline of Afro-Asian meetings (perhaps due to the overuse of official conferences of developing nations) was illustrated at the anniversary meeting by the general lack of heads of state among the delegates and the paucity of publicity given the meeting throughout the world (with exceptions such as Indonesia). Over all, recent conferences have shown something of an about-face from the first years when the African states were on the outside and power was in the hands of Arab and Asian states. Exclusively Afro-Asian meetings appear to be on their way out.

At present, with the exception of Indonesia and to an extent North Vietnam, the Southeast Asian states have not been highly influential in Afro-Asian meetings. In fact, other states often do not participate in the multitude of official and unofficial conferences. The Indonesians have made a major effort to make up for the silence of their neighbors. Central to the Indonesian ideology is anti-imperialism and the unity of the oppressed Afro-Asian states, and the government of Indonesia has been anxious to place itself as the leader of the developing nations, and particularly of the neutralist bloc. In activating this policy Indonesia has participated in Afro-Asian meetings more often than any other Southeast Asian state and has played host to a variety of international conferences. She has hosted in the past few years special professional conferences such as the Afro-Asian Journalists, sports extravaganzas such as the Asian Games, and more recently the Ganefo Games (Games of the "New Emerging Forces"), and international political and social conferences such as the Bandung meeting of Asian-African states and Afro-Asian Islamic Conference, both held in 1965. Within the meetings, Indonesia's general line has been strongly anti-Western colonial and anti-capitalist combined with generally laudatory remarks for various facets of her own political philosophy. Recently, Indonesia has also attempted to gain support for specific policy lines such as her anti-Malaysia campaign.

Trade Relations: The final area to be considered is that of interregional trade. Here again interaction has not been great. Trade did increase between the two regions from 1956 to 1962 but has never been large. Using United Nations figures for trade between Southeast Asia and Africa and the Middle East (this is the best we have for several countries) exports to Africa and the Middle East in 1956 averaged 13.7 million U.S. dollars a quarter, while imports stand at 27.4 million. By 1962 the respective figures were 23.6 million and 28.9 million. Over these years the total of imports and exports amounted to less than 2½% of the trade of the respective regions. Of the Southeast Asian states, what is now Malaysia was the major trader with Africa, followed by Thailand and Burma. Trade was infinitesimal or non-existent between Africa and the Middle East and Brunei, Cambodia, Laos and Vietnam. Selectively using the three years between 1956 and 1962 there were no exports from Laos and Brunei and only in 1956 were there exports from Cambodia to the African and Middle Eastern regions. The story of imports was much the same.

❖   ❖   ❖   ❖   ❖

In sum, we can state that trade was very small in amount between both continents and that political relations have had little to do with trade balances. Whereas over half the trade is with the white-dominated governments of southern Africa, no Southeast Asian country has an embassy in those states and only Thailand and the Philippines have honorary consuls in the Union of South Africa. Elsewhere there is no particular correlation between diplomatic relations and trade activities.

In conclusion, in no particular area has any special international relationship grown between Africa and Southeast Asia. Nor have there been extensive efforts in recent years to intensify relations, with the exception of Indonesia. The only forum for continuing policy exchanges remains the United Nations. Even there the very size of the Afro-Asian caucus makes some types of contact difficult. Aside from Indonesia, relations between Africa and Southeast Asia remain sparse, sporadic and unspectacular.

45. U.S. ASSISTANCE TO LESS DEVELOPED COUNTRIES, 1956 - 65 *

k e n n e t h   m.   k a u f f m a n
a n d   h e l e n a   s t a l s o n

G L O S S A R Y

L.D.C.s—Less developed countries, which include:

NEAR EAST AND SOUTH ASIA. Afghanistan, Pakistan, India, Nepal, Ceylon; Cyprus, Greece, Turkey; Egypt, Iran, Iraq, Israel, Jordan, Lebanon, Saudi Arabia, Syria, Yemen.

EAST ASIA. All countries in the region (except Japan and Mainland China), plus the Trust Territories of the Pacific Islands.

AFRICA. All countries except Egypt and the Republic of South Africa.

LATIN AMERICA. All countries in the region.

In addition to the L.D.C.s covered in U.S. aid statistics, DAC aid figures include Malta, Spain and Jugoslavia.

DAC—Development Assistance Committee. Members: Australia, Austria, Belgium, Canada, Denmark, France, West Germany, Italy, Japan, Netherlands, Norway, Portugal, Sweden, the United Kingdom and the United States. An agency of the O.E.C.D. (Organization for Economic Coöperation and Development).

NET FLOWS—Disbursements of economic grants and loans (maturity of one year or more) to L.D.C.s and to multilateral agencies, minus repayments of principal. Data are on a calendar-year basis.

G.N.P.—Gross National Product.

P.L. 480—The Public Law establishing the program now called "Food for Peace."

From the jumble of terms that are used to describe the U.S. aid-giving process, two have been chosen—"commitments" be-

* From "U.S. Assistance to Less Developed Countries, 1956–65" by Kenneth M. Kauffman and Helena Stalson, *Foreign Affairs*, Vol. 45, No. 4 (July, 1967), pp. 715–25. Reprinted by special permission from *Foreign Affairs*, July 1967. Copyright by the Council on Foreign Relations, Inc., New York.

cause they are an indicator of intentions, and "expenditures" because they measure the amounts used by recipients.

COMMITMENTS: (1) Authorization of long-term loans and grants; (2) in the case of agricultural commodities under P.L. 480, the planned uses of the local currencies acquired through sales, the authorization of grants and donations, or the long-term credits for dollar sales; (3) obligation of funds to international organizations and capital subscriptions to the Inter-American Development Bank, the International Development Association and the International Finance Corporation. Commitments are on a fiscal-year basis, July 1 through June 30.

EXPENDITURES: (1) Dollars disbursed by the U.S. Government to the account of a foreign government or entity, or (2) the dollar equivalents of goods shipped or delivered, services rendered or foreign currencies disbursed; not including disbursements by international agencies of funds to which the United States has contributed. Expenditures are on a calendar-year basis.

Commitments will usually exceed expenditures because of (1) time lags, (2) the inclusion of a large part of the annual average of $200 million in commitments for non-regional funds (chiefly contributions to international agencies) that do not appear in expenditures since they are not assignable to L.D.C.s, and (3) the valuation of some items in P.L. 480 aid at higher prices in the commitment figures. Inclusion in expenditures of the net accumulation of foreign currencies, a portion of which is excluded in commitments, reduces the difference between the two measures.

In the great debate as to the obligations of the highly industrialized nations to the less developed countries (L.D.C.s), it is not always easy to find relevant and consistent information on the actual amounts of foreign aid provided by the United States. This is so chiefly because of the variety of American aid programs and the variety of ways in which their activities are recorded. The reduction of this diversity to a relatively few figures means some loss of precision but is justified by the need for some kind of straightforward measurement. While a considerable body of informed opinion, in the United States and abroad, holds that the growing gap between the rich nations and the poor nations may lead to disaster, this view appears to be moving against the current of public and Congressional opinion. To meet this issue it may be useful to have in one place an annotated set of figures on U.S. Government aid as well as a summary of total world aid to the L.D.C.s in the decade 1956–65.

The most striking facts revealed by the data can be summarized in eleven points:

1. Official economic aid to all L.D.C.s from all sources (including communist countries) averaged $6.7 billion a year between 1961 and 1965.

2. During the 1956–65 decade, member countries of the Development Assistance Committee (DAC), which account for about 90 percent of all economic aid, provided over $50 billion of official economic assistance for L.D.C.s. The U.S. share was 58 percent of this total.

3. The net flow from all DAC countries was 45 percent higher in the second quinquennium than in the first.

4. U.S. commitments of economic assistance rose 60 percent between the first and second halves of the decade—from $2.5 billion to $4.0 billion a year. But the rising trend in annual commitments ended in 1962.

5. U.S. commitments of economic assistance to L.D.C.s and multilateral agencies rose from 0.54 percent to 0.68 percent of G.N.P. between 1956–60 and 1961–65. But from a 1962 high of 0.76 percent, they fell steadily to 0.60 percent of G.N.P. in 1965.

6. Net U.S. bilateral economic assistance expenditures for L.D.C.s rose more than 50 percent between the two halves of the decade—from an average of $2.1 billion a year to $3.2 billion a year.

7. U.S. military aid to L.D.C.s averaged $1.3 billion a year in both halves of the decade.

8. Between the first and second halves, U.S. economic aid to East Asia declined in absolute amounts. The proportions and amounts going to Africa, Latin America and to non-regional funds rose.

9. Large countries have tended to rank high in total aid but low in per capita aid.

10. Over the decade the terms of U.S. assistance hardened. Aid was increasingly tied to procurement in the United States. Loans rose from 42 percent to 60 percent of bilateral commitments between the first and second halves of the period. From the middle of the decade loans increasingly became repayable in dollars and interest rates on these loans rose toward the end of the period.

11. During 1963–65 interest and principal repayments amounted to nearly half of U.S. gross bilateral economic aid expenditures in Latin America, and to about 12 percent in the rest of the L.D.C.s.

According to DAC, total world flows (net) to all the L.D.C.s from all official sources—multilateral and bilateral—averaged $6.7 billion a year from 1961 to 1965. In 1965 they reached $7.4 billion.[1] Of the total flow about 90 percent came from fifteen DAC member countries. For these countries data covering the 1956–65 period are shown below.

[1] Total net flows of economic aid to L.D.C.s, from non-communist and communist countries, from official and private sources, were estimated by DAC (in billions of dollars):

	1960	1961	1962	1963	1964	1965
Total	7.7	9.0	8.6	9.4	9.9	11.0
Total, excluding private bilateral flows	4.9	6.0	6.4	7.0	6.9	7.4

TABLE I

Net Flow of Official Financial Resources to Less Developed
Countries and Multilateral Agencies

(*in billions of U.S. dollars*)

	1956–60	1961–65	1956–65
All DAC	21.0	30.5	51.5
United States	11.7	18.1	29.8
All other DAC	9.3	12.4	21.7

In the decade covered, DAC countries provided some $50 billion of economic assistance for the L.D.C.s.[2] Between 1956–60 and 1961–65 the amounts increased by 45 percent. Although this was a significant improvement in the level of aid, the 1966 DAC Chairman's report cautioned against the presumption that there is a rising trend in the total volume of economic assistance. From several donor countries there were disquieting reports of disenchantment with aid, which may affect budgetary appropriations for both bilateral and multilateral programs.

SOURCES

Table I. O.E.C.D., Development Assistance Committee, "Development Assistance Efforts and Policies, 1966 Review," Report by Willard L. Thorp, Chairman (Paris, 1966), p. 148.

Footnotes 1 and 3. Same, p. 30 and 160.

Tables II, IIIA, IIIB, IV, V and VIII. U.S. Agency for International Development, "U.S. Overseas Loans and Grants and Assistance from International Organizations: Obligations and Loan Authorizations, July 1, 1945–June 30, 1965" (1966), and the Agency's 1963 report covering the period July 1, 1945–June 30, 1962; U.S. Department of Commerce, *Foreign Grants and Credits by the United States Government*, December issues; U.S. National Advisory Council on International Monetary and Financial Problems, semiannual reports to the Congress and the President; U.S. Foreign Claims Settlement Commission, semiannual reports to the Congress. Population estimates from the U.N.

Table VI. U.S. Agency for International Development. Figures are for A.I.D. expenditures in all countries, including a few not here considered as L.D.C.s.

Table VII. U.S. Department of Commerce, *Survey of Current Business*, June 1966.

[2] Amounts provided to multilateral agencies go partly to more developed countries. Unlike the data cited in footnote 1, the figures in Table I measure flows *to* multilateral agencies and not *from* them to the L.D.C.s.

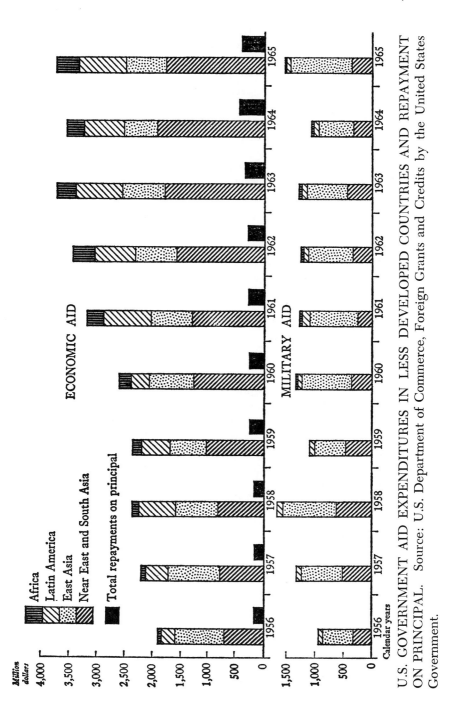

U.S. GOVERNMENT AID EXPENDITURES IN LESS DEVELOPED COUNTRIES AND REPAYMENT ON PRINCIPAL. Source: U.S. Department of Commerce, Foreign Grants and Credits by the United States Government.

TABLE II

U.S. ASSISTANCE TO L.D.C.s—ANNUAL AVERAGES

(*in billions of dollars*)

	Commitments[a]	Expenditures[b]		
	Economic	Economic		Military
		(gross)[c]	(net)[d]	
1956–60	2.5	2.3	2.1	1.3
1961–65	4.0	3.5	3.2	1.3
Decade	3.3	2.9	2.6	1.3

a Fiscal years; includes non-regional commitments.
b Calendar years; excludes non-regional expenditures.
c Gross aid, before repayment of principal.
d Net aid, after repayment of principal.

Consequently it is not certain whether the flow of official aid will continue to rise.

As far as official U.S. aid is concerned, commitments of economic assistance increased by 60 percent between 1956–60 and 1961–65, and net expenditures rose 52 percent. Military aid, however, remained the same in the first and second halves of the ten-year period.

In Table IIIA the percentage distribution of economic assistance commitments is shown by broad regions. There were distinct changes between the first and second halves of the decade. Only the Near East and South Asia maintained about the same relative share. The East Asian share fell from 33 percent of the total to 15 percent; it was the only region to experience a decline in the dollar value of commitments—from $4.1 billion to $2.9 billion—owing in large part to the decline in the aid programs for the Philippines and Taiwan. Africa's share increased 116 percent as five newly independent countries received aid for the first time in 1959 and another thirteen for the first time in 1961. Latin America's share rose 40 percent, and the share of non-regional commitments 90 percent. The broad pattern of commitments (above) is reflected in the data on expenditures shown in Tables IIIB and VIII. (Discrepancies are the result of differences in coverage, valuation and timing.)

TABLE IIIA

DISTRIBUTION OF U.S. ECONOMIC ASSISTANCE TO L.D.C.s

(*commitments expressed in percentages*)

	1956–60	1961–65	1956–65
Near East and South Asia	40.4	42.1	41.5
East Asia	32.7	14.5	21.4
Africa	4.9	10.6	8.5
Latin America	17.7	24.8	22.1
Non-regional and multilateral	4.2	8.0	6.5
Total—in billions of dollars	12.4	20.2	32.6

TABLE IIIB

DISTRIBUTION OF U.S. ASSISTANCE TO L.D.C.s[a]

(expenditures in billions of dollars)

	Economic			Military	Total
	1956–60	1961–65	1956–65	1956–65	1956–65
Near East and South Asia	4.6	8.4	13.0	4.2	17.2
East Asia	4.1	3.6	7.7	7.8	15.5
Africa	0.5	1.7	2.2	0.2	2.4
Latin America	2.2	4.0	6.2	0.8	7.0
Total	11.5	17.7	29.2	13.0	42.2

[a] Gross aid, before repayment of principal; excluding expenditures by international agencies.

Between the first and second halves of the 1956–65 decade there was a definite shift in the sources of U.S. economic aid. As shown in Table IV, the Agency for International Development and its predecessors and the Export-Import Bank declined in relative importance, while P.L. 480 (Food for Peace) and others increased. The substantial rise in "other" commitments mainly reflects growing contributions to multilateral agencies.

TABLE IV

SOURCE OF U.S. ECONOMIC ASSISTANCE COMMITMENTS TO L.D.C.s

	1956–60		1961–65		1956–65	
	$ bill.	%	$ bill.	%	$ bill.	%
A.I.D.	7.2	58	9.7	48	16.9	52
Export-Import Bank	1.6	13	1.8	9	3.4	11
P.L. 480	3.0	24	6.3	31	9.2	28
Other	0.6	5	2.4	12	3.1	10
Total	12.4		20.2		32.6	

In Table V twenty countries are listed in order of the total amount of U.S. economic assistance received between 1956–65. These nations accounted for 80 percent of U.S. economic aid expenditures in L.D.C.s during the decade. The table shows both total and per capita expenditures for the ten years and for the entire post-World War II period. Figures in parentheses are rankings.

There are striking differences between total aid expenditures in a country and assistance per capita. India is first in total but nineteenth in per capita aid among the first twenty recipients. Pakistan and Brazil rank high in total but low in per capita assistance. Conversely, Israel, Jordan and Laos are rather far down the list of total aid but rank first, second and third in aid per capita. Evidently countries with large populations tend to receive more aid, but not nearly in proportion to the number of their inhabitants.

TABLE V

U.S. ECONOMIC ASSISTANCE EXPENDITURES, BY MAJOR RECIPIENTS

	1956–65		1945–65	
	Total ($ mill.)	Per capita[a] ($)	Total ($ mill.)	Per capita[a] ($)
1. India	5,011	10.29 (19)	5,431 (1)	11.16 (19)
2. Pakistan	2,504	24.34 (13)	2,681 (3)	26.06 (17)
3. Korea	2,473	87.22 (6)	3,881 (2)	136.88 (7)
4. Viet Nam	2,085	129.31 (4)	2,335 (5)	144.82 (6)
5. Brazil	1,746	21.23 (16)	2,389 (4)	29.05 (15)
6. Turkey	1,417	45.14 (9)	1,848 (7)	58.87 (9)
7. Egypt	1,041	35.17 (10)	1,084 (10)	36.62 (11)
8. Taiwan	888	71.45 (7)	2,263 (6)	182.07 (5)
9. Chile	797	93.03 (5)	939 (12)	109.61 (8)
10. Israel	640	249.71 (1)	1,044 (11)	407.34 (1)
11. Colombia	571	31.60 (12)	640 (16)	35.42 (12)
12. Iran	568	24.24 (14)	792 (15)	33.81 (14)
13. Indonesia	547	5.23 (20)	805 (14)	7.70 (20)
14. Mexico	529	12.39 (17)	859 (13)	20.12 (18)
15. Argentina	511	22.86 (15)	611 (17)	27.34 (16)
16. Jordan	452	228.74 (2)	483 (18)	244.43 (2)
17. Morocco	435	32.65 (11)	471 (19)	35.35 (13)
18. Greece	424	49.58 (8)	1,760 (8)	205.82 (4)
19. Laos	396	198.00 (3)	435 (20)	217.50 (3)
20. Philippines	373	11.53 (18)	1,268 (9)	39.20 (10)

[a] Per capita data are based on estimated 1965 population.

There have also been a few significant changes in the ranking of countries. Compared to their positions over the entire period 1945–65, Chile, Colombia, Egypt and Iran in the last ten years have moved up in the ranking of total aid received, while Greece and the Philippines have gone down.

Over the ten-year period, 1956–65, the terms of U.S. economic assistance have become progressively harder. During the first quinquennium, 42 percent of bilateral economic aid commitments were loans; in the second, 60 percent. Grants accounted for 81 percent of economic aid expenditures in 1956, 64 percent in 1960 and 43 percent in 1965. The grant component of expenditures fell precipitously in the Near East and South Asia from 77 percent in 1956 to 53 percent in 1960 and 27 percent in 1965. Grants were a more stable proportion of expenditures in East Asia, constituting 91–95 percent in the first half of the decade and 83–85 percent in the second half. In Latin America the grant portion was lower throughout the period, and there was no marked trend; grants formed 26 percent of the total for the decade. For Africa, grants averaged 71 percent of economic assistance expenditures for the ten-year period. The proportion rose steadily from 54 percent in 1956 to 78 percent in 1963. In 1965 the proportion fell to the 1956 figure—54 percent.

During the first half of the period principal and interest on most U.S. economic assistance loans were repayable in local currency—except for Export-Import Bank loans which have always been repayable in dollars. In the second half of the decade service on A.I.D. loans became payable in dollars. Since 1962, commodities provided under P.L. 480 have increasingly had to be paid for in dollars and by 1971 the bulk of this kind of assistance will be on dollar terms.

Although average interest rates were lower and grace periods longer on A.I.D. loans made during the second half of the decade, the advantages of this from the point of view of most L.D.C.s were offset by the requirement to repay in dollars. Moreover, within the 1961–65 period interest rates have risen as a result of legislative action. For the softest A.I.D. loan (forty-year maturity) from 1961–63 a charge of 0.75 percent per year was made. In 1964 the rate rose to 1 percent during the ten-year grace period and 2 percent thereafter. In 1965 the rate subsequent to the grace period increased to 2.5 percent.

A.I.D. soft loans are made to L.D.C.s whose balance-of-payments positions do not warrant harder terms. To countries that are better able to service debt, A.I.D. tends to use twenty-year loans at 3.5 percent interest. The Export-Import Bank follows commercial interest rates more closely. Its loans for the last several years have averaged thirteen years maturity; interest has been 5.5 percent.

Although in 1965, of all the major DAC aid donors the United States was still giving the best overall loan terms, the gap had narrowed appreciably since 1962. While the weighted average interest rates on U.S. official bilateral loan commitments had risen from 2.5 percent to 3.3 percent, the rate for all DAC member countries was 3.6 in both years.[3]

A major change in policy came toward the middle of the decade when A.I.D. loans were tied to procurement in the United States. In the second half of the decade vigorous efforts were made to link other A.I.D. expenditures to purchases of U.S. goods and services. As Table VI shows, these policies have resulted in a decline of A.I.D. spending abroad from 60 percent to 20 percent of the total between 1961 and 1965. Naturally this has diminished the direct contribution of aid to

[3]   Terms for DAC members as a whole became harder in 1965. The 1966 DAC review shows the following history of terms.

Loan terms (*weighted averages*)		*1962*	*1963*	*1964*	*1965*
Maturity (in years):	DAC total	23.6	24.8	28.4	22.2
	United States	28.6	32.5	33.4	28.0
Interest (in percent):	DAC total	3.6	3.4	3.0	3.6
	United States	2.5	2.0	2.5	3.3

TABLE VI
GROSS A.I.D. EXPENDITURES

Fiscal year	Total ($ mill.)	Amounts spent abroad ($ mill.)	%
1961	1,801	1,065	59
1962	1,849	983	53
1963	2,074	799	39
1964	2,022	515	25
1965	2,091	411	20
1966	2,202	503	23

deficits in the U.S. balance of payments, but it also has been regarded by recipients as a hardening of the conditions of U.S. aid and undoubtedly has reduced the amount of goods and services that recipients obtain per dollar of aid.

Table VII compares U.S. bilateral economic aid expenditures with principal and interest payments by the L.D.C.s over the last three years of the decade. In Latin America, debt service in recent years has amounted to nearly half of gross U.S. aid expenditures. In other parts of the less developed world service payments have been rising, but still constitute a rather small proportion of gross aid. For the L.D.C.s as a whole, the cost of servicing U.S. loans averaged 19 percent of gross aid from U.S. sources.

Principal and interest in Table VII include payments in local currencies. For most countries these do not constitute as great a burden as dollar payments, but with the shift to loans repayable in dollars, and as the impact of higher interest rates begins to affect payments, the L.D.C.s will be faced with sharply rising dollar obligations. This will reduce the net outflow from the United States, but it necessarily will also reduce the effect of U.S. assistance. If gross loans to L.D.C.s were forthcoming at a

TABLE VII
U.S. ECONOMIC ASSISTANCE EXPENDITURES AND DEBT SERVICE

Calendar year	Latin America			Asia and Africa		
	Gross expenditures	Principal and interest payments	Principal and interest as % of expenditures	Gross expenditures	Principal and interest payments	Principal and interest as % of expenditures
	($ millions)		(%)	($ millions)		(%)
1963	816	375	46	2,912	275	9
1964	729	405	56	2,840	355	13
1965	856	347	41	2,891	367	13
Total	2,401	1,127	47	8,643	997	12

TABLE VIII. U.S. Economic and Military Aid Expenditures in Less Developed Countries, Calendar Years 1956–1965. *In millions of dollars or dollar equivalents.*

	1956	1957	1958	1959	1960	1961	1962	1963	1964	1965	Total 1956–65
Economic											
Loans	306	497	802	777	773	1,449	1,657	1,844	1,919	2,120	12,144
Grants	1,270	1,276	1,344	1,339	1,399	1,601	1,635	1,648	1,647	1,571	14,730
	1,576	1,773	2,146	2,116	2,172	3,050	3,292	3,492	3,566	3,691	26,874
Net accumulation of foreign currency claims	328	426	230	256	453	160	165	236	3	56	2,313
Total, economic	1,904	2,199	2,376	2,372	2,625	3,210	3,457	3,728	3,569	3,747	29,187
Repayment of principal	162	186	189	242	253	285	303	384	469	404	2,877
Economic, net	1,742	2,013	2,187	2,130	2,372	2,925	3,154	3,344	3,100	3,344	26,311
Military[a]	960	1,329	1,697	1,099	1,378	1,294	1,263	1,302	1,078	1,568	12,968
Total (bilateral), gross	2,864	3,528	4,073	3,471	4,003	4,504	4,720	5,030	4,647	5,315	42,155
net	2,702	3,342	3,884	3,229	3,750	4,219	4,417	4,646	4,178	4,911	39,278
Multilateral and non-regional[b]	96	84	75	88	172	183	340	291	292	503	2,124

[a] Including transfers of excess stocks.
[b] Commitments of U.S. funds in grant form.

NOTES TO TABLE VIII

N.B. The data on expenditures are taken, for the most part, from annual volumes and hence are not revised figures.

ECONOMIC AID: Programs of the Agency for International Development and its predecessor agencies, the Social Progress Trust Fund, Peace Corps, and "other" programs; Export-Import Bank long-term loans (including credits extended to refinance principal payments, excluding advances by others whether or not guaranteed by the Bank); Food for Peace (P.L. 480) programs—grants and loans, including donations through private welfare agencies and also including some portion of grants of local currency for common defense (Sec. 104c) which, when transferred as cash grants, are considered as economic aid. Economic aid here excludes payment on war damage claims to the Philippines and operations of the U.S. Exchange Stabilization Fund.

Loans are disbursements of new credits. *Grants* are net grants. *Net accumulation of foreign currency claims* is the total of the local currencies acquired through sales of agricultural products, less the amounts used for grants and credits to the L.D.C.s and for U.S. purposes. *Repayment of principal* includes repayment in both dollars and local currencies on dollar and local currency loans. It excludes repayment of lend-lease silver by India and Pakistan.

MILITARY AID. Primarily grants under the Military Assistance Program, but also including small amounts of other military aid. Excess stocks of military equipment (included at their acquisition value) are not charged to MAP funds. Military aid includes the portion of local currency funds acquired through P.L. 480 Title I sales, allocated to Sec. 104c uses (common defense) and used by the United States for purchases of military supplies and services. Military aid excludes credits provided to finance the sale of military supplies and services; these credits are included under economic loans. It also excludes defense support/supporting assistance, which is regarded as economic aid extended for the purpose of meeting political and security objectives.

MULTILATERAL AND NON-REGIONAL AID: Grants and subscriptions to the United Nations and related agencies, to the Inter-American Development Bank, the International Development Association, and the International Finance Corporation, and to non-regional economic programs.

constant amount each year on the average terms offered by A.I.D. and the Export-Import Bank in the early 1960s, in five years repayments of principal and interest would amount to about 15 percent of new gross loans, in ten years to about 35 percent and in fifteen years to 60 percent. It is virtually inevitable, therefore, that the United States and other donors will soon be forced to consider the consequences of the mounting burden of the L.D.C.s' debt service.

APPENDIX

Selected Data on Transitional Societies°

° Data compiled from United Nations and other sources

State	Former colony of:	Date of inde- pendence	Area (sq. miles)	Population	Popu- lation density (per sq. mi.)	Per cent urban populati (over 100,000
LATIN AMERICA						
Argentina	Spain	1816	1,072,067	21,688,000	20.6	58.2
Bolivia	Spain	1825	424,163	3,697,000	8.6	9.2
Brazil	Portugal	1822	3,286,470	81,301,000	25.2	17.6
Chile	Spain	1818	286,397	8,567,000	29.7	35.6
Colombia	Spain	1824	439,512	17,787,000	35.1	32.1
Costa Rica	Spain	1848	19,652	1,443,000	70.8	22.5
Cuba	Spain	1898	44,218	7,631,000	165.9	25.4
Dominican Republic	Spain	1865	18,703	3,573,000	184.6	11.0
Ecuador	Spain	1830	105,684	5,084,000	46.1	18.0
El Salvador	Spain	1821	8,260	2,928,000	341.9	9.2
Guatemala	Spain	1839	42,042	4,343,000	101.8	10.5
Guyana	Great Britain	1966	83,000	640,000	7.7	
Haiti	France	1804	10,714	4,660,000	424.7	5.7
Honduras	Spain	1838	43,277	2,163,000	48.3	6.4
Jamaica	Great Britain	1962	4,411	1,773,000	392.2	21.4
Mexico	Spain	1821	761,600	40,913,000	52.1	20.2
Nicaragua	Spain	1838	57,143	1,655,000	27.9	14.3
Panama	Spain	1903	28,753	1,218,000	42.1	26.1
Paraguay	Spain	1811	157,047	2,030,000	12.4	15.5
Peru	Spain	1821-1824	496,222	11,650,000	22.9	15.7
Trinidad and Tobago	Great Britain	1962	1,980	949,000	478.3	
Uruguay	Spain	1825	72,172	2,719,000	35.4	44.7
Venezuela	Spain	1821	352,142	8,722,000	23.9	33.6
SUB-SAHARAN AFRICA						
Burundi	Belgian Man.- Trust	1962	10,747	2,369,000	225.2	
Cameroon	French Man.- Trust	1960	183,376	5,103,000	24.9	3.3
Central African Republic	France	1960	241,313	1,352,000	5.4	8.3
Chad	France	1960	534,363	3,300,000	3.8	
Congo (Brazzaville)	France	1960	134,749	826,000	6.2	16.2
Congo (Leopoldville)	Belgium	1960	905,063	15,627,000	17.1	5.5
Dahomey	France	1960	44,696	2,300,000	50.3	4.2
Ethiopia	—	—	457,142	22,200,000	48.6	2.2
Gabon	France	1960	102,317	462,000	4.5	
Gambia	Great Britain	1965	3,997	330,000	73.0	

Gross domestic product per capita	Rate of annual growth in real gross domestic product	Rate of annual population growth	Per cent illiterate	Number of persons per:				
				News-papers	Radio	Tele-phone	Doctor	Motor-ized vehicles
544	-2.8	1.7	8.6	7	4	15	670	17
84		1.2	69.2	38	11	189	3,900	87
156	1.5	3.1	51.2	18	17	67	2,500	47
457	3.5	2.6	16.4	8	5	36	1,600	48
298	2.7	2.2		17	8	47	2,400	84
260		4.1	15.7	11	18	70	2,200	41
300		2.1		11	5	34	1,200	58
201		3.5		37	23	129		119
189	0.6	3.0	32.7	19	30	115	2,600	163
178		2.8	51.0	20	9	142	4,800	92
270	1.9	3.1	72.0	32	20	217	4,900	97
			20.0		16	68		
85		2.3	90.0	166	221	1059	11,000	561
193	2.0	3.0	55.0	50	17	233		155
390	1.3	1.6	18.1	15	9	42	2,500	25
394	1.7	3.1	34.6	9	6	62	1,800	41
198	9.2	2.9	50.4	15	17	120	2,800	106
427	2.9	2.9	26.7	13	6	32	2,500	36
117	2.2	2.6	25.7	27	12	156	1,700	
220	3.7	2.2	39.4	21	5	92	1,700	61
650	7.3	2.9		12		27	2,400	15
476		1.7	9.7	6	3	17	870	13
716	0.6	4.0	34.2	13	7	36	1,400	22
		4.3					66,000	
64		2.6		500		1248	29,000	163
93		2.3		3333	67	656	33,000	
53		.5		3333	179	1334	56,000	
99				1000		115	15,000	
110	3.0	2.2	84.6	500	446	520	63,000	
61				1000	65	735	24,000	261
·		1.7	70.0	1000	148	1242	96,000	1115
216		1.8	87.6		15	164	6,600	
		1.4		200	132	322	16,000	220

State	Former colony of:	Date of independence	Area (sq. miles)	Population	Population density (per sq. mi.)	Per cent urban population (over 100,000)
Ghana	Great Britain	1960	92,100	7,740,000	81.4	9.3
Guinea	France	1958	94,926	3,420,000	35.4	3.9
Ivory Coast	France	1960	124,502	3,750,000	29.6	4.3
Kenya	Great Britain	1963	224,960	9,365,000	40.5	5.3
Malagasy	France	1960	230,035	6,100,000	26.5	4.3
Malawi	British Protectorate	1964		3,753,000		
Mali	France	1960	464,874	4,576,000	9.5	2.4
Mauritania	France	1960	419,229	900,000	1.9	
Niger	France	1960	489,206	3,250,000	6.5	
Nigeria	Great Britain	1960	356,669	56,400,000	155.9	8.3
Rhodesia	Great Britain	1965		4,216,000		
Rwanda	Belgian Man.-Trust	1962	10,169	3,018,000	285.2	
Senegal	France	1960	76,124	3,400,000	44.1	11.7
Sierra Leone	Great Britain	1961	27,925	2,180,354	78.1	5.2
Somalia	Italy - Great Britain	1960	246,201	2,500,000	9.1	4.2
Tanzania			362,844	9,087,577	27.5	1.3
Tanganyika	Great Britain	1961		8,788,486		
Zanzibar	Great Britain	1963		299,111		
Togo	French Man.-Trust	1960	21,853	1,642,000	73.4	
Uganda	Great Britain	1962	93,981	7,551,000	76.5	1.5
Union of South Africa	Great Britain	1910	472,359	17,892,000	37.0	23.1
Zambia	Great Britain	1964		3,710,000		6.2
MIDDLE EAST						
Afghanistan	—		250,966	14,736,379	58.6	4.3
Algeria	France	1962	919,591	10,670,000	11.7	16.6
Iran	—	——	636,363	22,860,000	34.9	19.2
Iraq	British Mandate	1932	167,568	7,004,000	40.9	25.7
Israel	British Mandate	1948		2,563,000		30.2
Jordan	British Mandate	1946	37,297	1,898,000	49.9	12.2
Kuwait	British Protectorate	1961		410,000		32.9
Lebanon	French Mandate	1941	4,015	2,152,000	536.0	23.2
Liberia	U.S. Supported		43,000	1,066,000	24.2	
Libya	Italy	1951	679,358	1,559,000	2.3	22.6
Malta	Great Britain	1964		319,000		
Morocco	France	1956	174,471	12,959,000	74.3	16.1
Saudi Arabia	—		872,722	7,000,000	8.0	6.6
Sudan	British Control	1956	967,491	13,540,000	13.6	2.3
Syria	French Mandate		71,228	5,399,000	75.8	27.2

Gross domestic product per capita	Rate of annual growth in real gross domestic product	Rate of annual population growth	Per cent illiterate	Number of persons per:				
				Newspapers	Radio	Telephone	Doctor	Motorized vehicles
204		4.1		35	15	251	21,000	180
74		3.0		5000	85	1028	19,000	
118		3.5		250		303	25,000	274
88		3.3		111	94	195	11,000	120
70		3.0		111	21	345	9,400	118
							35,000	321
57		3.5		2000	458	1135	39,000	95
60		4.0			30		26,000	
64		3.2		3333	162	1911	65,000	613
102	2.5	5.7		100	141	961	27,000	829
		-1.2		32			6,200	26
		2.6						
152			94.4	166	22	140	21,000	
				143	237	472	22,000	214
45				1000	96	1190	30,000	
						479		
79		1.8		333	313		16,000	214
		1.2		200	37		7,900	
75				111	260	629	34,000	
75	0.1	2.5		125	76	467	15,900	238
605		2.5	68.5	17	16	17	2,000	14
		2.8		143			9,200	70
72		2.8		250	589	1602	32,000	899
180	5.0	2.9		45	7	66	5,500	32
160		2.4	87.2	66	14	142	3,800	150
187		2.8	85.4	83	70	117	4,900	93
	6.2	7.6	15.8	6	4	13	400	32
204		2.7	67.6	37	31	75	5,900	144
		10.6		250	4	23	1,000	6
153		3.0		10		23	1,000	25
		1.4	91.1	333	11		16,000	
162		3.7		143	18	129	5,800	35
		0.5		9	4	16	780	13
144	-0.1	2.9	86.2	58	21	92	9,700	63
		1.9		500		264	13,000	
80	3.5	2.8	95.6	200		413	29,000	351
142	8.4	4.2	64.6	111		79	5,200	158

State	Former colony of:	Date of independence	Area (sq. miles)	Population	Population density (per sq. mi.)	Per cent urban populatio (over 100,000)
Tunisia	France	1956	59,952	4,565,000	66.1	8.5
Turkey	—	—	301,380	32,005,000	103.3	10.2
United Arab Republic (Egypt)	British Protectorate	1922	386,100	28,900,000	72.4	25.3
Yemen	—	—	75,290	5,000,000	66.4	
ASIA						
Burma	Great Britain	1948	261,789	24,732,000	92.6	4.1
Cambodia	France	1954	66,607	5,740,000	86.1	7.2
Ceylon	Great Britain	1948	25,332	10,965,000	419.4	4.7
China (Mainland)	—	—	3,691,502	686,400,000	203.2	8.6
China (Taiwan)	—	—	13,952	12,429,000	865.1	26.3
India	Great Britain	1947	1,261,416	471,624,000	373.9	8.3
Indonesia	Netherlands	1949	575,893	100,045,000	173.7	9.4
Laos	France	1954	91,428	1,882,000	32.8	8.1
Maldive Islands	Great Britain	1965		94,527		
Malaysia	Great Britain	1963	128,207	9,137,000	64.5	7.4
Malaya				7,810,000		
Sabah				507,000		
Sarawak				820,000		
North Korea	—	—	46,814	11,100,000	237.0	6.0
North Vietnam	France	1954	60,156	15,715,000	261.2	10.7
Pakistan	Great Britain	1947	365,529	102,885,000	275.7	6.7
Philippines	Spain–United States	1946	115,707	32,345,000	270.3	9.6
Singapore	Great Britain	1963		1,865,000		100.0
South Korea	—	—	38,452	28,353,000	718.6	23.2
South Vietnam	France	1954	65,948	15,715,000	232.4	9.1
Thailand	—	—	198,455	30,591,000	149.7	6.2
Western Samoa	New Zealand Man.-Trust	1962		122,000		

Gross domestic product per capita	Rate of annual growth in real gross domestic product	Rate of annual population growth	Per cent illiterate	Number of persons per:				
				Newspapers	Radio	Telephone	Doctor	Motorized vehicles
199	2.5	2.2	86.6	35	16	100	9,600	56
292	1.8	2.9	61.9	22	20	111	5,700	217
146		2.4	73.7	58	14	110	2,600	267
		2.6						
75	-0.2		42.9	111	121	1190	9,600	563
	-4.6	2.2		125		1481	25,000	
141	1.4	2.6		27	27	267	4,600	96
				52	86		8,700	
121	3.6	2.9	46.1	15	11	93	1,700	513
74	0.2	2.0	72.2	3333	153	692	5,800	720
73	1.5	1.5	57.1	90	80	676	41,000	260
		2.4	63.2	90	85	1772	38,000	
		1.9						
222	3.1	2.5	53.0	15	23	79	6,500	46
		3.4	76.5	27	25	101	12,000	52
		2.5	78.5	40	16	128	14,000	141
		2.2			18			
		3.4	35.5				7,857	
79	4.0	2.1	81.2	200	259	959	11,000	857
127	1.4	3.1	28.1	55	273	221		161
322		4.5	50.2	3	13	25	2,400	17
124	1.9	2.9	17.8	18	17	167	2,900	911
73			29.4	26	226	751	29,000	
112	2.4	3.2	32.3	90		554	10,000	231
		3.3			21	98	2,600	90